FIZZ!

T0289767

THE CLASSIC WINE LIBRARY

There is something uniquely satisfying about a good wine book, preferably read with a glass of the said wine in hand. The Classic Wine Library is a series of wine books written by authors who are both knowledgeable and passionate about their subject. Each title in The Classic Wine Library covers a wine region, country or type and together the books are designed to form a comprehensive guide to the world of wine as well as an enjoyable read, appealing to wine professionals, wine lovers, tourists, armchair travellers and wine trade students alike.

Other titles in the series include:
Port and the Douro, Richard Mayson
Sherry, Julian Jeffs
Madeira: The islands and their wines, Richard Mayson
The wines of Austria, Stephen Brook
The story of Champagne, Nicholas Faith
Côte d'Or: The wines and winemakers of the heart of Burgundy,
     Raymond Blake
The wines of Canada, Rod Phillips
Rosé: Understanding the pink wine revolution, Elizabeth Gabay MW
Amarone and the fine wines of Verona, Michael Garner
The wines of Greece, Konstantinos Lazarakis MW
Wines of the Languedoc, Rosemary George MW
The wines of northern Spain, Sarah Jane Evans MW
The wines of New Zealand, Rebecca Gibb MW
The wines of Bulgaria, Romania and Moldova, Caroline Gilby MW
Sake and the wines of Japan, Anthony Rose
The wines of Great Britain, Stephen Skelton MW
The wines of Chablis and the Grand Auxerrois, Rosemary George MW
The wines of Germany, Anne Krebiehl MW
The wines of Georgia, Lisa Granik MW
The wines of South Africa, Jim Clarke
The wines of Portugal, Richard Mayson
The wines of Roussillon, Rosemary George MW

FIZZ!

Champagne and Sparkling Wines of the World

ANTHONY ROSE

ACADEMIE DU VIN LIBRARY

Anthony Rose is an award-winning wine and sake critic who contributes to publications including *Decanter*, *The World of Fine Wine*, Financial Times How to Spend It online and *The Oxford Companion to Wine*, and reviews sparkling wines for The Real Review. He is Regional Chair of the southern Italy panel at the Decanter World Wine Awards, and teaches a sake consumer course at Sake No Hana in London. He was the wine correspondent of the print version of the *Independent* from start to finish (1986–2016) and is a founding member of The Wine Gang (www.thewinegang.com). His book *Sake and the wines of Japan* was shortlisted for best drink book at the Fortnum & Mason Food and Drink Awards 2019. In 2017, he was a Finalist in the Pink Lady Photographer of the Year Awards. Anthony lives in south London. Find him online at www.anthonyrosewine.com and on twitter: @anthonyrosewine.

First published in 2022 by Infinite Ideas Limited
This edition published 2024 by Académie du Vin Library Ltd
academieduvinlibrary.com

A CIP catalogue record for this book is available from the British Library

ISBN 978–1–913141–77–6

The five dominant sparkling wine production methods (page 29) modified from Kemp, B., et al., 'Chemical compounds and mechanisms involved in the formation and stabilization of foam in sparkling wines'. *Critical Reviews in Food Science and Nutrition* 59(13): 2072–94.

The traditional method (page 31) redrawn from original supplied courtesy of Comité Interprofessionnel du Vin de Champagne.

Chemical processes during second ferment (page 42) adapted from Kemp, B., et al., 'Effect of production phase on bottle-fermented sparkling wine quality'. *Journal of Agricultural and Food Chemistry*, 63(1): 19–38.

Map of Tasmania, page 80, redrawn from map supplied courtesy of Wine Tasmania.

Map of Champagne, page 142, modified from map supplied courtesy of CIVC.

Geological map of the south of England (plate section page 1), modified from Geological map of the British Islands based on the work of the Geological Survey under Permit Number CP21/035 British Geological Survey © UKRI.

All photos © Anthony Rose

Illustrations drawn by Darren Lingard

Printed in Great Britain

CONTENTS

INTRODUCTION: ON SPARKLING FORM

What distinguishes sparkling wine from still wine? In a word, bubbles. The thrill of the sparkle brings an extra dimension to wine in the vivacious dance of touch and dissolution on the tongue in myriad pinprick bursts of aroma and flavour. Other words for the gravity-defying upward surge of fizz in the glass, including mousse, effervescence, foam, sparkle, all convey a fleetingly indulgent sense of exuberance, vivacity, fun and joie de vivre. Almost all sparkling wine is best enjoyed chilled. Like sea-spray on a hot day, the cool explosion of bubble on tongue seals the refreshing deal.

Who ever thought that putting bubbles into wine was a good idea? Until they burst onto the scene, literally, wine was minding its own business as a serious alcoholic beverage enjoyed by kings, emperors, noblemen, monks and others who could afford the luxurious fermented juice of the grape. Like balloons and candy floss, meringues and marshmallows, bubbles are frivolous things, here this minute, gone the next. What in heaven's name is the point of them? And why reduce a fine wine from the serious to the superficial?

When fizz first started to sit up for attention in the seventeenth century, it must have taken a leap of the imagination to think that bubbles in wine could possibly be a good thing. In fact they were frowned upon. But they were also new, frivolous, decadent and fashionable. The trendsetting proponents of the bubble were cocking a snook at the traditionalists for their po-faced devotion to the serious still wines of Clos Vougeot from Burgundy and Sillery from Champagne. 'Don't be Sillery, just be silly,' as they might have said.

1

While the idea that bubbles get us merry more quickly has never been proven scientifically, decadent society of the time realized it intuitively. Madame de Pompadour, one of Louis XV's *maîtresses en titre* (head mistresses), is reputed to have said 'Champagne is the only wine that leaves a woman beautiful after drinking it.' Serena Sutcliffe MW comments: 'Advice such as this from one of the famous *horizontales* should be taken seriously.' The fashion for fizz caught on, and sparkling wine has never ceased to be stylish.

We rarely give bubbles in wine a second thought today. Centuries of enjoyment of sparkling wines have left us with the happy legacy of bubbles coursing through our veins. It is only with the benefit of hindsight that we can see quite how ingenious an achievement putting the bubble into the bottle and keeping it there really was. Without the bubbles, Champagne, a wine made in chilly northerly climes, would have been impossibly tart and light to drink; the trick was turning it into something not just palatable but also enchantingly ephemeral and enduringly exciting.

In the beginning it was merely an extension of the observation of nature. The first curious minds that noticed that wine that had gone into hibernation over winter and bubbled up as temperatures rose in the following spring started experimenting with ways of capturing that sparkle. It was hit-and-miss for over a century but once the commercial genie was out of the bottle, the addition of sugar and yeast – and patience – became the core of an evolutionary process designed to trap those golden bubbles back inside.

The story of fizz has been one of image and prestige reinforced by generous PR and marketing budgets. Illustrated by posters of the louche and the loose, sparkling wine was first and foremost a wine of celebration, a fun drink for toasting the signing of treaties, the conquest of mountains and the celebration of royal weddings. At worst, it was – and still is – a foaming liquid endorsed by A-list celebrities to be sprayed over Grand Prix winners and footballing victors and smashed over the bows of new ships. While it's a brilliant wheeze, this triumph of style over substance can blind us to the realities of sparkling wine as a drink in its own right. Perish the thought that it might be drunk with food.

While big can be beautiful, and there's no better example than Dom Pérignon, for a growing number of consumers, sparkling wine has morphed beyond the superficial to the quality and character of the product itself. In the twenty-first century, the message of sparkling wine is often more orientated towards the human story of the grower and the land. Where big brands rely on consistency year in year out to ram home the message of continuity, growers' sparkling wines, broadly based on their own vineyards, have brought about a growing appreciation of fizz as a wine in its own right.

A renewed focus on the local origin of the grapes in Champagne has in turn led to a similar outlook in other regions and countries producing fizz. Even the legendary *champenois* grower Anselme Selosse has said: 'For me, Champagne is not the best sparkling wine. There are no best sparkling wines. Each personality is its own. There is no universal best.' The current move towards single parcel or vineyard vinification, riper fruit and lower yields, use of natural yeasts and fermentation in oak, is based on a disdain for convention and a return to traditional practices. The proliferation of sparkling wines with no sugar added or with low dosage is a return to an almost forgotten phenomenon, and this time round, climate change is playing an unsolicited walk-on part.

Whether innovation or a return to tradition, the current sparkling wine phenomenon is symptomatic of the trend towards the treatment of fizz as a wine in its own right. According to the Napa Valley producer Paula Kornell, 'I believe that we're all much more accustomed to drinking sparkling wine on a normal basis now, that this isn't something that's just for special occasions.' Even the historical idea that non-vintage fizz must show continuity of style is under fire as producers are more willing to acknowledge differences based on a back-to-basics approach towards authenticity and uniqueness of terroir.

Consumers are increasingly interested in the artisanal approach, along with issues such as climate change, sustainability and biodiversity. A growing desire for greater transparency is being met by a more informative mindset on the part of producers, big and small, keen to feed this new curiosity and match it with greater clarity, albeit from diverse perspectives and with different objectives. Greater attention is being paid to QR codes and back labels featuring tirage and disgorgement dates, details of varietal composition, percentages of vintages and the like. Gone are the days when Krug could market its Champagne with the condescending slogan 'Krug is Krug'.

This book is not trying to cover all the bases. In selecting which producers to profile, I have been conscious that there are many books on Champagne but far fewer on wines in the sparkling realm beyond it. It's not just that Champagne has for centuries been where the glamour lies, but until recently, the sparkling wines of the world outside Champagne haven't been particularly remarkable other than as, shall we say, Champagne substitutes. I am aware that a number of producers that I, and doubtless others, would like to have included have been squeezed out by the constraints of space.

In the *Observer* (18 April 2021), David Williams wrote: 'Prosecco's rise is just a part of what has been a golden age for sparkling wines. In the early 2000s, Champagne was responsible for almost all the best sparkling wines in the world; in the years since, producers from Austria, Germany, Canada, Tasmania, Catalonia, Franciacorta and Trentino in northern Italy, and, perhaps most promising of all, southern England, have all emerged to challenge the northern French region's hegemony with some truly spellbinding bottles.' Perhaps he was strapped for space because he might also have mentioned South Africa, California, Slovenia, Croatia, New Zealand and Japan.

This is not coincidental. The spectacular rise of Prosecco, from sales of 60 million to 600 million bottles over the past two decades, has fed consumer aspirations to the glam lifestyle without having to beg, steal or borrow. As the UK's Chancellor of the Exchequer, Rishi Sunak, said when he reduced sparkling wine duty in his autumn budget of 27 October 2021, 'it's clear [sparkling wines] are no longer the preserve of wealthy elites'. Buoyed by results in competitions and growing consumer awareness, producers in emerging countries and regions have taken advantage of climate change and consumer trends to try their hand at making bubbles and finding, perhaps as much to their surprise as ours, that they're really rather good at it.

Terroir no longer has to be reverentially whispered with a French accent. Once regarded as little more than country cousins attempting, at best, to reproduce Champagne itself, today's producers of fizz have become confident exponents of the style. Where once sparkling wine was regarded as a wine of celebration, today it comes in a range of styles in which celebration may play a role but is not the be-all and end-all. A growing global thirst for fizz, abetted by a serious approach to making sparkling wine from quality grapes, has resulted in a reappraisal of the style. Now that fizz can be enjoyed as an aperitif, an ice breaker or with food, it has become a wine for all occasions.

Thanks to the long-established pre-eminence of Champagne, the challenge to its position as the nonpareil of the sparkling wine world has taken a while to materialize, but materialize it has. None of this is to deny the place of Champagne either in this book or in our fridge doors. The tradition, heritage and prestige associated with Champagne will always influence perceptions of quality. Rightly so. In its best expression, Champagne remains a yardstick of incredible achievement for both consumers and producers, but it is merely one yardstick. Its very familiarity can sometimes obscure the fact that sparkling wines from emerging wine countries and regions don't have to be Champagne imitators and can express the character of fizz in different ways.

As Corinne Seely, the winemaker at Hampshire's Exton Park, points out: 'As a French winemaker, I am certainly not in the UK to make a pale copy of Champagne. We are perhaps making a new category of bubbles and that is unbelievably exciting! It is almost like creating a new style in fashion.' In this book I aim to shine a light on this new sparkling wine phenomenon beyond the frontiers of Champagne, focusing on the newcomers, exploring how they've carved out an identity for themselves and reviewing their direction of travel, with all the excitement that the genuine prospect of a new sparkling wine world order brings.

PART 1
ANATOMY OF THE BUBBLE

1

A BRIEF HISTORY OF THE BUBBLE

THE DAY THEY INVENTED CHAMPAGNE

In 1992 I was a member of a trade and press group visiting Moldova at the request of the Moldovan government to assess the country's potential for bringing its wine to the West. The majority of the group was French, so they pricked up their ears when Tom Stevenson, a leading Champagne authority, got up during a dinner in the cavernous sparkling wine cellars of Cricova to make a speech on the origins of Champagne. Fascination turned to indignation as Mr Stevenson informed us that it was the British, not the French, who invented Champagne. An affront needing to be avenged, the French contingent struck up the Marseillaise in the bus back to the hotel. Stevenson and I sat at the back quietly humming 'Greensleeves'. An international incident was narrowly averted.

Sparkling wine was already part of the language by the time Dom Pierre Pérignon took up his post in the Abbey of Hautvillers in 1668 at the age of 29. In a paper presented on 17 December 1662 to the newly formed Royal Society, 'Some Observations Concerning the Ordering of Wines', the Oxford-educated Dr Christopher Merret noted: 'Our wine coopers of recent times add vast quantities of sugar and molasses to all sorts of wines to make the drink brisk and sparkling.'

Merret learnt about the method of creating bubbles by adding sugar from the cidermakers of Hereford, Somerset and Gloucester. '[It] comes into the glass with a speedy vanishing nittiness which evaporates with a sparkling and whizzing noise,' said the cidermaker Silas Taylor. Just a week before Merret presented his paper, the Reverend John Beale's 'Aphorisms on Cider', read to the Royal Society on 10 December 1662, said that 'bottling is the next best improver' for cider and that 'two to three raisins into every bottle' plus 'a walnut of sugar' was a recipe guaranteed to produce a second fermentation.

The crusading Pope Urban II, born in Châtillon-sur-Marne in Champagne, brought fame to the wines of Aÿ on his accession in 1088. The region's two main grape varieties were Gouais, used for the red *vins de Montagne*, and the pinkish grey Fromenteau, destined for the white *vins de Rivière*. Lavish banquets at the coronations of Louis XI in 1461, of Louis XII in 1498, Francis I in 1515 and Francis II in 1559 were washed down with wines from Burgundy and Champagne. It wasn't until Henri III was crowned in 1575 that, for the first time, only the still wines of Champagne were served. Louis XIII served only Champagne wines at his coronation by the archbishop of Reims in 1610. His successor Louis XIV was partial to them but when his doctor, Guy-Crescent Fagon, insisted he only drink burgundy for health reasons – Champagne being too acidic – this set the stage for the transformation of Champagne into a new kind of drink altogether: one with bubbles.

In 1662, the same year that Merret presented his Royal Society paper, the dashing epicurean Charles de Margeutel de Saint Denis, seigneur de Saint-Évremond, arrived in London after being banished from the court of French king Louis XIV for rubbing his educator and minister Cardinal Mazarin up the wrong way. Along with the Marquis de Bois-Dauphin and the Comte d'Olonne, Évremond was a founder of the dining club nicknamed 'the three coteaux'. The English court of Charles II at the time was effectively a satellite of the court of Louis XIV at Versailles. As a friend of Charles II and an ambassador for the still wines from the Côte des Blancs and the Montagne de Reims, in particular from Aÿ, Hautvillers, Sillery and Avenay, the merry Marquis regarded it as his mission to introduce these wines to Restoration London. A year later, the satirist Samuel Butler referred to brisk Champagne in his satirical poem *Hudibras*:

That shall infuse eternal spring,
And everiasting flourishing:
Drink every letter on't in stum.
And make it brisk champaign become.

In contrast to the fortified wines, Port and Sherry, Sillery, imported in cask, was popular with the grandees who frequented London cafés, and at society hostesses' suppers, for its refreshing prickle on the tongue. It's no coincidence that ice houses first became fashionable during the reign of Charles II. In ritualistic scenes worthy of *Eyes Wide Shut*, the Marquis de Sillery used young girls dressed as priestesses of Bacchus to present him with his best bottles. This is likely to have been similar to tocane (also known as tocanne), a traditionally fermented, notoriously acidic rose-coloured sparkling wine from Aÿ, which was already in demand by 1675. With its light, perky acidity, it became as fashionable a new phenomenon as today's natural wines. In 1676, the English playwright Sir George Etheridge wrote in his Restoration comedy *The Man of Mode*:

> To the mall and the park, where we love till 'tis dark,
> Then sparkling champaign puts an end to their reign;
> It quickly recovers poor languishing lovers,
> makes us frolick and gay and drown our sorrows;
> But alas we relapse again on the morrow

Verre anglais, as the French called it, was stronger than French glass and better able to withstand the pressure caused by a second fermentation in the bottle. In 1625 King James I prohibited the use of English oaks for firewood since they were needed for shipbuilding by the Royal Navy in the war effort against the French. Thanks to this, glassmakers such as Sir Robert Mansell turned to coal-fired furnaces reinforced with iron and manganese for smelting glassware, making the hand-blown bottles stronger than anything that the French glass manufacturers of the period were capable of. Wine glasses too were fortified with lead oxide so that by the end of the seventeenth century, the upper middle classes and landed gentry were using lead crystal vessels.

Sir Kenelm Digby's Newnham glassworks produced a style of bottle initially adopted by the nearby cider and perry producers for its strength and shape. Using a wind tunnel to heat his coal-fired furnace to ferocious levels, he made a bottle strong enough to hold sparkling cider. The glass was dark and, protected in this way from the light, the cider was given a shelf life that extended to two or three years. This strong, dark glass was used to form an onion-shaped bottle with a long neck, the strong rim of which was capable of holding a stopper in place with the string tied to a ring of glass around the neck. Before cork came along, the stopper was a wooden toggle wrapped in hemp and soaked in tallow.

The introduction of the cork, which, like strong glass, was in use by the English before the French, proved revolutionary. Corks were first held in place by hemp string, before wire or staples became the norm.

TASTING THE STARS

It is clear that by the time Dom Pierre Pérignon entered the scene, the sparkling wine die was cast. However, following the French Revolution at the end of the eighteenth century, Dom Grossard, who had been a monk at Hautvillers before the abbey's suppression during the Revolution, put such a gloss on Pérignon's achievements that it was easy for Comte Pierre Gabriel Chandon de Briailles, son-in-law of Jean-Rémy Moët, to burnish the story when he bought the ruins of Hautvillers in 1822. The cult of Dom Pérignon was duly instigated and with the restoration of the site and the addition of a museum, 'art and nature, together with generations of clever propaganda, combine to seduce the visitor into the delusion that Champagne was invented here during the near half-century between 1668 and 1714 when Dom Pérignon was procurator of the Abbey,' says Nicholas Faith in *The story of Champagne*.

Dom Pérignon wasn't primed to look for sparkling wine, although he did stick a few bottles upside down in the sand to have a go at capturing the elusive sparkle that surged in the barrel as the yeasts awoke from hibernation in spring. The fact is that Champagne was not so much an invention as an evolutionary process. In the late seventeenth and early eighteenth century, no one had a clue how secondary fermentation actually worked. Its development was the cumulative result of a number of processes devised by a series of clever people over a very long period of time. To be fair, while Dom Pérignon's famous quote 'come quickly, I am drinking the stars' is probably apocryphal, his intuition may have told him that the gentle sparkle he found as the wines refermented was the effect of the earth's gravitational pull.

While he may not have invented sparkling wine, Pérignon was a pioneer in several respects. Conscious of the potential of the region's chalk soils, he was meticulous about pruning for low yields, and harvesting selectively for optimum ripeness and freshness in the morning before temperatures rose. In the vineyard he preferred mules and donkeys to horses for their calmer nature. He placed the *pressoir* (he had access to four presses) closer to the vineyard itself for rapid press runs. Using the first pressing and keeping skin contact to a minimum helped produce a delicate, bright white wine from Pinot Noir. White grapes had less flavour and a tendency to referment and prematurely age. By blending wines from the abbey's 10 hectares of vineyards with the many grapes derived from the *dîme*, the fraction of the tenant's crop to which the abbey had the rights, he was able to create a wine of superior quality.

The fact that by the turn of the century the wines from Hautvillers were worth four times that of ordinary Champagne wines was strong evidence that the teetotal, vegetarian monk was a master viticulturalist, winemaker, taster and blender. He also imported strong glass from England and cork from Spain to help with the process of ageing in bottle. But Dom Pérignon was not alone in his endeavours. A younger contemporary of Pérignon, Frère Jean Oudart, was a winemaking pioneer at the Abbé de Pierry with control over vineyards, latterly *grands crus*, in Pierry, Cramant and Chouilly in the Côte des Blancs.

A decree of 25 May 1728 allowing Champagne to be transported in bottle and subsequent decrees standardizing the size, weight and capacity of bottles and the secure tying of the cork (*ficelage*) helped lay the foundation for Champagne as an industry. By the beginning of the French Revolution, nine of the firms familiar today had been established: Ruinart (1729), Chanoine Frère (1730), Taittinger, then called Forst Furneaux (1734), Moët & Chandon (1743), Henri Abelé, then Van der Veken (1757), Lanson, then Delamotte (1760), Roederer, then Dubois Père et Fils (1765), Clicquot (1772) and Heidsieck (1785). Champagne was the only wine to be served at the Fête de la Fédération held on the Champs de Mars on 14 July 1790 to toast the outcome of the French Revolution; and Memmie Jacquesson opened up for business in Châlons-sur-Marne in 1798.

CHAMPAGNE TAKES OFF

While Champagne fuelled the debauchery of the court of the French Regent, Philippe Duc d'Orléans, and was a drink beloved of the eighteenth century's metropolitan elite and the aristocracy, it was still at best a hit-and-miss affair. As a *mousseux*, or *saute-bouchon*, its effervescence developed naturally. In his *Origine et Développement du Vin de Champagne* (1848), Armand Maizière observed that by the beginning of the eighteenth century, putting the sparkle into Champagne was a precarious business beset by the technical problems of mass breakages, defective corks and frequent lack of effervescence.

By 1800, 300,000 bottles a year were being produced. But technical progress and the rise of an appreciative European middle class wanting in on the action would soon transform Champagne from a luxury confined to an aristocratic elite into an international commodity. In 1807, the emperor Napoleon visited Jean-Rémy Moët, Mayor of Épernay. The ill wind of Napoleon's incessant wars blew its benefits into the cellars of Reims and Épernay as Russians developed a taste for the bubble and Champagne salesmen followed Napoleon's military campaigns through Europe to set up networks with a thirsty new clientèle in Austria, Prussia and Poland.

'Today they drink, tomorrow they will pay,' Madame Clicquot is reported to have said, after Reims and Épernay fell to the Russians and the Prussians in 1814. Sure enough, before long, her salesman, Louis Bohne, had the Russian tongue hanging out with the Halley's comet vintage of 1811 and as their sales rose to 30,000 bottles, Clicquot and Roederer together were to turn Russia into an export market second only to Britain. T. G. Shaw, a Victorian British wine merchant, wrote: 'I have heard it alleged of the Russians that they keep their windows open when they have a party in order that those in and out of the house may hear the reports of the Champagne bottles, and so become duly impressed by the style of the entertainment.'

Newcomers poured into Reims and Épernay from Switzerland and Germany. Soon after the restoration of the Bourbon monarchy in 1814, demand saw 25 firms elbowing each other for space along Épernay's Rue de Commerce, later to become the Avenue de Champagne. To the existing names, those of many of today's leading houses were added: Henriot (1808), Joseph Perrier (1825), Mumm (1827), Bollinger (1829), Pommery (1836), Krug (1843), Pol Roger (1849), Mercier (1858) and Gratien (1864). It was the merchants who created the demand and made a success of Champagne as a brand. The legacy of Champagne branding explains in part why it has taken so long for Champagne to achieve recognition as a wine of terroir.

Nonetheless, early attempts to classify Champagne's terroirs foreshadowed the Échelle des Crus, created in 1911. On his trip to the region in 1788, Thomas Jefferson, later to become third President of the United States, remarked on the quality of *crus* such as Aÿ, Hautvillers, Cramant, Avize and Le Mesnil. In 1816, André Jullien ranked *crus* into five categories of quality, rating Verzy, Verzenay, Mailly, Saint-Basle, Bouzy and Clos Saint-Thierry in the top rank of Champagne's red grapes, and Sillery, Aÿ, Mareuil, Hautvillers, Pierry and Dizy at the head of the region's white grapes. By 1880, the price per hectare of Aÿ and Dizy was running at 40,000–50,000 francs, Bouzy and Ambonnay 38,000–40,000 francs and Le Mesnil 22,000–25,000 francs.

In 1828, the first Champagne Stakes horse race was run in England. By 1853, over ten million bottles were being produced per year, nearly eight million of which were destined for export, with some 2.5 million delivered in France to wine merchants and consumers. Exports to England were boosted by Napoleon III's Free Trade Agreement of 1860 and the consequent lowering of import duty taxes. Impressive as the resulting growth was, even the increasing production figures pale into insignificance compared to the golden age to come: the Belle Époque. As the Australian author Rob Walters puts it: 'Sweet, cold and bubbly, Champagne was to become the world's first mass party drug.'

TECHNICAL BREAKTHROUGH

While the global dissemination of Champagne was due to the many indefatigable and often colourful salesmen who took their product to the client, rivalry between the houses and the growing competition for new markets acted as a spur to all the houses to achieve the many technical breakthroughs that led, ultimately, to quality improvements. Among new technical developments, it's impossible to overestimate the importance of the *liqueur de tirage*. In his *Traité théorique et pratique sur la Culture de la Vigne* of 1801, Napoleon's Minister of the Interior, the scientist Jean-Antoine Chaptal, had already been advocating the addition of sugar to wine to increase its alcoholic strength and thereby stabilize a product of dubious quality and limited shelf life.

Chaptalization apart, by 1830, adding sugar had become a regular practice to get the second fermentation under way. The problem was that it increased the rate of bottle shatter. Breakages were running at an average of 20 per cent but in 1828 and again in 1835, excessive sugar addition led to a huge proportion of bottles being smashed. Champagne's cellars must have sounded as though there was a war on and indeed, without a mask, you took your life in your hands. 'I know of one cellar in which there are three men who have each lost an eye owing to this case,' wrote T. G. Shaw.

Before the *liqueur de tirage* was introduced to the process, Champagne sparkled because its natural effervescence had been captured in the bottle with the continuation of the first fermentation. In 1836, the invention of the saccharometer by Jean-Baptiste François, a pharmacist from Châlons-sur-Marne, resulted in the development of a precise formula for measuring the sugar in the base wine before it underwent a second fermentation in the bottle. This, combined with Pasteur's discovery of the role of yeast in 1857, and assisted by stronger bottles, better corks and wire muzzles to hold the cork in place, led Champagne production to achieve stable secondary fermentation, and the incidence of smashed bottles was brought under tighter control. However, a way of removing the sediment while still preserving the carbon dioxide in the wine had yet to be devised.

RIDDLE-ME-REE

In the process known as *remuage*, or riddling, the yeast particles that stick stubbornly to the side of the bottle are gradually coaxed into the upside-down neck and onto the cork. This process was discovered by Barbe-Nicole Clicquot Ponsardin following the death of her husband in 1805. The 27-year-old widow designed a wooden table with holes carved in it to hold inverted bottles while she tapped and tweaked them to get the stubborn sediment to move down towards the cork. Legend has it that this all happened in her kitchen, but more likely, the experimental table that had great holes gouged out of it was in the Clicquot cellars – otherwise dining chez Clicquot might have been something of a gamble.

Madame Clicquot then hired the services of the skilled chef de cave Antoine Müller, who hit upon the ingenious solution of carving the holes in the table at a 45 degree angle. In this way, the bottle could be twisted sharply and continually until the bottle was perpendicular and the sediment duly sat on the cork, ready to be removed. This in turn led to the creation of the rectangular *pupitre*, two boards joined at the top by a hinge to form an inverted V, and with it a whole new profession of *remueurs*. Madame Clicquot managed to keep the process secret at least until 1821 and the extra clarity her Champagnes had for this period of time gave her a competitive advantage over her rivals. By 1850, use of the *pupitre* was standard practice and repetitive strain injury a more likely common cause for complaint among cellar workers than shattered glass.

This still left the tricky problem of disgorgement. Once the sediment was removed, it left a bone dry, often tart, wine. Sugar had to be added to make it more palatable, particularly to the sweet of tooth, such as the Russians, who liked as much as 250–330 grams per litre of sugar, leading to a drink 'only good for savages and children', according to George Saintsbury. Scandinavia, France, Germany and the USA came next down the sweetness pecking order. Drunk before and during a meal in the UK, the British preferred the driest style, although at 22–66 grams per litre, it was still way above what we know as dry today. The first dosage machine was invented in 1844, allowing a measured amount of dissolved sugar and wine or brandy to be added following disgorgement to create the final balance. Brandy was routinely used because when the alcoholic strength was reduced by the addition of sugar, the alcoholic balance had to be redressed through the incorporation of brandy.

After the London wine merchant, a Mr Burne, tasted and enjoyed the 1846 vintage of Perrier-Jouët in its natural, unsweetened state, he surmised that this drier style might just go well with food, especially since the English were already amply supplied with sweet and sticky wines in the shape of Sherry and Port. Unfortunately, he found the wine so difficult to sell that 'eventually Mr Burne drank it all himself, every single bottle of it,' according to André Simon. The excellent 1865 vintage was shipped almost unsweetened by Ayala and Bollinger and became an instant hit with the Prince of Wales. Clicquot waited until after the widow's death in 1866 before shipping a dry version, but it was the outstanding vintage of 1874 that sealed the fate of sweet Champagne. Although George Saintsbury confessed that he didn't share 'the prevailing mania for Pommery', Madame Pommery's 1874 vintage was the catalyst that reconciled the sweet Champagne drinker to the drier style. It was to take another century however before brut Champagne was to dominate the market.

It was also a time when the commercial success of Champagne was threatened on two fronts, first by variable quality and second by the expansion of sparkling wine production. It wasn't just the capricious vintage variations that made the quality of Champagne so uneven and price so up and down. According to the British writer Cyrus Redding: 'In 1818 there were effervescing wines sold (by the producer in Champagne) at from one franc 25 cents to one franc 50 cents; these wines were of a very inferior quality, and being sweetened with sugar and spirit, could only answer for instant consumption ... Some of the growers and merchants never keep any Champagne but of the best quality, and never sell under three francs. These are the best persons of whom to buy.'

The problem wasn't due just to Champagnes of inferior quality but also to those of dubious origin. Legitimate and illegitimate imitators were rife. Writing in 1870, the Bristol wine merchant Charles Tovey tells of seeing 'a very large number of casks of White Loire Wine at the railway station at Aÿ'. Eventually, following a lawsuit by the Grandes Marques, in 1887, the Court of Appeal in Angers decreed: 'Henceforth the term "Champagne" or "Champagne wines" shall refer exclusively to wine produced in, and sourced from, the ancient province of Champagne, an area with specific boundaries that shall neither be extended nor contracted.'

One of the most important developments in the process was yet to come: disgorgement by freezing (*à la glace*) invented by one Armand Walfart, in 1884. Essentially, the ingenious new technique required the use of a shallow, refrigerated tray containing brine and held at -20°C. The neck of an inverted bottle is dipped into the liquid, temporarily freezing the wine and sediment collected on the bottom on the cork. The bottle is then turned upright and as the cork is removed, the plug of ice with sediment attached is ejected by the pressure in the bottle. The remaining wine is 'stunned' by the chill and stays in the bottle, allowing the liqueur d'expédition to be added and the bottle resealed.

Thanks to Walfart's innovation, eventually patented in 1896, and of course, ever-growing demand, production soared to 30 million bottles by the end of the century, and 39 million by 1910. By 1906–7, Champagne held stocks of 121 million bottles, with 23 million exported and 10 million drunk in France. In 1902, Mumm sent 1.5 million bottles across the Atlantic to the United States, where sales quadrupled between 1900 and 1909. After Britain, it had become Champagne's biggest export market. It was the heyday of Champagne's vineyards too. Before phylloxera struck and economic decline set in, there were an estimated 60,000 hectares of vineyards planted, almost twice the current figure.

CONSPICUOUS CONSUMPTION

Fin de siècle hedonism mirrored earlier excesses in a dizzying whirl of endless, conspicuous consumption by the nouveau riche bourgeoisie of Paris, London and New York. If ever there was a symbol of this decadence, it was the Champagne Mercier cask. Taking 19 years to construct under the supervision of the aptly named cooper, M. Jolibois, Eugène

Mercier created the largest barrel in the world for the 1889 Exposition Universelle in Paris. On 7 May 1889, the 20-tonne cask, constructed from 170 Hungarian oaks and containing the equivalent of 200,000 bottles, was drawn through Paris by 24 white Morvan oxen, making its grandiose entrance to a rapturous reception after the enforced widening of the entrance to the exhibition hall.

In London, Escoffier's Savoy Hotel wine list offered Bollinger, Deutz and Clicquot vintages ranging from 1884 to 1893, while other hotels and restaurants rushed to add Champagne to their lists. According to Colonel Newnham-Davis in his guide to London restaurants: 'in London … ladies as a rule will consider a dinner at a restaurant incomplete without Champagne. Ninety-nine out of a hundred Englishmen, in ordering a little dinner for two, turn instinctively to the Champagne page of the wine card.' Vintage Champagne made its mark in the 1880s and the Gay Nineties became the peak of Champagne's popularity. Champagne overflowed during the Belle Époque at the turn of the new century when going out to fancy restaurants and cafés, to cabaret and music hall to see and be seen, was the order of the day.

Labels linked Champagne to love, marriage, sports and leisure. One label showing two cyclists in hot pursuit of a young female cyclist with windswept hair announced: 'Grand Vin des Cyclistes. Fin de

Siècle'. Champagne fuelled art nouveau, haute couture, the Decadent movement's writers and poets and the Bohemian lifestyle symbolized by dancers such as La Goulue and Jane Avril, who modelled for Toulouse-Lautrec. During the Dreyfus affair, a Champagne Anti-Juif (Anti-Jew Champagne) was launched to exploit anti-Semitic sentiment. Approaching war was met by the indefatigable marketeers of Champagne with new labels of flags, soldiers and battles to fit the relevant importing country.

A RIOTOUS TIME

Imports to the UK peaked at 9.6 million bottles in 1897. Even in 1906, the UK was still the biggest importer at 7 million bottles, a figure not achieved again until 1982. 'It was the last fling of an age that was to end in the trenches,' as Serena Sutcliffe puts it. The *fin de siècle* marked the beginning of a series of economic and political disasters that were to ravage the Champagne region for a long time to come. The phylloxera louse arrived late in Champagne, in 1890, to the tolling of bells. Le Comte Gaston Chandon set fire to the vines of one of his growers, M. Piot-Husson, in an effort to eradicate the pest. This was of course in vain, since as we now know it was only *vinifera* grafted onto American rootstock that would resist phylloxera. At Moët's École de Viticulture, set up in 1899 in Épernay, an army of vignerons was trained in the art of grafting, but the region's vineyards were not entirely reconstituted until the 1920s.

Grape prices fell by 80 per cent between 1889 and 1902 and, with the exception of the excellent vintages of 1904 and 1906, a series of rot- and mildew-affected vintages from 1902 through to the disastrous 1910 vintage culminated in the Champagne riots of 1910 and 1911. With supply under threat but demand still strong, new vineyards were being planted. At the same time, a number of merchants were looking to sources such as the Loire, Chablis and Picpoul for their grape supplies. Some producers were mixing in apple juice and there were even rumours that some were buying rhubarb from England to make their wine. Figures from growers in the Marne showed that in each of the years 1907–10, Champagne sales considerably outstripped production of Marne Wines. With the ballooning of counterfeit Champagne, provenance had become a major issue and boundaries had to be drawn.

In 1908, the drawing of the boundaries of Champagne included the *départements* of Marne and parts of the Aisne, representing an area of some 15,000 hectares, but left out the Aube region to the south. Nonetheless, growers in the Aube continued to sell their grapes to Champagne houses. Growers in the Marne who had lost out in earlier poor vintages realized that some houses were still buying grapes from Aube growers, who had been generally better off during the lean years thanks to a marginally warmer climate. When the Marne growers converged in Épernay and blocked grape shipments, the government reacted quickly, passing a law in 1911 restricting the use of Aube grapes.

Aubois growers reacted with fury, marching into Troyes with hoes made into lances. Thirty-six local mayors resigned and 8,000 growers marched through the streets of Bar-sur-Aube, set fire to their tax returns and burnt an effigy of the prime minister, Monis. When the government backed down, the Marne growers in turn became incensed and marched on Épernay. Riots broke out in Damery, Dizy, Cumières and Hautvillers. Growers intercepted trucks from the Loire and pushed them into the Marne. They went on the rampage in Aÿ, ransacking the cellars and houses of merchants suspected of buying grapes from elsewhere, smashing barrels of wine, setting buildings on fire and turning the streets into rivers of Champagne.

The government had to draft 40,000 troops into Épernay to restore order. By June 1911, a compromise was reached by which the Aube was to be given the temporary title of 'Champagne Deuxième Zone'. In the same year, the Échelle des Crus was established to regulate the price of grapes. The full price would be paid to *grand cru* growers and between 80 and 99 per cent to growers in *premier cru* villages, with the scale sliding down to villages initially ranked as low as 22.5 per cent. Eventually, the minimum percentage increased to 80 per cent, but once the price of grapes was no longer fixed, in 1990, the Échelle lost its raison d'être and was abolished in 2010. The relevance of the Échelle des Crus today remains only insofar as it classifies 17 *grand cru* and 42 *premier cru* villages.

Long before the new law restoring the Aube to Champagne came into effect (it took until a law passed on 22 July 1927, defining the zone of Champagne production, followed by the creation of the official appellation of Champagne in 1936), German troops marched into Reims, entering the city on 3 September 1914 and reaching Épernay three days later. Heroically, the harvest was picked in the so-called blood vintages of 1914 and 1915 even though the great coronation city itself, reduced to rubble, had to be evacuated. The wine continued to be made and many thousands inhabited Champagne's subterranean chalk cellars, where interconnecting passageways were cut between rival companies, Veuve Clicquot, Pommery, Mumm and Ruinart. By the end of the war, 100 civilians from a pre-war population of 120,000 remained.

ONWARDS AND UPWARDS

In the postwar era, Champagne lost many of its most important markets. The October Revolution of 1917 put paid to the autocracy of Tsar Nicholas II and his bubble-loving court. Vodka, the drink of the proletariat, took the place of Champagne, resulting in a 10 per cent loss of sales. Thanks to Prohibition, brought in on 1 July 1919, Champagne lost its route to the United States. In the same year, the French government laid the groundwork for the AOC system and the decimation of the region's vineyards, reduced from 60,000 to just 12,000 hectares by 1919, gave growers the opportunity to replant with phylloxera-resistant rootstock in more suitable locations.

For a while, the Roaring Twenties kept Champagne afloat, but the great Depression of the late 1920s and early 1930s put paid to any hopes of a longer-term revival. The Second World War brought further devastation to Champagne with the occupation of the region from May 1940 until its liberation on 28 August 1944. The only silver lining was the establishment of a Bureau de Répartition for Champagne during the occupation at the request of Robert-Jean de Vogüé and Maurice Doyard to the Vichy government. The Germans had to work with the Bureau to get Champagne for the Wehrmacht and bars, restaurants, hotels and brothels, in Paris mostly, but also for consumption in Germany. Knowing that the Bureau de Répartition would be too linked to the war and the Vichy government, in 1941 the two presidents asked Vichy to change the name to Comité Interprofessional du Vin de Champagne (CIVC). This was an important step in creating a fulcrum between the competing demands of the Champagne houses and the growers who supplied them, regulating grape prices, controlling quality, instigating future planning and setting up protection mechanisms. On 8 May 1945, the signing of Germany's unconditional surrender was celebrated with six cases of 1934 Pommery. As Don and Petie Kladstrup have noted, 'the last explosions of the war were the popping of Champagne corks'.

After the war, Champagne's fortunes moved in cycles of boom and decline. Surges in sales such as those in 1967, 1973 and 1989 were buffeted by crashes and slumps due to circumstances beyond their control such as the student riots of 1968, the oil crisis of 1974, the stock-market crash of 1987 and the Gulf War of 1991. At the same time, a generation that had known only lean years in Champagne welcomed the increased use of chemicals and intensive farming with open arms. In 1951, the average yield was 2,900 kilograms per hectare. By 2019, thanks to a greater consistency of yield brought about initially by intensive agriculture and subsequently by global warming, yields had more than trebled to 10,200 kilograms per hectare.

A strategy to reduce the effect of volatility by targeting export countries resulted in a peak of sales of 185 million bottles in the late 1970s and a further boom, to 249 million bottles in 1989. By the turn of the millennium, the sales figure rose to 327 million bottles. Whenever one bubble bursts, in the end it always turns out to be the hiatus between two corks popping. That is the story of Champagne.

Not until the early 1970s did brut Champagnes begin to dominate the market. By the mid-1990s producers had begun to lower the sugar levels in their non-vintage brut wines in response to a taste for drier Champagne, aided by warmer climate conditions. The trend to drier styles accelerated after the heatwave 2003 harvest, encouraged by the increased use of reserve wines in this low-yielding vintage. Producers have lowered dosages to maintain styles owing to riper and better grapes, increased use of reserve wines and longer lees contact times, but also to create drier Champagne. Today, a level close to 8–9 grams per litre, a 2–3 grams per litre drop since 1991, is generally deemed ideal to balance current acidities, enhance fruit flavours, and provide a dry enough style for global tastes.

By the early 1970s, the world of Champagne was changing significantly. Large financial groups began to acquire or dismantle the independent houses at a rapid rate. At the same time, the growth of supermarket monoliths was creating a demand for large volumes and low prices. It's no coincidence that a reaction against brand-led commercialism and a desire for wines of terroir marked the rise to prominence of Champagne's growers. Big brands continue to dominate the market, but thanks to a small band of pioneering growers, a renewed focus on the vineyard has resulted in more conscientious vineyard management and winemaking and less emphasis on bubbles per se. The resulting focus on Champagne as a wine has not only had positive consequences for Champagne itself, but also inspired confidence in the potential for authenticity and excellence among aspiring fizz producers around the globe.

The bubble beyond Champagne

According to the historian Benoît Musset, the first recorded mention of sparkling wine is found in an Egyptian papyrus document dated AD 522. Sparkling wines were considered flawed, and secondary fermentation in spring is listed as one of the factors making wines unfit for sale. In the 1201 miracle play *Le Jeu de Saint Nicolas*, Jehan Bodel portrays characters in an inn, with one commenting: 'see how it devours its bubbles, how it sparkles, shimmers and bounces'. Épernay wine is described in a 1320 poem by Watriquet de Couvin as 'sparkling on the tongue, clear, quivering, strong, fine and fresh'. In Limoux in France's south-west, the Benedictine monks of the Abbaye de Saint-Hilaire mentioned the distribution of Blanquette de Limoux in cork-stoppered flasks in 1531 (although the 1544 accounts of the Sire d'Arques referred to the grape variety rather than a sparkling wine as such).

Champagne's pre-eminence as a sparkling wine region in the eighteenth century provoked envy and inspired competition. Seeing that Champagne had stolen a sparkling march on burgundy, the Dijon agronomist, Edme Beguillet, describes Champagne, in 1770, as 'the only industry capable of bringing previously non-existent wines out of obscurity, and bestowing reputation on a previously unknown product.' In 1845, the champenois had become so concerned at imitations that a lawsuit brought by a group of Champagne houses resulted in the French Cour de Cassation banning the use of the name Champagne as a generic label for French sparkling wines. Cyrus Redding listed Die, Saint-Péray, Limoux, Anjou and Belfort among French regions making fizz in the first half of the nineteenth century. By the late 1800s, the roster had expanded beyond French borders to include Italy, Germany, Russia, Switzerland, Hungary, Spain, Australia and the USA. Mass production was helped by the introduction of the moulded bottle in 1882.

Australia's first serious attempts at sparkling wine began in the late 1840s when Edward Cory and William Burnett showed their 'champagnes' at the Hunter Valley Vignerons Association, following which New South Wales, Victoria and South Australia were soon to get in on the act. By the 1880s, French winemaker Auguste d'Argent of the Victorian Champagne Company, was making 'Sparkling Burgundy' and Charles Pierlot was brought out by the sparkling wine pioneer Hans Irvine from Pommery and Greno Champagne in 1890. Mark Twain observed the Australian weakness for 'champagne' and visited the extensive cellars at Great Western In 1895. Another Frenchman, Edmond Mazure, made sparkling 'burgundy' at Auldana near Adelaide in the early 1890s, subsequently producing an array of sparkling wines under the La Perouse label in the 1910s.

Sparkling wine production was already sufficiently established in America by the mid-nineteenth century for the wine merchant T. G. Shaw, writing in 1864, to conclude: 'The most important vineyards are those of Ohio, Missouri and Indiana, but the most celebrated is in Cincinnati'. In 1842, Nicholas Longworth, a Cincinnati lawyer, produced sparkling Catawba after a batch of wine accidentally went through a second fermentation. He became rich enough to bring in winemaking savoir-faire and technology from Champagne, but alas, the first Frenchman to arrive drowned in the Ohio River, while the second lost 42,000 out of 50,000 bottles in one season to burst bottles. Third time lucky, a M. Fournier arrived in 1852 and Longworth was soon producing 100,000 bottles a year. Longworth sent a case to the abolitionist poet Henry Wadsworth Longfellow, who described it as having 'a taste more divine, more dulcet, delicious and dreamy [than Champagne]'.

While the first New York 'champagne' was made in 1865 by Joseph Masson, who called it sparkling Catawba, he and his brother Jules made a cuvée in 1870, which was mistaken at a meeting of Pleasant Valley growers for a 'great champagne of the West' (i.e. California). While the eastern states were making merry with fizz, Pierre Sainsevain, on returning from Champagne, set up a winery in San Jose for bottle-fermented 'sparkling California'. At the same time, Agoston Haraszthy sent his son Arpad to Champagne to learn the tricks of the fizz trade at De Venoge. Arpad was later to produce Eclipse, one of the most successful American sparkling wines of the 1870s. Meanwhile, Paul Masson, who left Burgundy for California in 1878 at the age of 19, was to become known as the 'Champagne King of California' after establishing the Paul Masson Champagne Company in 1892.

The sparkling wine industry was bubbling under in nineteenth-century Europe too. Georg Kessler, who had worked for Madame Clicquot, left in 1826 to found the firm of GC Kessler in Esslingen and, with it, the German sparkling wine industry was born. Carlo Gancia is believed to have cut his sparkling winemaking teeth at de Venoge in 1848, returning to his native Piemonte to create the first 'Italian champagne' in 1865. Prosecco's future was foretold after Federico Martinotti developed a prototype of the tank method, allowing refermentation of the base wines in *autoclavi* (large pressurized tanks). The *metodo Martinotti* was patented in 1895 before Eugène Charmat took up the baton and patented the Charmat method in 1907. While the claim for the first

Spanish sparkling wine belongs to Antoni Gali Comas in around 1850, the first to pioneer a bottle-fermented sparkling wine from local Penedès varieties was Josep Raventós in 1872.

In Pozsony (now Bratislava), Johann Evangelist Hubert returned from Napoleon's campaigns in Russia to make sparkling wine. The company that became Hubert was founded in 1825 by Mihály Schönburger and János Fischer and won the award for best Hungarian sparkling wine in 1842. The first sparkling producer on the Pest side of Budapest was founded in 1852, but domestic fizz production didn't really take off until later in the nineteenth century. In neighbouring Slovenia, sparkling history dates back to 1852 when the first traditional method bubbles appeared in Radgona (today in Austria), a tradition continued by Radgonske Gorice on the Slovenian side of the border. In Moldova, it's reported that Prince Paravichini made 'an extremely pure champagne probably from the Iaidzhi variety [possibly Chasselas] in Akkerman in 1825 and, famously, Henri Roederer founded what became the Odessa Sparkling Wine Factory in 1896.

Today it's almost impossible to imagine a time when wine was drunk with no thought of the bubble. As is clear from the early history of so many countries, either through visits to the region by fizz-struck pioneering spirits or the importation of champenois savoir-faire and technology, we have Champagne to thank for inspiring production of sparkling wine around the globe and enriching our capacity for enjoying bubbles for all seasons and occasions.

2

THE ESSENCE OF EFFERVESCENCE: AN INTRODUCTION TO SPARKLING WINE TECHNIQUES

THE TRADITIONAL METHOD

The method most associated with quality is the traditional method, also often referred to as the classic method. It was known as the *méthode champenoise* until 31 August 1994 when European Union regulations phased out its use for sparkling wine other than Champagne. Imitation in this case was not deemed the best form of flattery by the champenois. For this method, the base wine undergoes its second fermentation in the bottle in which it is eventually sold. The step-by-step processes involved in the traditional method are explored further below.

THE TRANSFER METHOD

A sparkling wine made using the transfer method can undergo its second fermentation in the bottle, and in this way be called bottle-fermented, but the difference between this and the traditional method is that after fermentation in bottle and time spent on lees, transfer method fizz is transferred to a pressurized tank to be filtered and put into fresh bottles (so is not therefore fermented in the bottle in which it is sold). Known as *transvasage* in Champagne, this method cuts out the traditional method's riddling and disgorgement processes and is used for airline quarter bottles (splits), some half-bottles and most larger formats than the jeroboam. According to Ed Carr of Tasmania's House of Arras, 'it allows maturation on yeast lees with some economic efficiencies for larger blends, but more advantageous is the ability to blend from different tirage wines at the decant stage and refill the final sparkling wine into different bottle types'.

THE TANK METHOD

The tank method is essentially a cost-effective method of producing the second fermentation and therefore ideally suited to the production of large volumes of sparkling wine. It was originally developed by Federico Martinotti in Italy (and is still known there as the Martinotti method), but was adapted by Eugène Charmat in 1907 and has therefore more commonly become known as the Charmat method, or *cuve close*. In this method, the base wine is transferred to a pressurized tank where it undergoes its second fermentation and the tank is sealed to keep in the bubbles. When the second fermentation is completed, the wine is filtered and bottled under pressure. Most Prosecco is made by the tank method. In a variation of this method, for lower alcohol fizz such as Moscato d'Asti for instance, there is just one fermentation. Yeast is added to the grape juice in a pressurized tank and, once it reaches the desired level of alcohol, the wine is chilled, filtered and bottled under pressure. The Russian continuous method, an adaptation of the tank method using interconnected pressurized tanks, is becoming increasingly rare.

ANCESTRAL METHOD

The ancestral method is the oldest and therefore, counterintuitively, the most traditional method of making sparkling wine. It's also known as the artisanal method, the rural method, *méthode gaillacoise* or *pétillant naturel*, hence the term pet nat to describe its currently fashionable incarnation. In Italy, it is known as *col fondo*, or *sui lieviti*, and is growing in popularity in the Prosecco DOCG sub-regions. In this method, there is no second fermentation or added *liqueur de tirage*. Carbon dioxide is produced by the natural sugars in the grapes and fermentation is stopped during the first fermentation by chilling down the wine, which is then transferred to a sparkling wine bottle. If it's riddled, filtered and

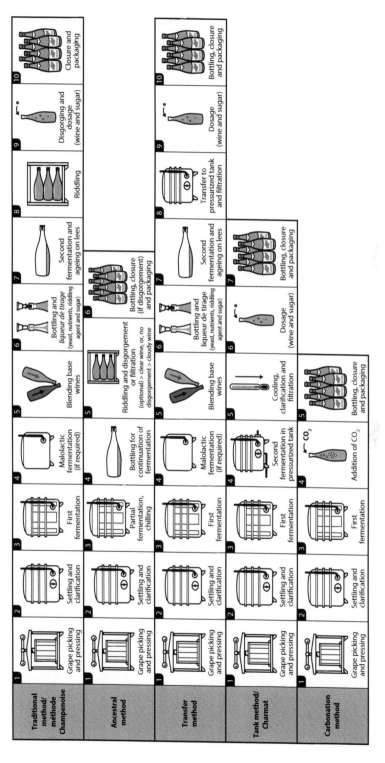

Summary diagram of the five dominant sparkling wine production methods

disgorged, it comes out clear. The desired end result is a highly quaffable, clear or slightly cloudy sparkling wine.

CARBONATION

Carbonation is the addition of bubbles from an external source, as in the case of fizzy drinks like lemonade, and consequently is also known pejoratively as the bicycle pump method. Injecting a wine with carbon dioxide is the cheapest method of producing sparkling wine and it has no quality associations. The method is normally thought of as producing large 'toad's eye' bubbles, but employed skilfully, it can deceive you into thinking that a superior process has been deployed.

A DETAILED INTRODUCTION TO THE TRADITIONAL METHOD

The *méthode champenoise*, or traditional method, is the Rolls-Royce of sparkling wine processes. Used to make premium sparkling wine, the process involves a double fermentation. The first takes place just like any other fermentation in tank, barrel or fermenting vessel of choice. The second fermentation is unique to sparkling wine. It involves fermenting the wine in the bottle it will eventually be sold in with a top-up of sugar, yeast, nutrients and riddling aids to create alcohol and carbon dioxide. The dissolved carbon dioxide trapped in the bottle is the sparkle in embryo. The process has taken centuries to develop, so it is perhaps not surprising to learn that there's more to the double bubble than meets the eye.

The press
Once tested for the required level of ripeness by tasting and analysis, grapes for the highest quality sparkling wines are normally hand-harvested, often in the early morning, into bins small enough to avoid crushing and premature oxidation. What amounts to ripeness could fill a book in itself. Suffice to say that the potential alcohol is typically between 9.5 and 11.5 per cent, the aim being to optimize fruit flavour and natural acidity and ensure that sugar ripeness (potential alcohol) and physiological ripeness are in sync.

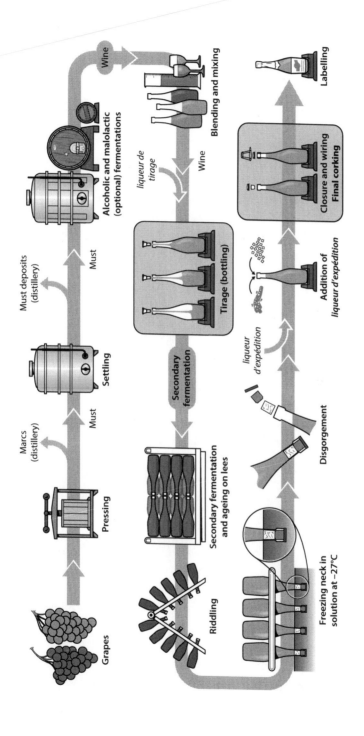

The traditional method

The pressing of the grapes is vitally important in obtaining a juice with optimum sugars, acids, minerals and vitamins from grapes so assiduously nurtured over the many months leading to harvest. The grapes are now almost always pressed in whole bunches for minimal damage to the skins, and the stalks of the bunches can help in preserving the gentle environment in which the juice is extracted and allowed to drain rapidly. In the case of black grapes, the pressing has to be done so gently as to avoid staining the juice with the red pigments of the grapeskins. This accounts for the mandatory hand-harvesting requirement in regions such as Champagne, Franciacorta and PDO England.

One of the most commonly used presses is the Coquard, which is a hydraulic press. It has a plate that presses either vertically down or in a horizontal or inclined horizontal configuration. The traditional method is to use thin-layer, wide, shallow basket presses where the maximum thickness of the skins being pressed is no more than 700 millimetres so that the juice can be extracted at low-applied pressures. In this way, the main causes of premature ageing in sparkling wine, high pH in pressings and bitterness from the skins, are minimized (although see the section on climate change, page 54).

Traditionally, juices pressed in this way were handled in a gently oxidative way. Most oxygen at this early stage is used up by the phenolics, and doesn't make it to fermentation. Modern technology with inert gas (nitrogen) allows producers the option of protecting the juice, which may be useful for fresher, fruitier styles, although a winemaker can adjust later if a more oxidative regime is required. 'Oxygen at the early stage is a style point rather than necessarily linked to fermentation,' says Nyetimber's Brad Greatrix. 'We're very relaxed about oxygen at the juice stage. Our view is that oxygenation early on helps to make a more stable wine in the long-term for ageing.'

The Coquard PTX (*pressoir traditionnel inox*) press in 2- and 4-tonne models is the modern stainless steel version of the traditional basket press, allowing for a rapid flow of the juice and making it easier to clean and to work with. Its latest model, the PAI press (*plateau automatique et incliné*) is a tilted plate press, with a capacity of 2, 4, 6, 8 and 12 tonnes. This allows for an extremely gentle pressing for the extraction of low solids, low colour, low tannins and ultra-pure juices. The plate presses in a horizontal direction, but leans back on itself, and so, as the plate retracts, the grapes slip down onto the floor of the press, and when the inclined plate moves forward again, the grapes buckle up in a new configuration. The mixing action needed between each subsequent pressing action is as gentle as possible 'and definitely more gentle than getting in with a pitchfork,' says Greatrix.

Pneumatic presses are increasingly common. They have a flexible membrane that inflates and presses the grapes against the outer wall of the drum, enabling the juice to drain away quickly and leave the tannins behind. Each type of press has its devotees, and proponents of the new Coquard will tell you that it's more gentle than the pneumatic presses.

The pressing programme is split into press fractions, each representing a gradual increase in pressure on the fruit. Traditionally, the press fractions are broken down into the cuvée, the first, most gentle pressing, followed by what prior to the Second World War was called *vin de suite* and is now known as the *taille*, the second pressing in the cycle. Finally comes the *rebêche* which, as the name implies (we get the word 'rubbish' from it), extracts the most phenolics and is discarded for distillation either by law, as in Champagne or, if not required by law, by general practice. In Champagne, the measures of the first pressing, or cuvée, and the second pressing (*taille*) are based on a 4,000 kilogram or four tonne batch of grapes, known as the *marc*.

The pressing percentages required by the Comité Champagne are 51.25 per cent of the batch for the cuvée, or 20.5 hectolitres per 4,000 kilogram *marc*, with 5 hectolitres of *taille*, which is 12.5 per cent of the 4,000 kilogram original load, a total therefore of 63.75 per cent. The cuvée is the purest juice, rich in sugar and malic and tartaric acidity. The taille is fruity but lower in acidity. A harsher third pressing, confusingly called the *deuxième taille*, which represented the last 116 litres of juice, was dropped in 1992 in Champagne and most premium sparkling wine producers don't use it. The corresponding figures for the cuvée are 66.7 per cent in Cava (60 per cent for Cava de paraje) and 60 per cent for Franciacorta.

Most producers will actually run the first 50–100 litres off into the *taille*. There are some smaller growers though who can't afford the luxury of discarding the *taille* and yet still manage to produce good sparkling wines. In practice, most producers effectively extract 500 litres per tonne in the first pressing, although some may reduce that to 400–450 litres for a *coeur de cuvée* (highest quality fraction), while those also producing still wines may add the *taille* to lower level wines, still and sparkling. After pressing, the juice is then pumped or drains by gravity to settling vats where it generally remains for a period of between 12 and 48 hours for the juice to clear, although some solids may be kept for the second fermentation. Sulphur dioxide (SO2) is generally added as an anti-oxidant. The clarified juice is pumped or gravity-fed to the fermenting vessel.

The first fermentation

After the pressing of the grapes into fractions and the settling of the juices, the first fermentation takes place in the fermenting vessel of choice, be it stainless steel, concrete, plastic or oak barrels, or a mix of different vessels. Until stainless steel came along, Champagne was routinely fermented in oak barrels. Barrels all but disappeared and temperature-controlled stainless steel became the norm, but recent times have seen many producers returning to barrel-fermentation for the complexity and even freshness that micro-oxygenation in barrel can bring.

As a general rule, producers are keen to avoid the influence of new oak flavours, but some like the flavour of oak and encourage it. Using larger barrels or avoiding new oak can help to prevent overt flavours of oak. Using different types of fermenting vessel can increase blending options before the second fermentation. Trendy concrete or oak eggs, clay amphorae and Georgian kvevri have also begun to make an appearance, but the jury remains out on their effectiveness.

Grapes from different plots are normally vinified separately and cool-fermented, typically for 10–14 days at an average temperature of between 15 and 20°C. Together with yeast-nourishing nutrients, most producers will use reliable, neutral yeasts they later use in the second fermentation as recommended for the particular variety. Such yeasts are also chosen for their compatibility with malolactic fermentation and second fermentation. Some producers prefer natural yeasts in the first fermentation but there's no hard-and-fast rule. Proponents of non-inoculated fermentations like the complexity they believe results in their use, and some believe they impart a certain *goût de terroir*, the taste, that is, derived from the vineyard itself.

As the grapes arrive at the winery with relatively low potential alcohol, the first fermentation may be boosted by sugar to raise the alcoholic strength a notch before the second fermentation. Chaptalization using cane or beet sugar is common in cool-climate sparkling wine regions such as Champagne and England. It is not permitted in California (except for the second fermentation) or in Cava production, but rectified concentrated grape must (RCGM) can be used for Cava in challenging vintages. Roughly 16 grams per litre of sugar contributes an extra 1% abv.

During the first fermentation, the resulting carbon dioxide is released and disperses into the earth's atmosphere. At the end of the first fermentation, or simultaneous with it, many sparkling wines undergo malolactic fermentation, essentially the biological conversion of tart malic acidity into softer lactic acidity. It is also done to improve stability and add creaminess of texture. In order to achieve freshness, aroma and texture, part of the base wine may go through malolactic fermentation and be blended with wine that has not undergone malolactic fermentation. There are significant exceptions to the general rule, if it is such, that malolactic fermentation is desirable and the roster of producers avoiding it, in part or entirely, is growing significantly in the light of climate change.

The assembly line: blending

The base wines are normally aged on their lees for a few months before the all-important blending takes place in the winter after harvest in preparation for the second fermentation. This ageing on the lees is a critical step in the formation of texture, with oak also used on occasion to bring an oxidative note or perhaps even some of the vanilla-like flavour of the cask to create more building blocks for the eventual blending process.

The *sine qua non* of pretty much all blending at this stage is to enhance complexity and achieve a cuvée of bright aroma and flavour, rounded texture and balancing acidity in preparation for the addition of the *liqueur de tirage*. The base wine is stabilized and clarified, with some producers using fining or clarifying agents; low sulphur dioxide is also important to ensure a good second fermentation. While the winemaker is looking to the final result in his or her blending, he or she has to be conscious at the same time of the requirements of the second fermentation, knowing that the *liqueur de tirage* and *liqueur d'expédition* are yet to be added, at the tirage and disgorgement stages respectively.

Since it's unusual for a single base wine to contain the necessary criteria for the blend in enough quantity, vineyard lots or parcels are generally blended together to obtain the required quality, quantity and consistency. The most commercially important cuvée in the sparkling wine producer's range is more often than not the non-vintage brut, so the more building blocks, the merrier, as it were. It takes experience, skill and intuition to recognize the different character of each parcel and how they can combine in a consistent or recognizable house style. Even then, blending may also involve using different press fractions and types of fermentation according to vessel and whether or not malolactic fermentation is carried out. And I haven't mentioned reserve wine yet.

The selection of grape varieties for the non-vintage cuvée house style is critical, but diversity of terroir and the vagaries of climate affect each variety differently according to vineyard and vintage. Producers creating cross-village or cross-regional blends, therefore have many strings to their bow when creating their wines. You might hear a Champagne producer talking about the components of the blend based on varying aspects of different vineyards for acidity, for body, for elegance, for aroma and for flavour. Much the same is also true for newer producers still finding their feet in the sparkling wine world. In England, Nyetimber and Gusbourne for instance rely on vineyards in more than one county to bring different characteristics. Ridgeview and Digby also rely on the differences their growers across a number of different counties bring to the party.

Vintage too can substantially change the proportion of a blend depending on how certain varieties have performed in any particular vintage. Just as Bordeaux has an insurance policy in its sheaf of different grape varieties, so Champagne operates in a similar way with its three major varieties. In a year when, for instance, Pinot Noir has been difficult, as it was in 2010, you may find a house like Dom Pérignon discarding a large quantity of its Pinot Noir in favour of Chardonnay, and vice versa. In a vintage of both quality and quantity, more wine may be set aside as part of the future reserve wine storage programme.

The addition of reserve wines

Blending for non-vintage sparkling wines (and some vintage wines outside Champagne) involves the addition of reserve wines. The art of knowing your reserves and what they can bring to the blend to create a whole that's greater than the sum of the individual parts requires experience and skill. As part of the blending process, the addition of reserve wines to the non-vintage cuvées can be critical in determining the house style. By law, vintage Champagne has to contain 100 per cent of that vintage, and so there is no room for reserve wines – although I have come across the occasional vintage with some (whisper it quietly) reserve wine, such as Charles Heidsieck's Champagne Charlie, always the black sheep.

Reserve wines come from earlier vintages held back to bring consistency of style and quality and add character and complexity to a non-vintage sparkling wine before it goes from the first stage of fermentation to its second, sparkle-inducing fermentation. In a year of inferior or variable quality, reserve wines can make all the difference. It's this legacy of vintage variation that's behind the 'insurance policy' of the reserve wine. While no reserve wine can be added to vintage wine in Champagne, up to 15 per cent is permitted in the rest of the EU and up to 5 per cent in the USA.

The reserve wine is a building block of the blending process in non-vintage sparkling wine and the best growers and winemakers know and nurture their reserves as if they were their own children. If the comparison sounds a bit glib, it isn't meant to be. Not all reserves are created equal and the age of the reserve wine is one of the many factors that can make a difference to the final blend. An older reserve may add complexity. A younger reserve refreshed on a regular basis may be the key to consistency in the non-vintage cuvée of a big company. With more than one bottling, the producer may play with different proportions of reserves.

Reserve wines under the microscope

In recent years, declining sales in Champagne leading to higher levels of stock and more available reserve wine could be a factor behind its increased use of reserve wines. Technological improvements in the ability to maintain quality wines suited to ageing as reserves is another important factor. The quality of the reserve wine may derive from its composition, which is more often than not the longer-lasting Pinot Noir or Chardonnay rather than Meunier.

According to Patrick Schmitt MW, there is a correlation between the increased use of reserve wines in Champagne from around 15 per cent to around 30 per cent in the two decades between 1991 and 2011 and the reduction of some 3 grams per litre in dosage over the period. In his Classic Wine Library book *The story of Champagne*, the late Nicholas Faith makes a similar point: 'increased use of reserve wines helps not only to provide better structure and roundness of the wine but also acts to reduce even further the use of sugar'. It's fair to say though that the jury is out on this correlation. In Franciacorta for instance, where dosage tends to be low, so also are reserve wine proportions, suggesting that the ripeness of the base wine may have an effect on the proportion of reserve wine used.

At Charles Heidsieck, the late Daniel Thibault added as much as 40 per cent reserve wine with an average age of 10 years to the Brut Réserve to bring about greater richness, mellowness and complexity. Thanks in part to Thibault, the trend is towards holding increased quantities of reserve wine. That has spread to smaller houses and growers with the means to hold significant reserves. A 2018 Master of Wine research survey by Tim Triptree MW found that smaller volume houses producing fewer than 50,000 bottles have an average of 34.9 per cent reserve wines, contradicting the belief that only larger houses have significant reserve stocks. Paul Bara, Francis Egly, Emmanuel Lassaigne, Pierre Péters and Larmandier-Bernier are among growers and houses using 40–50 per cent or more of reserve wine in their non-vintage blends.

This is by no means exclusive to Champagne. A number of English sparkling wine producers are building up their reserves for both quality reasons and contingency plans. Exton Park's Corinne Seely started her library of reserve wines with the 2011 vintage. In 2020, she released three new reserve blends (RB) each of whose names, RB 32, RB 28 and RB 23, are based on the number of reserve wines in the cuvée. At Langham Estate in Dorset, Justin Langham recently sank seven 4,000-litre concrete tanks into the ground to build his reserve wine storage capacity. Taking its cue from Champagne, this is the logical new reality for English wine. The same trend is going on in most of the countries starting to take their sparkling wines seriously.

Krug holds its many reserve wines in stainless steel tanks, but the type of vessel used for holding reserve wines varies according to the predilection and requirements of the producer. In addition to stainless steel, the most common storage method, some producers such as Roederer hold their younger reserves in stainless steel and older reserves in large oak vats of between 3,000 and 10,000 litres. Similarly, Domaine Chandon in Australia has reserves in both stainless steel and large oak barrels. Others, notably Bollinger, use magnums, 800,000 of them, to store their reserves, which they refresh with a small topping up of sugar and yeast.

Reserve wines are an essential tool in the winemaking armoury because they can be used for a variety of different purposes. Being older, they can take the rough edges off a younger vintage base wine, all the more so when the base wine needs bolstering to bring it into line with the desired minimum quality criteria. They can also be used constructively in a hot year to freshen up the blend or, in a challenging year, to add backbone. They can increase the available quantity of the final cuvée where there's an unexpected shortfall.

The perpetual reserve

The perpetual reserve is a portion of the reserve held in tank or barrel that is drawn off as required, with the tank or barrel then topped up, or refreshed, with the current vintage. The perpetual reserve provides a stylistic addition to build complexity, and you can't help feeling that by bringing older vintages into the blend, sparkling wine producers are also adding something of their own territorial DNA, their soul, not to put too fine a point on it, to the blend.

One of the first to create a perpetual reserve, Bruno Paillard now uses three different ones, kept in stainless steel and barrel, with the same varietal make-up of his three multi-vintage blends, Première Cuvée, Rosé and Grand Cru Blanc de Blancs. Each year the reserves are refreshed not just with the wine of the new harvest but a proportion of the blend itself which is surplus to requirements. Pierre Péters' perpetual reserve is stored in three types of container: stainless steel, concrete and 45 hectolitre Stockinger casks, and the results are outstanding.

Drappier too keeps five large wooden vats to enrich its non-vintage wines and Bérèche uses its perpetual reserve of equal parts Chardonnay, Pinot Noir and Meunier for the Reflet d'Antan and non-vintage cuvée. AR Lenoble started out with 225-litre barrels and tanks, subsequently adding 5,000-litre wooden vats to allow for an ageing process and more recently again, in 2010, added magnums under cork and staple. At Devaux, in the Aube, chef de cave, Michel Parisot, started his perpetual reserve with a Chardonnay from Chouilly in the Côte des Blancs, keeping it in stainless steel on its fine lees and replenishing a third with a wine from the same village every year. To that he added another perpetual reserve, a blend of Pinot Noir and Chardonnay, kept in a 14,000 litre vat.

Few Champagne producers use a genuine criadera-style Sherry solera even though they might call it that. Although they work with perpetual reserves, at least three producers label their Champagnes 'solera', namely Fabrice Pouillon, R. Dumont and Nathalie Falmet, as does Dopff au Moulin in Alsace. Anselme Selosse, however, uses both a perpetual reserve and an actual solera system. The perpetual reserve is kept in a 1,800-litre foudre, the proportion of new wine changing every year. In contrast, the solera, used for his Substance, is contained in three 5,000 litre stainless steel tanks which are used like criaderas in Jerez, while the mini-soleras for his six single vineyard Champagnes consist of one criadera and the solera itself.

The second fermentation

After the blend is made, the wine is cold stabilized to induce crystallization of potassium bitartrate (from the tartaric acid) and, optionally, but normally, filtered. It is then time to add the *liqueur de tirage*, that is, wine, cane or beet sugar, yeast, nutrients and riddling aids for the second fermentation. This is the tirage stage. Where in the first fermentation the type of yeast used is an off-the-peg Champagne yeast or natural yeast, the second fermentation requires a specialized traditional method yeast.

Most sparkling wine producers use an active dried Champagne yeast or their own in-house yeast. A special yeast is required at this stage because it's entering an alcoholic, high acid environment and must also submit to low-temperature, high pressure fermentation in the bottle. It also needs to be of a kind that makes it easy for the winemaker to remove it at the end of the process. In addition to yeast, the liqueur contains a mix of the wine with yeast nutrients such as diammonium phosphate or thiamin, riddling aids known as adjuvants, and sugar, often in the form of rectified concentrated grape must (RCGM).

Once the *liqueur de tirage* has been added, the bottle is sealed with a polyethylene bidule stopper and crown cap or, occasionally, a natural cork and agrafe (iron clip), and laid down horizontally in a cool, dark cellar to allow minimum infiltration of light or vibration disturbance. The point of the bidule is to help in collecting the lees at the end of the riddling process, making for an easier, cleaner disgorgement when in due course the frozen plug of yeast is removed from the neck of the bottle. The addition of 22–24 grams per litre of sugar results in the formation of 11–12 grams per litre of carbon dioxide, which yields a pressure of around six to seven atmospheres at 20°C before disgorgement.

As a temporary closure for the second fermentation, the varying range of permeability of the crown cap will allow minuscule amounts of oxygen to enter the bottle during ageing to enhance aromatic and sensory features. If the aim is long lees ageing, the crown cap may be at the lowest rate of oxygen ingress to reduce the impact of oxidation while the bottle is maturing in the cellar. During the second fermentation, in which the bottles are laid on their side to complete the fermentation process, the yeasts ferment at around 10–20°C and consume the sugar to create alcohol (typically an extra 1.5%, so reaching 12–12.5% abv) and carbon dioxide. The actual *prise de mousse*, literally, the capture of the sparkle, usually takes some four to eight weeks but can take up to six months.

During the disgorgement process some carbon dioxide is lost, meaning that the final pressure will typically be between four and six atmospheres. Before the term crémant was appropriated by non-Champagne producers, a crémant style at lower pressure, for instance Mumm's Crémant de Cramant, was often much sought after. Some *blancs de blancs*, notably Roederer Vintage and Pierre Gimonnet's Gastronome, are bottled at lower pressure. Cédric Bouchard is typically looking for 4.5 atmospheres of pressure as he thinks that too much carbon dioxide can get in the way of the wine. So, for a softer style, a producer might use sugar at less than 20 grams per litre in the *liqueur de tirage* to reduce the atmospheric pressure accordingly.

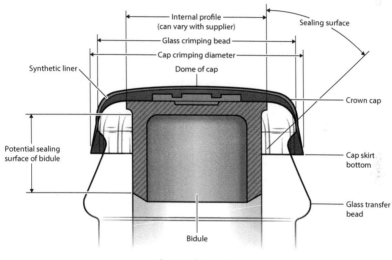

Crown Cap parts

Autolysis

Once sealed in its final resting place, the bottle is laid flat in a metal cage and the wine is left to mature on the dead yeast, or lees, dispersing the yeast so that eventually, the job of disgorgement will be easier. Also called stillages, the French refer to these cages as *sur lattes*. In turning grape sugar into alcohol and carbon dioxide, yeast cells have to work hard for a living; they spend their short lives on the conversion process and when they have done their work, they die.

In the second fermentation, a new battalion of yeasts joins the *liqueur de tirage* for a second round of hard labour, in which they too self-destruct when, after some six months, their work is done. Two to four months after the completion of the second fermentation, as the yeast cell walls degrade, enzymes get involved, starting to break the cells down, releasing compounds into the wine. These are a mixture of cell wall compounds known as mannoproteins and internal cell components such as peptides, fatty acids, nucleotides and amino acids. During this long, slow microbiological process, which can take anything from several months to many years, these compounds work both to transform the wine into something rather different in aroma and flavour, such as the delicious aromas and flavours we call toasty, biscuity, brioche-like, nutty and so on, while also ensuring a stable foam quality that delivers body and texture.

Despite the many studies on autolysis, it's still not known for sure what the rates and drivers are of the transformation of varietal aromas and flavours into more complex characters during the lees-ageing process. Resulting from the reaction between amino acids and trace reducing sugars, the Maillard reaction is thought to be responsible for some of the flavours in the brioche, biscuit and toast spectrum. According to Hannah Charnock, a PhD candidate of Brock University, Canada, 'while the yeasts will preferentially consume glucose during autolysis, there may be residual fructose available to participate in the Maillard reaction once various amino acids, proteins and/or polypeptides are released from yeast cells'.

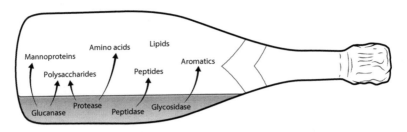

Chemical processes during the second fermentation of sparkling wine

Francis Egly, a grower who harvests his grapes very ripe, believes that 'it's somewhere between the third and fourth year in the bottle that a Champagne starts to lose its fermentation and yeast notes. Only after this time is the terroir truly able to express itself.' As fruit becomes riper, there is a suggestion that such longer lees-ageing may not only not always be necessary but can even militate against the required harmony, energy and freshness of a bottle-fermented wine. Jérôme Prévost, who typically makes very ripe base wines, doesn't age his wines especially long. Similarly, when English producer Ridgeview released its Oak Reserve NV, its first oaked cuvée, to great acclaim in the autumn of 2020, it had spent a mere 11 months ageing in bottle. At Nyetimber they believe each wine has an optimum time on lees, and it's possible to go too far.

Following the breakdown of the yeast cells and ageing on the lees, the sediment in the wines is loosened in an optional process known as *poignettage*. The wines are then placed either in traditional pupitres, wooden riddling frames with a hole for turning bottles from horizontal to vertical or, far more commonly today, in large gyropalettes, automated riddling machines that replicate the labour intensive work of hand riddling. Riddling should be used as a tool to optimize lees contact because the lees development in vertical, or *sur pointe*, bottles is dramatically slowed compared to horizontally stored bottles. While hand-riddling may take 8–10 weeks to complete, a gyropalette, which might typically hold 504 bottles, can do the job of moving the yeast deposit into the neck of the bottle in five to seven days, or in advanced cases, just one hour.

Disgorgement

There is a critical moment in the life of a bottle-fermented sparkling wine. After months, or even years, slumbering quietly in their serried rows, these wines are about to receive a rude awakening, a process that Champagne producer Bruno Paillard calls 'a sort of trauma, like a patient who undergoes a medical operation'. The inverted bottle is unceremoniously plunged into a shallow bath of freezing brine and the top inch or so of the neck frozen in a glycol or calcium chloride solution to between -25°C and -27°C for 8–10 minutes. The process allows the crown cap to be removed and the pressure to propel the bidule containing the yeast plug out of the neck with minimal loss of wine and carbon dioxide. Most traditional method sparkling wines are disgorged in this way. If, however, the bottle was sealed with a cork and agrafe (the metal clip that secures the cork under the lip of the bottle neck), the wine is normally disgorged by hand, or *à la volée*. Given that a machine can deal with several thousand bottles an hour, it goes without saying that this is much more labour intensive and requires skilful work to avoid a greater loss of wine.

This emergent stage culminates in the addition of the *liqueur d'expédition*. The amount of sugar added, normally cane or beet, obviously depends on the desired level of additional sweetness the producer is looking for in the style. Sugar implies extra sweetness but a typical addition of say 8 grams per litre will not so much sweeten the wine as fine-tune its balance and structure. If a brut wine tastes on the sweet side, the winemaker has more than likely overdone the dosage, perhaps to compensate for the perceived or actual acidity in the wine.

This is especially true where the grapes haven't quite ripened sufficiently in a mediocre vintage or where they've been picked too early. There is a growing trend to add very little or even no sugar for a very dry style, but the addition of sugar at this stage not only adjusts the sweetness level, but also contributes to the convalescence, as Bruno Paillard calls it, once the wine has been disgorged. The older the wine, the longer the rebalancing needed. Why is this?

This is because the Maillard reaction, also sometimes known as micro-maderization, is thought to continue even after disgorgement, albeit more slowly, in the presence of sugar and amino acids. Adding to the aromas and flavours of the second fermentation, it brings extra nuances of vanilla, toastiness, spice and candied fruit. According to Bruno Paillard, there are five or six 'lives' or stages of evolution after disgorgement: fruity, floral, spicy/nutty, baked bread/toasty and finally candied and caramelized fruit. Even a good non-vintage wine can taste a lot richer and more delicious if it is left for a year or two after purchase. If it's already late-disgorged, it should ideally need little further ageing.

As for the type of *liqueur d'expédition* itself, again much depends on the style preference of the producer and precisely what the aim is in terms of balance, freshness, house style and structure for longevity. Seasoning is the operative word because just as a sprinkling of salt and pepper can make a dish so much more appetizing, as little as 1 per cent liqueur can make a difference to the end product. And most bigger producers disgorge each non-vintage blend more than once during the year, even on occasion adding a little less dosage as the wine gets more bottle age. It's worth bearing in mind that the dosage and residual sugar are not necessarily the same. Even in a wine that's fermented dry there may still be 2–3 grams per litre of residual sugar, in which case the residual sugar will be a few grams higher than the dosage.

A spoonful of sugar: the dosage

Somebody wiser than I once observed that 'dosage is one of the most misunderstood aspects of Champagne'. Why? Because it's often assumed that the addition of sugar after disgorgement only has the effect of adding sweetness. But the aim of the dosage is as much to season the resulting fizz for complexity, balance and increased longevity as it is to sweeten it. The dosage is in effect the winemaker's last throw of the dice in defining and refining his or her wine style.

The dosage is as often as not the same as the wine that's in the bottle it's added to, with the addition of finishing tools for aroma and texture such as tannins, gum arabic and mannoproteins. Some producers might prepare a syrup of cane or beet sugar, oaked or unoaked white wine, or brandy (illegal in Champagne). Mumm uses barrel-fermented wine for its prestige cuvée, René Lalou. A winery might look to its perpetual reserve or solera system for added complexity. Catalonia's Gramona uses a one-hundred-year-old solera to bring about the required nutty, or oxidative, undertone to its Imperial Gran Reserva Brut. In Canada, Magnotta uses sparkling icewine.

The trend of the last 30 years has been for producers to adjust their dosage downwards in line with warmer climatic conditions, riper harvests and lower acids. At the same time, a rising proportion of reserve wine (in non-vintage Champagne and sparkling wine) and longer ageing on the lees in bottle also contribute to an extra roundness that reduces the need for a higher dosage. Raising glycerol levels by manipulating fermentation temperatures, adding texture through bâtonnage on base wines and oak ageing for the dosage can also be contributory factors. Since 1991, Champagne's ten biggest brands have dropped their dosage by 25 per cent on average, based on an average drop of 3 grams per litre, from 12 grams per litre to 9 grams per litre. Moët & Chandon alone has dropped its dosage from 13 grams per litre in 1998 to 9 grams per litre today.

Closure

During the addition of the liqueur care is taken to minimize oxidation given that a tiny amount of oxygen enters at the moment of disgorgement. Next comes the corking. Oxygen is of course the enemy of wine once it's been exposed to air and since that's exactly what happens at the disgorgement stage, typically, sulphur dioxide or sometimes Vitamin

C, is added at this stage to prevent oxidation. There is a trend towards adding less sulphur dioxide or even none at all, and some claim that the failure to add any sulphur dioxide is responsible for a growing tendency towards premature oxidation in sparkling wines.

In 2003, the CIVC showed that it was not only potential oxidation that was a problem but the variation in the amount of dissolved oxygen from one bottle to the next. In the same year, Bertrand Robillard demonstrated at Moët & Chandon that the level of foam is the main factor that determines the amount of air intake. And so trials using the continuous stream form of jetting, a process already used in the brewing industry, were carried out at Moët. By 2009 nitrogen-based pulse-jetting had been patented by LBM Industries. Effectively what this does is to inject a precisely metered micro-pulse of sulphited water into the bottle neck to induce foaming which continues all the way up to the lip of the bottle, reducing oxygen ingress in the neck space with the insertion of the cork while the foam is high. With all oxygen thereby ejected, the cork is then inserted, compressing the carbon dioxide. It is estimated that jetting can reduce the dissolved oxygen from eight parts per million to one part per million. According to Tom Stevenson, 'jetting is the most important development in sparkling wine technology for more than 100 years.' It's now used by, among others, Moët, Bollinger, Nyetimber and Veuve Clicquot.

It seems a little counterintuitive that after its long and arduous journey from grape to disgorgement the liquid in the bottle should now have to encounter yet another potential danger. It has to come into contact with an alien substance, aka cork, and it needs to trust that the cork will be its friend and companion for months if not years to come. The cork has to be applied accurately to the neck of the bottle if oxidation is not to become an issue. And in order to resist the pressure from inside the bottle, which at an average of five to six atmospheres is about the same as that of a London double-decker bus tyre, it has to be tied down securely to prevent it from escaping prematurely.

A sparkling wine cork is essentially an agglutination of cork granules stuck together with or without two or three discs of natural or agglomerated cork. About a third of the cork remains outside the neck so that it can be securely tied down, literally, by a four-legged steel wire cage, or muzzle. The muzzle comes topped with a tin cap preventing the 'cheesewire effect' of the steel cutting into the cork. Natural cork is variable in porosity and a potential victim of cork taint or TCA. A popular preventative innovation is the Mytik DIAM. Made from technical micro-agglomerate cork granules, it is deemed to be the most reliable solution to the problem of cork taint. Many of the big brands have adopted the Mytik DIAM, which has varying levels of oxygen ingress, according to the manufacturing process. After resting for a minimum period as required by the producer, the fizz is finally ready to be labelled, packed up and sent off to market.

Same magnum, same vintage, cork variability
(the magnum on the right was far superior)

A date with disgorgement

Whether or not the date of disgorgement is declared by the producer is a controversial issue, but it needn't be. The most common arguments against declaration are the claim that a non-vintage fizz is consistent year in year out, that consumers aren't interested in technical details or that consumers might be deceived into thinking that the disgorgement date on the back label looks like a sell-by date. I've even been told that 'each cuvée has its own personality and we will then adapt the time spent on the lees and after disgorging to achieve the best quality', as if the latter were a genuine reason for not doing it.

In the case of traditional method fizz, the date of tirage and the date of disgorgement both signify something useful for consumers. In a vintage sparkling wine where the date of the harvest is known, the date of disgorgement tells us how long the wine has spent on its lees and how much post-disgorgement age it has. In the case of non-vintage, in addition to the date of disgorgement, the date the wine was bottled for its second fermentation tells us how long the wine has been developing on its lees, which is important information for those who want to know if they should drink now or hang on to it for an occasion they have in mind.

As consumers become more sophisticated, they rightly want more information, especially if they're going to cellar a few bottles for some beneficial post-disgorgement ageing. According to Jancis Robinson writing in the *Financial Times* (12 July 2019), 'many of the Champagne houses are underestimating the increasing sophistication of their customers. As for the myth that non-vintage blends are consistent from year to year, this was prominently busted back in 2011 when Krug acknowledged how intricately their Grande Cuvée blend varied from year to year and announced that henceforth they were to put a code on the back of each different lot.'

Bruno Paillard saw the writing on the wall and became the first to put the date of disgorgement on the back label in 1983. Some but by no means all producers have since followed suit, although there's a growing trend towards doing it. As Champagne Palmer says: 'we are not putting the disgorgement date on the back label yet but, because of the growing transparency expectation from consumers, we are moving in that direction.' The scannable QR code is another option for communicating details to those who want it.

Conveying this information should be seen not as a screen to hide behind but as an opportunity to communicate. Producers have everything to gain by showing consumers the respect they deserve when they fork out a not inconsiderable sum for the privilege of drinking that producer's fizz. Anything is surely better than the deathless guff still too often seen on the back of the label: 'a miracle of delicacy, this vintage brut delights with the subtle balance of sparkle and fullness.' That really is the extent of the information on the back label of one well-known brand's vintage Champagne. Useful? You decide.

3

IN THE VINEYARD

THE SPARKLING WINE SEASON

Starting out with the givens of location, grape variety, clone and root-stock, the job of the viticulturalist is to manage all the necessary processes required in the vineyard and take account of the variables, not least the weather. In the case of sparkling wine, the potential alcohol at harvest has to be low enough to accommodate the extra 1–2 per cent alcohol created by the second fermentation. Achieving flavour ripeness (with tartaric and malic acid in roughly equal proportions) at relatively low potential alcohol is a difficult balancing act that requires the right grape varieties and can only be achieved with a helping hand from Mother Nature. Only a cool climate with the minimum amount of heat distributed over a sufficiently long growing season (conventionally 100 days) can ripen the grape in such a way that it has accumulated sufficient sugar and yet remains low enough in potential alcohol when picked to be able to accommodate not just one, but two fermentations.

Different soils contain varying amounts of nutrients and many need supplementary nutrients to ensure balanced, healthy vine growth. Chalk for instance, while it has great water absorption and transmission capacity and reflects sunlight efficiently, is a high-alkaline soil that is lacking in organic matter and doesn't hold much iron. Compaction has to be avoided to ensure adequate aeration. Soils need minerals and the capacity to transmit those nutrients to the vine for its development. Among the minerals required for healthy vine growth are iron, magnesium, boron, zinc, nitrogen, potassium and phosphorus. Soil samples will tell the vineyard manager what nutrients are required and what cover crops should be grown in order to encourage microbial life and add nitrogen. Sheep in winter can provide manure and, as it were, mow the lawn. 'We are worm farmers and sun farmers as much as grape farmers,' says Exton Park's Fred Langdale.

In winter the vineyard manager needs to prune for the balanced growth of the vine to achieve the optimum yield. Cordon spur pruning has one permanent horizontal arm (Cordon de Royat) along which a number of canes are typically pruned back to two buds, or two arms (Cordon double). The Chablis cane pruning system has three to five branches from which a short cane is retained, growing from the central trunk, and generally brings higher yields. Guyot is cane pruning, with one cane and one spur (single guyot) or two canes and two spurs (double guyot). Vallée de la Marne (for Meunier) is cane pruning. Only Cordon de Royat and Chablis can be used in *grand* and *premier cru* vineyards in Champagne.

Climate change is resulting in earlier budbreak in spring, increasing the threat of exposure to spring frosts. Just a short period below 0°C can be devastating, especially if there is more than one frost event. Throughout Europe, 2020 and 2021 were brutal as night-time temperatures fell below zero in the spring. With later budburst than many of Europe's classic wine regions, England got off relatively lightly, but England had severe frost problems of its own in 2016 and 2019. Combating frost is based on displacing cold air with fans, candles or driving frost-busting machines that blow warm air through the vineyard, the latter contributing to the climate change that caused the problem in the first place. Ploughing at this time can encourage the roots to delve deeper into the soil, and a variety of cover crops add nutrients, helping to balance growth, protect against soil erosion and encourage microbial life.

Sap rising in the vine, Langham Estate, Dorset, England

With the trellis adjusted to expose the canopy to sunlight and create ventilation to protect against mildew and rot, good early summer weather at flowering allows for an even fruit set. Leaf removal after flowering is a method of opening up the canopy to sunlight, while bunch-thinning after flowering maximizes the energy in the grape. The summer months are crucial for the ripening of the grapes and the process of *véraison*, the changing of the colour in the grapes. With best practice in mind, vineyard managers are increasingly using organic-based products to feed the leaves for the maintenance of photosynthesis and keeping mildew, both powdery and downy, and botrytis at bay.

As harvest approaches, in Champagne a data summary is notified to technical teams who supply pre-harvest meetings with harvest date estimates. The Comité Champagne sets the harvest dates, whereas elsewhere producers rely on their weather stations and apps. The start date is dictated by technique and measurement, but growers are increasingly tasting before deciding when to analyse for average weight, estimated sugar and total acidity. Grapes are manually picked, by law in most quality-orientated appellations such as Champagne and England PDO, in order to retain whole, undamaged bunches for pressing and, in black grapes, to avoid any colouring of the must. It's also the case that phenolic compounds from the grapeskins can have an adverse effect on foaming properties. Some producers opt to pay by the hour rather than by crate in order to ensure a critical sorting in the vineyard for health and avoiding moisture before the bunches are brought in for pressing.

Veraison - Pinot Noir changing colour, Josef Chromy, Tasmania, Australia

THE TERROIR OF THE BUBBLE

It may sound like a statement of the obvious to say that sparkling wine begins in the vineyard, but a blinkered focus on the process alone can obscure the simple fact that good sparkling wines are made from the right kind of grapes grown in the most suitable of locations; in a word, terroir. Bubbles may all look identical in the glass but not all bubbles are created equal. The potential for quality and authenticity varies according to the nature of the terroir and human input. That's the inescapable logic behind, for instance, Champagne's Échelle des Crus, in which grape prices were fixed on a sliding scale based on an informal but long-standing hierarchy with the most prized terroirs commanding the highest prices.

At first glance however, the notion of terroir as it relates to sparkling wine is in some respects a paradox. Two major features of sparkling wine threaten to derail the terroir argument. The first is the blend, the second the process itself. Blending is the *sine qua non* of sparkling wine thanks to the vagaries of climate, the multiplicity of vineyard sources and the crafting of a consistent house style year in year out. Rare is the fizz that goes to its second fermentation without some form of blending, whether of permutation of grape variety, vineyard, vintage or reserve wine. In addition, whether native yeasts or commercial yeasts are used, what type of fermenting vessel is deployed and whether or not the wine undergoes malolactic fermentation all play their part in the resulting base wine.

Once the first fermentation has been carried out, does blending automatically obscure the characteristics of vineyard location? Robert Walters, a champion of terroir, argues that blending in Champagne, where the houses dominate the market, has always been a necessary expedient in the face of commercial realities. It's true that blending is a prerequisite for creating large, consistent brand volumes, but there's an element of special pleading in his argument that the region's best wines – 'every bit as great, as complex, as terroir rich, as delicious and moving as the finest Burgundies' – come from growers alone.

The author of *Champagne*, Peter Liem, makes the case for a strong link between blending and terroir, saying: 'terroir is no less important in a blended wine than in a single vineyard wine. What changes is its role.' He points out that vineyard sources are used specifically for their contrasting characteristics and the fine distinctions they can bring to the blend. Far from being a negation of terroir, blending in this way is, rather, an enhancement of it. Nyetimber's Brad Greatrix agrees: 'We like our vineyards to show through in our wines – since we work with 100 per cent estate-owned sites it's a way to ensure inimitable wines. Blending in and of itself needn't overwhelm terroir.'

Whether house or grower, an experienced producer understands the potential of specific sites to bring their varied characteristics to the blend. Discussing his various vineyards, Rodolphe Péters states that Le Mesnil is 'austere', Avize shows 'ripe citrus, candied citrus peel', Oger is 'elegant, white flowers, orange blossom, white pear' and Cramant shows 'creamy vanilla, cinnamon, saffron'. In the knowledge of the relative freshness of Cuis, the structure of Cramant and voluptuousness of Chouilly, the top Côte des Blancs grower, Didier Gimonnet, blends all three. Exton Park in Kent is a single vineyard on chalk, and while each cuvée blends different grape varieties, single parcels and a library of vintage reserves, for winemaker Corinne Seely, 'you always find in Exton Park an iodine taste, a saltiness'.

Recognizing vineyard origin through the prism of the sparkling wine process itself is more of a challenge. Even if we acknowledge that a greater focus on the vineyard is bringing a more precise sense of place to the wine, the question still arises: to what extent does the alchemical process by which base wine is transformed into liquid golden bubbles preserve the expression of terroir, if at all? Put more prosaically, is it possible to reconcile the many steps taken to influence flavour – among them autolysis, long lees-ageing and dosage with oak-aged wines or brandy – with an expression of place? And to what extent does the language of descriptors developed for the perception of bubble-related characteristics intrude on the expression of terroir?

In a world in which intervention in the vineyard and the cellar is increasingly seen as manipulation, it's easy to assume that less intervention leads to wines better placed to express their terroir. But since all wine processes involve an interpretation of the terroir of some sort – without the hand of man or woman there would be no expression of terroir – why should the second fermentation be the pantomime villain? In the view of Exton Park's Corinne Seely, 'I don't think that the second fermentation of sparkling wines in the bottle has any more impact on terroir flavours than the first alcoholic fermentation. It is likely that the terroir is even more pronounced in sparkling wine made from one terroir than in the *vin clair* – the still wine – it is made from.'

The purpose of the second fermentation is not simply to add bubbles for the sake of it but to bring complexity, depth, length and harmony. If it enhances subtlety and transparency in a wine, why should these characteristics not lead to recognition of the wine's origin and enhance the expression of place? Comparing the process with bâton-nage in Burgundy, Corinne Seely believes that autolysis, while bring-ing aroma, body, richness and texture, doesn't alter the provenance. For Mark Driver at Rathfinny in Sussex, 'the fundamentals of terroir – soil, microclimate and vineyard practices – are the key drivers for us. We try to practice low intervention and add nuances through malolactic fer-mentation and longer bottle ageing and let the fruit sing.'

So rather than the second fermentation detracting from a wine's ter-roir expression, the opposite, with the second fermentation helping to create a complete and fully expressive wine, is more likely to be the case. Compare a *vin clair* with the finished article. It's logical then to conclude that given the extent to which the DNA of the wine's origins is preserved in the sparkling wine process, the resulting fizz is indeed no less an authentic product of its terroir than any other wine. However much human input with all its complexities appears to be doing its best to disguise the vineyard location, in working in fact to interpret its iden-tity as faithfully as possible, it allows us, the consumer, to identify and appreciate a good bubble when we taste it.

CLIMATE AND FIZZ

An existential threat

The year 2020 was Europe's warmest on record – and then came 2021. If you blinked, you may have missed Japan's cherry blossom season, the spring awakening, which peaked at its earliest date since records began 1,200 years ago. Perhaps you were not aware of the heat dome in Lytton, British Columbia that broke Canada's temperature record with a brutal high of 49.6°C, Sicily's record 48.8°C, Montoro in Spain's 47.4°C, or the catastrophic July flash floods that killed more than 170 people in western Germany, or the raging wildfires in Siberia, California, Greece, Turkey and Algeria, or that almost a year's worth of rain fell in Zhengzhou, China, in three days, leaving 51 dead. If only there were some sign of a climate crisis.

After an 11,000-year period of climate stability, planet Earth is warm-ing up. Apart from the direct impact on precipitation and rainfall caused by the warming of the earth's atmosphere, climate change is also bring-ing with it more frequent extreme weather events: heatwaves, drought, wildfires, hurricanes, monsoons, flash floods, frost, hail and a significant rise in sea levels with all the catastrophic damage that such unpredictable extremes entail. It goes without saying that climate change is having knock-on effects for wine producers such as vine shutdown, a growing risk of fungal disease, sunburn and, most significant of all, disparities between the speed of the uptake of sugar and physiological ripeness.

An increase in potential alcohol and a corresponding decrease in acid levels will have long-term consequences for the flavour, freshness and longevity of sparkling wine. The key element of climate for fizz is the link between temperature and the ripening of the grapes used. A cool climate, preferably accompanied by a notable day and night temperature difference, is the prerequisite for encouraging the required development of natural acidity in the grape. In a cool climate, if the growing season between flowering and harvest is long enough, it allows the grapes to ripen to produce a base wine of between around 9.5–11.5 per cent alcohol. This base wine needs to have sufficient flavour and natural acidity to allow retention of freshness and balance following a second fermentation.

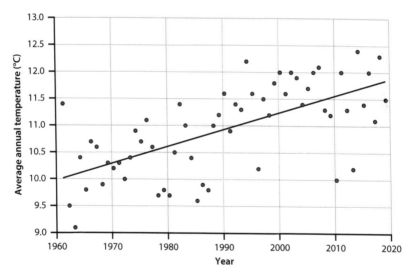

Champagne average annual temperatures 1960–2020

A common metric for the growing season temperature (GST) is to take the average temperature for the seven month growing season from spring to harvest. Typically, the average figure to qualify for very cool climate is between 13.5°C and 14.4°C, while between 14.5°C and 15.5°C is cool. The correlation between heat summation and vine development is subject to other influences, however. Frost or winter freezing where there's an average of below 0.5°C may rule out an area that might otherwise have potential. Additional factors include sunlight intensity, rainfall, humidity, soil moisture and, most relevant perhaps in the context of climate change, extremes of temperature. The effects of climate in any given location will vary according to the specifics of the location.

In climatic terms, the sparkling wine benchmark is Champagne, which, at 49°N, is at the margins for grape-growing. Like that of most sparkling wine regions, the climate is mainly maritime, thanks to the influence of the Atlantic, so summers are generally warm and rainfall is steady. At the same time, there is a continental climate influence, manifesting itself mainly in the potential for hard frosts, damaging hail and extreme heat spikes in the summer.

Over 300 years of sparkling wine history and today's multi-billion pound industry is predicated on the assumption that Champagne has the perfect climate for sparkling wine thanks to an average annual temperature of 10°C. Since the 1990s however, changes in the climate have accelerated. Harvests have been getting earlier. Natural alcohol has risen by 0.7 per cent by volume while total acidity has fallen by 1.3 grams per litre. The traditional period of 100 days between flowering and harvesting has reduced substantially over the past 70 years. Beginning around mid-September, the harvest is starting a week to three weeks earlier than at the end of the 1980s. Cyril Brun, Charles Heidsieck's chef de cave, recently warned that finding ways to preserve freshness in Champagne will be one of its biggest challenges. To conclude that climate change is an existential threat to Champagne is no exaggeration.

As we've seen from the section on the traditional method, because of earlier ripening and higher sugars induced by climate change, there's a growing trend towards the option of only partial malolactic fermentation or blocking malolactic altogether in order to retain the wine's natural backbone and freshness. Clover Hill in Tasmania, Graham Beck in the South African Cape's warm, sunny Robertson region, Colet in Spain, the Loire's Bouvet Ladubay, Ambriel in England and Gancia in Piemonte are among many who avoid malolactic fermentation to retain as much bright acidity in the wines as possible. Louis Roederer Champagne and Chapel Down in Kent are among another expanding group who, with acids in danger of becoming too low in warm years, will do a partial malolactic fermentation, depending on vintage conditions, to maintain freshness.

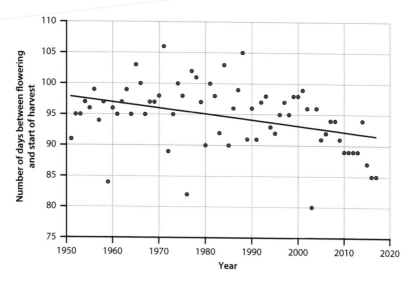

*Champagne number of days between flowering and
the start of harvest 1950–2020*

There is a school of thought too that suggests that a judicious amount of bitterness caused by an increase in tannins may compensate for the lower levels of acidity induced by climate change. In Cyril Brun's view, 'in the light of global warming, a higher level of ripe bitterness in warm vintages like 2005, 2006, 2009 and 2015, provides support to the acidity and helps with the ageing process'. In the case of his 2008 Charles Heidsieck Rosé for instance, he says 'you need a bit of positive bitterness to ensure length and ageing'. Moët & Chandon's Benoît Gouez makes a similar point when he says, in talking about vintages with low acidity like 2003, 'stylistically a winemaker can replace some acidity with bitterness'.

Responding to reduced day to night temperature differences in warmer summers, measures such as the use of new grape varieties and adapting the viticulture and the winemaking are being looked at. One region that has already added a new grape variety to the roster is Franciacorta in Italy, where the ancient Erbamat grape was added to the Franciacorta Production Code in 2017 (and allowed up to 10 per cent in blends) for its distinct acidity. In Slovenia, the native Rumeni Plavec grape is being harnessed for its notable acidity and local distinction.

It's an ill wind

If climate change is 'the curse that keeps on taking', as Mark Carney, UN special envoy for climate action, has put it, there is a sense in which the alteration in climate also brings with it clouds with silver linings. As cold regions start to warm up, new regions or pockets of regions are emerging where extreme cold has become just about warm enough to ripen grapes for sparkling wine. Instead of spending sleepless nights worrying about getting enough sugar into the grapes and avoiding excessive acidity, today's vineyard manager is as likely to be having nightmares about the rapid accumulation of sugar at the expense of acidity.

A gradual change in climate has mitigated the strident acidity that once made English wine hard to love. After Peter Hall planted his Breaky Bottom vineyard in East Sussex in 1974, he struggled for years with adverse conditions. He says that the 1970s and 1980s were 'BAW: Bloody Awful Weather, rainy and cold, with difficult vintages producing small yields.' Into the 1990s and the twenty-first century, the climate changed for the better, from a vine growing perspective, and after 20 years of making still wines, in 1995 Peter made the successful leap from still wines to fizz. 'What the change has meant to viticulturalists,' says English wine expert Stephen Skelton MW, 'is that once marginal varieties – Pinot Noir and Chardonnay being the most widely planted – have suddenly started to move into the mainstream. Natural sugars have increased, acids are still high, but nowhere near as high as they were.'

Prosecco DOCG has experienced a similar phenomenon. The harvest has gradually crept forward and now takes place in mid to late September, sometimes earlier. Other Italian regions have looked to the skies. In Piemonte, sparkling wine producers have found a haven, if not heaven, in the high ground of Alta Langa. At altitudes of 250–500 metres or higher, Alta Langa today is recognized as the new *terra cognita* for Italian traditional method sparkling wine. At Soalheiro in Portugal, altitude has been key to coping with the current and future impact of climate change, with recent new plantings at 1,100 metres above sea level. In Spain, Cava producers such as Can Sala, Torres, Loxarel and Juvé & Camps, have found that by ascending to 700–900 metres in the highlands of Mediona and the foothills of the Pyrenees, they experience a longer growing season, which brings more freshness and vitality to their Cavas.

As Australia has found with Tasmania's maritime climate, proximity to the cold influence of the Southern Ocean is a significant factor in the development of vineyards suited to flavour accumulation with the necessary accompanying juicy acidity. Faced with the threat of heatwaves and forest wildfires, California's fizz producers have increasingly inched closer to oceanic influences to meet the challenge of climate change. On Canada's Atlantic seaboard east of Maine, Nova Scotia is one of the new frontiers of Canadian fizz thanks to the moderating influence of Atlantic saltwater breezes. A hot area such as Robertson in South Africa's Cape works for fizz thanks to the cooling breeze that blows up from the Breede River mouth at the Indian Ocean.

'Indicative' maps in Tom Stevenson and Essi Avellan's *World Encyclopedia of Champagne and Sparkling Wine* suggest that, with latitude, altitude and proximity to the oceans in mind, southern Chile and Argentina, parts of Bolivia and Lesotho, north-east Germany and large swaths of New Zealand's South Island could be the new frontiers of sparkling wine. I wouldn't rule out Argentina and Chile's Patagonia, or Ningxia in the central-north of China, or Japan's Yamagata or Hokkaido either. It's no coincidence that these two cold-climate prefectures in Japan's far north are already starting to produce some of the country's finest fizz.

AN A TO X OF SPARKLING WINE GRAPE VARIETIES

There are three main types of grape variety suited to sparkling wine, but what all the best ones have in common is the ability to ripen with good natural acidity. In the first category are the neutral grape varieties that make for the perfect sparkling base wine but don't impart much if anything in the way of specific varietal character. Then there are the aromatic varieties such as Riesling, Bacchus, Muscat and Sauvignon Blanc, which endow a fizz with specific varietal aromatic character. And finally there are indigenous varieties used for reasons of tradition and authenticity.

Principal white varieties

Alvarinho. The same grape as Spain's Albariño and one of the major grapes in Vinho Verde from north-west Portugal, whose sparkling wines, *espumante*, made by the traditional method, must be aged for at least nine months.

Arbane. Also known as Arbanne, this is one of Champagne's rare, almost forgotten varieties. A few houses include it in their cuvées, but its low-yielding properties are not appreciated by the majority of the champenois.

Chardonnay. Early budding, easy to grow, with good sugar levels and high acidity, Chardonnay is not just the classic white grape variety of Champagne, but loved by sparkling wine producers the world over for its blending potential, suitability for traditional method sparkling wine and the way it can develop complexity with age.

Trellis post, Nyetimber, West Sussex, England

Chenin Blanc. Chenin's naturally high acidity makes it an excellent candidate for traditional method sparkling wines in the Loire Valley and South Africa.

Erbamat. Thanks to climate change, this historic, late-ripening variety has had a make-over in Franciacorta, where it has been reintroduced to add acidity, forming up to 10 per cent of a blend.

Furmint. The Hungarian grape of Tokaji, also known as Šipon in Slovenia, recognized as a great base wine for sparkling wine with its high acidity and relative neutrality.

Glera. Glera was called Prosecco until 2009, when the ingenious Italians made Prosecco a designation of origin based on the name of a village in the province of Trieste to ward off competitors. Cultivated principally in the province of Treviso for light, fragrant, tank method (principally) fizz.

Grüner Veltliner. Austria's signature grape for quality white wines is also used for refreshing, light- to medium-bodied sparkling wines.

Koshu. Grown mostly in Yamanashi prefecture, Japan's native pink-skinned white grape is a *Vitis vinifera* containing a proportion of the Asian wild grape *Vitis davidii*.

Macabeo. Delicate, versatile and exceptionally terroir-sensitive, this Catalan variety is one of the principal white varieties in Cava blends with Xarel·lo and Parellada.

Mauzac. Specific to south-west France, Mauzac is used for the dry, sweet and sparkling wines of Limoux and Gaillac.

Muscat. This aromatic white variety is used for Asti Spumante, Moscato d'Asti and Clarette de Die and widely used around the world for light, sweet, grapey fizz.

Parellada. Native, fairly neutral Catalan variety, late-ripening and well-adapted to the high parts of the Penedès, capable of bringing delicacy to a Cava blend.

Petit Meslier. A crossing of Savagnin and Gouais Blanc, this is one of the rare, almost-forgotten historic grapes of Champagne, once prized, particularly in the Aube, for its acid-retentive properties. Champagne Gratiot Delugny's Bulles d'Avenir is pure Petit Meslier.

Pinot Blanc. Permitted but rare in Champagne although Vouette & Sorbée's Textures is made from it. More common in Alsace, England, Germany and Franciacorta, where its relative neutrality and plentiful acidity make it a useful blender.

Riesling. Riesling can make for high quality German Sekt, where it often shows the floral and petrolly aromatic qualities of the variety.

Seyval Blanc. An early ripening hybrid grape (Seibel 5656 × Rayon d'Or) once more popular in England than it is now.

Xarel·lo. The first to bud, but with the longest cycle of all Catalan varieties, it has the best balance of sugar and acidity at harvest and is shown to be the white grape variety with the highest amount of resveratrol and other potent antioxidants. Aromatic and flavoursome, its acidity brings structure, allowing lengthy ageing.

Principal red varieties

Lambrusco. The main varieties for quality sparkling red Lambrusco are the light, high-acid Lambrusco di Sorbara and the darker, fuller-bodied, more tannic Lambrusco Grasparossa.

Meunier. Earlier ripening than Pinot Noir, Meunier is the predominant variety in Champagne's Vallée de la Marne and is becoming increasingly popular in England. Although largely a blender, there are also some pure Meunier cuvées, notably from Champagne producers Michel Loriot, Bérêche et Fils, Françoise Bedel, Chartogne-Taillet, Egly-Ouriet, Gosset, Tarlant, Jérôme Prévost and Geoffroy and, in England, Fox & Fox, Exton Park, Hambledon, Langham Estate and Oxney.

Monastrell. Catalan variety bringing aromatic complexity, texture and colour to the blend.

Pinot Noir. Predominant in the *grands crus* of the Montagne de Reims and a big player in the Aube, the Burgundian variety has been adopted by most of the major sparkling wine producers around the world.

Syrah/Shiraz. Most red bubbles made in Australia come from Shiraz, which makes a dark-coloured, spicy, full-bodied sparkling red, often off-dry to semi-sweet in its more commercial incarnation, to mask the tannins.

Teran. High acid Mediterranean variety common in Istria and Slovenia and good for refreshing sparkling reds.

Trepat. Sometimes described as the Catalan Pinot Noir, the native grape of DO Conca de Barbera is an early budding, thin-skinned variety, which, planted at high altitude, brings herbal aromas, bright fruit and elegance to pink Cava.

4

ASPECTS OF SPARKLING WINE

PUTTING ON THE STYLE – A GUIDE TO SPARKLING WINE STYLES

Non-vintage

As the name suggests, a non-vintage (NV) sparkling wine is a blend of two or more different years, although it can be from one harvest without the producer declaring it as such. The addition of reserve wines from previous vintages allows the producer to achieve continuity of style and quality and to bring an added degree of complexity to the party. The actual percentage blended varies from producer to producer and can be as much as (sometimes more than) 40 per cent of the blend. To try to stand out from the crowd, some producers prefer to call this blend multi-vintage, or MV, but non-vintage is in no way pejorative and can be superior precisely because it is a blend of more than one harvest.

Vintage

Vintage sparkling wines are a snapshot of a single harvest. Typically, a producer actually 'declares' a vintage in an exceptional year because they believe in its quality and want to convey the character of the vintage without needing to bolster it with wine from previous harvests. There's no hard and fast rule though and some producers declare a vintage as much as a marketing exercise as a badge of quality. Vintage Champagne must come from 100 per cent of that year's harvest (apart from the *liqueur d'expédition*), while in the rest of the EU and many other countries, there is a 15 per cent leeway; no more than 15 per cent can be added for sparkling wines imported into the EU. Vintage fizz usually spends longer on the lees than non-vintage, with regulations in place to guarantee it.

Blanc de blancs

Blanc de blancs is a sparkling wine blended exclusively from white grapes, Chardonnay almost exclusively in Champagne. Other French regions might include their own local grape, such as Chenin Blanc in the Loire, Mauzac in Blanquette de Limoux and Gaillac, Sémillon and Sauvignon Blanc in Bordeaux, Clairette in Crémant de Die and Marsanne and Roussanne in Saint-Péray. Cava has its own indigenous white varieties in Xarel·lo, Parellada and Macabeo, while recently taking Chardonnay on board in blends. In Italy, Prosecco's *blanc de blancs* is made from the Glera grape and Franciacorta has recently incorporated the native Erbamat into its production code. Riesling is in common use in Germany, Furmint in Hungary, Rebula and other local high acid varieties in Slovenia, while Japan uses its own native Koshu for most of its *blanc de blancs*. Most sparkling wine countries follow the Champagne model in full or in part.

Riddling (remuage), Heiko Bamberger, Nahe, Germany

Blanc de noirs

Blanc de noirs is a sparkling wine blended from red grapes. In the case of Champagne, the blend has to be exclusively from Pinot Noir and Meunier. Outside Champagne, a proportion of white grapes, according to the rules of the region, can be blended in. Most sparkling wine countries have adopted the Champagne varieties, but some regions with older traditions and pride in their native varieties have given priority to those varieties: Lambrusco di Sorbara in Lambrusco, Baga in Bairrada, Mavrud and Melnik in Bulgaria, Teran in Slovenia, and in Germany Frühburgunder, aka Pinot Précoce, a mutation of Pinot Noir.

Prestige cuvée

A prestige cuvée, or de luxe cuvée, is the crème de la crème of a sparkling wine producer's range, whether non-vintage or vintage. Most are vintage but Krug Grande Cuvée, Laurent-Perrier Grande Siècle, Cattier Clos du Mesnil and Rare are all blends of multiple vintages. A prestige cuvée must be a selection of the very best raw material from the best years and made with consummate skill. Dom Pérignon apart, it's generally made in relatively small quantities and on top of perfect contents, it comes wrapped in stunning livery and endowed with a very high price tag. Because most are made in small quantities and age well, prestige cuvées tend also to be much sought after on the secondary market.

Late disgorged/recently disgorged

One of the ultimate expressions of the prestige cuvée is the late-disgorged style. Bollinger was the first to come up with a late-disgorged cuvée when it released the 1952 Grand Année as RD, or recently disgorged, in 1961. Since then, many houses have come up with their own versions of wines that have spent a decade or more on the lees. The longer the dead yeast cells interact with the wine, the more complex the aromas and flavours become and the process can continue actively for ten years or more. The aim is therefore to highlight the aroma, flavour and texture-altering effects of leaving the lees to work its magic in the bottle.

Red

On my first visit to Australia in 1989, the wine writer James Halliday served a bottle of sparkling burgundy, as it was then called. It was in fact a sparkling Australian Shiraz, made using the traditional method, and aged for long enough to soften into a red that resembled Burgundy, only with fizz, hence the name. There are few such traditional styles around today, but the commercialization of Aussie red bubbles, made from Shiraz, Pinot Noir, Cabernet Sauvignon, Merlot, Durif and Chambourcin, using the traditional, transfer, tank or carbonation methods, is becoming popular. Lambrusco, the traditional frothing speciality of Emilia-Romagna made by both Charmat and *metodo classico*, is distinguished by its lightness and freshness.

As sweet as you are

With its relatively light alcohol level, refreshing acidity and off-dry residual sugar content in the region of 15 grams per litre, Prosecco has been the barnstorming phenomenon of the century and led the way back to the mass market for off-dry sparkling wines. Some of the most delicious sparkling wines in a sweeter style, Asti Spumante and its lower-in-alcohol counterpart, Moscato d'Asti, made by the tank method, can be delightfully fragrant, light and refreshing. A few producers have tried to make traditional method demi-sec and the sweeter doux style work, but any excessive sugar makes a fizz too heavy for its own good. This doesn't appear to be an issue in the case of the likes of Moët Ice and Pommery Pop, successfully aimed at young people and the nightclub lifestyle.

Sparkling rosé

Because of the wide range of approaches to making and marketing it, sparkling rosé probably courts more controversy than any other style of fizz. Ruinart was the first Champagne house to sell rosé, in 1764, and Veuve Clicquot the first house to export it, to Switzerland, in 1775. Historically, elderberry juice was added to rosé, 'la teinture de Fisme', but it was forbidden in the early part of the twentieth century. Perhaps it was America's sparkling pink Cold Duck and its association with Coco Chanel's little black dress and the dancing, drinking, smoking flapper that led Mme Bollinger to consider pink Champagne deeply suspect, causing her to declare 'Champagne is white'.

That sniffy attitude continues among a handful of 'purists', but it's difficult to maintain in the light of the vast improvement in pink Champagne and sparkling wine. No longer just an afterthought or 'a girly thing', it's down to producers taking the style more seriously in the face of growing demand and a reduction in dosage due to warmer growing seasons and an improvement in the ripeness of black grapes. 'Rosé is now more than a fashion,' said Dominique Demarville, while still chef de cave at Veuve Clicquot. The evidence lies both in the contribution of quality rosé Champagne producers Laurent-Perrier, Gosset and Billecart-Salmon and the proliferation of prestige cuvée, grower and single-vineyard pink Champagnes. Today pink Champagne accounts for some 10 per cent of all Champagne made.

In most Champagnes, rosé is made by blending in around 10–15 per cent red wine specially made soft and aromatic for the purpose. At their two wineries dedicated to red wine production, in Épernay and the Aube, Moët & Chandon use thermovinification (heat treatment) for Rosé Impérial for gentle tannins and aroma extraction. The main alternative is *saignée*, or maceration of uncrushed black grapes on the skins for a short time, as Laurent-Perrier does, as does Moët & Chandon for its Grand Vintage Rosé. The latter process has to be carefully managed to avoid excessive tannins, but a little extra firmness can make them ideal with food. The range of colours is 50 shades of Farrow & Ball, and counting.

In suspense – barrels held up by straps, Langham Estate, England

Sparkling rosé in both non-vintage and vintage is one of the most promising categories for the emerging English sparkling wine category. Hush Heath's Balfour Rosé was one of the first to show the potential and today, most top English wineries are now making high quality rosés; among them are Ambriel, Digby, Exton Park, Chapel Down, Gusbourne, Henners, Harrow & Hope, Langham, Raimes, Ridgeview,

The Grange and Wiston Estate. We are beginning to see a promising new prestige rosé category emerging, most notably from Nyetimber with its 1086 Vintage Rosé and Hambledon's Première Cuvée DZ.

Thanks to the demand for rosé Cava, Trepat and Pinot Noir were introduced in 1998, since when production of pink Cava has reached a similar percentage to that of pink Champagne. Trepat, with its fragrant berry-like aromas, can only be used for rosé production. As in Champagne, pink Cavas are being taken more seriously. In Catalunya the styles are becoming drier with brut nature such as Gramona's Argent, Vilarnau's Brut Reserva Rosé and Agusti Torelló Mata's Rosé Reserva, increasingly popular. Garnacha and Monastrell can also be used. Recaredo for instance use over two-thirds Monastrell in their brut nature. As evidence of the growing seriousness of rosé in Italy, Franciacorta rosé must spend a minimum of 24 months on the lees, vintage rosé a minimum of 30 months on the lees and rosé riserva a minimum of 60 months on the lees. In 2021, Prosecco Rosé DOC was launched, authorizing the use of 10–15 per cent Pinot Noir with the traditional Glera grape.

Brut nature/zero dosage

If rosé courts controversy, the brut nature styles divides opinions even more. In 2019, the writer Terry Theise claimed that a generation of younger 'anti-dosage militants … are sucking charm, grace and complexity from thousands of Champagnes because they have fervently decided that sugar in all contexts is evil'. Creating cuvées with zéro dosage isn't the exclusive province of 'anti-dosage militants' and there are some very good examples of the type. When Bruno Paillard first produced a Champagne without dosage some 30 years ago, it flopped. He vowed never to produce another, but thanks to climate change and the maturity of certain vineyards he thought might suit the style, in 2018 he brought out an excellent Dosage Zéro largely based on Meunier.

In Champagne, Ayala, Drappier, Gimonnet, Pol Roger, Billecart-Salmon, Laurent-Perrier, Philipponnat and Roederer are among well-known producers that have more or less successfully incorporated low or no sugar cuvées to their ranges. Equally, growers like Jacques Lassaigne, Vouette & Sorbée, Tarlant and Roses de Jeanne eschew dosage either because they believe that their richly concentrated Champagnes don't need it or because they feel that sugar masks terroir. If it's too tart, the relative austerity of the zero dosage fizz can be hard to love. Thanks to its generosity of fruit, Franciacorta fizz can be highly successful without dosage and the same is true for a growing number of sparklers from Spain and Italy. Gusbourne's Natural Brut and Hambledon's Première Cuvée DZ could be the harbingers of a new trend in England too.

Pet nat

Pet nat, or *pétillant naturel* to give it its grown-up name, is an increasingly popular style of fizz. Unlike sparkling wines made in a tank, pet nats are fermented in the bottle, but they are very different animals from traditional method sparklers, not least because they tend to highlight grape varieties not normally found in more traditional sparkling wines, often showcasing blends of native varieties. Instead of having the yeast removed as in the traditional method, pet nat retains the yeast. It may be, and often is, a bit cloudy, which, for aficionados, is all part of the fun.

The genesis of pet nat began with France's *méthode ancestrale*, or *méthode rurale*. In this early traditional method, young wine is bottled before all its residual sugar has been fermented to dryness. The wine has no sugar added and undergoes just a single fermentation, continuing to ferment in the bottle, usually on its lees deposit, producing bubbles from the carbon dioxide emitted during that primary fermentation. At around 2.5 to 3 atmospheres of pressure, the result is less fizzy than Champagne. It was most often demi-sec, a touch of sweetness being the result of unfermented sugars remaining in the bottle. A couple of classic examples of this early style remain: Blanquette de Limoux, and the rarer but interesting Bugey-Cerdon.

Pet nat has become popular, especially among producers of natural wines, where its fun style fits the ethos and the lifestyle. It's generally less expensive to make than traditional method, at least in part because it doesn't need to undergo a second fermentation and extended lees ageing, not to mention the accompanying processes of riddling, disgorgement and filtration. However, this doesn't mean that pet nats can never benefit from a little bottle age.

Today's pet nats are for the most part dry or drier than the traditional styles. In this, control over the fermentation is paramount and winemaking can still be a bit hit-and-miss with reductive winemaking not uncommon (splashing the wine into a carafe can help). Often, fruit and a mineral-like texture are accompanied by noticeable acidity, balancing out any residual sweetness. However, a little residual sweetness can help to keep the alcohol levels to a relatively low 10–12 per cent. Most examples are sealed with a crown cap, so the wines can sensibly be stored standing up.

Some producers disgorge the sediment and filter before bottling, but most pet nat is bottled with its sediment, or lees, intact. The lees remain in the bottle until consumed so you can stand the bottle in the fridge while chilling to allow the sediment to fall to the bottom. However, most producers counsel gently shaking the bottle before opening to distribute the sediment. The effect is to bring added texture to the wine which will of course look cloudy.

The modern incarnation of pet nat took off in France's Loire region (where in Central Touraine it has acquired its own AOC), quickly followed by the Jura in eastern France, both hotbeds for natural wine. Another region with good examples is Austria's Burgenland from the natural wine producers around the Neusiedlersee. The style has spread throughout Europe. Apart from usual suspects such as Spain, Italy and Germany, Czech Republic, Hungary and Slovakia have also started to make some exciting examples, and a growing number of pet nats are emerging from South Australia and from California and Vermont in North America.

A glass half full

I have some sympathy with the view of one wine writer who declared: 'unpretentious glasses say spontaneity, fun and pleasure while delicate expensive ones say one-upmanship and pedantry; they are for the sort of people who say "stemware" instead of glass, or "timepiece" for watch'. Some sympathy but not much. If you're going to spend good money on a pricey sparkling wine, then the wine – and you – deserve a glass that will enhance the enjoyment of the experience. A good sparkling wine glass has the capacity (pun intended) to reward you time and again.

The best glass for enjoying sparkling wine is one that holds its bubbles for as long as possible. This was the purpose of the long, narrow flute, which retains the bubbles, especially those that shoot straight up your nose in an explosion of aromatic molecules. A narrow flute is best for light sparkling wines, a broader flute such as a sommelier flute better for allowing the aromas of the wine to waft upwards in scent-carrying effervescence. For that reason, sparkling wine glasses are now being made to accommodate the best of both worlds with an effervescence point (or nucleation point) to encourage a steady stream of bubbles and a broader surface area.

(left) Effervescence points in Schott Zwiesel Vina 77 Sommelier flute; (right) bubbles rising from the nucleation point – see how they grow.

The scientific term nucleation is much used in the beer sector. One of the most extreme examples of nucleation is the Peroni beer glass where an elaborate design is laser etched onto the inside of the base, producing the bubbles all over that base and ensuring a maximum feed throughout the entire glass, up to the head. On a perfectly smooth glass surface, there's no reason for a bubble to grow, so an etching at the bottom of the glass is important. Early effervescence points were achieved using actual glass points (which could create hygiene issues), while modern nucleation points are created by using laser etched dots. These are difficult to see – so do not detract from the glass – and they are easy to clean with no danger of breakage or of the etching eroding. Where nucleation points are at the base of the glass, bubbles have more time to grow as they rise through the liquid and so are larger and more visible at the top. Such glasses can prolong the sparkle and enhance presentation by encouraging the bubbles to spiral up from a particular point. I would advocate getting in a few if you want to get the most from your glassware. Among the best are Riedel Veritas and Superleggero and Schott Zwiesel Vina 77 Sommelier flute and Bar Special 772ep.

THE SCIENCE OF THE BUBBLE

What is a bubble? We know a bubble when we see one but do we know what a bubble is and how it works in the bottle and our glass? A bubble is in essence a pocket of gas enclosed in liquid. In a Champagne bottle, there are typically five or six atmospheres of pressure. When you open the bottle, the pressure is suddenly released. The trapped gas which had been dissolved in the liquid escapes and this results in a release of bubbles. The carbon dioxide must escape until the pressure in the air void matches the pressure in the liquid. At that point a stasis is reached and gas ceases to escape the liquid. Millions of bubbles need to escape for equilibrium to be restored.

When sparkling wine is poured into a glass, it can escape both through the surface and through bubble formation. Most of it escapes unnoticed through the surface but a percentage escapes as bubbles, depending on the shape of the glass, surface area and how clean the glass is. Bubbles don't come from nothing. In any pressurized gas environment like a Champagne bottle, what bubbles need is a place to get started, a bubble production site, also known as a nucleation or effervescence point. According to Gérard Liger-Belair, nucleation sites are as much able to form from impurities stuck on the glass as scratches or irregularities in the glass itself. Most nucleation sites, Liger-Belair tells us, are elongated, hollow, roughly cylindrical cellulose fibres cast off from paper or cloth that floated onto the glass from the surrounding air or stayed on the glass after being wiped dry. These particles trap tiny air-pockets when the sparkling wine is poured. The tiny trapped air pockets in the scratch or impurity are inflated by carbon dioxide escaping from the depressurized liquid. As more gas concentrates it gradually gains the buoyancy to overcome the attachment forces. As the bubble detaches, it expands and becomes increasingly buoyant while a small gas pocket that remains trapped allows new bubbles to nucleate. As it expands, the bubble's buoyancy increases, allowing it to accelerate its progress through the super-saturated liquid towards the surface of the glass on a journey lasting from one to five seconds. When the bubbles reach the top of the glass, they burst at the surface, delivering a refreshing spray to the atmosphere while the liquid flows outwards and then back down the sides to the bottom of the glass. This effervescence however, says Liger-Belair, is easily spoilt by the presence of fatty molecules coming into contact with the bubbles as they reach the surface. So eating crisps or peanuts while you sip, or wearing lipstick, for instance, could cause the bubbles to collapse rapidly after the first sip. Quality wines tend to have smaller bubbles, which Liger-Belair links to a reduction in carbon dioxide during the long ageing process, which in turn means slower bubble growth.

By the time you put an opened bottle in the fridge, it has already lost a lot of the gas that it had but putting it in the fridge makes it easier for the remaining gas to stay put. According to bubble scientist Helen Czerski, when you cool down liquid and the gas around it, you slow down the gas molecules bouncing around in the liquid like bumper cars, making it harder for the carbon dioxide to escape because it's protected in the liquid. A Champagne stopper will also slow it down because it raises the carbon dioxide pressure in the neck space. By limiting the volume, you're trapping your carbon dioxide molecules, making it more likely that they'll bump into the surface and go back down.

Light strike

Light strike occurs when a wine is exposed to light in the ultraviolet and blue light end of the spectrum. The light reacts with the naturally occurring amino acids in a wine, transforming them into unpleasant volatile compounds with off-flavours, smelling of cooked cabbage, dishwater, old potatoes or damp cardboard. With their lower phenolic content than red wine, white and rosé wines are more susceptible to this phenomenon.

Even a relatively short exposure to light, including the normal form of artificial light used by retailers, is sufficient to damage wine and the transformation can occur in as little as 60 minutes of exposure to light. Wines that are most at risk come in clear glass bottles, making white and rosé doubly susceptible, especially sparkling versions, with the extra amino acids from lees-ageing. Brown glass provides 99.9 per cent protection from UV and 90.5 per cent from all harmful light. Amber glass blocks out 90 per cent or more of harmful light, green glass up to 50 per cent, clear glass just 10 per cent. Thinner glass bottles may be more environmentally friendly but thinner glass reduces the bottle's protective properties.

So why do Champagne and other sparkling wine producers still bottle their wines in clear glass? Cosmetics, in a word. Allowing all wavelengths of visible light to pass through transparent glass shows the true colour of the wine in the bottle and when it sparkles, pink bubbles especially, it can be a beautiful thing. For many producers, it's part of the brand image. Take Roederer Cristal for instance. There's no one more receptive to criticism than its winemaker Jean-Baptiste Lécaillon. He won't change the bottle though because it's been part of Cristal's identity ever since it was bottled in clear glass for Tsar Alexander II of Russia in 1876. Instead, he wraps the clear glass bottle in a 98 per cent protective, UV-resistant orange cellophane. Ca' del Bosco has followed suit with a similar wrapping for its Prestige Cuvées.

English and Trento DOC producers have been ahead of the game perhaps because they never had clear bottles as part of their brand identity. Nyetimber switched to dark amber bottles in 2008. Winemaker Brad Greatrix, who is passionate about eradicating light strike says: 'There are plenty of delicious/ amazing wines in clear glass, but their quality is resting on a house of cards.' After trials with rosé, Chapel Down changed to ebony glass. In classic Italian style, Alta Langa's Gancia fizz, already bottled in dark glass, is tightly wrapped in a foil film resembling a matt cloth material, with a different colour foil for each cuvée. The Slovenian winery Radgonske Gorice has gone even further. Its Untouched by Light, for which night-vision goggles were used for harvest, bottle rotation and packing, is housed in a black light-proof bottle in a 100 per cent recyclable vacuum-sealed bag.

What can be done to mitigate the effects of lightstrike? Avoid buying sparkling white or rosé in a clear glass bottle for one thing, especially if it looks as if it has been gathering dust in the shop for some time. If a clear glass bottle comes with a box or protective wrap, keep it in its protective clothing for as long as possible. At home, keep wines in as dark a place as possible. If you're eating out, at a picnic for instance, keep the wine away from direct sunlight, preferably in a bag or box.

PART 2

COUNTRY INTRODUCTIONS AND PROFILES

5

AUSTRALIA AND NEW ZEALAND

AUSTRALIA

I could hardly miss Seppelt when I stopped by for a visit on my first wine trip to Australia in 1989 because the name Seppelt Great Western Champagne Cellars was proudly affixed to the Victoria winery in gigantic lettering. In the soft granite caves of the Grampians, excavated by miners during the gold rush era of the mid-nineteenth century, with its winemaker, Ian McKenzie, I tasted a Seppelt's champagne made not from Chardonnay or Pinot Noir, but from the Ondenc grape, which was valued for its naturally high acidity.

Australia's first attempts at sparkling wine production in the late 1840s – the 'champagnes' of Edward Cory (Gostwyck) and William Burnett (Glenview) – were well-received at the Hunter Valley Vignerons Association. In the 1880s and 1890s, French winemakers Auguste d'Argent, Charles Pierlot and Edmond Mazure were all pressed into sparkling wine service. Hans Irvine had bought Joseph Best's vineyard in 1888, envisaging producing fizz for the local and export markets. 'I am confident that in several districts of Australia, champagne wines can be produced that will compare favourably with the best champagne wines in the world', he wrote. By 1900, his Great Western Champagne had won a gold medal at the Paris Exhibition and was Australia's leading sparkling wine brand.

Penfolds acquired Minchinbury Champagne Cellars in 1912, installing Leo Buring as its head winemaker. Six years later, Hans Irvine sold the Great Western Champagne company to Benno Seppelt. Seppelt's Great Western became even more famous after 1932 when Colin Preece created Seppelt's champagne and a distinct and enduring 'sparkling burgundy' style based on Shiraz. The 1950s saw many traditional-method sparkling wines replaced by cheaper Charmat-method fizz, including Cold Duck. With the help of Günter Prass, a German sparkling specialist, Colin Gramp's Orlando winery pumped out Barossa Pearl, a light fizz not dissimilar to today's Prosecco, but made from Eden Valley Riesling, Barossa Semillon and Muscat, with Muscatel and Frontignan juice getting the second fermentation under way.

It took until the 1980s for the modern industry to be transformed by a shift to cooler climates and a demand for higher quality fizz. Great Western's Salinger, a Chardonnay–Pinot Noir blend, led the charge, followed by good value Aussie fizz in big volumes: Angas Brut, Orlando Carrington and Trilogy, Seaview Brut, Hardys Brut and Killawarra. The Champagne houses were on the scent. After an extensive search for the right spot by the late Dr Tony Jordan, Moët & Chandon established its Green Point Vineyards outpost, today's Chandon Australia, in Victoria's Yarra Valley in 1985. Soon after, Roederer entered into a joint venture in Tasmania with Heemskerk, for the development of a 25-hectare vineyard, Bollinger took a stake in Petaluma in the Adelaide Hills and Deutz teamed up with Yalumba.

To achieve flavour and aroma characters closer to those of Champagne, new vineyards were planted in regions with lower average temperatures, good elevation and longer growing seasons. In addition to Yarra Valley, Tasmania and Adelaide Hills, the main regions included the foothills of the Australian Alps, Macedon Ranges, Strathbogie Ranges and Mornington Peninsula in Victoria, Orange and Tumbarumba in New South Wales, and Pemberton and Margaret River in Western Australia. More recently the elevated subalpine region of King Valley in Victoria has become a stronghold of Australian Prosecco. A legal squabble with the EU means that this has limited export opportunities to Europe but, made in Charmat, traditional method and pet nat styles, it's a big hit with Australian consumers.

Australia today produces around seven million cases of fizz, the lion's share of which is sparkling white, mostly based on Chardonnay and Pinot Noir and, to a lesser extent, Meunier. Apart from the classic Champagne varieties, grapes used include Semillon, Chenin Blanc, Riesling, Crouchen, Trebbiano, Prosecco and Muscat Gordo Blanco.

Dry brut is the standard style, with dosage no higher than 12 grams per litre, but sparkling rosé and sweeter moscato styles are popular too. One distinctive style making waves is pet nat, a subset of the natural wine movement. Based on the ancestral method (see page 28), pet nats are all the rage with younger drinkers; winemakers such as Bryan Martin at Ravensworth, Jauma, BK Wines, Dirt Candy, Cavedon and Tim Wildman, with Astro Bunny, are leading the way.

Australia has been producing sparkling red wines based on Shiraz for well over a century. Originally called 'sparkling burgundy' for its resemblance, usually after a period of maturation, to, yes, burgundy, these joyfully frothing, crimson-red bubbles can also be made from Pinot Noir, Cabernet Sauvignon, Merlot, Durif and Chambourcin, using the traditional, transfer, tank or carbonation methods. To absorb any potential bitterness from the tannins and create a smoother mouthfeel, dosage tends to run from off-dry to medium-sweet and, in some cases, fortified wines are used.

A TOUR D'HORIZON OF THE REGIONS

Tasmania

After two miserable summer days of rain and cold on my first trip to Tasmania in 1991, I cut my losses and headed, partner and small son in tow, for the Sunshine Coast of Queensland. It was no surprise to find that the weather forecast on a second visit in 2006 showed that rain was due while mainland Australia was bathed in glorious sunshine. More recently, as a guest judge at the 29th Annual Tasmanian Wine Show in 2019, our little twin-engine plane hovered over pastures so verdant they must have seemed like home to the first English convicts and free settlers to arrive in nineteenth-century Van Diemen's Land. I was no longer surprised as to why the island's cool climate gave it such an advantage in producing crisp dry whites and flavour-intense fizz over many of Australia's mainland vineyards.

Located south of mainland Australia at 41–43°S, Tasmania's potential, thanks to its cool, temperate climate and hilly terrain, has been harnessed for elegantly refined sparkling wine. A protective rain shadow that runs across the centre and the east yields long sunshine hours with mild spring and summer temperatures, warm autumn days and cool nights, which lead to slow ripening and good acid retention, producing flavour accumulation and an elegant, juicy acidity that brings finesse and delicacy. Almost all vineyards need supplementary irrigation and the westerly winds of the Roaring Forties can upset flowering, one of the hazards of nature that has to be overcome.

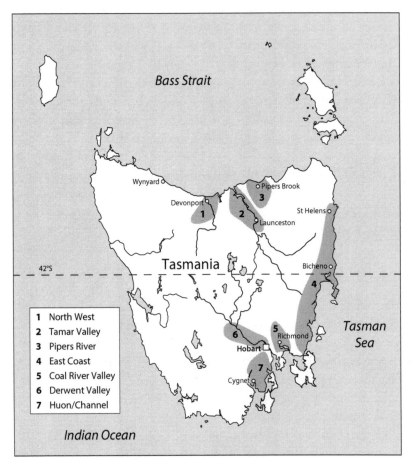

Wine-producing regions of Tasmania

Tasmania's modern wine era began when the French hydroelectric engineer Jean Miguet planted his 1.3 hectare La Provence vineyard in northern Tasmania, and the Italian businessman Claudio Alcorso founded Moorilla Estate on the banks of the Derwent River in 1958. The island's vineyards were subsequently developed piecemeal mainly around Launceston and Hobart by immigrants looking for a patch of dirt to invest in, farmers diversifying into wine and mainland exiles making a lifestyle choice. Sparkling wine took off when Louis Roederer agreed to a joint venture in 1986 after Graham Wiltshire suggested trialling sparkling wines based on Pinot Noir and Chardonnay at Heemskerk near Piper's River. Around the same time, Swiss vigneron Bernard Rochaix established Rochecombe with Alf Edgecombe and, in 1987, Taltarni's Dominique Portet planted 13 hectares of Chardonnay and Pinot Noir at Clover Hill overlooking the Bass Strait.

As mainland companies started to pay top dollar for their base wines from Tasmania, Hardys' (now Accolade's) chief sparkling winemaker, Ed Carr spotted the potential. His premium House of Arras label, the first all-Tasmania vintage of which was 1988, is today one of Tasmania's finest brands and is renowned for its late-disgorged fizz. Jansz Méthode Tasmanoise cheekily doffs its cap to its original Heemskerk/Louis Roederer blueprint, delivering a classic range of traditional method Tasmanian sparkling wines; and the pioneering Dr Andrew Pirie has stamped his authority on Tasmania's sparkling wine movement at Liliputian-sized Apogee.

Some 60 per cent of all Tasmania's Chardonnay and 45 per cent of its Pinot Noir goes to fizz. With recognition of significant site variation thanks to diverse soils, aspects, altitudes and climatic differences, sparkling wine production has expanded to cooler regions such as Piper's River and the northern coast (inland from Devonport), including the inland parts of the Tamar Valley; the Derwent Valley centred on Hobart, and the southernmost, cold-climate Huon Valley. There is sandstone and schist in the Derwent Valley, red to grey sandy loam on the east coast, quartzite and white sands over clay in the Coal River Valley; Pipers River boasts free-draining red clay loam over clay and Tamar Valley is gravelly basalt on a clay and limestone base.

Among boutique wineries making waves, Stefano Lubiana, Delamere and Josef Chromy make some of the leanest, cleanest fizz on the island. Moorilla is making impressively bone dry sparkling wines and Hobart-based Henskens Rankin is an exciting newcomer to watch. Larger-scale companies such as Hardys, Kreglinger, Yalumba (with Jansz Méthode Tasmanoise) and Brown Brothers (Pirie Tasmania) are contributing grape-growing prowess and winemaking savoir-faire. Combining local research into viticulture and winemaking with a focus on clones, modern equipment and winemaking techniques, the Tasmanian sparkling wine industry has reached a level of sophistication that could scarcely have been imagined a generation ago.

Adelaide Hills

The elevated Adelaide Hills region is renowned for its coolish climate and winter-dominant rainfall. Much of the region has good underground water supplies. Altitude allows Chardonnay and Pinot Noir to retain acid levels and develop flavour. Low-lying areas with heavy soils provide potential for greater vigour, while higher, well-drained stony soils allow vigour control. Notable Adelaide Hills sparkling wine producers include K1 by Geoff Hardy, Deviation Road, Daosa, Sidewood and Croser by Petaluma.

King Valley

Home to many so-called alternative varieties, including Prosecco, Arneis, Pinot Grigio, Sangiovese and Nebbiolo, Victoria's King Valley is the centre of Australian Prosecco. After the Second World War the region was settled by Italian immigrants and tobacco farmers, among them Otto Dal Zotto, originally from Valdobbiadene, who specialized in Italian varieties after establishing Dal Zotto in 1987. He planted a vineyard with Prosecco at Whitfield in 1999 and began a new category of Australian fizz. Although barely 20 years old, Australian Prosecco has boomed, with other producers including Brown Brothers, de Bortoli and Pizzini.

Yarra Valley

'Colonized' by Moët & Chandon at Green Point in the 1980s, the Yarra Valley's cool climate conditions and varied altitudes and exposures contribute to a long growing season, making it ideal for Chardonnay and Pinot Noir. Typically, winter- and spring-dominant rainfall and cool, dry, humid summers allow optimum ripening and high acidities. Soils are varied, with loamy sand to clay loam and rocky, red-brown clay subsoils, and deep, fertile red volcanic soils on the southern side of the valley. Notable Yarra Valley sparkling wine producers include Chandon Australia, Yarra Burn, Yering Station (Yarrabank) and Dominique Portet.

Other regions

Many wineries in Australia have invested in sparkling wine production. Although cool-climate traditional method styles and pet nat lead the fine wine conversation, fizz is also produced in Barossa Valley, McLaren

Vale, Coonawarra, Limestone Coast and Langhorne Creek in South Australia; Great Western and Rutherglen in Victoria; and the Hunter Valley in New South Wales, where the craze for Australian sparkling wine started in the 1840s.

Producers

Apogee

Lebrina, Tasmania

www.apogeetasmania.com

Andrew Pirie and his brother David first bought land in Tasmania in 1973 and planted Pipers Brook Vineyard. He completed his doctoral thesis on viticulture soon after and is now recognized as one of Tasmania's foremost wine pioneers. In his restless quest for terroir, he selected the best index for predicting vine ripening in cool climates in a paper at the Cool Climate Symposium in Hobart in 2012. After spotting a For Sale sign in Lebrina in the Pipers River district, Pirie acquired the 'boutique' property in order to establish a sparkling wine project based on a deliberately manageable, hand-tended 2-hectare vineyard planted to 67 per cent Pinot Noir, 20 per cent Chardonnay and 13 per cent Meunier with the aim of turning out *grand cru*-quality sparkling wine.

With a growing season temperature index (GST) of 14.5°C, the cool temperature in this region is crucial, being close to Aÿ in Champagne, and several clones such as 777, 521 and 115 are planted, including one clone from Champagne. The unique two-layered Scott Henry trellis system is 2.2 metres high and 2.2 metres wide, producing double the leaf area of the standard Tasmania vineyard, for maximum vine health, sunlight exposure and photosynthesis. According to Pirie, the moisture supply to the vine and the rate of evaporation are among the most critical factors in determining the style and tannin profile of the resulting wines. Production is limited to between 10,000 and 20,000 bottles a year, reflecting a philosophy based on the average size of a holding in Champagne.

The wines are vintage Deluxe Brut, a traditional-method sparkling wine, oxidatively pressed and partially oak-fermented, with around 35 per cent Pinot Noir, 40 per cent Chardonnay and the balance from Meunier, and a Deluxe Rosé Vintage Brut consisting of 90 per cent Pinot Noir and 10 per cent Chardonnay with 30 months on lees. As close to an expression of terroir as a Tasmanian sparkling wine comes, the most recent releases of the Deluxe Vintage Brut, 2014 and 2015, show complex aromatics and creamy textures with a refreshingly dry, salty tang. The same vintages of the Deluxe Rosé Vintage Brut display the subtle toastiness of bottle-aged Pinot Noir balanced by delicately dry, textured cherry and raspberry notes. In the definition on Apogee's website, Apogee is the zenith or highest point and with wines like these, Andrew Pirie is approaching the pinnacle.

Chandon Australia

Coldstream, Victoria

www.chandon.com.au

In the late 1980s, Dr Tony Jordan made a splash with the 2001 Z*D, a groundbreaking zero dosage *blanc de blancs* stoppered with a stainless steel crown seal aimed at eliminating cork taint. It was just one of the things that set Chandon apart. Chandon today makes a wide range: non-vintage, vintage, rosé, late-disgorged, rich, dessert, Pinot Gris, Pinot Shiraz, and even a ladies-who-lunch Chandon Garden Spritz to be drunk with orange bitters, ice and lemon. All fit the model of wine-making facility and cellar door tourist attraction, with panoramic views of the Yarra Valley from a high-class restaurant very much part of the Napa Valley-esque 'Chandon experience'.

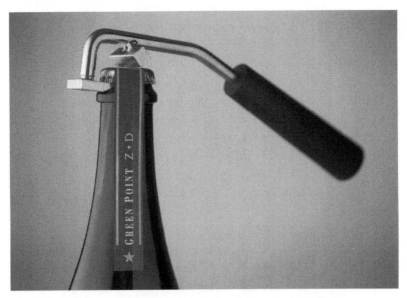

Stainless steel crown cap pioneered by Dr Tony Jordan,
Green Point Z.D., Chandon Australia

Chandon has largely stuck with its Victorian roots for its vineyard sources. Apart from its own 40-hectare Green Point vineyard, the lion's share comes from super-cool-climate vineyards, the first at 700 metres in 80 hectares on granitic sands in the high Strathbogie ranges, the second the 85-hectare Whitlands vineyard in the King Valley, which is mostly volcanic, deep, free-draining soils at 800 metres. With their high natural malic acidity, these two vineyards bring the structure that Dan Buckle and Glenn Thompson, respectively chief winemaker and sparkling wine-maker, are aiming for. The remaining half of its supply comes from some 40 growers in the Yarra Valley, King Valley, Strathbogie and Tasmania.

After a mix of hand and machine picking, with a press in the vine-yard in remote sites, fermentation takes place in stainless steel to main-tain brightness and freshness, with a small amount of oak fermentation. There are some 130 blending components, plus the reserve wines, from which to create the final blends. The winemaking team is given carte blanche with no interference from its owner Moët Hennessy in Champagne. The vintage wines are aged for between three and ten years with little added reserve wine.

Both the Chandon NV Brut and the NV Brut Rosé are excellent value sparkling wines. With 20 per cent reserve wine and around 7 grams per litre dosage, the emphasis in both cases is on freshness and delicacy of fruit. The former is redolent of French toast and citrus, while the rosé has berry fruit and savoury dryness. The vintage sparklers are impres-sive, with the Blanc de Blancs Brut outstanding for its complexity and mouthwatering acidity and the Blanc de Noirs Brut charmingly floral and fragrant with plump Pinot Noir vinosity. The most impressive fizz is the Chardonnay–Pinot Noir Chandon Late Disgorged, whose toasty rich, fine-textured fruit is seamlessly balanced after ten years maturation.

Josef Chromy Wines

Relbia, Tasmania

www.josefchromy.com.au

The drama of Joe Chromy and his escape as a 19-year-old from commu-nist Prague in 1950 is worthy of a John le Carré novel but, suffice to say, Chromy is one of life's survivors. After building a new life in Tasmania and establishing several successful ventures, involving Heemskerk, Jansz and Tamar Ridge, Chromy made his third foray into the Tasmanian wine industry when in 2004 he bought the 60-hectare Old Stornoway Vineyard in Relbia, close to Launceston. The first two vintages were made at Andrew Hood by Jeremy Dineen, who came on board to run the Relbia winery before leaving at the end of 2020 to do his own thing.

'The larger crops tend to make the better sparkling wines with subtler flavours and less phenolics; deeper, richer soils are better suited for fizz too, as it produces larger bunches and berries,' says Dineen. Irrigation is usually needed and everything is tasted before picking because while Dineen looks for delicacy in the skins and the juices, 'all the measurements in the world won't tell you what it tastes like and that's the important thing'. Depending on the blocks, varieties, clones and crop loads, picking takes place over three weeks with around 11 per cent potential alcohol for the sparkling Pinot Noir and Chardonnay.

Josef Chromy's fizz is Pinot-dominant and stainless steel fermented, with little or no oak and low dosage. None of the wines go through malolactic fermentation. The result is a lean, clean style of fizz. According to Dineen, 'the combination of Pinot dominance gives a robustness and retaining that natural malic acidity brings greater finesse with more zing, primary red apple skins and subtle perfumed fruits rather than bruised fruit'. Kept in stainless steel on the lees, Josef Chromy's reserve wines go back to 2008.

In the NV Tasmanian Cuvée, which spends from 18 to 30 months on the lees, there are subtle aromatics and a Cox's appley mousse, with tangy freshness. The Vintage Tasmania, a *blanc de noirs*, is juicy in its crunchy berry fruit mousse, and the Late Disgorged Sparkling displays superb, malty–toasty aromas with a superfine mousse imbued with a savoury, dry, appley bite. Chromy's Pepik Sekt is a sparkling Riesling whose aromatic citrusy character with its limey zip and zing, is mouthwateringly delicious.

Clover Hill Wines

Lebrina, Tasmania

www.cloverhillwines.com.au

Taltarni's Dominique Portet came in search of cool climate terroir for sparkling wine in 1985, opting for a 66-hectare property at Lebrina in the Pipers River for its mild summers and long autumns days. In the following year, Clover Hill was established by the Goelet family. The first varietal planting, a Penfolds clone Chardonnay introduced by vineyard manager Chris Smith in 1987, produced the inaugural award-winning 1991 Clover Hill Blanc de Blancs. Then came more Chardonnay, along with Pinot Noir, and finally Meunier, of which there are now 5 hectares.

The Goelet family took the Clover Hill vineyard to full production capacity of around 10,000 cases in 1996 and from 1997, Dominique Portet played no further part.

From Clover Hill's stunning cellar door, opened in December 2017, the restaurant terrace looks out over steeply sloping vineyards towards the Bass Strait in the far distance. The free-draining soils, of which some 22 hectares are planted to vines, are red volcanic clay over shallow bedrock. Despite heavy rainfall between October and December, little ground water is retained. For Clover Hill's aim of retaining bright fruit quality, picking is at as low a potential alcohol as possible and no oak is used or malolactic fermentation carried out. Clover Hill Vintage Brut was poured for the wedding of Tasmanian-born Princess Mary and Prince Frederick of Denmark in 2004 and selected for the Australian visit of Queen Elizabeth II and the Duke of Edinburgh in 2011.

Clover Hill cellar door

Until 2015 Clover Hill was producing exclusively vintage sparkling, before adding a NV Cuvée and NV Cuvée Rosé. A perpetual reserve is used for the NV wines. The non-vintage Clover Hill range includes a bright, appley Tasmanian Cuvée NV and a pale-skinned Tasmanian Cuvée Rosé NV with an emphasis on texture and light raspberry notes. Vintage wines start with the briochey Vintage Brut, with its briny tang, while the Cuvée Exceptionelle Blanc de Blancs is distinctly saline and savoury. The Cuvée Exceptionelle Rosé shows lipsmacking strawberry notes and the all-Chardonnay Clover Hill Cuvée Prestige is complex in aroma with lemon and lime citrus notes and a savoury hint of saline-streaked butterscotch.

Coldstream Hills

Coldstream, Yarra Valley, Victoria

www.coldstreamhills.com.au

In 1988 I met the Australian wine writer James Halliday at the Qantas Cup in Napa Valley, where his Reserve Pinot Noir swept all before it. I visited Coldstream Hills the following year with Oz Clarke. This was just four years after Halliday and his wife Suzanne had founded Coldstream Hills with the Amphitheatre and House Block planted just a year after the building of the winery and the planting of G Block with Pinot Noir, Chardonnay and Cabernet Sauvignon. Plantings expanded in the 1990s to include the Upper Yarra Valley Vineyard, the Briarston Vineyard and the Fernhill Vineyard, and a temperature-controlled barrel cellar was built in 1999. The first fizz was a 1995 *blanc de noirs*.

Today, the estate is owned by Treasury Wine Estates, with Andrew Fleming and Greg Jarratt heading up the winemaking. Fruit from the estate's Deer Farm Vineyard in the Upper Yarra is used to make the fizz. The cooler south-facing aspects of the vineyard provide vibrant citrus for Chardonnay and perfume and structure for Pinot Noir. For Fleming, the trick, especially in warmer years such as 2016, and with climate change gathering pace, is to manage the vineyard by picking early, on flavour, at around 10.5 per cent potential alcohol. The wines are whole-bunch pressed and fermented in stainless steel. Malolactic fermentation, if done, is carried out in colder years, such as 2011.

The vintage Coldstream Hills Pinot Noir Chardonnay is typically made up from two blending components and spends 3–3.5 years on its lees with a dosage of around 6 grams per litre. The vintage fizz shows hints of brioche and Champagne-like complexity, with pristine fruit richness balanced by a fine blade of acidity. Only released in outstanding Chardonnay vintages, notably 2011 and 2015, the vintage Chardonnay-dominant Coldstream Hills Blanc de Blancs, a single vineyard fizz from the Deer Farm Vineyard, spends four years on the lees with a dosage of 6 grams per litre for a fine-textured, creamy mousse and vivid fruit quality.

Delamere

Pipers Brook, Tasmania

www.delamerevineyards.com.au

The Delamere vineyard was established in 1983 by Richard Richardson and his wife Dallas, following the French close-planting pattern with 1.5 metres between the vines, and expanded to 3 hectares over the next three years. When Shane Holloway, an Adelaide University winemaking graduate, acquired the Pipers River property in 2007 with a minimum of equipment and a lot of stock, there were 6.5 hectares of vineyard, planted three-fifths to Pinot Noir and two-fifths to Chardonnay with 7,500 vines per hectare in the estate's deep red, fertile Ferrosol soils. In 2012, he was joined by Fran Austin, who had been the winemaker at Bay of Fires. Another 5 hectares were planted in 2013, fifty-fifty Chardonnay and Pinot Noir, with 2 hectares of Meunier to follow.

There are now six sparkling wines in the portfolio, made only from estate grown fruit. The vines for the sparkling wine range are mostly east-facing and cane-pruned, with a low fruiting wire for low yields, while ground heat adds to ripeness and flavour. To the original clones, Shane and Fran have added 115, 114 and 777 of Pinot Noir for lower yields, along with moderate yielding Chardonnay clones 76 and 95 and higher yielding I10V1. After the grapes are hand picked at about 10–10.5 per cent potential alcohol, winemaking is carried out in batches to build as much time on the lees as possible in the non-vintage wine. Around 20 per cent reserve wine is held in small format barrel, tank and foudres. Most wines undergo at least a proportion of malolactic fermentation for balance and approachability.

With 18 months on the lees and around 4 grams per litre dosage, the NV Cuvée is an elegantly melony, appetizingly balanced fizz, its non-vintage counterpart, the pure Pinot Noir NV Rosé charmingly floral, fragrant and strawberryish. Disgorged after six years, the prestige cuvée Rosé is strawberry-rich with a savoury hint of saline dryness. Delamere's *blanc de blancs*, with full malolactic fermentation, displays elegant notes of biscuit and brioche, a creamy mousse and a hint of salinity, while with nearly ten years on the lees and no malolactic fermentation, the Late Disgorged Blanc de Blancs shows a fine malty bouquet, a smoky-savoury superfine mousse and tight, fresh zestiness. Quite a wine!

House of Arras

Bay of Fires Cellar Door, Pipers River, Tasmania

houseofarras.com.au

Named for the famous tapestry town in France, Arras is Australia's premier sparkling wine producer; almost all its fruit comes from Tasmania. After identifying Tasmania as the place with the best potential for fizz, Ed Carr arrived in the mid-1990s with an open cheque book from BRL Hardy (Accolade today). Vineyards such as Pipers Brook Vineyards, Meadowbank and Delamere were already planted to Chardonnay and Pinot Noir. Convinced that Tasmania's cool maritime island climate and sunny ultra-violet light were perfectly suited to growing the raw material for great fizz, Carr persuaded more growers to plant the Champagne varieties and Hardys to produce a Tasmanian prestige cuvée. In December 2002, the seminal 1998 Arras became the first vintage to be made entirely from Tasmanian fruit.

Together with sister winery Bay of Fires, House of Arras sources some 800 tonnes of grapes from regions selected for their cool climate locations. Carr particularly favours the east coast and the south for the subtly different influences each region brings to the blend. Arras is also planting in the cool Piper's River region. Vineyards are generally planted on their own roots, so there's no rootstock work, but Arras has done much work on clonal selection, with I10V1, a Davis clone, for Chardonnay and MV6, the Busby clone, for Pinot Noir favourites, together with an unknown clone of Meunier selected from an Accolade Wines vineyard in the Upper Yarra Valley.

Arras aims to pick at 11–11.5 per cent alcohol as Carr is looking for ripeness with no risk of herbal notes. Fruit destined for traditional method fizz is hand-harvested. The grapes are transported to Bay of Fires, pressed and the juice shipped to Hardys' Tintara winery in McLaren Vale. Arras' top cuvées, the vintage wines (Late Disgorged, Grand Vintage, Blanc de Blancs, Rosé) and the Brut Elite, are traditional method. Bottle fermented/transfer method allows blending options with economies of scale. After malolactic fermentation, the wines spend between 30 months and 15 years on the lees. Up to 10 per cent new oak is used in the traditional-method fizz and some older oak for up to 25 per cent of blends. Reserve wines up to five years old are built up in 2,500 litre French *foudres*. Dosage is on the way down, varying from some 9 grams per litre for the Premium Cuvée to 2–4 grams per litre for the traditional-method cuvées.

The wines in the Arras range are all blends. The complex, expansively creamy Arras Brut Elite NV Cuvée, with Meunier to fill out the mid-palate, won the trophy for the best non-vintage sparkling at the 2020 Tasmanian Wine Show (and Best Australian Sparkling Wine at the 2019 and 2020 Champagne and Sparkling Wine World Championships, CSWWC). The crisp Arras Blanc de Blancs NV Brut, with its vivid citrus-zesty acidity is a multi-regional blend of pure Chardonnay. The Chardonnay-based Arras Grand Vintage, which spends around seven years on the lees is delightfully rich and complex while the Arras Vintage Rosé is a wine of superb summer pudding richness and sensual texture. The Arras Late Disgorged Cuvée is Ed Carr's answer to Bollinger R.D. All in all, some 780,000 bottles are produced.

Jansz Tasmania

Jansz Wine Room and Interpretive Centre
Pipers Brook, Tasmania
www.jansz.com.au

Jansz Tasmania was originally established north of Launceston in 1975 as Heemskerk, the name of the seventeenth century Dutch explorer Abel Janszoon Tasman's ship. It was planted by Graham Wiltshire who, with co-owner Bill Fesq, was joined by Champagne Roederer in 1986. The first Jansz, labelled Cuvée 1989, containing 85 per cent 1989 fruit, blended with oak-aged wines from the 1987 and 1988 vintages, was launched in 1990. The estate was acquired by Josef Chromy, who sold the Heemskerk group to Dr Andrew Pirie in February 1998. In the same year, Pirie disposed of the Jansz brand to the Hill Smith family, who put the talented winemaker Natalie Fryar in charge in January 2001. Early Jansz wines were primarily Chardonnay-dominant blends but trials with Pinot Noir led to the birth of Jansz Tasmania Premium Rosé in 2005.

With ideal conditions for sparkling wine thanks to the moderating influence of the Bass Strait, the Jansz vineyard, resting on a bed of free-draining, red basalt soils, lies on the northern Tasmanian Wine route in Pipers River. All vintage wines come from the nine blocks planted to 10.27 hectares of Chardonnay and nine blocks to over 9.3 hectares of Pinot Noir. Including the 19.6-hectare Jansz Pipers River Estate vineyard itself, Jansz covers just over 100 hectares with three other vineyards: Glenview at White Hills, Pontos Hills in the Coal River Valley and Woodside at Forcett. Grapes are also bought from external growers for the light, crisp, refreshing Chardonnay-dominated Premium NV and the creamy Pinot Noir-dominated Premium NV Rosé. After hand-picking, crushing and fermentation, the wines are transported to South Australia for bottle fermentation and lees ageing before emerging with the Jansz signature 'méthode Tasmanoise' label.

With Jennifer Doyle at the winemaking helm today, Jansz produces a strong range of sparkling wines. The Tasmania Vintage Cuvée, a blend of almost equal Chardonnay and Pinot Noir, fermented for seven months in older oak, spends four years on lees for subtle briochey nuttiness and a mouthwateringly grapefruity 'sea spray' feel. The vintage Single Vineyard Chardonnay, rich in apple and peach fruitiness, is savoury and dry. Barrel-fermented for seven months and aged for more than three years on the lees, Jansz Tasmania Vintage Rosé, a pure Pinot Noir, shows a spicy raspberryish fragrance and soft berry fruit mousse.

Jansz Tasmania's limited edition Late Disgorged is aged on the lees for eight years for an enveloping toasty mousse and briney dryness. If you're lucky enough ever to try the 1992 Jansz Brut Cuvée 92, Heemskerk, this mature 'Champagney' Tassie fizz is full of toast and honey, like a mature, truffley Champagne only richer and more powerful. The latest wine to join the fold, Jansz Tasmania Pontos Hills Vintage Cuvée, is a 2017 field blend of Chardonnay, Pinot Noir and Meunier, first released to celebrate the inaugural vintage at the custom built Jansz Pontos Hills Winery in 2021.

Jean-Claude Rouzaud, Mark Fesq, Jean-Baptiste Lécaillon and Graham Wiltshire – launch of Jansz in The Examiner, *28 October 1991*

Stefano Lubiana

Granton, Tasmania
www.slw.com.au

From a winemaking family in Istria, Steve Lubiana's parents emigrated to Melbourne after the Second World War in 1950. After buying an old distillery at Moorook in the Riverland and converting it to wine, the family ran a thriving business supplying table wine to the immigrant community of Italians and Greeks. Steve (Stefano), graduated from Roseworthy in 1985 and did a stint in Champagne with Bauchet Frères in Bisseuil, returning to Australia for the 1987 vintage.

After taking over the family business, Steve decided to branch out on his own. The search for a location for sparkling wine brought him to Tasmania where, in the winter of 1991 in a dry, cool spot 25 minutes north of Hobart, he planted a hectare of Pinot Noir and Chardonnay. His first vintage was in 1993. After unsuccessfully trialling organics, he tried again, becoming biodynamic in 2013, using local preparations. 'Ultimately it makes for better acidity and greater clarity and definition in the wine,' says Steve.

Together with his wife, Monique, and son Marco, a University of Adelaide graduate, he has 25 hectares planted, mostly to Pinot Noir, although the fizz has become Chardonnay dominant as he can't make enough Pinot Noir to keep up with demand for his still reds. Soils, of grey, gravelly, silty loam over clay, are poor. Irrigation helps keep the canopy green and vigorous, helping to maintain freshness and avoid overt varietal characters while promoting the desired texture. Thanks to climate change, the growing season is gradually becoming earlier and rainfall less, with extremes of temperature more common and lower acidities burning off some of the malic acidity.

With around 15 per cent reserve wines, the NV Brut Reserve, fermented partially in oak, is a Pinot Noir–Chardonnay blend, spending two years on its lees. It's fresh with a subtle hint of biscuit, quite Champagne-like in character, with a full-flavoured mousse and balancing lively freshness. A similar blend, the Grande Vintage (no reserve wines, no malolactic fermentation) is deliciously toasty, with oodles of kumquat and citrus peel fruit in a cushion of fine mousse, deriving its complexity from five years on the lees. There's nowhere better to enjoy the Lubiana range than its delightful hilltop restaurant, the Osteria.

Moorilla

Hobart, Tasmania

www.moorilla.com.au

If one winery visit is all you have time for on a trip to Tasmania's capital of Hobart, Moorilla beckons as the all-singing-all-dancing wine experience. A member of Ultimate Wine Experiences Australia, Moorilla is remarkable for its history, its beautiful Derwent River location, its chalets, its museum, its brewery cellar door, its two restaurants, The Source and Faro, its ferry transfer, its experiences, and its wines. Did I mention the wines? Moorilla crushes around 220 tonnes of grapes (including recently bought Domaine A), roughly a quarter of which are destined for sparkling wine.

Moorilla was established in 1948 by a peripatetic Italian, Claudio Alcorso, who was incarcerated during the Second World War as an enemy alien. On release, he bought 19 hectares of land and, in 1958, against the advice of the locals, planted Riesling cuttings from David Wynn's Coonawarra vineyard, making his first wine in 1962. In 1995, it was bought by a controversial Tasmanian, David Walsh, in his own words 'a gambler and museum-less maths nerd', who opened the Moorilla Museum of Antiquities in 1999 'to properly store my nascent collection of African antiquities and coins'.

The Moorilla Vineyard itself is only 2.5 hectares, sitting just above sea level on a diverse mix of soils, with a three-week picking window across the vineyard. Moorilla also owns the 15-hectare St Matthias vineyard at Rosevears in the Tamar Valley, planted initially to 4 hectares in 1983 by Launceston pharmacist Laurie Wing and his wife Adelle, where cool breezes and ancient volcanic and newer clay soils ensure long ripening conditions for wines with good acid balance.

After he came on board in 2007 to run the new low-tech, small batch winery, Canadian winemaker Conor van der Reest's techniques, such as switching the balance in the wines away from sugar and towards acidity, provoked scepticism. Over a decade on, the vintage 2008s and 2009s only now being released are showing how well they have aged, with no malolactic fermentation, and how pristine they can be. From 2013 van der Reest started using some oak with the aim of softening the wines and that has worked.

The Praxis Riesling spends just 6–9 months on its lees for crisply refreshing appley aromas and a lipsmacking, tangy, limey fruit quality. The Muse Extra Brut, with roughly two-thirds Chardonnay and a third

Pinot Noir, spends four years on the lees, receiving a low 5 grams per litre dosage for a fizz with evolved biscuity aromatic notes and grapefruit zesty acidity. The Cloth Label Late Disgorged Extra Brut (made by Alan Ferry and Conor), comprising just over half Pinot Noir and under half Chardonnay with ten years on the lees, undergoes partial malolactic fermentation, producing a fizz that is still fresh, with a smoky, malty bouquet and fine-textured richness.

Pipers Brook

Pipers Brook, Tasmania

www.kreglingerwineestates.com

Pipers Brook was founded by Dr Andrew Pirie in 1974 after he and his brother David first came to Tasmania and dropped anchor here in the belief that the location was Australia's best terroir not just for Pinot Noir but for sparkling wines too. He launched his first sparkling wine under the Pirie name in 1995, taking the brand with him when he moved to Tamar Ridge. However, it remained with Tamar Ridge when Brown Brothers took over. Acquired by the Belgian owned G & C Kreglinger (the original brothers, George and Christian) in 2001, Pipers Brook today has three fizz labels, Ninth Island, Pipers Brook and Kreglinger.

Since Luke Whittle took the helm as senior winemaker in 2016 (and chief winemaker for Kreglinger Wine Estates in 2019), with Natalie Fryar consulting, there is less reserve wine in the non-vintage blends than hitherto. Pipers Brook crushes some 1,400 tonnes of fruit from 180 hectares and just over a third of that, around 36,000 cases, is sparkling wine. Ninth Island Tasmania NV Cuvée is attractively citrusy with a squeeze of lemon and lime for freshness; its counterpart, the Ninth Island Tasmania Rosé NV Cuvée shows plenty of strawberries and cream fruit and texture.

From the Pipers Brook Vineyard and the nearby Hills Vineyard, half of Pipers Brook Vintage is barrel-fermented and spends two years on the lees for a complex, rich mousse and lipsmacking acidity. The jewel in the Pipers Brook crown is the Kreglinger range, derived from 6 hectares of close-spaced Chardonnay and Pinot Noir in the steep, east-facing Hills Vineyard. Fully barrel-fermented, Kreglinger Vintage Brut, with three years on the lees, shows subtle biscuity notes and a silky textured, full-flavoured mousse. It's complemented by a pure Pinot Noir Vintage Rosé and Brut de Blancs and magnums of Late Disgorged Kreglinger beckon at the cellar door.

Tamar Ridge

Rosevears, Tasmania

www.tamarridge.com.au

Tamar Ridge Wines was established by Josef Chromy in 1994 on the western bank of the Tamar River. The 22-hectare vineyard at Kayena was developed with the help of the Australian viticulturalist Dr Richard Smart and retained by Chromy after he sold the Heemskerk Wine Group in 1998. A new winery was opened in time for the 1999 vintage and after the winery was sold in 2002 to the controversial wood-chipping company Gunns, Tamar Ridge's talented young winemaker Mike Fogarty left. Andrew Pirie was lured on board, and when Gunns decided to uncouple the wine business in 2010, the Australian wine industry breathed a collective sigh of relief at Brown Brothers' acquisition.

The Pirie name is used for the fizz, an NV Brut, a Vintage Brut and Vintage Rosé, while the Tamar Ridge brand is retained for the still wines. Winemaker Tom Wallace and assistant Anthony DeAmicis source fruit from the Hazards Vineyard on the east coast, the Kayena Vineyard (comprising over 30 distinct Pinot Noir sites) and, more recently, the Whitehills Vineyard. Pinot Noir and Chardonnay are hand-picked, producing some 480–500 litres per tonne, and the base wine is shipped to Victoria for tirage. Pure Pinot Noir with a good proportion of Whitehills fruit is used for the copper-bronze Pirie Rosé Brut with its lightly toasty, ripe berry fruit quality, and mouthfilling mousse.

A blend of mainly Chardonnay plus Pinot Noir, the Pirie NV Brut shows fresh aromatics and a full-flavoured, mouthfilling mousse with a lively, fresh, appley fruit quality and background nougat, while a more mature Pirie NV Brut from museum stock spends three to four years on the lees, with 10 per cent reserve wine, and 10 per cent oak, for a seductive Champagne-like aroma and deliciously oxidative, nutty notes. With some six years on the lees, the Pirie Vintage Brut, a half Chardonnay, half Pinot Noir blend of the three best vineyards, displays a toasty, velvet-textured mousse in an expansively creamy mouthful.

NEW ZEALAND

Sparkling wine production in New Zealand got off to an inauspicious start. Most of the early pioneers were focused on table wines and when they turned their attention to fizz, it was usually made from Müller-Thurgau or Palomino, using the tank method, and bore uninspiring names such as Cold Duck, Marque Vue and Montana Pearl. Gisborne was at the heart of production, mainly for the region's ability to grow Chardonnay and Müller-Thurgau at yields allowing for budget-friendly fizz.

In a generation, New Zealand fizz has been transformed. Attention has turned to cooler-climate vineyards mostly in Marlborough and latterly Central Otago for quality traditional method fizz. Hunters, No.1 Family Estate and Nautilus were early adopters, producing fruit of exemplary quality and laying down bottles with extended lees-ageing. In Central Otago, Rippon Vineyards released the region's first bottle-fermented sparkling wine, Emma, in 1993, to great acclaim. Quartz Reef's Rudi Bauer and Clotilde Chauvet were convinced the cool climate and precise winemaking would deliver wines of great elegance and today Akarua and Amisfield too produce notable examples.

The distraction of sparkling Sauvignon Blanc, launched in the wake of the Sauvignon Blanc glut of 2008, did little for the country's growing reputation for quality fizz. Today, New Zealand's dynamic wine industry continues to focus on quality, exploring new ways to market bottle-fermented sparkling wines to the world. Méthode Marlborough is a collaboration of 12 producers working to promote the wines at home and overseas. Wines must be made by the traditional method, using any combination of Chardonnay, Pinot Noir and Meunier, and aged on lees for a minimum of 18 months before disgorging.

Producers are also mindful of the potential impact of climate change and have demonstrated an awareness and ability to take pre-emptive measures to ensure that quality remains high. Clive Jones (Nautilus Estate) is exploring options of sourcing fruit from cooler sites such as Marlborough's Awatere Valley and focusing on high acidity Pinot Noir clones such as 10/5 and Abel. He and others also adapt vineyard management techniques to retain more canopy and therefore shading. While fizz only represents about 2 per cent of wine production (and less than 1 per cent of the exports), a focus by agile winemakers on quality and innovation ensures a bright future for the country's sparkling wines.

Producers

Cloudy Bay Vineyards
Blenheim, Marlborough
www.cloudybay.co.nz

In 2016, Cloudy Bay's winemaker, Victor Joyeux, was visiting neighbouring Marlborough producer Fromm when Hätsch Kalberer, Fromm's winemaker, went to the cellar and brought up a mysterious bottle that they tasted blind. 'We all realized it was an old vintage of a sparkling wine; it had a beautiful golden colour, aromatically quite upfront with a bready, floral and nutty character. The wine had good balance, good fizz and was quite enjoyable. It turned out to be the 1987 Pelorus that was given to Hätsch in 1992 by Kevin Judd. What a real game changer for me to realize the potential of the wine.'

After its foundation by Australian David Hohnen of Cape Mentelle fame, Cloudy Bay's first release was the 1985 Sauvignon Blanc, a wine that garnered as much attention for its arresting label as for the wine itself. It was followed in 1987 by its inaugural sparkling wine, named after Pelorus Jack, a dolphin who was reputed to escort ships crossing the Cook Strait. Today, Cloudy Bay is owned by Moët Hennessy. Victor Joyeux, who came from France to Cloudy Bay in 2013 as assistant wine-maker, now oversees the sparkling wine programme, and is joined by winemakers from Champagne, who come to do a New Zealand harvest in an ongoing exchange of information and knowledge.

Joyeux thinks the marked temperature shift between night and day and the drying north-west winds from late spring to harvest that limit disease pressure explain 'the high level of aromatic intensity and bright natural acidity carried by our wines'. The fruit for Pelorus comes from the estate vineyards and six local growers in the Wairau Valley. The grapes are hand harvested and gently pressed, after which the first fer-mentation is carried out in neutral vessels, where it undergoes malolac-tic fermentation. The Pelorus range (NV, rosé and vintage) has evolved, with Joyeux in charge, to become more complex and distinctive. The use of 20–25 per cent reserve wine contributes complexity and depth. The accomplished, complex NV is kept *en tirage* for at least 30 months while the well-crafted NV Rosé receives less time on lees. Interestingly, although the time on lees is stated, the date of disgorgement is not.

Kumeu River Wines

Kumeu, Auckland

www.kumeuriver.co.nz

Maté Brajkovich founded Auckland's San Marino Vineyards in 1944, making table wines for the local market. In 1986 the family changed the name to Kumeu River Wines, the better to reflect its location. Today Maté's widow Melba and all four children work in the business. With a deserved reputation as New Zealand's leading Chardonnay producer, eldest son and winemaker Michael Brajkovich MW turned his attention to making a traditional method fizz modelled on the French crémant-style, feeling confident that their Kumeu vineyards would produce fruit of excellent potential if harvested early.

The proximity of large oceans both east and west of Auckland moderates the climate significantly, keeping temperatures cool and acidity high. The grapes are sourced from Kumeu River's own vineyards, the fruit hand-harvested and a crémant-specific pressing cycle of the Willmes press used. Only the first 630 litres of juice per tonne is used and the fermentation takes place in old 225 litre oak barrels using wild yeasts, followed by malolactic fermentation. After the second fermentation, bottles are hand-riddled and disgorged. Each bottle receives just 3.5 to 5 grams per litre of dosage, using ten-year-old, bottle-matured Chardonnay, administered via a sheep-drenching gun, which is (apparently) both practical and accurate.

The first cuvée, based principally on the 2012 vintage, was released in late 2017 as Kumeu Crémant, a blend of 60 per cent Chardonnay and 40 per cent Pinot Noir. Although a relatively recent addition to the portfolio, the style continues to evolve with each year's release. As time goes on, the aim is to introduce 30–35 per cent reserve wine into the blend. Kumeu Crémant is a precise wine, with a strong autolytic character but, as with all wines from Kumeu River, the focus is on quality of fruit and a distinctive sense of place. Pleasingly, the dates of both bottling and disgorgement are shown on the back label.

Nautilus Estate

Renwick, Marlborough

www.nautilusestate.com

Since 1998, Clive Jones has been chief winemaker at Marlborough's Nautilus Estate, which was established in 1985 by Australia's Hill Smith family. In a region of rapid evolution, this may help to explain why the quality of Nautilus Cuvée is both impressive and reliable. The first tirage of Nautilus Cuvée was laid down in 1991. While Jones saw his role as continuing to refine the wine, he was always determined to keep it as a Pinot Noir-dominant blend, something of a rarity in Marlborough, but a variety he thinks gives structure and a distinctive savoury edge to the final blend.

After it took the Best Sparkling Wine trophy at London's 1995 International Wine Challenge (IWC) and with the upcoming

Millennium celebrations in mind, Jones decided to increase production of Nautilus Cuvée. When the global over-supply forced Nautilus to keep wine *en tirage* for longer than originally intended, the enforced extended time on lees, from 18 months to 36 months, created a wine, typically 75 per cent Pinot Noir and 25 per cent Chardonnay, with a strongly autolytic character. The addition of 8–15 per cent reserve wine, matured in older oak barrels, added the depth, richness and intensity of a vintage fizz.

The original source, a 2.1-hectare, well-drained, loamy and sandy alluvium block off the eastern end of Rapaura road, still provides the major component for the blend. Trialling different clones, Jones continues to prefer the Swiss clone AM10/5 for the structure and backbone he seeks. Until the late 2000s, the Chardonnay component was clone 6 but was then changed to clone 96 from a vineyard at the western end of Rapaura road, whose lighter, stony, alluvial soils give additional subtlety and finesse. The grapes are handpicked and chilled overnight before being pressed through an open screen airbag press. An oxidative regime is used to avoid colour pick up, with fermentation generally taking around two weeks, and all base wines undergoing malolactic fermentation.

An impressive wine that is heavily influenced by the extended time on lees, with 6 grams per litre dosage, the autolytic character is beautifully judged, and the palate savoury yet delicate and precise. In late 2013 Nautilus released a Vintage Rosé, made from Pinot Noir clones 115 and 777 grown on the estate's own Opawa vineyard and kept on the lees for around 30–32 months. Look on the back label of a Nautilus Cuvée and you will see the month of tirage and disgorgement, which Jones believes is essential information for both on-premises customers and wine consumers.

No.1 Family Estate

Blenheim, Marlborough

www.no1familyestate.co.nz

The Le Brun family has done more to raise the profile of New Zealand as a source of premium sparkling wine than any other producer. Daniel Le Brun comes from Champagne, where his family has been growing grapes since 1684. Apparently destined, as the eldest son and twelfth-generation vigneron, to take over the family business from his father after graduating from the Champagne School in Avize, Le Brun visited Marlborough in 1978. 'I was immediately convinced this was the place to be,' he says. 'The soil and the climate reminded me of Champagne in the best vintage years though there was no winery infrastructure back then, just bare paddocks with almost desert-like conditions and a few dusty sheep.'

To finance the move, Le Brun sold some of his vineyards in Champagne to his brother. At a time when the Müller-Thurgau grape was predominant, he remained loyal to the classic Champagne varieties. While working in Rotorua, he met, fell in love with and married Adele. In 1980, together with their four-month-old daughter Virginie, they made the move to Marlborough, taking their 50,000 carefully tended vine cuttings with them. The cuttings went into cool storage until they could purchase 12 hectares to plant their first Marlborough vineyard. Today, they have been joined in the business by their daughter Virginie and son Remy.

No.1 Family Estate draws from both its own vineyards and those of contract growers. The estate vineyard lies in the riverbed of the old Wairau River, with soils ranging from river stones and gravels to a thin layer of sandy loams. Le Brun believes the combination of high sunshine hours, moderate rainfall and cool, dry autumns gives crisp, acid-driven wines that can age beautifully. Following hand harvesting, the grapes are gently pressed and fermented in neutral vessels using specialist equipment imported from Champagne. He operates a perpetual reserve for the non-vintage wines for consistency.

Most important, in volume terms, are the No.1 Assemblé, a blend of the three classic varieties and Cuvée No.1, a poised and detailed *blanc de blancs*. The NV Rosé and NV Reserve are produced in smaller quantities. The theme of family continues with the naming of the three ultra premium cuvées: Cuvée Remy, a powerful Pinot Noir-dominant blend, Cuvée Virginie, a precise Chardonnay-led blend and the stunning Cuvée Adele, its Swarovski crystal studded bottle inspired by the always beautifully groomed Adele. No.1 Family Estate's wines have time on lees on the back label and date of disgorgement of the current release is on both the tasting notes and the website. In recognition of his dedication to the art of creating superlative sparkling wines, Daniel Le Brun was awarded the Chevalier Order of Merit (1997) and Chevalier Order of Agricultural Merit (2006) by the French Government.

Quartz Reef Wines

Cromwell, Central Otago
www.quartzreef.co.nz

Originally from Austria, Rudi Bauer has lived in New Zealand since the mid-1980s. His winemaking career has taken him around New Zealand (Mission Estate, Rippon and Giesen) as well as overseas. But when he wanted to establish his own winery, his desire was to return to Central Otago. Focusing on the Bendigo sub-region, Quartz Reef was established in 1996 with John and Heather Perriam. They were joined by Clotilde Chauvet, Bauer's successor at Rippon, of Marc Chauvet Champagne. The success of both his Pinot Noir and his sparkling wine quickly resulted in the doubling of land under vine, from 15 to 30 hectares.

Since 1998, the grapes for Quartz Reef fizz have been sourced only from Central Otago. Extremes of light and marked diurnal temperature variation contribute to the focused cool-climate style so important in fine sparkling wine. The Bendigo Estate Vineyard site is a 15-hectare north-facing slope comprising arid clay, fine gravel and quartz soils. The remaining 15 hectares are opposite on a gently sloping terrace of mainly fine loess, clay and sandy loam. Bauer believes the unusually high amount of quartz has a strong impact on the vibrancy, clarity and acidity in the wines. All fruit is handpicked and whole bunch pressed before fermentation in stainless steel. The wine sits on its lees for six months before tirage bottling with malolactic fermentation not desired, though sometimes it happens. All bottles are riddled and disgorged by hand on site, and dosage, relatively low at no more than 2–4 grams per litre, uses estate liqueur.

A powerful advocate of biodynamic farming, Bauer wants the wines to be 'as precise as the fresh air and as pure as the crystal clear mountain streams of Central Otago', likening the acidity common to Quartz Reef fizz to 'a fibre optic cable carrying the precise laser-like flavours through the palate'. While the Quartz Reef Brut and Rosé Brut are fantastic wines, Bauer wanted to see what the estate was capable of and so set about producing his ultra-premium Vintage Blanc de Blancs. The wine spends 60 months on lees, has a dosage of under 4 grams per litre and is only made in limited quantities and in specific vintages. For those fortunate to secure a bottle, it vindicates Bauer's belief that Central Otago can produce exceptional traditional method fizz.

6

ENGLAND

Whatever winemaking was initiated in England by the Romans, its legacy clearly failed to impress King John who, on taking a sip of the wine made by the monks at Beaulieu in Hampshire, remarked: 'Send ships forthwith to fetch some good French wine.' Three centuries later, the good French wine that King Henry VIII enjoyed will have rolled onto ships in Bordeaux and off the Thames quay straight into his wine cellar (which can still be visited in Whitehall). Any thought of making something resembling drinkable wine would have been nipped in the bud by the Black Death, the Dissolution of the Monasteries and the Little Ice Age, which lasted from the early fourteenth through to the mid-nineteenth century, causing temperatures in the northern hemisphere to plunge.

However, around the time of the Second World War, there were stirrings in the vines. Edward Hyams planted a vineyard at Canterbury and George Ordish planted one at Yalding in Kent in 1939. Sir Guy Salisbury-Jones established three acres of vines at Hambledon and Ray Barrington Brock thought that Müller-Thurgau and the hybrid Seyval Blanc had a decent chance of ripening in Britain. Speaking of Müller-Thurgau, Dr Helmut Becker of Geisenheim counselled early ripening Germanic crossings destined to mark English wine out as borderline drinkable. 'Hell is Italian punctuality, German humour and English wine,' remarked the raconteur, Peter Ustinov, with a humour considerably drier than the wines of the time.

The first English vineyard I remember visiting was Yearlstone in Devon, whose then owner, Gillian Pearkes (pronounced pea-arks) established the vineyard by planting an assortment of weird but not necessarily wonderful grape varieties. She was typical of the obsessive hobbyist and stiff-upper-lipped retired colonel syndrome that made 'the heroic eccentricity', as Andrew Jefford called it, of England's fledgling cottage industry something of a laughing stock among wine connoisseurs.

Then in 1986 along came Adrian White, a businessman who bought Denbies Estate in Dorking from the fourth Lord Ashcombe and a handful of entrepreneurs like Chapel Down and Three Choirs prepared to show that English wine on a commercial scale was possible. Bottle-fermented bubbly was starting up, notably at Lamberhurst, with Pinot Noir, Pinot Blanc and Chardonnay, and Carr Taylor, albeit from grapes based on the Germanic varieties: Reichensteiner, Schönburger, Kerner and Huxelrebe.

After Champagne outlawed the term *méthode champenoise* for potential usurpers, the race was on for a suitable term for English bubbles. With the PR-minded David and Linda Carr Taylor, I organized a competition at the *Independent* newspaper. One ingenious suggestion, the FRED Method (F for fermentation, RE for remuage, and D for disgorgement), was rejected in favour of the Traditional © Method but that didn't cut the mustard with the producers either. Mike Roberts of Ridgeview wanted to call it Merret after Christopher Merret; Coates & Seely thought Britagne was the answer, but all the names suggested fell on fallow ground. So, English Classic Method Sparkling Wine it is.

Perhaps it was because they were from another country that Stuart and Sandy Moss were able to think outside the box. Medical equipment entrepreneurs who had come to England in the 1970s in search of antique English oak furniture, the Chicagoan couple ended up in 1986 buying Nyetimber. This medieval priory, with 42.5 hectares at West Chiltington in West Sussex, had once belonged to Henry VIII's fourth wife, Anne of Cleves. They took advice from Jean-Manuel Jacquinot, a champenois, planting the first grapes on greensand in 1988, expanding to 20 hectares of mostly Chardonnay, with 3 hectares of Pinot Noir and Meunier, in 1990 and 1991. Jacquinot was taken on to consult with Kit Lindlar, the winemaker. The first release, the 1992 Nyetimber Blanc de Blancs, was selected for Queen Elizabeth II's Golden Anniversary Lunch in 1997, while the follow-on 1993 vintage was even more successful.

Shortly after, Mike and Christine Roberts' Ridgeview planted 13 clones of Chardonnay, Pinot Noir and Meunier. A new winery was built at Ridgeview in 1997 and in 2000 Ridgeview won the UK

Trophy for England's Best Sparkling wine with the 1996 Cuveé Merret Bloomsbury. Professional sparkling wine ventures sprang up in England's southern counties: Camel Valley in Cornwall, Chapel Down, Hush Heath and Gusbourne Estate in Kent, Hattingley Valley, Hambledon and Coates & Seely in Hampshire and Wiston Estate in Sussex. Businessmen and bankers, couples seeking a new lifestyle and farmers keen to make a different sort of hay piled in. Many of today's English winemakers and viticulturalists cut their professional teeth at Plumpton College. A part-time wine course set up by Chris Foss in 1988 led to a partnership with the University of Brighton in the mid-1990s and today the college boasts a growing range of courses on viticulture and winemaking .

The champenois too have added to the gaiety of the nation. Duval-Leroy, Roederer and Billecart-Salmon were the first to take interest, though none actually made a purchase. The first Champagne house to the take the plunge was Vranken-Pommery which entered into a joint venture for its Louis Pommery cuvée with Hattingley Valley in 2014. It then established a 19-hectare site at Pinglestone Estate near Alresford in 2018, with a first crop in 2021. In 2017 and 2019, linking hands with the English wine merchant Hatch Mansfield, Champagne Taittinger planted an initial 28.5 hectares on a south-facing chalk soil apple farm in Kent, calling it Domaine Evremond after Charles II's fun-loving French friend. Significant ventures then, if not quite the second Norman conquest.

There was no Chardonnay among the 430 hectares of vines planted in 1984. The eight most widely planted varieties (accounting for 76 per cent of the vineyard area) were, in alphabetical order, Bacchus, Huxelrebe, Madeleine Angevine, Müller-Thurgau, Pinot Noir, Reichensteiner, Schönburger and Seyval Blanc. From small acorns, or rather vines, grow mighty vineyards, and the tally was an estimated 3,800 hectares in 2021. Wine GB's 2021 annual report showed that there were approximately 800 vineyards and 178 wineries, producing 8.7 million bottles in 2020 (down from 10.5 million in 2019), of which sparkling wines outnumbered still by seven to three. An estimated 5.5 million bottles were sold in 2019, 29 per cent at the cellar door and 7 per cent online, with the rest being sold through the wine trade. In 2020 sales looked to have increased by a further 30 per cent.

Chardonnay and Pinot Noir, 'which up until the mid-1990s would not have ripened well enough to produce viable crops of grapes,' according to

Stephen Skelton MW, now dominate. According to 2020 figures, Pinot Noir plantings took the number one spot with 1,155 hectares under vine (33 per cent), Chardonnay was number two at 1,120 hectares (32 per cent), Meunier came in third with 455 hectares under vine (13 per cent) followed by Bacchus with 175 hectares (5 per cent). Given that the UK doesn't feature in the International Organisation of Vine and Wine's vineyard surface area list of the world's top 25 countries, the UK wine industry makes a noise way out of proportion to its size.

So what has led to the rapid success of English wines, particularly the sparkling wines? People go on about England's chalky soils, and rightly so, but the soils haven't moved. What has changed is the climate. You only have to listen to the BBC's daily Shipping Forecast to agree with Dr Alistair Nesbitt, of Climate Change Consulting, who described England as 'an island of weather'. Despite a mild growing season and the warming effects of the Gulf Stream, lowish temperatures in the critical ripening period of July combined with rainfall before or during harvest used to make it difficult for English producers to achieve the ripeness levels and yields of their continental counterparts.

'The factor that has most influenced viticulture in Britain in the last three decades is that of climate change,' says Stephen Skelton MW. The pivotal years of 1989 and 1990 saw a gradual climb in Britain's temperatures. Where previously temperatures struggled to reach a maximum of 29°C, most years between 1994 and 2006 saw temperatures rising to 29°C or higher. The torrid 2003 vintage was the wake-up call that alerted wine producers throughout Europe to the dangers – and potential benefits – of climate change. Subsequent years have been mixed, but while the cold, wet vintage of 2012 bucked the trend, 2009 and 2014 were excellent and 2018 a watershed year of unprecedented high average yields of 50 hectolitres per hectare compared to the prior 10-year average of 20.6 hectolitres.

The changing climate has led not only to hotter summers, but also to a growing season that is starting earlier, with summer's warmth continuing into September. According to Gusbourne's Charlie Holland, 'We're seeing the direct effects of climate change here in that we can ripen the grapes to a level we never used to be able to. Even ten years ago, we didn't think we could get that level of ripeness.' The 2003 and 2009 harvests started in September in the first decade of the current century but in the following decade, the 2011, 2014, 2016, 2017, 2018 and 2019 harvests all began in September.

According to a Met Office report released on 29 July 2021, 'All of the top-ten warmest years for the UK in records back to 1884 have occurred since 2002, and, for central England, the twenty-first century so far has been warmer than the previous three centuries. 2020 was the first year to have temperature, rain and sunshine rankings all in the top 10.' While the ill wind of climate change appears to have handed England's merry new band of wine entrepreneurs a golden opportunity, extreme climate events such as unpredictable violent storms, high winds, flash flooding, hail and hard frosts threaten to rain on their parade.

Climate change apart, the most significant factor in the greater quality and consistency of English fizz is the choice of location. At Exton Park, Corinne Seely's research into the impact of the chalk on the juices has led her to believe that chalk has a significant impact. 'The distinctive style of English fizz is higher acidity than Champagne, and I find that this acidity lifts the flavours,' she says. Yet since acidity in Britain isn't (yet) the issue it is in Champagne, planting on chalk soils is by no means the panacea for English sparkling wine. Protection from frost and wind along with a southerly or south-easterly exposure to sunshine and good drainage are key elements, along with healthy soils with levels of organic matter that can help reduce the need for sprays and fertilizers.

Though chalk is talked up by some as the Holy Grail, those doing the talking are often closer to the Monty Python than the Arthurian version. As Champagne's Aube subregion shows, chalk is not necessarily a prerequisite for making great sparkling wine. England's soils are more diverse and nuanced than those of Champagne. In the right spot, and where all the major criteria for planting are met, greensand and both clayey and sandy soils with good drainage are as likely as chalk soils to produce fine English sparkling wines. Nyetimber in West Sussex is planted on a band of greensand, Hush Heath and Gusbourne in Kent are happy with their clay, Harrow & Hope in Buckinghamshire is content with its gravelly clay and Langham in Dorset enjoys its Kimmeridgian sub-strata.

Gusbourne is headquartered in Kent, where the soils are based on clay, but its holdings expand into Sussex, with chalk and flint soils. Winemaker Charlie Holland says that the two locations bring complementary features: 'There's a temptation to chase the chalk in England, but sometimes that misses the point. It's one part of the puzzle, but arguably not the most important factor. It can be a bit heavy in Kent in a hot year, while you can get brain-rinsing acidity in some years in

Sussex but, as a blending component, it's offset with riper fruit from here [Kent].' Matt Strugnell, Ridgeview's Plumpton-trained viticultur-alist, makes the point that 'while chalk works well in some cases, chalk sites tend to be quite exposed and it can be hard to get enough vigour; that means often having to give more organic matter to the soils and planting the right clones on the right rootstocks'.

In the vineyard, leaf removal after flowering to open up the canopy, and bunch-thinning, can help to induce earlier ripening. In the cellar, British producers making sparkling wine today lack for nothing when it comes to investment in the most up-to-date equipment and technical know-how. Extending lees-ageing and the building up of reserve wines as contributions to non-vintage and multi-vintage cuvées (and even in smaller proportions in vintage cuvées) are growing trends. Better-handled oak is increasingly commonplace and malolactic fermentation is generally applied to help soften the appley bite that comes naturally to English wine.

In 2020, the Great British Classic hallmark was introduced to distin-guish traditional method English Quality Sparkling from Charmat and other methods. PGI status exists for English/Welsh quality sparkling wine. In 2015, a Sussex group got together and applied for Protected Designation of Origin (PDO) for Sussex wine. Until the process is rati-fied, Sussex has a temporary protected status. Other groups have since applied for PDOs in the wake of the application. Some think it might dilute the English quality sparkling wine brand but a regional designa-tion based on a county such as Sussex is a logical first step towards defin-ing different styles based on terroir. Given the prospect of burgeoning wine tourism, it could also help kindle consumer enthusiasm for eating and drinking local.

From a standing start not much more than 30 years ago, English sparkling wine has come of age as a credible entity the world over. From a multiplicity of varied climates and soils, England's sparkling wine pro-ducers now make a variety of different styles. Leading the way are *blanc de blancs* (Chardonnay), with a growing number of impressive non-vin-tage and vintage wines, *blanc de noirs* (Pinot Noir and Meunier), along with rosé, demi-sec and oak-fermented fizz. A new millennial wave of producers, including the champenois themselves, has added to the crit-ical mass of those making quality sparkling wines with mouthwatering maritime freshness, whose delicious orchard apple and quince flavours, and vital tanginess characterize English fizz.

Producers

Albury Organic Vineyard

Albury, Surrey

www.alburyvineyard.com

After 30 years in the IT industry, Nick Wenman fulfilled a long-cherished dream of owning his own vineyard when he planted the 5-hectare Albury Vineyard in 2009. This planting comprised the traditional Champagne varieties, Chardonnay, Pinot Noir and Meunier, as well as some Seyval Blanc and Pinot Gris. Expert advice cautioned against going down the organic or biodynamic route, but Nick was determined to follow bio-dynamic principles. 'We have seen first-hand in France and Australia the difference between the quality of soil on biodynamic vineyards and that on chemically sprayed ones,' says Nick. 'Encouraging a natural harmony between the earth, the vine and the cosmos without the need to use systemic chemicals, it is the difference between living and dead soils.'

With a clay topsoil and a bedrock of chalk, the vineyard, mentioned in John Evelyn's 1670 diary, is located on the southern slopes of the North Downs in the Surrey Hills near Dorking. It is not a vigorous site and Nick believes the low yields contribute to the quality of the fruit and that wild ferments bring a sense of place to the wines. A first small harvest was in 2011 and the first sparkling wine made from a blend of the 2011 and 2012 harvests. A further 3 hectares were planted in 2020. Nick's daughter Lucy has joined the team as marketing and events manager, while Alex Valsecchi is one of the few female vineyard managers in England. Matthieu Elzinger, at premium contract winemakers Litmus Wines, heads up the winemaking.

A pneumatic press is used to create the classic Champagne fractions followed by fermentation in stainless steel with organic yeasts. The Classic Cuvée is a fine-textured Pinot-dominated blend with rich orchard apple fruit. The Blanc de Blancs is a blend of Chardonnay and Seyval Blanc, creating a 'quintessentially English' style that's almost chalky, with a sake-like sweetness and an explosion of lemon sherbet. Albury also produces small quantities of a Chablis-like bio-dynamic wild ferment Blanc de Blancs from Chardonnay fermented in a Nomblot concrete egg. The date of disgorgement hasn't yet been mentioned on the label but the plan is to do so from 2021. Albury is a member of the Vineyards of the Surrey Hills group (www.surreyhills-vineyards.co.uk).

Ambriel

Redfold Vineyards, Pulborough, West Sussex

www.ambrielsparkling.com

The 'lightbulb moment' came when Wendy and Charles Outhwaite were tasting a Nyetimber fizz they had been given. 'I thought it was amazing, not having enjoyed English wines until then,' says Wendy. When she announced to her family that she was leaving her career in law to start a winery, her parents were utterly bewildered and her daughter said: 'so, you're going to the country to die'. But Ambriel is no retirement project simply intended to make enough bubbles to keep them home, hosed and lubricated. That would be to under-estimate the commitment to a serious, professional wine endeavour by two smart and engaging individuals. Amateurish no, hands-on, definitely.

Before picking up the secateurs, Wendy was a high-powered QC and Charles a banker, retiring, respectively, in 2013 and 2019. They had always loved wine and felt sure that they had the energy and the will, even in retirement, to try to produce something that they loved. Luckily for them, their love of wine is shared by their three boys, although not their daughter. Over five years, they looked at various sites from Kent to Cornwall. 'When, irritatingly, my father-in-law said there's a perfect place in West Sussex, we thought, here we go, another wasted Saturday, but no, but this really is a fantastic site,' says Wendy.

In 2008, they set about planting 9.5 hectares to burgundian clones of the three Champagne varieties, 6 per cent Meunier with the rest half and half Chardonnay and Pinot Noir, building the winery to suit the size of the vineyard. Redfold Vineyards, to give it its proper name, is a sunny, south-facing site on free-draining greensand. Half a metre below the surface there are big greensand rocks which heat up, thereby retain-ing the warmth, especially through the night. The vineyards teem with beneficial insects encouraged by wildflower planting. From its highest point, 90 metres above sea level, you can see Chanctonbury Ring and the South Downs.

Charles and Wendy studied winemaking at Plumpton College and invited consultants to visit. Working with stainless steel and aged bur-gundy barrels, they vinify by clone in batches, pressing whole bunches, and they blend blind by tasting, two practices they think are 'slightly weird' but which suit their purpose. What isn't chosen for the blend is retained for the reserve wines, which are used in the Classic and Rosé but not the vintage wines. In the voluminous 2018 vintage, they also made a *blanc de blancs* and *blanc de noirs*.

Starting out Chardonnay dominant, the Classic Cuvée NV is now Pinot-dominant. In the absence of malolactic fermentation this is in part to avoid any excessive malic acidity that might come from Chardonnay. This is an outstanding blend of mouthwateringly savoury maltiness with a delightfully full-flavoured, tangy mousse. Made from the 777 Pinot Noir clone, pressed and left for 36 hours, the Rosé, a vinous wine with bubbles, shows an appealing fresh, crunchy, strawberry fruit quality. 'The wines we produce aren't designed to be Coca-Cola, but they're what we like and we hope others like them too,' they say.

Black Chalk

Cottonworth, Hampshire

www.blackchalkwine.co.uk

Based in the chalklands of Hampshire, chalk is at the heart of what this new family endeavour is about. Black Chalk symbolizes both the name used by the old masters to sketch out their ideas on canvas and the chalk soils. Jacob Leadley left his London job in 2009 to retrain as a winemaker at Plumpton College. After working at Hattingley Valley, he branched out on his own to create, with brother-in-law Andrew Seden, a fizz based on sourcing locally produced Chardonnay, Pinot Noir and Meunier from vineyards in Hampshire planted on shallow chalk soils. Two impressive debut releases, Black Chalk Classic 2015 and Black Chalk Wild Rose 2015, caught the eye.

In 2019, Black Chalk entered the next phase of expansion by leasing 12 hectares of vineyards in Hampshire's Test Valley from Fullerton Estate. Planted to Pinot Noir, Meunier, Chardonnay, Pinot Gris and Pinot Précoce, the four sites – Hide, Rivers, The Levels and The Circle – are all within a one-mile radius of the winery. They are particularly pleased with the 4.6-hectare Hide vineyard. Flanked on one side by woodland, it will be home to a new development of boutique, ultra-luxury treehouses. Since September 2019, a tasting room and shop have opened on the banks of the River Test 10 miles from Winchester and, having secured over one million pounds in funding, the new winery was completed in time for the 2020 harvest.

Jacob is assisted by new arrival Zoe Driver, who also cut her winemaking teeth at Hattingley Valley. In the winery, the grapes are whole-bunch pressed and cold settled before the primary fermentation takes place in stainless steel and oak barrels for softening acidity and additional complexity. The tasting phase determines whether or not a partial or full malolactic fermentation is to be done. Tirage takes place in early spring and the wines are then aged on the lees for at least 20 months and held after disgorgement for a further six months on cork before release. These are exciting times for Black Chalk, whose fine second releases bode well for the future.

Breaky Bottom Vineyard

Rodmell, Lewes, East Sussex

www.breakybottom.co.uk

Visiting Peter Hall at the end of the bone-crunching track to Breaky Bottom feels like a throwback to the days long before bubbles were a twinkle in any English winegrower's eye. He didn't conceive of making fizz until two decades after planting Müller-Thurgau and Seyval Blanc close to the coast in the Sussex South Downs National Park in 1974. Making only sparkling wine today, Peter is the living embodiment of the transition from the eccentric English hobby grower of yesteryear to today's professional fizz producer competing in a global market for a slice of the action. Such is the evolution of English wine.

Born in 1943, Peter grew up with his two brothers on his grandmother's mixed farm, the 26-room Rangeworthy Court in Gloucestershire. His French grandfather, Alex Mercier, taught him about wine. Between 1963 and 1965, he studied agriculture at Newcastle University, then worked for Harris Robinson, a farmer at Northease Farm in East Sussex. While bedding down some sheep one day, he came upon Breaky Bottom, an 1827 dilapidated stone and flint cottage owned by Northease Farm, nestling in a hollow between the folds of the surrounding hills. Peter fell for it and moved in, but after giving notice three years later, he fell for the farmer's daughter, married her and stayed on.

He was making a modest living out of a small pig unit and buying calves from nearby Lewes market when, while shopping in Lewes one day, he saw an advert for two books, *Growing Grapes* and *Wines From Your Vines*, by the Isle of Wight grower Nick Poulter. After devouring the books he invited Poulter to visit, before planting just under 1 hectare of Seyval Blanc and soon after, 1.2 hectares of Müller-Thurgau and more Seyval Blanc on the property's free-draining chalk, loam and flint soils. After 20 years of making still wines, Peter made the leap to fizz in 1995 with his Seyval Blanc, called Millennium Cuvée Maman Mercier in homage to his French–Italian mother. 'I had always thought Seyval, such a clean and straightforward variety with good acidity, would be nice with bubbles in. I'm glad I made the jump.'

Despite a series of disasters that would have tested the patience of a saint – a crop ruined by a contract winemaker, a harvest destroyed by his father-in-law's pesticide spray, an invasion of grape-munching pheasant and partridge and terrible flooding – he emerged from caravan exile in 2002 to plant a small amount of Chardonnay and some Pinot Noir and Meunier. Peter waits longer than most before picking, often into the third week in October, or even into November, until he thinks the grapes are fully ripe and to allow the acidity to soften. The grapes are pressed into a 1-tonne Bucher airbag press and both fermentations are carried out in the charming Sussex flint barn. After three years, often longer, on the lees, the bottles are sent to Simon Roberts at Ridgeview or Dermot Sugrue at Wiston Estate for disgorgement.

In homage to members of the family and individuals who have made an impact on him, Peter names each cuvée after them. The majestic 2010 Breaky Bottom Seyval Blanc Cuvée was named Koizumi Yakumo in honour of his great-great uncle, the travel writer Lafcadio Hearn (1850–1904) who became a Japanese citizen. The rich, toasted brioche-style 2014 Chardonnay–Pinot Noir–Meunier, is named after Michelle Moreau, sister of the French actress Jeanne Moreau, while the exceptional 2010 Chardonnay–Pinot Noir–Meunier, with its notes of smokiness and nuttiness is named for the engraver Reynolds Stone, his label designer. 'It was never my goal to make a lot of money and was certainly not my motivation,' says Peter, a perennial Old Holborn roll-up dangling from the ancient mariner lookalike's lips, 'but I'm blessed to have planted at Breaky Bottom.'

Bride Valley Vineyard

Litton Cheney, Dorset

www.bridevalleyvineyard.com

'Our hero was born with a silver spoon in his mouth,' says Simon Loftus of Steven Spurrier, in his 1985 book, *Abe's Sardines*, 'and has been one of the most innovative people in his chosen profession, achieving fame while losing great chunks of his fortune.' A film, *Bottle Shock* (which Steven Spurrier hated) was made about the seismic Judgment of Paris, starring Alan Rickman as Spurrier. Yet despite this recognition and his achievements as an indefatigable author and writer, earning him the Decanter

Man of the Year Award in 2017, and culminating in his memoir *Wine, A Way of Life*, Steven Spurrier was in many respects an unsung hero.

Following the growing success of English fizz such as Nyetimber and Ridgeview, Spurrier and his wife Bella, now chairman, decided to try turning a loss-making sheep farm into a profit-making vineyard by planting the Champagne varieties in Dorset's Jurassic coast soils. Working with a team from Burgundy's Boisset, an in-depth analysis of soils, slopes and exposition confirmed 10 blocks on exposed slopes covering 10 hectares as suitable for fizz. The brilliant Burgundian nurseryman, Pierre-Marie Guillaume supplied the vines. Between 2009 and 2013, 10 hectares were planted on a grid of 2.3 x 1 metre to 55 per cent Chardonnay with seven different clones, 25 per cent Pinot Noir with four and 20 per cent Meunier with two. Fercal and 41B rootstocks were matched to the climate and subsoil for a total of 42,000 vines. A further 1.2 hectares is set to follow.

At harvest, the grapes are handpicked and taken to Furleigh Estate, where Ian Edwards vinifies by the traditional method. Annual production is approximately 30–50,000 bottles. The first Bride Valley, the 2011, was released in 2014, and immediately sold out. Made up of 85 per cent sparkling and 15 per cent still wines, the range consists of a lower pressure Dorset Crémant, the excellent signature Blanc de Blancs Brut Reserve and the utterly delicious Rosé Bella. In 2018 the first still wines were produced, the Dorset Chardonnay and Dorset Pinot Noir, joined by the Dorset Pinot Noir Rosé in 2019.

The Court House, with an airy tasting room, gives access to the gardens with pieces from Steven's collection of modern sculptures. The Wine and Art Room is next door, with the newly created Club Room following the launch of The Club at Bride Valley in 2020. Tours and tastings are held throughout the spring and summer and lunches, dinners and picnics can be arranged for up to 24, by prior appointment. It may have taken double the predicted investment to get Bride Valley up and running, but as it enters its second decade, its success is a tribute to a very special poacher turned gamekeeper whose passing in March 2021 leaves English wine the poorer but cements the legend of one of the great men of wine.

Chapel Down Wines

Tenterden, Kent

www.chapeldown.com

Let's cut to the chase. After more than its fair share of ups and downs,

Chapel Down is today on course to becoming a UK sparkling wine superstar. Beginning as a 1980s vineyard on the Isle of Wight, a merger with Carr Taylor Vineyards and Lamberhurst Vineyards created the English Wines Group. With the Group facing financial problems by the turn of the millennium, the experienced Frazer Thompson was taken on in 2001 to inject some much-needed business sense into the company. Sales to British Airways accounted for 44 per cent of its turnover, and when the Gulf War started in 2003, the company almost went under.

Today, Chapel Down has created a secure structure by raising capital via share issues and crowdfunding. The visitor experience is second to none, with a well-designed shop, an airy tasting room and an excellent restaurant. In a spectacular about-turn, Chapel Down is increasingly using its own vineyards instead of largely sourcing grapes from vineyards spread throughout the country, and it has prospered since taking on the talented, Kent-born, Plumpton-trained winemaker Josh Donaghay-Spire in 2010. At the 2020 Decanter World Wine Awards (DWWA), the 2014 Kit's Coty Coeur de Cuvée and 2015 Three Graces were awarded platinum medals, while the 2014 Kit's Coty Blanc de Blancs and 2017 Kit's Coty Chardonnay won golds.

'Where we are on the North Downs, with altitude, south-facing exposure and chalk soils, we are in the Goldilocks Zone,' says Josh. 'We planted our flag on the North Downs and the quality of the fruit coming in now has never been better.' Chapel Down planted a bit more than a flag. Beginning in 2008, Kit's Coty, sloping south from 70–30 metres, was planted to 40 hectares, with 30 hectares of Chardonnay and Pinot Noir, and subsequent plantings of Bacchus and Meunier in 23 combinations of clones and rootstocks. In 2015, a further 44 hectares were planted at Court Lodge Farm near Boxley, 40 hectares at Street Farm in 2018 and 50 hectares at Boarley Farm in 2019, all to Chardonnay, Pinot Noir and Meunier. The long-term goal is to make 2.5 million bottles, roughly half of it fizz, from 280 hectares on the North Downs and 100 hectares from growers.

The most important change during Josh's ten-year tenure has been the quality of the grapes thanks to an increase in Chapel Down's own vineyard sources. The grapes are picked ripe and malolactic fermentation is normally carried out, but Josh is now looking at partial malolactic fermentation to maintain freshness. The average dosage has reduced from 10–12 grams per litre to 8–9 grams per litre. Since 2010, only the classic fizz grapes (and Pinot Blanc) have been used. Some reserve wines are used and a perpetual reserve is being built. The Champagne press cycle is followed in three 8-tonne and one 5-tonne Scharfenberger presses with only the first pressing used. Fermentation is with exclusively wild yeasts for Kit's Coty Coeur de Cuvée and a proportion for the Blanc de Blancs. Jetting technology at disgorgement has been installed.

The base wines spend six months on the lees and are blended in May following the harvest. The approachable Brut NV and Brut Rosé spend on average 18 months on the lees, the seductively toasty Three Graces some four years. There are five years on the lees for Kit's Coty Blanc de Blancs, a delicately proportioned wine with real finesse and savour, and the outstanding barrel-fermented Coeur de Cuvée, whose underlying nuttiness and savouriness is defined by energy and freshness. A mobile line, supplemented by a small bottling line, comes in from Champagne, bottling with DIAM Mytik Classic cork. The North Downs may not be England's Côte des Blancs quite yet but, as Josh says, 'Kit's Coty is a way of us seeing what you can achieve in England. The birth of a wine region is happening now in Kent and it means a lot to be a part of that in the county of your birth.'

Cottonworth Wines

Andover, Hampshire

www.cottonworth.co.uk

Located in the heart of the Test Valley in Hampshire, Cottonworth belongs to the Liddell family, who have been farming there for four generations. Over the past decade, they have planted Chardonnay, Pinot Noir and Meunier on south-west to south-east facing slopes. The lack of nutrients in the free-draining, water-retentive chalky soils helps in a gentle stressing of the vine required for the superior fruit the Liddells are after. A combination of exposure to the south-westerly wind, an altitude at 40 and 70 metres above sea level and a temperate climate are the additional prerequisites for fizz quality.

'I found myself standing amongst the vines apologizing to them for stealing their grapes after all their hard work,' says Hugh Liddell, who worked in Burgundy in 2004, where he gained a better understanding of the nebulous concept of terroir. He believes that while the concept of terroir is as yet not developed in Britain because of a lack of viticultural history and tradition, 'it allows us to pick and choose traditions and cultural methods in the vineyard and winery'.

England's high rainfall makes keeping vigour in check essential. With three different soil types on the property, with varying levels of chalk, Hugh aims to match different rootstocks to soil type in order to achieve medium growth vigour. He pays close attention to clones for their early ripening properties, with Champagne clones for Pinot aimed at achieving good acidity, yield and resistance to disease, and Burgundy clones used mainly for their sparkling rosé, but also to increase the quality of their white fizz. The end result, says Hugh Liddell, is that their Chardonnay is 'elegant, fruity and fresh', while Pinot Noir 'brings body and structure', with Meunier rounding out the other two when blended.

Digby Fine English

Arundel, West Sussex

www.digby-fine-english.com

Launched in 2013, Digby Fine English is the brainchild of American-born Trevor Clough and his British husband, Jason Humphries, who conceived the idea in the driveway of Chateau Sainte Michelle in Washington, after being captivated by the experience of visiting it and other West Coast sparkling wineries. 'How come we've never been offered a glass of English sparkling wine to try all the times we've eaten out in London if the wines are as good as the critics say?' they wondered. They conducted blind tastings on their return to London and, when English fizz beat most big-name Champagne brands, they decided to set about creating a world-class English fizz worthy of global acclaim, showcasing it in a setting befitting its luxurious status.

In May 2019, they opened the Digby Fine English Tasting Room in Arundel, within spitting distance of Arundel Castle, featuring Digby's well-travelled tasting counter and an exclusive Members' Room for up to 12 guests. 'We wanted this to be a space that matches the elegance and energy of our house style, as well as the exuberance and abandon of our brand,' says Trevor Clough. 'Our goal is nothing less than to help put English fizz on the world map.' In 2017, it became the fastest-selling English fizz in the US.

Digby sources and blends Chardonnay, Pinot Noir and Meunier grown in contracted vineyards in the chalk soils of Kent, Sussex and Hampshire. Wiston Estate's Dermot Sugrue carries out the fermentation, bottling, ageing and disgorging with Trevor Clough the head blender. In the Tasting Room, the Digby Tasting Flight includes three

50 millilitre pours of Digby sparkling wines or a Mini Tasting Flight of two 25 millilitre glasses of different Digby styles. To coincide with the opening of the Tasting Room, Digby Fine English launched the Kenelm Club, which includes three automatic wine shipments per year. And if you are wondering about the name, Sir Kenelm Digby was the innovative seventeenth century English courtier credited with inventing the modern wine bottle in the 1630s. Here's looking at you, Digby!

Exton Park Vineyard

Exton, Hampshire

www.extonparkvineyard.com

Without watercress, there would be no Exton Park. It's all down to Malcolm Isaac, the packaged fresh salads and watercress magnate, who sold his company, Vitacress, and bought the neighbouring 100-hectare estate of Exton Park in 2009. Overlooking the village of Exton in the Meon Valley, the vineyards occupy varying south- and south-east-facing aspects at altitudes of between 65 and 122 metres. The South Downs' chalky slopes had obvious potential for sparkling wine and the first vineyard was planted to 8 hectares of Chardonnay, Pinot Noir and Meunier. While at nearby Coates and Seely, Corinne Seely bought grapes from Exton Park and when she visited in 2009, she fell in love with the terroir and soon after became head winemaker.

After studying soils and their chemistry in Paris, Corinne's passion for terroir led her first to Château Lynch Bages and Domaine de Chevalier. In 2008, while travelling around the world as a freelance consultant, she discovered England. Isaac built a new winery to Corinne's specifications, with two Bucher presses and a series of small temperature-controlled tanks to allow individual plots to be processed separately. This tailor-made facility gives her a 'library' of wines from different plots and years from which to make the Reserve Blends, released in 2021. The most recent addition to the estate is Exton Hall, a two-storey building for high-end bespoke corporate events and wine dinners, with an open-plan kitchen diner, featuring an extraordinary spiral staircase.

The initial planting has expanded to 24.3 hectares, roughly half-and-half to Chardonnay and Pinot Noir with some 20 per cent Meunier. Under vineyard director Fred Langdale, the vineyard was planted at vine densities varying from 3,500 to 5,000 vines per hectare, each plot with different pruning systems and cover crops used to nourish and generate the best soil health. The exposition and airflow from south westerlies is also important in helping to keep powdery mildew, downy mildew and botrytis at bay. Frost, which affected over a third of the crop in 2017, can be a problem but the vineyard location helps to mitigate the risk. For maximum ripeness, yields are restricted to around 7 tonnes per hectare.

The grapes are pressed under nitrogen to maintain freshness. From the 2011 vintage, Corinne started to maintain a stock of reserve wines, using this 'archive of flavours' to craft each wine, with up to 32 reserves in each blend. Each bottle is branded with an RB (Reserve Blend) number representing the average number of reserve wines in each bottle. Corinne aims to keep the wines on the lees in bottle for three years and then another ten months after disgorgement. With a penchant for innovation, Exton Park pioneered wines such as the 2016 pure Pinot Meunier Rosé, which was awarded Gold at the IWC.

The new Reserve Blend range launched in April 2021 comprises the RB32 Brut, the RB23 Rosé and the RB28 Blanc de Noirs. At 60 per cent Pinot Noir and 40 per cent Chardonnay, the fine RB32 Brut shows fresh lime and grapefruit aromas with a full-flavoured green apple and citrus fruit tang. Exton Park RB28 Blanc de Noirs, a pure Pinot Noir, combines rich fruit sweetness with a zesty grapefruit twist. The Exton Park RB23 Rosé, a Pinot Noir and Meunier blend, shows cranberry-like fruit in a refreshingly crisp, summer pudding vein. In Corinne's view, Exton Park has created a new style of sparkling wine with its own personality. 'I'm not here to make Champagne,' she insists. 'English wine for me is about innovation, creation and freedom. I feel freer here. We are building a new industry. I want Exton Park to become one of the greatest ambassadors of England, like Bollinger is for France.'

Fox & Fox

Mayfield, East Sussex

www.foxandfox.wine

Gerard Fox was so inspired by the quality of an English sparkling wine he tried at a London reception in 2003 that he and his wife, Jonica, decided to put a south-facing field on their East Sussex property to good use as a vineyard. His enthusiasm and Jonica's concern that she knew nothing about growing vines led her to study winemaking at Plumpton College. Jonica is responsible for the vinegrowing, winemaking and marketing, while Gerard is chairman and tractor driver. Wines were only made from their own grapes until 2020 when they sold their Lakestreet vineyard. They now work with a number of Sussex growers.

They also completed a trial, interplanting new vines at the 1.5-hectare Hobdens vineyard planted in 2004 to double the vineyard density. The vineyard at Mayfield on the eastern side of Crowborough Hill (the highest point in East Sussex) is planted to Dijon and Champagne clones and sheltered from westerly weather systems. Soils are largely clay loam and greensand over sandstone with ironstone shale beds. The wines were made at Davenport Vineyards until 2019 when the winemaking moved to Bolney Wine Estate. Minimal intervention involves the careful management of acids at pressing and in the care taken after the first fermentation. There is no filtration and no malolactic fermentation and they are fanatical about their dosage trials to ensure balance.

Today Fox & Fox has a range of nine wines and an emerging reputation for moreishly drinkable fizz. From an average of 20,000 to 25,000 bottles, there is a varietal Collection Wine range based on Pinot Noir, Meunier, Chardonnay and Pinot Gris. The House Wine duo consists of Mosaic, a malty–toasty blend of Chardonnay and Pinot Noir with a full-flavoured rich mousse of energetic orchard fruit bubbles, and Mosaic Rosé. The Limited Editions range includes the CV (Chairman's Vat) Brut, a complex, lees-rich, savoury blend of Pinot Noir, Chardonnay and Pinot Gris, and Midnight Dark Dry Rosé Brut, which is mainly Pinot Noir. Their Essence Pure Chardonnay Brut 2011 achieved 97 points from Stephen Skelton MW and Tom Stevenson and the Tradition Blanc de Noirs Brut 2014 received 97 points from the DWWA. Every wine released since the 2013 vintage has won at least one gold medal.

The Grange

Itchen Stoke, Alresford, Hampshire

www.thegrangewine.co.uk

Five miles east of Winchester on the Hampshire Downs overlooking the River Itchen, The Grange is a family enterprise created in 2011 by four siblings, Zam, Rose, Lucy, Mark, and their father, John Ashburton, a former banker and current wine lover. The youngest, Zam Baring, who worked in TV in a previous life, is now the managing partner, working with vineyard manager and assistant, Phil Norman and Samuel Philippot respectively.

Two to three hundred years ago, the upper Itchen was channelled for the development of water-meadows, allowing the water emerging from chalk springs at a constant 10°C to trickle out and keep frosts at bay. Sheep that devoured the rich meadow grasses would fertilize the fields on the valley sides, allowing the farmer to grow a valuable crop of wheat or barley. Recently, The Grange has started to run sheep through the vineyard to help improve the soil structure and ecosystem.

At Burge's Field, 52,000 vines of Pinot Noir, Chardonnay and Meunier are grown. The south-facing slopes sit on a thin cap of gravelly clay beneath which lies a layer of chalk over 100 metres thick, laced with bands of hard silica flints. The chalk bedrock absorbs winter and spring rainwater which is stored to nourish the vine throughout the growing season. This, says Zam Baring, is what imparts 'a steely minerality, like rain on black flint' to the taste of their Chardonnay. Coates & Seely made the wines from their first harvest in 2014 and the 2015 harvest, handled by Emma Rice at Hattingley Valley, was made 85 per cent in stainless steel tanks and 15 per cent in oak barrels with 33 months of lees-ageing.

The newcomer's wines are impressive: The Grange Classic, a blend of Chardonnay, Pinot Noir and Meunier, shows good lees development for a biscuity aroma and orchard fruit flavours shot through with a sharp citrusy crispness and finishing on a tangy dry note. The pale coppery Grange Pink, based on Meunier, Pinot Noir and Chardonnay, is fragrant with a convincing complexity and richness of strawberry fruit, in no way confected, finishing with a crisply dry, cranberryish bite.

Gusbourne Estate

Appledore, Kent

www.gusbourne.com

Six miles from the Strait of Dover as the seagull flies, Gusbourne Estate sits on a south-facing slope off Kent's Romney Marsh. The rain shadow and low altitude help with warmth, protection and, crucially, ripeness. The estate goes back to 1410 when nobleman John de Goosebourne owned 58 hectares on this ancient pilgrimage route. The goose crest on the bottle is in homage to the Goosebourne family crest of three geese. For a long time an arable, fruit and vegetable farm, or 'turnip patch', Gusbourne was purchased in 2004 by South African orthopaedic surgeon, Andrew Weeber, who spotted the potential while visiting family locally and planted 20 hectares.

In 2013, Shellproof, the wine investment company of Conservative Party grandee Lord Ashcroft, bought Gusbourne for £7 million, investing a further £2.7 million in 2018. With the first cash injection, an additional 63 hectares were planted between 2013 and 2015, at Gusbourne and at the Goodwood Estate in Sussex. In the same year, Gusbourne announced a lease on another 25 hectares in Sussex. Relying on production from its own 15 vineyards, roughly 93 hectares are planted; two-thirds on Wealden clay and Tunbridge Wells sands in Kent, and one-third on chalk and flint soils in Sussex. About half is Chardonnay, 40 per cent Pinot Noir and 10 per cent Meunier.

At varying levels and with protection from woods, shrubs and trees, each Kent vineyard is very different, with more clay at the top of the hills and more silt and sand at the bottom, an ancient seabed. Since the Butness and Cherry Garden vineyards were planted in 2004, Boot Hill, planted in 2006–7, has come into its own as the best site for Chardonnay (Gusborne's Guinevere is one of England's top Chardonnays). Some vineyards might have up to 40 different clones. As the estate got bigger, it became possible to work out which were the best clones for which sites. Generally lower-yielding, with a level of ripeness not found anywhere else, the Burgundy clones work well, while on the chalk soils, the Champagne clones often prove superior.

According to Charlie Holland, winemaker with Gusbourne since 2013, 'you get ripeness, fullness, and a muscular character from Kent, while Sussex brings a more poised, perfumed style with higher acidity'. Broadly speaking, the cooler years work better in Kent, the warmer in Sussex. After 15 years, Gusbourne feels it has a proven track record of being able to ripen the crop. 'We like the clay here,' says Holland. 'Chalk often starts better in Sussex with its free-draining soils, but then in mid-season, the clay soils can overtake the chalk, and retain that heat and race away. We're usually one of the first out of the blocks in picking. Acidity is key, our calling card, and essential for freshness and vitality.'

Gusbourne works hard at the husbandry of its site, using grass and rotating cover crops to help with drainage, even planting daikon radish to soak up water. Manure is used to improve humification. Sensitive to the potential dangers of downy and powdery mildew and botrytis, Gusbourne is working hard on its green credentials by reducing spraying and herbicides to a minimum. With a vine density of round 4,000 vines per hectare, the vines are tall and spaced wide for maximizing photosynthesis. Yields are low compared to Champagne. Harvest takes place over three weeks, all handpicked by around one hundred Romanian and Bulgarian pickers.

From 40 blocks, Holland obtains over 200 different components. Ninety per cent is fermented in stainless steel and the remaining 10 per cent in three-quarters older oak and a quarter new oak casks. All the wines are vintage, with 5–7 per cent reserve wine if need be to add complexity. The dosage has dropped from 9 to around 7–8 grams per litre. After malolactic fermentation and second fermentation, the wines spend about three years on lees, although the aim is to extend that to four years for the *blanc de blancs*, even though they feel that some wines actually drink better after two years on lees ageing. The 2014 Rosé and Brut for instance, was 'beautiful with two- to two-and-a-half-years lees ageing'.

While the consistently fine Blanc de Blancs, with its textured richness and pristine fruit quality, is Gusbourne's signature wine, the generously fruity, yet saline, dry Brut Reserve and raspberries and cream-like Rosé have been more Pinot driven in recent years. The Chardonnay-dominant Brut Reserve Late Disgorged wines are particularly memorable, showing a complexity and longevity in their evolution that's subtly biscuity, balanced and elegantly restrained. A successful first zero dosage natural brut is a promising pointer to a new English wine trend. A variety of vineyard tours take in scenic vineyards, winery and the tasting room, which is open to visitors all year round. Gusbourne Reserved was created in 2021 to give members the chance to taste new wines and limited editions and receive invitations to members-only events.

Hambledon Wineries Ltd,

Hambledon, Hampshire

www.hambledonvineyard.co.uk

Located on the South Downs in Hampshire, Hambledon is one of the most historic names in English wine and not just because the rules of cricket were first laid down in Hambledon village in the eighteenth century. It was on its chalky slopes, 15 miles from the sea, that Major General Sir Guy Salisbury-Jones established England's oldest commercial vineyard in 1952. In 1999 it was bought by Ian Kellett, who studied winemaking at Plumpton College in Sussex before planting the slopes of Windmill Down to an initial 4 hectares of Chardonnay, Pinot Noir and Meunier in 2005, with a combination of 27 different clones and rootstocks.

After a team visited Pol Roger with a view to gaining insights from Champagne, funds were raised through a minority shareholder company and UK and EU government funding. The vineyard expanded to nearly 25 hectares and more recently to 80 hectares, with more Pinot

Noir and Meunier, taking Hambledon to a potential production figure of 500,000 bottles, the halfway point to its eventual, even more ambitious, target of one million bottles. The year 2011 saw the appointment of Hervé Jestin, formerly chef de cave at Duval-Leroy and, since 2015, of the Frenchman Felix Gabillet, who studied winemaking at Changins University in Switzerland.

All the wine is made with estate-grown, hand-harvested fruit. Malolactic fermentation and extended lees ageing are the trademarks of the Hambledon style. Felix Gabillet's aim, under the watchful eye of Hervé Jestin, is to fulfil Ian Kellett's ambition of producing the finest multi-vintage sparkling wine in England. With that in mind, Hambledon has added to the Classic Cuvée and Rosé a Première Cuvée and more recently a Première Cuvée DZ, which is like cherry jam on toast without the jammy sweetness.

The Hambledon Classic Cuvée is a finely chiselled wine, its creamy textured mousse supported by a hint of toastiness and refreshingly tangy vivacity. The excellent pale, coppery bronze Hambledon Rosé, a 90 per cent Chardonnay blend with 10 per cent red wine added, displays a berry-fruit fragrance with a touch of smoke, complemented by crunchy mulberry fruitiness. Worthy of its moniker, Première Cuvée, Hambledon's prestige fizz, boasts a lively English orchard fruit quality full of bite and energy, supported by a textured complexity.

Harrow & Hope Marlow Winery

Marlow, Buckinghamshire

www.harrowandhope.com

As we peered over the dead brown wood of the Harrow & Hope vineyard towards Marlow one chilly December morning in 2020, Henry Laithwaite was purring with contentment. He had not only won an IWC trophy for his 2015 Brut Reserve but, more importantly, brought in perhaps his best harvest yet. This was quite a turnaround for a man who had once thought of sparkling wine as a triumph of glitz over terroir.

After graduating in biology from Durham University and following stints in wineries in France and Australia, the purchase in 2008 of Château Verniotte in Castillon in 2008 proved not to be quite the idyll that he and his wife Kaye had anticipated. On their return to England, when his mother Barbara's Wyfold fizz (which he now makes) beat 82 rivals to win the prestigious Judgment of Parsons Green fizz awards in

2009, Henry calculated that making English fizz could indeed be a viable business. Instead of joining his father Tony Laithwaite at Direct Wines, he and Kaye bought 4 hectares near Marlow in 2010 and the remaining 2.5 hectares in 2012, building a winery for the inaugural 2013 vintage.

The main attraction of the Chiltern Hills location was the ancient south-facing Thames Valley terraces of free-draining, gravelly, clayey soils on a chalky bedrock, coupled with an elevation of 45–70 metres above sea level. The site was planted at a high density of 5,555 vines per hectare to 40 per cent Chardonnay on the chalkier soils, and 40 per cent Pinot Noir with 20 per cent Meunier in the more clayey parts, using Mercier Frères Champagne clones and rootstocks. The calcium in the soils helps to temper vigour, while pruning limits the number of buds per vine. 'Kilos per vine is the metric,' says Henry, and at an average of some 8 tonnes per hectare, this is close to the optimum yield for quality fruit and business viability. He is now growing on organic principles – no herbicides, no pesticides, mowing between rows – aiming for organic certification by 2023.

The cellar is equipped with a four-tonne Scharfenberger Europress and a battery of small 25-hectolitre stainless steel tanks in which separate lots are vinified based on clones and varieties. The first press fraction of just over 50 per cent is set aside for the fizz, with some 14 per cent of the second fraction used for the Brut NV and Rosé. Around 30 per cent of the wine is fermented, using wild yeasts since 2019, in 225-litre barriques, 300-litre hogsheads and 500-litre puncheons. The barrels also contain the reserve wines used for the NV. The wines undergo malolactic fermentation and remain on the lees for at least three years. Current annual production, due to be supplemented by the first all-Meunier cuvée in 2022, is around 40,000 bottles.

Like Jacquesson's system for its NV cuvée, the NV Brut Reserve is numbered according to the base year in the wine. No.4 is based on 2015, No.5 based on 2016 and so on. The Harrow & Hope Brut Reserve NV No. 4 and No. 5 are both blends of 40 per cent Pinot Noir, 40 per cent Chardonnay and 20 per cent Meunier. They remind me of Charles Heidsieck, with an almondy nuttiness and an intense toasty mousse dissolving on a steely knife-edge. The 70 per cent Pinot Noir, 30 per cent Meunier Blanc de Noirs Brut shows mouthwatering freshness and fine textural weight; the Blanc de Blancs Brut has smoky-chalky mineral intensity and savoury richness streaked with salinity. The Rosé

Brut maintains that consistency of quality, with a crunchy, cranberry-dry bite and delightful savoury fruit quality.

The name Harrow & Hope symbolizes the blood, sweat and tears of working the rock-hard, machine-crunching soils, along with optimism for a great and, as it were, not too harrowing, future. From an initial scepticism, Henry is now a convert to English fizz: 'The more I get into making sparkling wine, the more I genuinely believe that it can be a terroir-driven wine in its own right and the more I'm aiming to bring that out in my wines.'

Hattingley Valley

Nr Alresford, Hampshire

www.hattingleyvalley.com

Hattingley Valley was established by Simon Robinson, an ex-City solicitor, in 2008. The first 7.5-hectare site was planted to Chardonnay, Pinot Noir, Pinot Gris and Meunier with the help of vineyard consultant William Biddulph. Another 3-hectare site, which was planted in 2011, includes some Bacchus. Together with their own vineyard plantings, which are on south-facing solid chalk soils with patches of flinty loam and clay, long-term relationships with selected growers across the south have ensured a varied and reliable supply of grapes. Burnishing its environmental credentials, Hattingley not only claims to be the first winery to adopt solar power but its logo is based on the Silver-washed Fritillary, a rare butterfly found in the vineyards.

The development of Hattingley has been overseen by the effervescent Emma Rice, who is both winemaker and director. Emma started out in wine at The White Horse at Chilgrove when she was fifteen. A 1979 Krug served in double magnum four years later was her lightbulb moment. She then worked for Domaine Direct, became Hugh Johnson's editor at Mitchell Beazley and graduated from Plumpton College in 2006. After a stint at Cuvaison in Napa Valley and then at Tamar Ridge in Tasmania, she joined Hattingley Valley to become involved in the construction of the new custom-built, eco-friendly winery in time for the 2010 harvest.

After the pressing by Coquard press, around three-quarters of the juice is stainless steel fermented and a quarter, none of which goes through malolactic fermentation, fermented in Burgundy oak casks for mouthfeel and texture. Following the disastrous 2012 vintage 'when nothing ripened', Emma decided to build up the reserve wine; 2015 became the first year when the Classic Reserve became a true NV, with 18 per cent reserve wines. In addition to her own sparkling wine, Emma also makes fizz under contract, including Champagne Vranken-Pommery's Louis Pommery England.

The core range consists of a rosé, a *blanc de blancs*, and its most popular blend, the Classic Reserve, whose fine nutty aromas and Cox's apple and honeyed mousse finishes with a saline dryness. The Blanc de Blancs shows Chardonnay at its savoury best in the context of creamy-textured bubbles with good ageing potential. The Hattingley Valley Rosé is one of England's finest, blending Pinot Noir, Meunier and a small amount of Pinot Précoce in a pink fizz of bright fruit with a vivacious, crunchy strawberry bite to it. Her 2014 Kings Cuvée won Supreme Champion and Best Sparkling Wine at the 2020 WineGB awards. Twice winemaker of the Year, in 2014 and 2016, at what was the UKVA Competition (now the WineGB Awards), Emma still has her sights set on something higher: 'If I could produce something as good as that 1979 Krug, and I'm still trying, then I'll be happy.'

Henners Vineyard

Herstmonceux, East Sussex

www.hennersvineyard.co.uk

In 2011, after several years working in PR in London, Collette O' Leary changed career to retrain as a winemaker. At the time, vineyard plantings were increasing and English sparkling wine was beginning to make its mark not just at home but worldwide. After working at J Vineyards in California and Graham Beck in South Africa, Collette was sufficiently captivated by 'the magic of the bubble' to go on a winemaking course at Plumpton College, joining Henners, which is owned by wine merchant, Boutinot, in 2019.

Established in 2007 in the Sussex village of Herstmonceux, Henners Vineyard is located less than five miles from the south coast, looking out across the Pevensey Levels Nature Reserve in the shadow of the South Downs. Proximity to the English Channel brings a strong coastal influence to the 3-hectare vineyard, whose low altitude, free-draining clayey soils are planted to Chardonnay, Pinot Noir and Meunier. The balance of supply comes from partners growing 20 hectares of grapes across the south-east of England. Henners doesn't rely on a single site, soil or terroir, working with producers 'to create something greater than the sum of the individual parts,' says Collette, be they grapes grown on clay or chalk soils.

A horizontal pneumatic Willmes Merlin 5100 press allows Collette to macerate fruit overnight for the sparkling rosé and, while whole bunch pressing is the norm, gives her the flexibility to press destemmed fruit if necessary. She ferments mainly in stainless steel with around 5 per cent of base wines fermented in oak. The base wines go through malolactic fermentation and are kept on the lees until blending. She is also developing a reserve wine programme, keeping back at least two previous vintages for use at blending in the non-vintage and multi-vintage cuvées. 'We are taste-led, so the direction of travel is towards winemaking practices such as malolactic fermentation, use of oak, use of reserve wines and time on lees to reduce the need for higher dosage levels.'

The core range consists of the moreishly drinkable Henners NV Brut (Chardonnay, Pinot Noir and Meunier) and NV Rose (Pinot Noir and Meunier), both elegantly restrained with an almost Champagne-like balance. Vintage wines, such as the mouthwateringly complex Henners Vintage (Chardonnay and Pinot Noir) and Henners Blanc de Blancs (Chardonnay), are produced only in certain years when conditions align. Annual production is around 70,000 bottles with the capacity set to double to 140,000 after 2020. 'We take a contemporarily traditional approach to see how we can improve in the future – the aggregation of marginal gains,' says Collette, 'starting in the vineyard all the way through to pouring into the glass.'

Busi Jacobsohn Wine Estate

Eridge Green, East Sussex
www.busijacobsohn.com

When Douglas Jacobsohn retired from his job as CEO of a marine insurance business in 2014, he and his wife Susanna Busi Jacobsohn bought Blackdon Farm in East Sussex with its 21 hectares of land. With no great ambition other than to enjoy life in the countryside, they got to talking, at a curry night at their youngest son's school, with a parent who knew Hambledon Vineyard and introduced the Swedish couple to Ian Kellett, Hambledon's owner. 'We had no idea then that there were so many vineyards in England and after spending the day there, which was rather romantic, we decided to go for it.'

The land had been used for grazing and hay production for 500 years but given the substantial nutrients in the Wealden clay (clay and sandstone) soils, they had an intuition that it might be good for vines. Before planting the 5-hectare vineyard, 40 per cent each to Chardonnay and

Pinot Noir, 20 per cent to Meunier, the Busi Jacobsohns installed a new drainage system. English wine expert Stephen Skelton MW organized a soil analysis and arranged the sourcing of the vines, which come from Burgundy. The most important contributor to grape quality in their view is the vineyard microclimate, a south-west facing slope ranging from 87 to 113 metres above sea level.

While the Busi Jacobsohn wines are made by Simon Roberts, Susanna and Douglas are instrumental in deciding on the blend, the dosage and the disgorgement date. The debut vintage, 2017, was made in stainless steel, and gained several awards. Unimpressed by English wine, a French sommelier, Olivier Thevin, tasted the wine, commenting 'this is like the best Champagne', and now stocks and sells it. There are four sparkling wines in the range, the Classic Cuvée Brut, a rosé, the Blanc de Blancs, and the Blanc de Noirs. Production is between 25 and 35 tonnes. The old stable on the property has been converted to a guesthouse and in 2019 they built a storage barn and a tasting room with a balcony over-looking the vineyard.

Langham Wine Estate

Dorchester, Dorset

www.langhamwine.co.uk

North-west of Affpuddle and Briantspuddle and north of Puddletown and Tolpuddle sits Langham Wine Estate. Whence the puddles? Not from the rainfall which, though substantial, is no greater here than in any other part of England's south-west. According to Justin Langham, former chartered surveyor and owner, with his brother and sister, of Langham Wine Estate, the future Queen Victoria, as a young girl, was due to visit the area, which is bisected by the River Piddle. In order not to offend her delicate sensibilities, the name was hastily changed to Puddle. If true, but for her visit, we might today be talking about the Tolpiddle martyrs.

The Grade I listed Bingham's Melcombe manor house, bought by Justin's father in 1980, sits at the heart of the Langham Agricultural Enterprise, whose six farms cover over 1,000 hectares of largely arable land. Justin's interest in vineyards turned to enthusiasm as various winery visits convinced him that sparkling wine was the way forward. After attending Plumpton College, he decided in 2009 to plant Chardonnay, Pinot Noir and Meunier in a 10-hectare plot. The site, chosen for its slope 90 metres above sea level, its south-facing aspect and shelter from the wind, sits on Kimmeridgian chalk, but for Justin, 'chalk is the reason why our Chardonnay does so well for us, but it's not our USP; the mini-continental climate is equally important for optimum ripeness'.

Twelve miles from the Dorset coast, the vineyard at Crawthorne has expanded to 12 hectares planted to 65 per cent Chardonnay, 25 per cent Pinot Noir and the balance to Meunier. A second planting took place in 2011 and a further acre was planted, including four rows of Pinot Précoce, in 2018. Spaced at 2.5 by 1.2 metres, the vines are high-grafted, which helps with earlier ripening. Yields are low at, on average, 4.5 tonnes per hectare. The topsoil is shallow, with a cover crop helping fix nitrogen and the soil dries within a day after it rains, while the chalk retains the moisture. Vineyard manager Olly Whitfield, ex-Plumpton College and Exton Park, is trialling various different pruning techniques, including single Guyot, double Guyot and cordon spur for the best quality to quantity ratio.

Winemaker Tommy Grimshaw and owner Justin Langham

Winemaking is carried out in a rudimentary but characterful old barn by Tommy Grimshaw, who joined Langham in 2019, having started at Sharpham as a 17-year-old in 2013. A 3-tonne Scharfenberger does the pressing at 650 litres per tonne and another timbered barn houses a battery of varying sized stainless steel fermentation tanks along with a mix of Burgundy and Bordeaux barriques and puncheons, each suspended in mid-air by a strong purple ratchet strap invented by Justin. The first fermentation of some 90 parcels is made half in stainless steel and half in older barrels and 500-litre puncheons. All wines go through malo-lactic fermentation, and blending capacity, with the perpetual reserve Langham is building via seven 4,000-litre concrete tanks set into the ground, signals a gradual future shift from vintage to non-vintage.

In 2017, the Classic Cuvée was split into a Chardonnay-dominated cuvée, Corallian Extra Brut, and a Pinot Noir-dominated cuvée, Culver Extra Brut, both named after sub-strata in the chalk bedrock. Corallian is at once lemon-biscuity, intense and appetizingly bone dry; Culver shows more spicy berry aromatics and rounded, sumptuous berry fruit. The Blanc de Blancs has the finesse of Chardonnay with its refreshingly lemony acidity and saline, dry finish, and the pale, coppery salmon pink Rosé is a model of charming, liquid ripe raspberries and cream. An exciting pointer to the future is the Langham Pinot Meunier, a seductively floral crowd-pleaser of a fizz. Tommy also makes a sparkling white and rosé *col fondo* in keg, called Zig Zag. Back labels are exemplary, showing vintage, or vintage base in the case of non-vintage, grape varieties and date of disgorgement. Production is on average 55,000 bottles, a size that suits Justin well: 'My ambition isn't to be the biggest, but I do want to be the best.'

Louis Pommery England

New Alresford, Hampshire

www.louis-pommery.com

In the early 2010s, Paul François Vranken, owner of the Vranken Pommery Monopole Group, decided to launch the production of sparkling wine outside the Champagne region. Seeing the potential of English terroir, with its chalky soils and warming oceanic climate, for a long, slow ripening season, he launched Louis Pommery England. The Chardonnay–Pinot Noir–Meunier blend began with the 2015 harvest, in collaboration with Hattingley Valley under the direction of Thierry Gasco and Clément Pierlot (respectively the ninth and tenth cellarmasters at Pommery), who were joined in 2019 by Pierre-Hubert Crozat.

The first plantings came in 2017, in a single block of the Pinglestone Estate, whose free-draining flint and limestone soils are mostly planted on slopes with exposures ranging from south-east to west, through south. On the plateau at 90 metres, the limestone gives way to deeper clayey soils that are well-suited to Pinot Noir. Wind and drainage help guard against disease. There's a grass cover crop and herbicides and in-secticides are not used. Long hedges have been planted for landscaping and to protect the local wildlife, and beehives have been introduced. Between 2017 and 2019, a series of plantings were carried out to create a 30-hectare vineyard in a single plot using the Champagne grapes plus Pinot Gris. In 2019, a new 10-hectare estate was purchased in Lovington. The first Pinglestone Estate harvest was in 2020, on 12.5 hectares, and 2021 will see the remaining 17.5 hectares, planted in 2019, come into production.

The winemaking process involves a light Champagne-style pressing followed by a rapid decantation, before fermentation in stainless steel vats at low temperature and malolactic fermentation. Reserve wines are used in the Chardonnay-based blend for complexity with ageing on the lees adding further to it. The 'range' remains just one cuvée, and a successful one at that, Louis Pommery England. Output averages 30,000 bottles a year, starting in 2015, followed by two further cuvées based on the 2016 and 2017 harvests. The aim is to produce new cuvées as and when the Pinglestone Vineyard plantings come on stream. In August 2021, the estate was certified with the WineGB Sustainable Wines of Great Britain trademark.

Nyetimber

West Chiltington, West Sussex

www.nyetimber.com

With a view to making a traditional method sparkling wine of which England could be proud, Nyetimber, a medieval priory given by Henry VIII to his fourth wife, Anne of Cleves, was bought in 1986 by Stuart and Sandy Moss, medical equipment entrepreneurs from Chicago. The key to the Mosses' success lay in their belief that to achieve that objective, they would have to find the right location, to eschew England's predominant Germanic varieties in favour of the Champagne grapes and to submit to advice from the champenois, retaining Jean-Manuel Jacquinot from the eponymous Champagne house.

Some 16 hectares of Chardonnay, Pinot Noir and Meunier were planted on free-draining greensand between 1988 and 1991, with an emphasis on Chardonnay. Building on these foundations, Dutch busi-nessman Eric Heerema bought Nyetimber in 2006 from the pop im-presario Andy Hill, who had acquired it following the retirement of the Mosses in 2001. After receiving glowing reports on the Canadian winemaking couple Cherie Spriggs and Brad Greatrix, Heerema asked them for their CVs. The result? The talented wife and husband team were hired, filling the shoes of predecessors Kit Lindlar (1992–5), Stuart and Sandy Moss (1996– 2001), Peter Morgan (2002–3), Dermot Sugrue (2004–5) and Belinda Kemp (2006).

Nyetimber only produces sparkling wine from its own 260 hectares of vineyards, split across three counties. There are now eleven vineyards with 327 hectares under vine of which 260 hectares were producing in 2020. Six are in West Sussex (five on greensand, one on chalk), two in Hampshire (both chalk) and three in Kent (all chalk), which is slightly warmer. With a balance of 49 per cent Chardonnay, 35 per cent Pinot Noir and 16 per cent Meunier, each of the vineyards is sub-divided into parcels based on clones and rootstocks (of which there are some 30 different types), soil type and, ultimately, on taste. More recently, densities have been reduced to 4,500 vines per hectare to allow in more sunlight.

With largely single Guyot, cane-pruned vines, meticulously tended by Ben Kantsler and his vineyard team, all sites are carefully observed for frost and disease pressure. Sub-lots are hand-harvested into 15-kilo boxes, parcel by parcel, at an average 6 tonnes per hectare, pressed in Coquard PAI presses and kept separate during the fermentation process, with around 100 different base wines. After a tasting in January, they are evaluated in several more rounds. Oxygen is kept to a minimum and to limit the potential for oxidation at disgorgement, the latest jetting technology is used and DIAM Mytik technical corks inserted. The wines normally undergo malolactic fermentation 'for greater balance', but there is no strict rule.

The overall style is the culmination of intensity with a delicacy, a fruit presence with a lightness of touch. After three years on the lees, the Nyetimber Classic Cuvée MV, a blend of half Chardonnay with half Pinot Noir and Meunier shows light toast and brioche and a concentrated appley fizz, with creamy textured mousse and appley acidity flecked with a hint of honey. The vintage Blanc de Blancs displays notes of smoky oystershell, a pristine Chardonnay with honeycomb and lemony notes and a firm spine of saline minerality. Blending around three-quarters Pinot Noir and a quarter Chardonnay, Nyetimber Tillington Single Vineyard is a class act with a gentle saline streak to the finish.

A West Sussex and Hampshire blend of Pinot Noir, Chardonnay and Meunier with 10–20 per cent reserve wine and just over 15 per cent red wine blended in, Nyetimber's Classic Cuvée Rosé MV displays a voluptuous raspberry ripple fruit quality and seamless texture. At the top of the range, the prestige cuvées 1086 White and Rosé are more than worthy of the prestige name. The black grape-dominant white is a deliciously toasty drop, all creamy mousse and rich, tangy vinous fruit, verging on the salty; the rosé, three-quarters Pinot Noir and a quarter Chardonnay, is an intense, lightly toasty, summer pudding and cream delight, showing English sparkling rosé at its superlative best.

Oxney Organic Estate

Beckley, Rye, East Sussex
www.oxneyestate.com

Kristin Syltevik came to Britain in 1984 to work as an au pair and went on to work in PR. In 2007, Kristin sold the PR agency she had founded and, starting in 2009, she and her partner Paul Dobson, an ex-professional golfer, bought four farms and a vineyard to make sparkling wine in line with their vision of sustainable modern farming. They now own a 320-hectare, Soil Association-certified organic estate, with an approach to disease control aimed at producing naturally healthy fruit.

Oxney is located six miles from the English Channel just north of Rye. The vineyard topsoil is Tunbridge Wells Sand, a fine sand and silt loam, above clay. The first vines, Pinot Noir, Meunier and Chardonnay, were planted in April 2012 and more, including Seyval Blanc, over the following two years. The first classic sparkling was made in 2014. With the most recent planting in May 2018, including Pinot Précoce, Oxney has become the largest single estate organic vineyard in the UK with a planted area of 13.65 hectares. The east- and west-facing vineyard surrounds the winery and farm shop, and from a south-west slope stretches out towards an oak wood, creating a warm, protected microclimate.

Initially carried out by David Cowderoy, the winemaking today is done by Syltevik and Salvatore Leone. The grapes are handpicked and transported to the adjacent winery, where the sustainable approach is replicated in a focus on low intervention, using whole bunch pressing in small batches, natural yeasts and minimal filtration. Each variety and clone is pressed and fermented separately with a small proportion barrel-fermented. Dosage varies from zero to 9 grams per litre and all sparkling wines undergo malolactic fermentation. They have started printing disgorging dates on the back label.

The top tier sparkling wine range includes The Classic Brut, a bright, nutty, mouthwatering blend of Chardonnay, Pinot Noir and Meunier which won a gold medal at the 2020 IWC. They have also started making the delicious Classic Rosé (awarded gold for 2016 by Drinks Business), the Classic Blanc de Blancs, and a pure Meunier Classic Blanc de Noirs made for the first time in 2017. The NV Estate range comprises a white and a pink sparkling wine made with an estate blend of Seyval Blanc, Chardonnay, Pinot Noir and Meunier. Also worthy of note: Oxney makes a rather good still Chardonnay.

Raimes

Alresford, Hampshire

www.raimes.co.uk

Like many English farmers now grasping the nettle of growing grapes for fizz, Augusta and Robert Raimes are fifth generation farmers who have planted 4 hectares of Chardonnay, Pinot Noir and Meunier on the chalky soils of their family farm in Hampshire's South Downs National Park. The soils are so obviously suited to the production of fine sparkling wine that instead of accepting two offers to buy, they not only planted the Champagne varieties in 2011, but decided to turn to the talented Emma Rice at Hattingley Valley to make their wines for them.

Apart from growing grapes, the Raimes family continue farming wheat, barley and oilseed rape on the farm, which stretches from the water-meadows of the River Itchen to the rolling hills of the South Downs. Their historic Tichborne estate is also home to a herd of traditional pedigree horned Hereford cattle. They believe that in England's cooler climate, with its relatively long growing season, the impact of the chalk substratum brings a minerality that helps to achieve balance and finesse.

In recognition of the growing thirst for wine tourism and bringing the public in to appreciate the scenic beauty of this neck of the woods, the Raimes family run vineyard tours in their trusty Land Rover for private vineyard tour groups between May and September and private tasting groups all year round. For such a recent enterprise, Raimes is already making startlingly good wines, most notably the almost burgundian Classic Vintage Chardonnay and Meunier cuvée and the crunchy, mouthfilling Rosé Vintage Pinot Noir–Chardonnay blend. The wines can only get even better as the vines mature and the viticulture becomes second nature.

Rathfinny Wine Estate

Alfriston, East Sussex

www.rathfinnyestate.com

The name of Pinchemdown Farm was changed to Rathfinny after the estate was bought in the 1850s by a Mr Finny, an Irishman, who wanted it to sound Irish, 'rath' meaning a circular farm enclosure. Located in the South Downs National Park, between Brighton and Eastbourne, it was established in 2010 as Rathfinny Wine Estate by Mark and Sarah Driver on a working arable farm. They had one simple aim: to produce some of the world's finest quality sparkling wines. The first harvest was in 2014 and the first wines were released to substantial acclaim in 2018.

In a previous life, Mark was a stockbroker, his wife Sarah a city solicitor. After returning from a stint covering Asian markets in Hong Kong, Mark was researching a course for his daughter, Milli (who now runs marketing at Rathfinny). 'Looking at the UCAS website, we were getting increasingly desperate,' he recalls. 'As we got to V, I found a course in viticulture. I found it so fascinating that I bought six bottles of English fizz and six of Champagne. We had a boozy night with friends, ranking the wines in order of preference and the English mostly came out on top. I thought, OK, if consumers are telling me that English fizz is on a par with Champagne, then it can't be all bad.'

The eureka moment resulted in Mark signing up to a two-year wine production course at Plumpton College. During the course, he came across Rathfinny Farm in Cradle Valley. He looked up weather records, carried out soil analysis and drew up a plan. Despite issues with wind, two consultants gave the thumbs up and Mark set about hiring his team. Jonathan Médard, the first winemaker, has moved on and the winemaking is now headed up by Tony Milanowski, a graduate of Adelaide University and former Plumpton wine lecturer. The viticulture is managed by Cameron Roucher, a grape farmer and nurseryman from New Zealand.

Rathfinny is just three miles from the English Channel on a deep bedrock of chalk, absorbing water like a sponge throughout the year, keeping the vines nourished during the warm, dry summer months. A semi-continental maritime climate and proximity to the sea provides protection from late frosts. With good sunshine and moderate rainfall, a steady growing season allows the grapes to ripen fully. Running along the southern edge of the estate, the ridge sloping down from 120 metres to 30 metres on the valley floor protects the vines from the worst of the prevailing south westerlies, assisted by a windbreak of trees planted every 100 metres and a temporary metal 'hedge'.

Rathfinny's first 20 hectares of vines were planted in 2012, followed by another 20 hectares in 2013 and the same again in 2014. Five hectares were planted in 2015 and the balance in 2019 and 2020. The single-site vineyard of 93 hectares is currently planted to 45 per cent Pinot Noir, 35 per cent Chardonnay and 15 per cent Meunier plus a small amount of Pinot Gris for the Cradle Valley still wine. Initially Chardonnay was planted at the top of the vineyard and Pinot Noir at the bottom, but plantings at some 4,100 vines per hectare now alternate to help Mark understand which clones (both Champagne and Dijon) work best where. An average yield of 8 tonnes per hectare is achieved and, long term, the aim is to plant 135–150 hectares. Work has also been done to enhance wildlife habitats, reclaiming areas of natural chalk grassland and creating wildlife corridors to improve biodiversity.

In the capacious cellar, finished in 2013, Rathfinny's three Coquard PAI presses yield 55 per cent of the first fraction and 10 per cent of the second. The juice is moved by gravity for settling and then to temperature controlled, stainless steel tanks for fermentation. As many as forty separate parcels are fermented by clone, sometimes by block. The red wines used for the sparkling rosé are aged in used French oak and all the wines go through full malolactic fermentation. Tirage in the new bottling cellar follows blending in the spring and early summer. Dosage is on the low side at 3–5 grams per litre and cork is DIAM Mytik.

Rathfinny's four wines are all vintage-dated, aged for at least three years and independently qualitatively assessed to comply with the Sussex PDO. All four are impressive: the incisively fresh Classic Cuvée Brut has a lively mousse of finely balanced English orchard apple fruit; the vibrant, citrusy Blanc de Blancs Brut has leesy–nutty tones and concentrated apple and tropical fruit flavours, and the coppery cherry and strawberry-scented Rosé has summer pudding flavours. Last but by no means least, the superbly vinous, rich Blanc de Noirs is mouthwateringly savoury and dry. Production is currently 300,000 bottles, including some 1,000 magnums of each cuvée, with a target of one million. The disgorgement date is printed on the label, the tirage date laser printed onto the bottle. Champion of a Sussex PDO, Rathfinny has joined with nine Sussex wine producers to create bespoke self-driven wine routes under 'Sussex Modern'.

Ridgeview Wine Estate

Ditchling Common, Sussex
www.ridgeview.co.uk

After building a successful IT business from scratch in the 1980s into one of the biggest IBM dealers in the UK, Mike Roberts and his wife Christine were made an offer in the early 1990s that they couldn't refuse. The long-cherished idea of making their own wine was literally to bear fruit when they set up a seven-hectare vineyard planted to 13 clones of Chardonnay, Pinot Noir and Meunier with the modest aim of producing some 20,000 bottles a year. In the admittedly voluminous vintage of 2018, Ridgeview produced 400,000 bottles. What went so right?

Mike's research led him to the conclusion that southern England's soils, geography and cool climate had potential for quality bubbles. No expense was spared on the perfect site at Ditchling in East Sussex. A modern winery with an underground storage cellar designed for classic-variety, bottle-fermented sparkling wine was established in 1997. He and his son Simon trained at Plumpton College, taking on Kit Lindlar to make the first wines. To hone his winemaking skills, Simon went to Australia where he met his soon-to-be wife Mardi, who returned as Ridgeview's marketing director. Chris and Mike's daughter Tamara joined Ridgeview in 2004 and her husband followed in 2011, Tamara becoming CEO in 2013.

Ridgeview's first release, the 1996 Cuveé Merret Bloomsbury won the Gore-Browne Trophy, also won by Ridgeview in 2000, 2002, 2009, 2010 and 2011. Ridgeview's 2006 Blanc de Blancs was awarded the Decanter World's Best Sparkling Wine and in 2018 Ridgeview was named International Wine & Spirit Competition (IWSC) Winemaker of the Year. With their wines poured at the Queen's eightieth birthday, Diamond Jubilee and four State Banquets at Buckingham Palace, prestige continues to follow Ridgeview.

Ridgeview brings in grapes from 85 hectares based on its own 7 hectares, plus West Sussex (25 hectares), East Sussex (24 hectares) and the remainder from Suffolk, Surrey, Essex, Hampshire, Berkshire and Hertfordshire. The grapes are handpicked with harvest normally running from the more sheltered eastern side of the country and moving west. The home vineyard is mainly loamy clay, while the 12 vineyards from which Ridgeview sources its grapes include the excellent Tukker family site Tinwood in West Sussex, which is stony, and East Anglia which is sandy and flinty. Essex is quite chalky and there are new grape suppliers in northern Kent and one on the Kent coast, both of whose vineyards are chalky.

The grapes are pressed in 4-tonne Coquard and Wilmes presses and the wines fermented in a combination of stainless steel and a small number of oak barrels. Because of its range of sources, Ridgeview has a large number of small tanks for keeping lots separate. Since 2015, Simon has started to build the reserves for a 'true non-vintage blend'. He would normally put the wines through malolactic fermentation to soften the malic acidity but since the 2018 vintage, with its lower acidity levels, he hasn't routinely done so.

In addition to the reliable Bloomsbury, Cavendish and Fitzrovia range, the single-vineyard Blanc de Blancs is exceptional, a fizz full of toast and butterscotch scents, followed by an intense rich mouthful of savoury-rich, creamy fruit. Small limited-edition parcels are occasionally made, such as the almost burgundian Ridgeview Oak Reserve NV single vintage, launched on 5 October 2020, and a sumptuously toasty Blanc de Noirs Limited Release. Simon is also trialling a late-disgorged fizz. With a £2 million investment in 2019, including a new cellar on two floors for 16 gyropalettes, disgorging and dry goods, Ridgeview can cellar up to one million bottles, including those for contract clients such as Laithwaites' Windsor Great Park, and Waitrose's Leckford Estate. A number of blends are also made under bespoke labels: South Ridge for Laithwaites, Booths English Sparkling Wine and the Wine Society's Exhibition English Sparkling.

Simpsons Wine Estate

Barham, Canterbury, Kent
www.simpsonswine.com

If you've come across the Languedoc wines of Domaine de Sainte Rose, then you've made the vinous acquaintance of the Simpsons, Ruth and Charles, that is, who have been making award-winning wines there since 2002. Charles has a pharmaceutical background, Ruth, from the Grants whisky family, a humanitarian one. Used to southern French sunshine, they initially vowed never to make wine in England, but succumbed to an irresistible proposition: two warm, sunny, south-facing sites on prime chalk soils eight miles from the coast, with the right aspect, wind protection and a high number of frost-free days.

In 2014, after acquiring the 35.2-hectare site in the unspoilt Elham Valley in Kent's North Downs for around £800,000 in 2012, they planted the first 9.12 hectares of Chardonnay, Meunier and Pinot Noir. This is the Roman Road Vineyard, situated along the route the Romans marched during the AD 43 invasion, bringing their vines with them. A further 18.05 hectares were planted on the steeper, higher southern slopes of the village during 2016 and 2017; the Railway Hill Vineyard is named for the historic Canterbury to Folkestone light railway.

Yields have varied from just 25 tonnes in 2017, when they were hit by frost and had only one vineyard site in production, to 200 tonnes in 2018 and 2019, as the more recent plantings came on stream. The inaugural 2016 Chalklands Classic Cuvée won a gold medal in the 2019 Champagne and Sparkling Wine World Championships and the 2018 Roman Road Chardonnay won Best in Show and a Platinum Medal at the Decanter World Wine Awards 2020.

The winery is within walking distance of the two vineyard sites. Two pneumatic grape presses protect the delicacy of aroma and flavour of each grape variety. After the secondary fermentation, bottles mature for 15–36 months, helping to round out the acidity. A secret dosage completes the process. The result is the appetizing, orchard fruit-flavoured Chalklands Classic Cuvée, the impressively complex Flint Fields Blanc de Noirs Brut and the crowdpleasing, tutti-frutti Rosé. In 2018 and 2019, 120,000 bottles of traditional method sparkling wine and 60,000 bottles of still wine were made.

Wiston Estate

Washington, West Sussex

www.wistonestate.com

When I first visited the Goring family's Wiston estate on a bitingly cold January morning in 2019, the higgledy-piggledy old turkey shed buildings housing the winery could at best be described as unlovely. But then, the Goring family didn't get where they were as successful farmers of beef herds, grazing sheep, wheat, barley and oil seed rape by ostentatiousness. Careful husbandry of the 6,000 acres of farmland straddling the chalky slopes of the South Downs has kept the family going strong since 1743 and the reign of King George II, the last British monarch to participate in a battle (The Battle of Dettingen in Bavaria).

After Harry Goring (the father of Richard Goring and his brand ambassador wife Kirsty) married Pip in 1972, it was her idea to plant a vineyard to remind her of the Cape Winelands of her home, not to mention enjoy the liquid fruit of their endeavours. Goring was persuaded when Madame Duval, owner of Duval-Leroy Champagne, came to England in 2005 with a view to exploiting the chalk slopes herself. In 2006, 6.5 hectares were planted in small plots, half to Chardonnay, the other half to two thirds Pinot Noir and a third Meunier. Herbicides are eschewed with just a mechanical hoe to keep the weeds from running riot.

The wine was to have been made up the road at Nyetimber but when the Gorings met Dermot Sugrue, then at Nyetimber, Dermot joined Wiston (after working the 2006 vintage at Jacquinot & Fils in Champagne). Sugrue, a Plumpton College graduate, was particularly attracted by the fact that the Gorings were keen to produce a sparkling wine cuvée from their own chalk site. He obtained a Coquard press from Champagne and made Wiston's first vintage in 2008, released in 2012, with magnums released after late disgorgement in 2017. The 2013 Wiston Cuvée was released in 2017 and won the award for Best UK Sparkling Wine at the Decanter World Wine Awards and the IWSC. Her Majesty The Queen used the NV Brut in Nebuchadnezzar to launch the new *Britannia* at Southampton in March 2015 and Wiston received the accolade of Winery of the Year at the WineGB Awards 2018 and 2020.

Production is around 30,000 bottles for the Wiston NV, which sees some of the reserve wines accumulated from the start, with some 15,000 bottles of vintage, although substantially more from the plentiful 2018 vintage. Only about one-third of production is labelled Wiston Estate, with disgorgement date and dosage on the back label. Sugrue also vinifies under contract for clients such as Jenkyn Place. They are investing £3 million in a wholesale renovation project for the new cellars, tasting room and café. As Harry Goring says, 'No one seemed particularly interested in hundreds of acres of barley and wheat, but plant a vineyard and people are fascinated.'

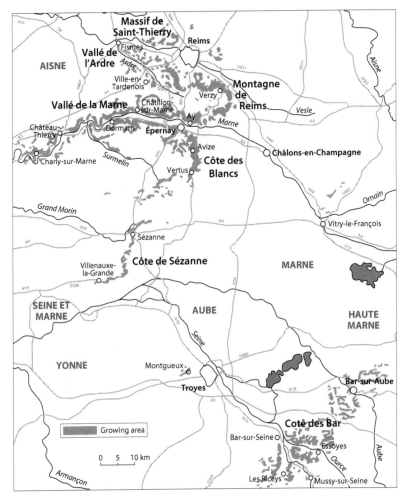

Map labels:

Massif de Saint-Thierry
Reims
Vallé de l'Ardre
AISNE
Fismes
Ville-en-Tardenois
Ardre
Montagne de Reims
Verzy
Vallé de la Marne
Châtillon-sur-Marne
Vesle
Château-Thierry
Dormans
Aÿ
Marne
Épernay
Charly-sur-Marne
Surmelin
Avize
Côte des Blancs
Châlons-en-Champagne
Vertus
Grand Morin
Vitry-le-François
Sézanne
MARNE
Côte de Sézanne
Villenauxe-la-Grande
Ornain
SEINE ET MARNE
AUBE
HAUTE MARNE
YONNE
Montgueux
Seine
Bar-sur-Aube
Troyes
Côte des Bar
Bar-sur-Seine
Essoyes
Armançon
Les Riceys
Mussy-sur-Seine
Ource
Aube

Growing area

0   5   10 km

The vineyards of Champagne

7

FRANCE

CHAMPAGNE

The Champagne appellation covers over 33,820 hectares in production, spread over 319 villages in the five departments of the Marne (66.4 per cent of plantings), Aube (23.4 per cent) and Aisne, Haute-Marne and Seine-et-Marne (10.2 per cent). The region's westernmost vineyards are closer to Paris than to Épernay, while the Côte des Bar down south in the Aube lies in a different terroir altogether. Pinot Noir accounts for 38 per cent of the appellation, 31 per cent is Meunier and 31 per cent is planted to Chardonnay The six main subregions of Champagne are the Montagne de Reims, Côte des Blancs, Côte de Sézanne, Grande Vallée, Vallée de la Marne and the Côte des Bar. Between them, they comprise 280,000 plots of vines, a mosaic of microterroirs each measuring on average 12 ares (100 square metres). Altitudes range from 90 to 300 metres above sea level. Seventeen villages are ranked *grand cru* and 42 *premier cru*.

Reims and Épernay sit at latitudes 49.5° and 49° north, respectively, where the average annual temperature is just 11°C (52°F). Champagne's vineyards are close to the northernmost limits of tolerance for a cold climate, receiving on average 1,650 annual hours of sunshine (but closer to 2,100 in hot years such as 1976 and 2003), compared to over 2,000 in Bordeaux and close to 2,000 in Burgundy. The region's dual climate is mainly oceanic, but with continental influences. Spring frosts are a potential danger during budburst, while winter frosts can destroy new buds and even the vines themselves. Since 1875, there have been 55 years when frost damage exceeded 1 per cent while in six vintages, it exceeded 40 per cent. Average annual rainfall varies between 674 millimetres (Épernay) and 604 millimetres (Reims).

The chalk hillsides of Champagne were formed when a vast sea covered the area during the Campanian era of the late Cretaceous Period 70 million years ago. The Paris Basin is a series of layers of concentric circles. The centre sank slowly under accumulated sediments of marine microorganisms consisting of tiny fossils and calcareous algae. A second seismic upheaval 10–11 million years ago raised the hills a further 150–300 metres, producing a sheer chain of undulating chalk hills containing the unique belemnite–micraster mix of dense white chalk that underlies the high forested plateau of the Montagne de Reims, the Vallée de la Marne and the Côte des Blancs. This chalk reservoir stores 300–400 litres of water per square metre, providing the vines with a steady water supply even in times of drought.

At the last count (2020), there were 16,200 growers, 130 cooperatives and 360 Champagne houses. Of the growers, 4,300 also produce their own Champagne. The houses dominate the market, while the cooperatives account for roughly one in every ten bottles of Champagne sold and include such excellent names as Beaumont des Crayères, Castelnau, De Saint Gall, Devaux, H. Blin, Jacquart, Le Mesnil, Mailly Grand Cru, Union Champagne and Palmer. The dominance of the houses increases in export markets where they represent around three-quarters of an export market of nearly 200 countries. In 2020, Champagne sales stood at 244 million bottles, down by 17.9 per cent on 2019. Non-vintage cuvées represent around 80 per cent of Champagne exports. The largest Champagne producer by volume is Moët & Chandon, part of Moët Hennessy, with a sales volume ten times that of its nearest competitors.

The DNA of Champagne's terroir is most apparent in 287 single vineyard Champagnes produced by growers whose terroir-based focus is, at least in some respects, the antithesis of the industry's blending bias. Krug's Clos du Mesnil, Billecart-Salmon's Clos Sainte-Hilaire and Philipponnat's Clos des Goisses are among cuvées produced from a single vineyard. Terroir-focused growers like Pascal Agrapart, Anselme Selosse, Tarlant and Francis Egly have singled out parcels within their vineyard holding for special attention because of their terroir origins. Others like Cédric Bouchard go further still, making wines that reflect a single vineyard parcel, grape variety and vintage.

Côte des Blancs

With 97 per cent of its 3,140 hectares of vineyards planted to Chardonnay, the aptly named Côte des Blancs is quintessential *blanc de blancs* Champagne country. Six of its eleven villages are *grands crus*: from north to south, Chouilly, Oiry, Cramant, Avize, Oger and Le Mesnil-sur-Oger. Its long, continuous slope, stretching for some 20 kilometres south of Épernay, faces mainly east and its bedrock of pure Cretaceous chalk, with shallow topsoils, is ideally suited to producing Chardonnay with freshness, finesse, balance and minerality. The middle portion of the slopes here are the tenderloin for Chardonnay.

Each village has its own character but in general, the farther south you head, the more taut, austere and saline the Chardonnays become. This is because the northern area vineyards contain a higher clay content, and Chouilly for instance is marginally warmer, while the more southerly vineyards, especially Oger and Le Mesnil-sur-Oger, contain more white chalk purity, although the sun-exposure of Oger makes it warmer than Le Mesnil. Despite its reputation for austerity, a single vineyard wine like Krug's Clos du Mesnil can be surprisingly opulent.

Leading producers: Agrapart, Claude Cazals, Guy Charlemagne, Diebolt-Vallois, Pascal Doquet, Doyard, Pierre Gimonnet, Gonet-Médeville, André Jacquart, Krug (Clos du Mesnil), Larmandier-Bernier, AR Lenoble, Lilbert, Jacquesson, Jean Milan, Le Mesnil, Pierre Moncuit, Pierre Péters, André Robert, Salon, Jacques Selosse, De Sousa, Aurélien Suenen, Union Champagne, Vazart-Coquart, J-L Vergnon, Veuve Fourny.

Montagne de Reims

Covering a vineyard area of some 8,280 hectares, the 97 villages of the Montagne de Reims fan out to west and east in a forested plateau on either side of the main north–south road running from Reims to Épernay. With ten *grands crus*, this vineyard area, lying on a deep bed of chalk, is made up of just over 40 per cent Pinot Noir, 34 per cent Meunier and 25 per cent Chardonnay and is best-known for the flavour, power and structure of its Pinot Noirs. To the east, sitting between the Vesle and Marne rivers, is the Grande Montagne, itself divided into four sections: the south-facing *grands crus*, including Bouzy, south-facing and warm, and Ambonnay; the east facing terroirs of Trépail and Villers-Marmery, known for Chardonnay; the north-facing *grands crus* of Verzenay and Verzy, and the northern *premier cru* of Ludes.

The Grande Montagne gives way to the Petite Montagne to the west, a Meunier stronghold with more sandy soils, with the Grande Vallée, effectively the southern flank of the Montagne de Reims, mostly facing south towards the Marne River. Generally speaking, the north-facing vineyards of the Montagne de Reims produce wines characterized by freshness, finesse and structure, while the southerly vineyards are more opulent. There are two smaller sub-regions here, the Massif de Saint-Thierry, noted for its sandy soils, and the Monts de Berru, a hill of chalk, sand, limestone and clay north-east of Reims.

Leading producers: Michel Arnould, Paul Bara, Bérèche, H. Billiot Fils, Cattier (Clos du Moulin), Chartogne-Taillet, Egly-Ouriet, Godmé, Krug (Clos d'Ambonnay), Benoît Lahaye, David Léclapart, Marie-Noëlle Ledru, Mailly Grand Cru, Arnaud Margaine, Benoît Marguet, Mouzon-Leroux, Pierre Paillard, Penet-Chardonnet, Eric Rodez, Jérôme Prévost, Frédéric Savard, Jean Vesselle, Vilmart.

Grande Vallée de la Marne

There are nine villages in the Grande Vallée, whose 1,830 hectares are made up of 65 per cent Pinot Noir, 19 per cent Chardonnay and 16 per cent Meunier. This relatively small but important subregion between the Vallée de la Marne to the east and the Montagne de Reims to the north is best-known for Pinot Noir, its power characterized by Philipponnat's historic, steep Clos des Goisses. Planted to 90 per cent Pinot Noir, the single *grand cru* of Aÿ is one of the region's most historic villages and would have been much on the lips of King Henry VIII of England. Although the Grande Vallée is often considered to be part of the Vallée de la Marne, it is a sufficiently distinct terroir to merit its own separate classification. Essentially, this is because the soils are more chalky compared to the clay-rich soils of the Vallée itself. 'It should really be seen as the southern flank of the Montagne de Reims,' according to Peter Liem.

Leading producers: Billecart-Salmon (Clos Sainte-Hilaire), Bollinger (Vieilles Vignes Françaises), Gaston Chiquet, René Geoffroy, Henri Giraud, Marc Hébrart, Jacquesson (Vauzelle Terme, Corne Bautray), Georges Laval, Philipponnat (Clos des Goisses), Roederer (Cristal Rosé).

Vallée de la Marne

The Vallée de la Marne, west of Cumières, is essentially Meunier country thanks to the area's mixture of clay, marl, sandy and limestone soils and a frost-prone microclimate. Its 11,500 hectares comprise 72 per cent Meunier, 16 per cent Pinot Noir and 12 per cent Chardonnay. This is a large, sprawling area of 81 villages, sitting to the north and south of the Marne River, that bisects Épernay and meanders for 64 kilometres from Cumières in the east to Saâcy-sur-Marne in the west. The vineyards of the *rive droite* ostensibly face south while the north-facing vineyards of the *rive gauche* can lay claim to higher natural acidity. In practice, exposures and altitudes on both sides vary considerably. The weather is cool, the area prone to botrytis and the clay soils are not as free-draining as the chalky soils of the Montagne and Côte des Blancs.

Leading producers: Apollonis, Dehours, Michel Loriot, Christophe Mignon, Moussé Fils, Franck Pascal, Tarlant.

Coteaux Sud d'Épernay, Coteaux du Morin, Côte de Sézanne, Vitryat and Montgueux

The Coteaux Sud d'Épernay, as the name suggests, lies immediately to the south of Épernay and consist of 11 villages covering a total of 1,200 hectares, comprising 47 per cent Meunier, 45 per cent Chardonnay and 8 per cent Pinot Noir planted in diverse soils. There are 18 villages in the Coteaux du Morin, which sits south of the Côte des Blancs; here 903 hectares are planted to 47 per cent Meunier, 40 per cent Chardonnay and 13 per cent Pinot Noir. Immediately south of the Coteaux lies the historic Côte de Sézanne, with 12 villages, an area of 1,479 hectares with a lot of clay in the soils, planted to 77 per cent Chardonnay, 18 per cent Pinot Noir and 5 per cent Meunier. East of these two small subregions, the Vitryat comprises 15 villages, whose 459 hectares, the best of which are on Turonian chalk soils, are planted to 98 per cent Chardonnay and 1 per cent each of Pinot Noir and Meunier. Montgueux, a small, sunny, south-facing chalk outcrop ('the hill of the Goths') 20 minutes to the west of Troyes in the Aube, covers 208 hectares, of which 90 per cent is planted to Chardonnay and 10 per cent to Pinot Noir.

Leading producers: Ulysse Collin, Didier Doué, Laherte Frères, Jacques Lassaigne, Bruno Michel, Taittinger (Les Folies de la Marquetterie).

Côte des Bar

Bisected in its south-western corner by the River Seine, the rolling hill-sides of the Côte des Bar comprise 63 villages and cover a vineyard area of 7,780 hectares, 23 per cent of the Champagne region, planted to 86 per cent Pinot Noir, 10 per cent Chardonnay and 4 per cent Meunier. This area is further divided into two subregions, the Barséquanais (Bar-sur-Seine) and the Bar-sur-Aubois (Bar-sur-Aube). As the closest sub-region of Champagne to Chablis, it's not entirely surprising that the soils are made up of the same Kimmeridgian marl, which comes from an older period, the Jurassic, than the Cretaceous chalk vineyards around Reims and Épernay. Within the Côte des Bar, in the steep, stony terroir of Les Riceys, the Alliance Riceys is a notable association of artisanal growers comprising Batisse-Lancelot, Pascal Manchin, Pehu Guiardel, Arnaud Tabourin and Philipaux Père et Fils.

Leading producers: Cédric Bouchard, Marie-Courtin, Devaux, Dosnon, Drappier, Charles Dufour, Pierre Gerbais, Nathalie Falmet, Fleury, Roses de Jeanne, Serge Mathieu, Val Frison, Vouette & Sorbée.

Producers

Champagne Agrapart
Avize
www.champagne-agrapart.com

If ever there was a grower who deserved to be called *homme de terroir*, it's Pascal Agrapart. Down to earth, literally, he is never so happy as when, with his son, he's fashioning his Champagnes by separately vinifying and blending the 70 or more small parcels spread over 12 hectares in seven *crus*, mostly in the Côte des Blancs, based 90 per cent on Chardonnay and 10 per cent on Pinot Noir. After graduating from the Lycée Viticole d'Avize, in 1981 Pascal returned to the domaine, founded in 1894, taking over from his father four years later. His terroir-based approach extends to ploughing to avoid compaction, cutting out herbicides and pesticides, adding compost made from local ingredients to enhance the organic life of the soil and organizing his pressings and tanks according to soil type.

Avize is the mainstay with the wines Complantée, Avizoise, Vénus and Expérience all exclusively from this *grand cru*, while 7 Crus, Terroirs and Minéral are blends – of the same vintage and soil type – that include Avize. Avizoise, first released in 1989, is from two plots with a layer of clay-rich topsoil over chalk. Minéral blends Bionnes in Cramant and

Champbouton in Avize, with the same poor, chalky soil types. Vénus (his horse of the same name, which has since died) highlights the benefit of working the soil by horse. The vines are more than 50 years old and both Minéral and Vénus are aged on the lees for between six and seven years. The wines are all *blancs de blancs*, except for 7 Crus Extra Brut, with 10 per cent Pinot Noir, and the Complantée, a field blend of the three major varieties along with Arbane, Petit Meslier and Pinot Blanc.

The wines are fermented in stainless steel and 600-litre oak hogsheads, neither fined nor filtered, and dosage is low. All wines go through malolactic fermentation. There is no dosage in the experimental Expérience Brut Nature, and the *liqueur de tirage* is made using unfermented juice from the same vineyard, La Fosse. Agrapart's wines, not least the aptly-named Minéral, exemplify the steely, mineral style of Champagne springing from Côte des Blancs chalk with low yields, picked at optimum ripeness to bring texture and balance.

Champagne Billecart-Salmon

Mareuil-sur-Aÿ

www.champagne-billecart.fr/en

Among the elite top Champagne houses, Billecart is *primus inter pares*, its discreet charm reinforced by its location, tucked away in a Mareuil-sur-Aÿ side street. The first recorded references to the Billecart family date back to 1545. The house itself was founded in 1818 following the marriage of Nicolas François Billecart and Elisabeth Salmon. In the wake of the Second World War, much Champagne had been consumed or shipped out by the Germans, but on his return Charles Roland-Billecart soldiered on. In 1952, when René Lamarle was at the winemaking helm, Charles' son Jean Roland-Billecart established the then revolutionary technique of double settling the must, in which an initial clarification is followed by a 48-hour cold settling at 4–5°C.

Billecart-Salmon had made rosé Champagne by the *saignée* method since the 1840s, but in the 1970s, Jean Roland-Billecart created a rosé Champagne which was a blend of white and red wine. This Brut Rosé, a blend of 40 per cent Chardonnay, 30 per cent Pinot Noir and 30 per cent Meunier, has today become the house's flagship cuvée, a pale, fresh, delicately balanced, berry fruity pink Champagne that's cemented its place in today's *art de vivre*.

François Roland-Billecart and his brother Antoine gradually rebuilt the house from 1973, buying new vineyards and joining forces in 2004 with the local financier Jean-Jacques Frey to bring in another 80 hectares of *grand cru* Ambonnay, Verzy and Verzenay in the Montagne de Reims and Mesnil and Avize in the Côte des Blancs. Nearly 30 years on, the house, now run by François' cousin Mathieu, makes 2.5 million bottles from an estate of 100 hectares, managing another 120 hectares and buying grapes by contract from families in around 100 hectares of vineyards. Mathieu is supported by a tasting committee of Jean, François and Antoine from the family and another four from the winemaking team.

Since the inauguration of a new *cuverie* in 2000, the house style has been amplified by the use of small thermoregulated tanks of 47 hectolitres. Some 280 individual parcels are fermented using only the first pressing to combine nuances of terroir with Billecart's sought-after freshness and elegance. Its brilliant long-term winemaker François Domi (replaced by Florent Nys in 2018) was instrumental in setting up a new *chai* of over 400 barriques in 2010 and 24 large oak vats in its bicentenary year, 2018. Oak complements the vinification process with a complex oxidative note and is the *sine qua non* of the justifiably popular Sous Bois, a one-third blend of Chardonnay, Pinot Noir and Meunier.

The wines are aged on their lees in Billecart's seventeenth and nineteenth century chalk cellars for three to four years for the non-vintage cuvées and eight to ten years for the vintage. Billecart's Pinot-dominated Vintage Brut and pure Chardonnay Blanc de Blancs are delicious, but it hits the high notes with its prestige cuvées, The Cuvée Nicolas François Billecart is richly textured and full-flavoured with a creamy mousse of delicious savoury nuttiness, the Louis Blanc de Blancs complex and elegant; Cuvée Elisabeth Salmon Rosé shows toasty complexity allied to a saline-streaked richness and impressive vinosity.

Created in 1995 in honour of the patron saint of the church in Mareuil-sur-Aÿ, Clos Saint-Hilaire is a single hectare plot of Pinot Noir planted on clay–limestone soils in a corner of Mareuil-sur-Aÿ and ploughed by draft horses. Allowing the roots to penetrate the soils results in smaller, concentrated grapes which, vinified in used burgundy oak casks and, with no dosage, reveal the true terroir. Each vintage of this intense, vinous *blanc de noirs* is distinctive, with a limited release of between 3,500 and 7,500 numbered bottles.

Champagne Bollinger

Aÿ

www.champagne-bollinger.com

Bollinger is synonymous with Aÿ and the DNA of its Champagnes is based primarily on Vallée de la Marne Pinot Noir from vineyards built up by the twentieth century's most famous Champagne widow, Tante Lily to her family, Madame Jacques to her staff. Following its foundation in 1829, the firm was awarded the Royal Warrant by the British Royal Family in 1884. It was over a century old when Touraine-born Lily Bollinger took over in 1942 at the age of 42, after her husband Jacques' death. Being polite to German officers while looking after the welfare of the company and growers, she weathered the vicissitudes of the Second World War, chain-smoking her way through roll-ups provided by head vigneron Jean Brunet.

Lily Bollinger acquired prime sites in Aÿ, Grauves, Bisseuil and Champvoisy to bring the estate closer to today's complement of 178 hectares, 85 percent in *grand* and *premier cru* sites. When houses introduced stainless steel in the 1960s, she stuck resolutely to her oak guns. So today, along with its pinot dominance, the use of 228-litre burgundy pièces, of which Bollinger have some 4,000, aged between three and ten years, is one of the defining characteristics of the Bollinger style. The barrels come from its partner Chanson, and Bollinger has started to cooper its own too, made after four years' drying from Champagne's Forêt de Cuis.

The distinctive character of Special Cuvée, roughly a fifth fermented in oak, the rest in stainless steel, results from a blend of three different years plus 5 per cent reserve wine from magnums, of which Bollinger has 800,000. Dosage has been reduced to around 7 grams per litre. For its greater complexity and ageability, the vintage Grande Année, so named from the 1976 vintage onwards, is a blend of 16 *crus*, 85–89 per cent *grand cru*, fermented entirely in oak, undergoing the second fermentation under natural cork as well as being riddled by hand and disgorged *à la volée* after some seven years on the lees. Jetting technology maintains post-disgorgement freshness.

Special Cuvée is complemented by the sumptuously strawberryish, toasty Brut Rosé launched in 2008, while Grande Année's pink mirror image is the Grande Année Rosé, which includes 5–8 per cent of red wine from Bollinger's La Côte aux Enfants vineyard in Aÿ. In 2020, it launched the new PN series to great acclaim with its seductive Bollinger

PN VZ15, a half oak, half stainless steel-fermented *blanc de noirs* mainly from Verzenay, with 20 per cent reserve wine. The PN Series, conceived in 2015 by Bollinger's chef de cave Gilles Descôtes, aims to create a new pure Pinot Noir NV Champagne every year to showcase Bollinger's Pinot Noir vineyards in Aÿ, Bouzy, Verzenay and Tauxières.

The outstanding R.D. (Recently Disgorged) launched by Lily Bollinger with the 1952 vintage in 1961, is in effect Grande Année with up to 20 years ageing on the lees. Another of Mme Bollinger's innovations was Vieilles Vignes Françaises, a remarkable *blanc de noirs* produced from two tiny plots of pre-phylloxera Pinot Noir planted *en foule*, by layering that is (provignage) in Aÿ's walled vineyards, Clos St-Jacques (21 ares) and Chaudes Terres (15 ares). BVVF is a gloriously vinous quintessence of Pinot Noir Champagne vouchsafed to the very few fortunate enough to be able to afford such hedonistic luxury.

Champagne Castelnau

Reims

www.champagne-castelnau.fr

Elisabeth Sarcelet rarely features in the glamorous pantheon of Champagne's winemakers, yet from humble intern in 1984 to becoming chef de cave in 2013, Elisabeth has been one of the longest serving winemakers in Champagne. Indeed, her contribution to the success of Castelnau was recognized when in 2016, the centenary of Castelnau's establishment, she was awarded the trophy for Winemaker of the Year. Elisabeth retired at the end of 2021, handing the pipette to Carine Bailleul, her long-term protegée.

Champagne Castelnau was launched in 1916 by a group of Épernay merchants who named it after General Edouard de Curières de Castelnau, a hero of the First World War. Popular in military and diplomatic circles of the 1920s, it morphed in 1962 into the Coopérative Régionale des Vins de Champagne. Today, 780 grape-growers own over 800 hectares in more than 150 different *crus*, bringing a great diversity of chalky subsoils mainly in the south-east corner of the Montagne around Bouzy and Trépail, and its vineyards benefit from varied climatic influences both oceanic and continental. Castelnau aims for a non-oxidative regime to preserve maximum freshness. Fermentation is typically in stainless steel and wines undergo a lengthy ageing on the lees, at least five years for the non-vintages and ten years for the vintages.

Its first prestige cuvée, the black grape-dominant, multi-vintage Hors Catégorie, was created in its anniversary year in 2016 and named after challenging mountain passes in the Tour de France, which it sponsors. The first edition was followed by Col de la Croix de Fer, altitude 2,067 metres (made June 2012, disgorged May 2017). A third edition in 2021, and perhaps the best to date, Col de la Madeleine, altitude 1,993 metres, is a selection of the best wines from 2008, 2010, 2011 and 2012, aged for six years to produce a richly gastronomic style bolstered by a tangy hint of bitterness, like a burgundy with bubbles. Tirage and disgorgement dates are printed on the back labels of Hors Catégorie and the Oenothèque collection, which includes 1995, 1996, 1998 and 2000, in magnum only. Annual production is around one million bottles.

Champagne Cattier

Chigny Les Roses

www.cattier.com

The family house of Cattier can trace its roots back to 1625 although production at its HQ in the Montagne de Reims village of Chigny-les-Roses started in 1918 under Jean Cattier. Returning home in 1916 as a wounded veteran, Jean released his first Champagne at the end of the war in 1918. Jean-Jacques Cattier took over the reins in 1971 and now runs Cattier with his son, Alexandre, representing the eleventh generation. Two fifths of the family's wines come from its 33 hectares in Chigny-les-Roses and the surrounding area, the rest from growers in the Montagne de Reims and Côte des Blancs. Based largely on Pinot Noir and Meunier, Cattier's Champagnes are voluptuously full-bodied and fleshy.

Across the main road from Chigny-les-Roses, the jewel in the Cattier crown is the 2.2-hectare Clos du Moulin, a walled vineyard that once belonged to Allart de Maisonneuve, an officer serving under Louis XV. Cattier's first harvest of Clos du Moulin, in 1951, was bottled in 1952 and released in 1956. A blend of 50 per cent Chardonnay and 50 per cent Pinot Noir, Clos du Moulin blends three good vintages, aged for between seven and ten years. The latest iterations are a blend of 2012 (65 per cent of the blend), 2009 (23 per cent) and 2008 (12 per cent), and a centenary cuvée, aged for more than 20 years, based on the 1999 (roughly 65 per cent of the blend), 1998 (around 23 per cent) and 1996 (12 per cent) vintages. There is also now a delicious 55 per cent Pinot Noir and 45 per cent Chardonnay Clos du Moulin Rosé.

Horses plough the soil to oxygenate it, and the vineyard is registered as HVE, with no use of herbicides. Eight tonnes of grapes go into the two Coquard presses at the winery at Rilly-la-Montagne, four for the old one in Chigny-les-Roses. All wines go through malolactic fermentation and dosage is on the low side at around 6 grams per litre. Some 600,000–700,000 bottles of Cattier Champagne are made annually, including on average 12,000–15,000 numbered bottles of Clos du Moulin (which is not produced every year).

To reach Cattier's 150-year-old subterranean cellars 30 metres below ground, you have to descend 119 steps. The cellar holds 1.5 million bottles and magnums. They look like any other Champagne bottles until you come across serried ranks of dazzling gold, silver and pink metallized bottles lying at a jaunty angle in their racks, as if ingots of silver and gold had been fashioned in the shape of Champagne bottles and hidden deep underground. This is the rap artist Jay-Z's brand Armand de Brignac, bought from Cattier in 2014.

Inspired by the swashbuckling hero of a novel read by Alexandre's grandmother Nelly, the name de Brignac was extended to Armand de Brignac by his aunt, Liliane. The garish label itself was created by Jean Cattier, but only used when a limited-edition silver bottle was made for the futuristic fashion designer André Courrèges. In 2000, Alexandre's father Jean-Jacques revived the process, adding the Ace of Spades icon and marketing the wine to a younger crowd. On cue, along came Jay-Z after a falling out with Roederer. To be fair, the Champagne is excellent. In 2020, its Blanc de Blancs was voted the number 1 Champagne in the world in the Best Wine of The World competition hosted by TastingBook.com. The Cattier family could scarcely believe their good fortune if they hadn't made one from it.

Champagne La Closerie

Gueux

www.champagnelacloserie.fr

Jérôme Prévost was more interested in drinking Champagne than making it, but when his mother told him that he didn't have it in him, it was all the motivation he needed to rise to the challenge. He became inspired to make wine after joining a group of young vignerons known as Valoriser (meaning 'to create value'). He was introduced to Anselme Selosse and the two men clicked, no doubt due to their artistic temperaments, and Selosse invited Prévost to work with him and make his wine in his winery, which he did, until 2003. After that he became a *garagiste*, making wine literally in the garage behind his house.

West of Reims, Prévost has 2 hectares of old-vine Meunier in the single vineyard Les Béguines. Despite the tiny size of his estate, Prévost's La Closerie Champagnes have received worldwide acclaim for their terroir character and ability to age. The soil is a unique Paleocene-era mix of fossil-rich Thanet sands and limestone and very much part of the diverse tapestry of soils that creates the potential for wines of terroir. Prévost hasn't used insecticides since 1994, or herbicides since 1996. With the microbial life of the soil encouraged, and natural yeast used, he achieves a particularly savoury cuvée with underlying saline notes full of energy that is quite different from most common or garden Meunier Champagne.

Prévost began Les Béguines in 1998, although it's not vintage-dated. The wines are fermented in 450- to 600-litre demi-muids, bringing an oxidative note. Reducing the tirage liqueur from 24.5 grams to 23 grams dials down the pressure and he doesn't rack, filter or stabilize. Dosage is low at around 2.5 grams per litre. Believing that lees ageing is a staging post on the way to post-disgorgement ageing, Prévost ages his wines on the lees for a minimum amount of time. Les Béguines, austere at first, needs at least two to three years of post-disgorgement ageing. His rosé, Fac Simile, is a rich, low dosage Champagne of great vinosity that also needs time after disgorgement. Annual production of only 13,000 or so bottles adds to the exclusivity.

Champagne Deutz

Aÿ

www.champagne-deutz.com

Deutz, which I used to pronounce as 'doyts' but now know as the francophone 'derts', is one of the small but perfectly formed Champagne elite. The Classic NV Brut of this Aÿ-based house is reliably on song with its full flavoured, textural roundness and finesse, and it excels in its *blanc de blancs*, rosé and vintage wines, but it really kicks into full gear with its single parcel cuvées, Hommage à William Deutz La Côte Glacière and Hommage à William Deutz Meurtet, along with two exceptional flagship cuvées in Amour de Deutz and Cuvée William Deutz.

Hommage and Cuvée William are named in honour of William Deutz, one of Madame Bollinger's clerks from Prussia, who relocated from his native Aix-La-Chapelle to join forces with Pierre-Hubert Geldermann in 1843 to create Deutz & Geldermann on the southern slopes of the Montagne de Reims. In recent times, after André Lallier-Deutz bought Delas and spread his sparkling wings to California and New Zealand, hard times kicked in in the wake of the crash that followed the Gulf War. The firm was bought by Roederer in 1993, which sold off Maison Deutz in California's Arroyo Grande in 1997.

Since taking over in 1996, Fabrice Rosset, Roederer's former MD, has expanded production from just over a half a million to nearly two-and-a-half million bottles. Under chef de cave Michel Davesne, the vineyard management too has expanded beyond the house's own 46 hectares to working with 60 suppliers spanning another 250–300 hectares. Each parcel is pressed and vinified separately using only the free run and first press juice and the wines, which undergo malolactic fermentation, are stored in small stainless steel vats to preserve freshness until the blending. Deutz Brut Classic and Brut Rosé account for 80 per cent of production, while up to 40 per cent of each harvest is held back for the reserve wines. Tirage ageing is in Deutz's two miles of subterranean chalk cellars.

When I last tasted Cuvée William Deutz, the 2006, disgorged in 2015, was still full of vigour and the 2002 a monument of complex, toasty amplitude complemented by a minerally streak. The more mature cuvées were remarkable, the 1996 a slick of richness underpinned by an eyewatering Granny Smith smear of tartness, a magnificent 1995 displaying wonderful development, light toast and a touch of honey, and an equally impressive 1988 was all toast and apples dipped in honey, with mouthwateringly superdry, minerally complexity.

Despite challenging weather conditions in 2010, Deutz made a blend of two Pinot Noir parcels derived from the La Côte Glacière and Meurtet parcels in the heart of the Maison Deutz' vineyards in Aÿ. The wine, 2010 Hommage à William Deutz Parcelles d'Aÿ, was aged for seven years on its lees. Since the 2012 vintage, La Côte Glacière and Meurtet have been separated into two exceptional single vineyard Pinot Noir-based cuvées. My favourite, if I had to pick one, is La Côte Glacière, whose origins recall Alfred de Vigny's 1853 poem 'La bouteille à la mer': 'The mousse of Aï glows with the light of happiness; At the very bottom of the glass, he catches a glimpse of France.'

Dom Pérignon

Épernay
www.domperignon.com

That a multi-million bottle production prestige cuvée Champagne can be talked about in the same breath as Krug and Cristal owes much to the creative energy of Richard Geoffroy, chef de cave of Moët & Chandon's prestige brand for nearly three decades until a youthful Vincent Chaperon stepped into his shoes at the end of 2018. Geoffroy took Dom Pérignon and created a separate luxury brand, doubling the number of vintage releases, burnishing its credentials as a celebrity-endorsed icon and establishing the late-disgorged series Plénitudes (originally Oenothèque), designed to show the revitalizing effects of late disgorgement.

The first cuvée of Dom Pérignon was the 1921, although it didn't assume the name until 1936 when Robert-Jean de Vogüé, Moët's marketing director, decided to use the brand name given by Mercier to Moët & Chandon in 1927 on Francine Duran-Mercier's marriage to Paul Chandon-Moët. A year before, in 1935, Moët had shipped Cuvée Centenaire, which bore an identical bottle and shield-shaped label that included Deletain's vine shoot and grape bunch motif, for Simon Brothers in London. It was initially produced only from vineyards owned by the Abbé de Hautvillers and bought by Moët in 1822, but production grew when Moët bought Lanson's vineyards in the 1990s.

With 550 hectares of *grand cru* and 250 hectares of *premier cru* vineyards, Dom Pérignon is a Chardonnay–Pinot Noir blend from as many as 20 different villages. Some 16 are *grand cru*, including Chouilly, Cramant, Avize and Le Mesnil for the Chardonnay component, and Aÿ, Bouzy, Mailly and Verzenay for the Pinot Noir. Average yields are around 10 tonnes per hectare. The wine is made in the same Épernay premises as Moët but the winemaking team is separate. The reductive style of winemaking, in stainless steel only with a steadily decreasing dosage, results in an elegant Champagne of great depth of flavour and longevity. Its rosé counterpart, first launched with the 1959 vintage, uses more Pinot Noir and often demands longer ageing.

For Geoffroy, the 'yin-yang' aim in blending was 'to restore a state of duality, of youth and maturity, of rigour and generosity, of apparent fragility and a statement of presence'. According to Vincent Chaperon, Dom Pérignon is made with a 'blossoming' in the first year aimed at capturing the consistency of Dom Pérignon's 'signature' and the inconsistency of climate in a harmonious whole. Second, the blending builds during the picking, the pressing and the pre-blending juices in the vats, culminating in the tasting. The third commitment is to complexity brought about by maturation. Not surprisingly Dom Pérignon has shown best in the recent excellent vintages of 2002, 2008 and 2012, the latter so effortlessly seamless and crowd-pleasing that it may even be the best from a trio of greats.

Geoffroy's legacy is the creation of different peak times for the enjoyment of Dom Pérignon based on the revitalizing effects of leaving the lees in the bottle to work its magic. Dom Pérignon is aged for seven to eight years, P2 for 10–12 years, while P3 is released 30 years or longer after the vintage. Dom Pérignon and Dom Pérignon P2 are 'twins', but there are differences between the two. The wine for P2, accounting for less than 10 per cent of Dom Pérignon but growing, is set apart from the start with a cork stopper for greater complexity and vibrancy. Generally P2 receives a lower dosage thanks to the extra richness engendered by maturation.

Dom Pérignon

Champagne Drappier

Urville, Côte des Bar

www.champagne-drappier.com

Drappier was Charles de Gaulle's favourite Champagne when he retired to nearby Colombey-Les-Deux-Eglises. (And it was mine too after I stopped off in Urville and ended up carting home two cases of Drappier Rosé Champagne in half-bottles, which proceeded to fill theatre and concert interval needs.) South-east of the delightful Aube capital of Troyes, Urville is a sleepy rural village in an undulating countryside of Limousin cows, green pasture and woodland and rustic names like Ource and Arce. Originally a family of drapers (hence Drappier), a Drappier ancestor settled in Urville to establish the estate, selling wines in the nineteenth century to the likes of Moët & Chandon, Veuve Clicquot and Heidsieck.

Memories framed in sepia-tinted photos hark back to 1911, when riots rocked this tranquil spot, which was much loved and painted by Renoir. During the stand-off, Michel Drappier's grandfather, George Collot, nicknamed Père Pinot for planting Pinot Fin, a strain of Pinot Noir, made a peace offering of Champagne and soon soldiers and growers were sitting down together playing cards. Michel's father, André, introduced the more frost-resistant Meunier after damaging frosts in the 1950s and when Michel arrived in 1979 after studying at Dijon and Beaune, he brought in Chardonnay. On Kimmeridgian limestone and marl soils, the 62-hectare estate is now over two-thirds Pinot Noir, nearly a third Chardonnay and Meunier with a smattering of Pinot Blanc, Arbanne, Petit Meslier and Fromenteau. Parcels in Pierry, Coulommes-la-Montagne, Mesnil-sur-Oger and Chouilly help to bring freshness and Drappier lease and buy in grapes for a total annual production of around 1.5 million bottles.

On his arrival, Michel moved towards lower intervention in the vineyard with no herbicides or fungicides. After gentle pressing by Coquard press, fermentation is in stainless steel with reduced levels of sulphur (there is even a 100 per cent Pinot Noir Brut Nature Sans Soufre) and a return to oak barrels, with barriques and larger oak casks from the Forêt de Tronçais. Since 2002, Michel has built up a perpetual reserve in five 5,000-litre foudres based on Urville Pinot Noir, and a series of further reserves separated by variety, vintage and *cru*. Drappier specializes in large-format bottles including the Primat (27 litres) and the Melchizedek (30 litres), an Aubois monster that should perhaps be named an Oh Boy. The result of Michel's back-to-the-future philosophy is finely crafted Champagnes based on the personality of Aube Pinot Noir, with red fruit characters par excellence.

Champagne Egly-Ouriet

Ambonnay

contact@egly-ouriet.fr

Francis Egly, fourth-generation head of Ambonnay grower–producer Egly-Ouriet, is a thoughtful perfectionist on a constant quest for ripe fruit with help from a *grand cru* terroir in which vines are on average 40 years old. With burgundy as his model, he bottles at lower atmospheres than the traditional five. After returning home from his studies, Francis started working with his father Michel in 1982, at a time when his father sold most of his fruit to the négociant. Bottling increased, and in 1989 he made an experimental bottling of a Pinot Noir-based *blanc de noirs*. A watershed moment, it was met with great acclaim. From 1990, he started to pick his grapes fully ripe, stopping filtration in 1995 and fining in 1996. Gradually, burgundy oak maturation was introduced.

Francis Egly aims for low yields as one of the keys to ripeness. He avoids insecticides, ploughs regularly, uses only organic compost, practises shoot-thinning and green harvesting and harvests late. His cool, thick-walled, capacious concrete cellars, built in 2006, are gravity-fed and temperature controlled. After partial or whole fermentation in oak, with no fining or filtration, and malolactic fermentation avoided in warm years, his wines are left to age on the lees in barrel and spend at least 48 months on the lees with some cuvées aged for 100 or more months. There is a high level of reserve wine in the blends (40–50 per cent) and low dosage, depending on the year.

Egly has 10 hectares in *grand cru*, mostly Ambonnay, also Bouzy, Verzenay and Verzy planted, on south-east-facing chalky clay over deep chalk, to 70 per cent Pinot Noir and 30 per cent Chardonnay. His 1.5 hectares in Bisseuil *premier cru* is the source of Les Vignes de Bisseuil (70 per cent Chardonnay, 15 per cent Pinot Noir and 15 per cent Meunier). From the family of his wife, Annick, Les Vignes de Vrigny is a 100 per cent Meunier cuvée made from 2 hectares of sandy-clay *premier cru* vineyards. From 3.5 hectares in Trigny, a new cuvée, Les Prémices, is one-third each Pinot Noir, Meunier and Chardonnay. Egly blends 70 per cent Pinot Noir and 30 per cent Chardonnay for his full-flavoured, densely textured brut tradition and rosé. The V.P. Extra Brut is given lengthy ageing on the lees, while the quintessentially Pinot Noir Blanc de Noirs Vieilles Vignes Grand Cru, made from old vines in the Ambonnay *lieu-dit* of Les Crayères, is his cuvée prestige, his calling card and the wine that's earned him cult status.

Champagne Geoffroy

Aÿ

www.champagne-geoffroy.com

Originally from Cumières in the Vallée de la Marne, with roots going back to the seventeenth century, the Geoffroy family started to produce their own Champagnes at the beginning of the 1950s when Roger Geoffroy and his wife Julienne decided to add value to grape-growing. Their son René developed the vineyards with the help of his wife Bernadette. When their son Jean-Baptiste returned to the family estate after viticultural college in the late 1980s, he and his wife, Karine, decided to relocate to expanded premises in Aÿ, where Champagne Geoffroy is a founding member of the Terres et Vins grouping.

Eleven of the estate's 14 hectares remain in *premier cru* Cumières, where 35 plots of Chardonnay (24 per cent), Meunier (34 per cent) and Pinot Noir (42 per cent), benefit from sunlit exposures, while the remaining 3 hectares are in Damery, Hautvillers and Fleury-la-Rivière. The soils are ploughed for aeration and herbicides avoided, organic manure is used and grass is allowed to grow between the rows. Picked at optimum ripeness, the grapes are pressed and vinified by plot in a range of tanks and different sized casks. Blends are decided on tasting and Jean-Baptiste avoids malolactic fermentation to maintain freshness. Bottles are stored in deep chalk cellars for between three and eight years, depending on the vintage.

The dosage varies according to style, from zero for the Pureté Brut Nature, a blend of 50 per cent Meunier, 40 per cent Pinot Noir and 10 per cent Chardonnay, to 10 grams per litre for the pure Pinot Noir Rosé de Saignée Brut Premier Cru. A relative newcomer to the range, Les Houtrants Complantés is a non-vintage field blend with Petit Meslier and Arbanne blended with the three main varieties. From a single *lieu-dit* in Cumières, Les Tiersaudes is pure Meunier. Vintages are kept separate in magnum and blended, the first release being a blend of 2008, 2009, 2010 and 2011. The wines are deliciously fresh and fruity with a degree of intensity, especially in the old vine, flagship Terre Millésime, and a seriousness of purpose that Jean-Baptiste and Karine are hoping will be continued by the next generation, daughters Margaux, Sacha, Rosalie, Colombine and Azalée.

Champagne Pierre Gimonnet

Cuis

www.champagne-gimonnet.com

The Gimonnets were originally grape growers, until the depression of 1929 led Olivier and Didier's grandfather, Pierre, to start bottling. However, after joining the family firm in 1955, it was their father, Michel, who took Gimonnet to the next level with his intuitive understanding of the expression each parcel could bring to their Champagnes. Today, Gimonnet is a name to be reckoned with. True horny-handed sons of terroir, Olivier and Didier are among the biggest growers in the region, with 29 hectares of vines in the Côte des Blancs' Cuis and Vertus and the *grands crus* of Cramant, Chouilly, Oger and Aÿ. Their meticulous focus on Chardonnay makes them a leading exponent of the *blanc de blancs* style.

More than two-thirds of their *grand cru* vines are over 40 years old, helping via low yields to bring about the ripeness and concentration that they – and we – are looking for. Rather than base their Champagnes on single vineyards for the *grands crus*, which they find can be too rich and powerful, they prefer to blend with a proportion of grapes from their 14 hectares of Cuis fruit, which provides the racy backbone, freshness, texture and 'soul' they aim to express. Fermentation in stainless steel in small tanks allows for blending by parcel. Reserve wines are stored after a micro-fermentation in the bottle to maintain freshness; the process is labour-intensive but serves their purpose.

Two-thirds of the range is non-vintage, the other third is best characterized by their classic Fleuron, a blend of Cramant, Chouilly and Cuis. The zero dosage version of the flagship Cuvée Fleuron, Oenophile Non-Dosé Premier Cru, is stainless steel-fermented and spends five to six years on the lees, combining lees-aged honeycomb and light toast richness of texture with a vivid bone-dry freshness. The Perlé de Gimonnet 'Gastronome' Premier Cru, intended for drinking with food, is made with lower pressure to create a creamy mousse. The prestige cuvées, the Special Club Vintage Collection and the three Special Club vintage *grands crus*, Oger, Cramant and Chouilly, are intensely vinous, balanced expressions of the Côte des Blancs in all its diverse glory.

Champagne Henri Giraud

Aÿ

www.champagne-giraud.com

In the days when the words, or scores at least, of wine writing guru Robert Parker were accepted like tablets of stone, his proclamation that Champagne Giraud was the finest house no one had ever heard of ensured that everyone thereafter heard loud and clear about a house that had been quietly but effectively ploughing a furrow, or several, for generations. Since Claude Giraud came on board, he has taken the house, with its 12 hectares of vineyards in Aÿ, to new levels of distinction.

It was the 1990 Fut de Chêne that took the world by storm, thanks in part to the reintroduction of Argonne oak from the forest of Argonne north-east of Aÿ. Claude engaged the knowledgeable cooper Camille Gauthier to cut and dry Argonne oak staves, which were sent to various coopers for construction into casks. His identification of 10 different plots (among them Châtrices, Beaulieu and Lachalade) was not for marketing but rather because he felt instinctively that the wood brings a gentler texture and blends well as part of the terroir. Around a third of Claude's production now relies on Argonne oak for its vinification.

That Fut de Chêne has now been replaced by his rich, firm prestige cuvée Argönne (the umlaut is a tribute to Aÿ), made only in new Argonne oak; a proportion of the revenue derived from it contributes to the forest's sustainability. Pinot Noir and oak dominant and on the oxidative side, these are wines of substantial vinosity made to be drunk with food. This is especially true of the Homage au Pinot Noir, which is smokily aromatic and richly toasty with a crunchy berry bite. The exception is Esprit de Giraud which, although still Pinot Noir based, is lighter and fresher – and cheaper – in more of an aperitif style, albeit still thoroughly appetizing.

Champagne Gosset

Épernay

www.champagne-gosset.com

Eighty-four years before Dom Pierre Pérignon set foot in the Abbey of Hautvillers, Pierre Gosset, the alderman of Aÿ, was the first to open a winery in the Champagne region. Since this was a century before the *méthode champenoise* was established, his *vin de champagne* was a still wine. Gosset has been one of the most traditional Champagne houses and although sold to the Renaud-Cointreau group in 1993, continuity of style was maintained by its brilliant winemaker Jean-Pierre Mareigner during his tenure of over 30 years until his death in 2016. Today, the chef de cave is Odilon de Varine, who joined Champagne Gosset in 2006, assisted by deputy cellarmaster, Gabrielle Malagu.

With no vineyards of its own, Champagne Gosset sources grapes from 140 hectares spread over a patchwork of terroirs and varied soils, albeit 75 per cent limestone subsoils. Gosset uses only the first pressing and, in its modern Épernay cellars, employs stainless steel for the first fermentation, working the lees to bring depth and richness to the base wine. Malolactic fermentation is avoided for 'the transparent expression of each parcel' and the dosage has come significantly down from its 12–13 grams per litre in the 1990s. Since the Cointreau acquisition, production has doubled to almost one million bottles, with rosé accounting for thirty per cent.

From the core range, the Grand Blanc de Blancs Brut stands out, a zesty, fresh and toasty 15-village blend. A special parcel, the Grand Blanc de Noirs Extra Brut is a superb, complex expression of Pinot Noir mostly from the *grand cru* vineyards of Aÿ, Ambonnay and Verzy. Also from a special parcel, a vinously rich pure Meunier, Grand Blanc de Meunier NV, was introduced by Odilon de Varine in 2018. The top-of-the range prestige line, Célébris Extra Brut, first launched in 1988, is aged for ten years on the lees to give it a delectably toasty creaminess. The 2008 Célébris Rosé is a worthy counterpart. Two new wines with extended lees-ageing have been added to the range, the better of which is the superbly savoury 12 Ans de Cave à minima. A niche rosé cuvée, Petite Douceur Rosé, is extra dry with a generous fruitiness.

Champagne Grand Siècle

Tours-sur-Marne

www.grandsiecle.com

Named after the era of Louis XIV, Grand Siècle is the jewel in the Laurent-Perrier crown. Even the elegant long-necked bottle is a replica of a 1705 handblown bottle from the Roi Soleil's reign. Although it dates back to 1812, it was only after the Second World War that Laurent-Perrier burst onto the scene, when the flamboyant resistance fighter Bernard de Nonancourt, aged 28, was appointed Chairman and Chief Executive of a house then ranked ninety-eighth in Champagne. At a time when a blend of vintage years was virtually unknown, de Nonancourt created a multi-vintage prestige cuvée based on the three exceptional years of 1952, 1953 and 1955, which was released in 1960 on the three-hundredth anniversary of Louis XIV's marriage.

Exclusively made from *grand cru* grapes, Grand Siècle is composed of Chardonnay, typically 55 per cent, and Pinot Noir, 45 per cent, blended by Laurent-Perrier's chef de cave, Michel Fauconnet, before being aged in bottle and magnum for between 10 and 13 years, in Laurent-Perrier's subterranean cellars. The Chardonnay comes from the Côte des Blancs vineyards of Le Mesnil, Oger, Avize, Chouilly and Cramant, while the Pinot Noir is sourced from Ambonnay, Bouzy, Mailly, Verzenay, Verzy and Louvois in the Montagne de Reims, and Tours sur Marne in the Vallée de la Marne. The new, dedicated Grand Siècle winery contains

14 stainless steel tanks each with a capacity of 110 hectolitres. For the second fermentation, the wine is sealed with cork and clip.

With no indication of the chosen vintages, how could collectors know which iteration of Grand Siècle they were buying or indeed how long to cellar it for? When the twenty-second iteration of Grand Siècle was released in magnum and the twenty-fourth iteration in bottle for the first time, the vintage blends were indicated on the website and in accompanying literature. A special cuvée, Les Réserves Grand Siècle N°571J made in limited edition magnums and, for the first time ever, in jeroboams, was originally launched to celebrate the house's bicentenary. A selection of 1995 (60 per cent), 1993 (20 per cent) and 1990 (20 per cent), it was kept for 16 years on lees before being manually riddled on pupitres with labelling by hand.

Current iterations based on a different trio of outstanding vintages include the Grand Siècle Iteration, #22, a blend of 2004 (55 per cent), 2002 (30 per cent) and 1999 (15 per cent), Les Réserves Grand Siècle iteration #17 (1995, 1993 and 1990) and Grand Siècle Iteration #24. The latter, consisting of 60 per cent of the 2007, 20 per cent of the 2006 and 20 per cent of the 2004 vintage, shows aromas of almond blossom and spice, followed by a featherbed mousse of expansively creamy bubbles whose delicacy and freshness belie its savoury, dry finish; evidence, if it were needed, that Grand Siècle, always complex and elegant, is one of Champagne's prestige cuvée greats.

Champagne Alfred Gratien

Épernay

www.alfredgratien.com

I am not ashamed to admit that Alfred Gratien, in the form of The Wine Society's own-label Champagne since 1906, has long been my own house Champagne. The year 1906 was the year after the first Jaeger, Gaston, became cellarmaster, handing the job down to his son, Charles and in turn, Jean-Pierre in 1966. Alfred Gratien originally founded sparkling wine ventures in Saumur and Épernay in 1864. Both businesses were bought by the German Sekt producer Henkell & Söhnlein in 2000, yet, with the addition of a new *cuverie* for blending and storage, the brand has remained staunchly traditional under Nicolas Jaeger, who joined his father in 1990 before becoming chef de cave in 2007.

The estate owns just 1.56 hectares of vineyards, *grand* and *premier cru*, in the Côte des Blancs, making up the rest of its needs through long-term contracts with around one hundred loyal grape growers. With continuity across four generations, one of the keys to the Gratien style is entire *sous-bois* oak vinification in used 228-litre Chablis barrels. The biscuity aromatics are the hallmark of the Brut NV style with a fair whack of Meunier from excellent sites in the Marne Valley. The Chardonnay proportion has increased recently and only the first pressing is used. The vintage wines too include a substantial proportion of Chardonnay, much of it from Le Mesnil, Cramant and Chouilly.

Each *cru* is vinified separately and in order to preserve the bright fruit character during lees ageing, during maturation (in some 1,000 barrels) the cuvées do not undergo malolactic fermentation. Alfred Gratien has always used corks, not crown caps, for the maturation of its vintage Champagnes. As Nicolas Jaeger explains, 'the permeability of the cork as well as its suppleness preserve freshness while encouraging the micro-oxygenation that's crucial for the wine's development'. Over 1.3 million bottles are left to rest in the house's chalk cellars, classic brut cuvées for four years, vintages for ten years and the cuvée Paradis for six to seven years.

Champagne Charles Heidsieck

Reims

www.charlesheidsieck.com

'Cette porte doit rester imperativement fermée', says the warning sign. As the Fort Knox-like steel door in Charles Heidsieck's Reims garden snaps shut, 116 chalk steps take you 65 feet down to its second century Gallo-Roman chalk cellars, where the company's 47 Bond-like echo chambers are chock full of rare old vintages. After the Descours family's EPI Group purchased the company from Rémy Cointreau in 2011 for the sum of €412 million, along with its bigger sibling, Piper-Heidsieck, Stephen Leroux, its urbane MD, grasped the nettle of restoring the house to its former glory. The first in a series of rare older vintages, the Collection Crayères, was released in 2017, two years after Cyril Brun, Guide Hachette's Winemaker of the year 2020, was appointed new chef de cave.

Charles Heidsieck's flamboyant founder Charles-Camille was known as Champagne Charlie by American high society after his success in selling 25,000 cases of Champagne in America by the beginning of the American Civil War. In 1862, when the wheeler-dealer was caught in possession of letters from French textile companies offering to supply clothing to the Confederate armies, he was arrested and flung in jail for four months. He returned to France in 1863 a bankrupt but, through an unlikely stroke of good fortune, he inherited a third of Denver, Colorado, allowing him to buy Charles Heidsieck Champagne.

Its first prestige cuvée, the 1955 Cuvée Royale, was launched in 1963, but when Joseph Henriot and his cousin Jean-Marc Heidsieck decided that it was not in keeping with the style of the house, they charged chef de cave Daniel Thibault with creating a new prestige cuvée that would push the style and elegance envelope. The result, Champagne Charlie, an intuitive distillation of the best of each vintage, was made in five vintages (1979, 1981, 1982, 1983 and 1985) before Thibault's untimely death in 2002 at the age of 55. It was then discontinued when Charles Heidsieck was absorbed in 1985 by Rémy Cointreau, which happened to have Krug in its portfolio.

Thibault's enduring legacy is Charles Heidsieck Brut Réserve. It has been sourced from 60 different *crus* since the 2007 harvest, with over 100 individual cuvées fermented in stainless steel to create the house style. Sixty per cent is a blend of equal proportions of Chardonnay, Pinot Noir and Meunier and 40 per cent consists of reserve wines with an average age of ten years. In a distinctive bottle shape modelled on Crayère No. 9, it is neither oxidative nor reductive but, as a 2020 London tasting of eight Brut Réserves, Mis en Cave, from 2017 (base 2016) back to 1987 (base 1986) showed, it is consistently aromatic, fleshy, butterscotchy, creamy and delicious. Alas, while the term Mis en Cave represented the year of bottling following the vintage of the base wine, it had to be relegated to the back label when the Comité Champagne thought it could be confused with vintage.

The remarkable consistency of quality continues with the Blanc des Millénaires, an all-Chardonnay prestige cuvée that was itself overshadowed by Champagne Charlie in the two overlapping vintages of 1983 and 1985. The 2004 vintage is still young, while in great vintages such as 1983, 1985 and 1995, it ages beautifully, turning into a wine of super-toasty fruit and exotic richness while retaining its freshness. Stephen Leroux has indicated, tantalizingly, that Champagne Charlie is to be reincarnated: 'We have purchased the bottle and done the mould again and Champagne Charlie will be on the market once again,' he promises.

Champagne Henriot

Reims

www.champagne-henriot.com

Linked principally to high quality Chardonnay, Henriot's range, from non-vintage via vintage to its two prestige cuvées, is one of the top drawer Champagnes. Much of the credit must go the late Joseph Henriot, wheeler-dealer extraordinaire, who bought and sold Charles Heidsieck then exchanged Henriot for a share in Veuve Clicquot in 1985 and then bought back the family firm in 1994, only without the vineyards, which Louis Vuitton Moët Hennessy (LVMH) hung on to. Since his uncle's death in 2015, Gilles de Larouzière Henriot – eighth generation of the Henriot family – has been at the Henriot helm.

Since the reacquisition, the house has invested in 36 hectares of real estate, sourcing the rest of its requirements from another 150 hectares in a wide diversity of terroirs. In particular there is Chardonnay from the Côte des Blancs and northern Montagne de Reims, while Pinot Noir comes mainly from Mailly, Verzy and Verzenay in the Montagne and vineyards in the Côte des Bar. Freshness and elegance were the watch-words for Henriot's recently departed cellarmaster Laurent Fresnet, who took over from Odilon de Varine in 2006, before leaving for Mumm in 2019. His successor, Champagne-born Alice Tétienne, who has worked at Krug, Nicolas Feuillatte and Laurent Perrier, followed as cheffe de cave in February 2020.

The many plots from which Henriot sources its grapes are vinified separately in stainless steel and all cuvées typically undergo malolactic fermentation. The consistent Brut Souverain and the delicate and complex Blanc de Blancs receive 40–50 per cent reserve wines, while the elegantly fresh and tangy Rosé receives a little less. Wines then spend between three and five years on the lees. The lipsmackingly toasty *grand cru*-based Millésimé spends six years on the lees, and prestige cuvée, Cuvée Hemera, also a blend of *grands crus*, with 50 per cent each of Chardonnay and Pinot Noir, at least 12 years. Dosage is systematically reduced from 9 grams per litre for the Rosé, to 8 grams per litre or so for Brut Souverain and Blanc de Blancs, 6 grams per litre for the Millésimé, and just 5 grams per litre for Cuvée Hemera.

My first experience of Henriot's prestige cuvée was buying three magnums of Baron Philippe de Rothschild for a relative song from under the nose of Christie's auctioneer, the late Michael Broadbent (after the auction, he said he would have snapped it up if I hadn't). The name was changed to Cuvée des Enchanteleurs before its delightful, almost white burgundy-like incarnation, Cuvée Hemera, appeared under Laurent Fresnet. Cuve 38 is a cuvée made entirely from the perpetual reserve of

Chardonnay built up in a single tank (numbered 38) by Joseph Henriot from 1990 onwards. Bottled in 2007 and released in 2014, this luxurious collector's item is released only in magnum, with the last four digits of the lot code indicating the month and year of disgorgement.

Champagne André Jacquart

Vertus, Côte des Blancs

www.champagne-andre-jacquart.com

Not to be confused with the massive cooperative Champagne Jacquart, André Jacquart started the domaine-bottling of Champagnes in Le Mesnil-sur-Oger on the Côtes des Blancs in 1958. The modern story begins in 2004 when Marie, the daughter of Pascal Doyard and Chantal Jacquart, moved to larger premises in Vertus. Combining the two inherited properties of her parents gave her 24 hectares to play with. Most of the 200 vineyard parcels are located in Le Mesnil and Oger and the rest are in Vertus (4 hectares), the Aube (2 hectares) and the Aisne (2 hectares).

Vineyard management is as close to organic as possible, and thanks to careful cultivation of the soils, Marie has achieved a step change in quality since taking over from her parents. In the cellar, there are two Coquard PAI presses while some 200 burgundy and Champagne oak casks testify to a substantial degree of oak fermentation, which can be tasted in the wines, all *blancs de blancs* except for the rosé. The wines are kept on the lees for up to eight months before tirage and end up super-dry, thanks to low dosage and the blocking of the malolactic fermentation. Ageing on the lees is four years for the non-vintage and five to eight years for the vintage.

The Vertus Premier Cru Brut NV, with 20 per cent reserve wine, 60 per cent barrel-fermented and held in tank for eight months, shows nutty crème fraîche aromas and creamy mousse. Both the bone dry Le Mesnil Grand Cru Brut Nature and its counterpart Le Mesnil Grand Cru NV are distinctively oaky with an elegantly dry, smoky mousse. Deep pink and strawberryish with an appetizingly dry vinosity, the Rosé de Saignée Experience Premier Cru NV is made from 80 per cent Pinot Noir from Vertus and 20 per cent Chardonnay from Le Mesnil with a maceration of 24 hours in the press and barrel-fermented. On average, the estate produces 100,000 bottles a year, using only Côte des Blancs fruit.

Champagne Jacquesson

Dizy

www.champagnejacquesson.com

Jacquesson is a tale of two golden eras. In the first, after its establishment in Châlons-sur-Marne by Memmie Jacquesson in the ninth year after the start of the French Revolution, Jacquesson was lionized by Napoleon Bonaparte, who awarded it a gold medal on one of his visits. By the time of the Paris World Exhibition in 1867, it was producing more than one million bottles. But it lost its mojo after the death of Adolphe Jacquesson in 1875. Set on the road to recovery by the de Tassigny family in 1925, when they moved the firm to Reims, it has returned to top form since it was acquired in 1974 by two brothers, Jean-Hervé and Laurent Chiquet, moving to Dizy, since when it has become a hugely impressive boutique house of uncompromising quality standards.

Jacquesson is nominally a négociant but has the feel of a grower. Its 28 hectares of vineyards, 17 hectares in the Grande Vallée and 11 hectares in the Côte des Blancs, provide it with some 80 per cent of its needs, allowing it to control the all-important aspects of viticulture from pruning to crushing. It sets great store by its management of the vineyards by traditional growing methods aimed at reducing the potential vigour of the soil and maximizing ripeness and health: little or no fertilizer, ploughing of the soil, sowing and mowing of grass between rows. Production has shrunk from upwards of 400,000 bottles 20 years ago to 250,000 today.

Attention to detail in the vineyard is accompanied by an equal focus in the cellar. Only the first pressing is used, the juice fermented in 500 litre neutral oak casks. Resting on its lees, the wine is stirred weekly, clarification occurs naturally and malolactic fermentation is routinely carried out. The first in a series of blends, Cuvée 728, was based on the 2000 vintage and named for the production number of the Cuvée n°1 made in 1898 to celebrate the house's one-hundredth anniversary. With around 20 per cent reserve wines, it's a blend of Jacquesson's three *grand cru* vineyards in Aÿ, Avize and Oiry and two *premiers crus*, Dizy and Hautvillers, vinified in oak casks and nearly always unfiltered, disgorged after four years with low dosage.

Its vintage Champagnes are single-vineyard wines, reflecting both the character of the vineyard and the vintage. Best-known is the Grand Cru Avize Champ Caïn, a *blanc de blancs* of exceptional finesse and minerality. In contrast, the Vauzelles Terme from a tiny 0.3-hectare parcel in Aÿ, is made from pure Pinot Noir, the 2002 being a particularly good example. Corne Bautray, from Jacquesson's home village of Dizy, is a *blanc de blancs* so good that it defies its location on pebble and clay soils, while Terres Rouges is a richly full-bodied *blanc de noirs* made from pure Pinot Noir. There is a late-disgorged version of the Cuvée, D.T., and late disgorged versions of the single vineyard Champagnes.

Champagne René Jolly

Landreville

www.jollychamp.com

René Jolly was established in 1737 in Landreville, in the Kimmeridgian terroir of the Côte des Bar, famous for its Pinot Noir. The family are proud of the fact that their ancestor Jean-Baptiste Jolly fought in the Crimean war under Napoleon III and was decorated by Queen Victoria. Since 2000, the family-owned business has been run by Pierre-Eric Jolly, who was born in Troyes in 1974 and who also heads up the Route du Champagne, which organizes local events. Certified for HVE level 3, Jolly works without chemical fertilizers and produces the Champagnes exclusively from the house's 14 hectares of vineyards across five plots in Landreville, planted 77 per cent to Pinot Noir and 23 per cent to Chardonnay. Annual production is 40,000 bottles.

Grapes are harvested as late as possible and pressed by traditional Coquard press with only the cuvée used. Cellar work is traditional with no filtration. The *liqueur d'expédition* is home-made and disgorgement is *à la volée*. The wines undergo malolactic fermentation, remaining on the lees for between three and fourteen years. The local oak used to make their barrels imparts a gently smoky and delicate vanilla flavour from twice-toasting at a low temperature, giving their Editio cuvée, whose base spends eight weeks in cask, its distinctive flavour. Editio is also aged on cork rather than crown cap. The Jolly wines are aptly named, crowd-pleasing Champagnes, if not overly complex, in particular the Blanc de Noirs. The Editio is a step up, a non-vintage prestige blend of 50 per cent Pinot Noir and 50 per cent Chardonnay with a rich mousse that combines dried fruit and smoky undertones in an opulent, winey Champagne that ticks all the right boxes.

Champagne Krug

Reims

www.krug.com

'I began my fancy for it with a '65', wrote George Saintsbury in his *Notes on a Cellar Book*, recalling Krug 'as being, though dry, that "winy wine" as Thackeray describes it.' In a diary entry in 1848, Joseph Krug's founding principle was that, faced with the challenges of climatic variation, there should always be two Champagnes of equal quality: vintage on the one hand, 'Champagne of circumstances', and on the other a cuvée that would transcend vintage 'to re-create the most generous expression of Champagne every year regardless of annual variations in climate'. After the Second World War, when winemaking was modernizing, Paul Krug, the current director Olivier's grandfather, continued to ferment in seasoned French oak barrels of 205 litres and, going against the grain, as it were, he included a substantial proportion of Meunier in the final blend.

So it is that Krug Grande Cuvée, a blend of wines from several vintage years, aims at capturing the most generous expression of Champagne regardless of vintage. The name changed from Private Cuvée to Grande Cuvée when Krug joined Rémy Martin to bring stability and the financing of Krug's huge stock along with access to new markets. The result is that the first job of cheffe de cave Julie Cavil and her tasting committee is to select the broadest spectrum of character from more than 120, sometimes up to 250 wines, 80 per cent from contracted growers, to then create from the crème de le crème of the year a prestige cuvée of richness of aroma and flavour, with six to ten years of ageing on the lees.

Varying proportions of its raw material come from some 20–25 villages, the most important being Le Mesnil and Avize for Chardonnay and Aÿ, Ambonnay and Les Riceys in the Aube for Pinot Noir, not forgetting Meunier, much of which comes from Sainte Gemme and Leuvrigny in the Vallée de la Marne. Krug is committed to sustainable viticulture and works with a close network of growers who farm without using herbicides while their vineyards are fertilized organically and grassed between the rows.

Under the stewardship of Maggie Henriquez and sixth generation Olivier Krug, a six-digit back-label ID code was created, from 2011, to reveal Krug's back story and technical data on the website. Musical pairing experiences are also a *sine qua non*. In 2016, they came up with the innovative Édition concept for KGC, the first being the 163rd Édition (based on their one-hundred-and-sixty-third uninterrupted vintage), created around a specific vintage with, typically, between 35 and 50 per cent of reserve wine from their reserves of 150 wines held in stainless steel from 13 vintages. Five editions later, the 167th Édition, recreated around the 2011 vintage with 42 per cent reserve wine going back to 1995, showed sweet aromatic toasty notes and bags of textured energy. Based on the excellent 2012 vintage, the 168th Édition, a blend of 52 per cent Pinot Noir, 35 per cent Chardonnay and 13 per cent Meunier from 198 wines with 42 per cent reserve wines from 10 vintages dating back to 1996 is, in a word, fabulous.

The aim on vintage, in Olivier's words, is 'not necessarily the best but the most eloquent wine of the year'. Thus, 2004 is a wine of vivacity and tension, 2006 nuttier, yet softer, with citrusy freshness and 2008 complex and full of verve, the best of the three. Aside from the Rosé and the Collection, the latter essentially later-disgorged releases, the two sparkling gems lie in Krug's single vineyard Clos du Mesnil and Clos d'Ambonnay. Described as 'the Romanée-Conti of Champagne' for its exceptional vinosity, Clos du Mesnil is a 1.87-hectare, east-facing walled Chardonnay vineyard in Le Mesnil, originally purchased to add backbone and minerality to KGC. Not made in every vintage, it produced sublime wines in 1982, 1988, 1996, 2000 and 2002.

Admirers of the Pinot Noirs of Ambonnay in the Montagne de Reims, Henri and Rémi Krug acquired the tiny 0.685-hectare walled garden vineyard of Clos d'Ambonnay from an existing supplier in the mid-1990s to keep its big brother, Clos du Mesnil, company. Launched with the spicy, vinous 1995 vintage, there have been four further vintages released to date: a rich and youthfully tangy 1996, a smoother 1998, a very fine 2000 and the excellent 2002, probably the best of the lot. Only 3,000–4,000 bottles are made and they are all exceedingly expensive, but then they are Krug and Krug achieves an unparalleled level of distinction.

Champagne Larmandier-Bernier

Vertus

www.larmandier.fr

'Good Champagnes conform to the rules. Really great Champagnes often break them.' Emblazoned across their website, this is a clear statement of intent from Pierre Larmandier. The Larmandier family have cultivated vines in the Côte des Blancs since the nineteenth century.

In the early twentieth century, Larmandier was famous both for its Champagne and its Cramant Nature still wine. The son of Philippe Larmandier and Elisabeth Bernier, Pierre was born in Vertus, graduating from the Audencia Business school in 1988 and returning to run the estate, to be joined in 2017 by his son Arthur, who graduated from Rennes Business School in 2016.

Larmandier-Bernier operate exclusively from their 14.5 hectares in Vertus, 1.5 hectares in Avize and 2 hectares in Cramant, split between 90 per cent Chardonnay and 10 per cent Pinot Noir. Influenced by his wife Sophie, and Anselme Selosse, Pierre adopted biodynamic practices from 1992, using native yeasts from 1999 and becoming certified organic in 2003. A biodynamic practitioner for 25 years, Larmandier-Bernier has learnt to be patient in picking the grapes fully ripe from some fifty parcels. In the new winery, built in 2010, the grapes are pressed gently by pneumatic press followed by fermentation with native yeasts, mostly in oak casks and vats, and a year-long stay on the lees in Stockinger barrels and vats. The perpetual reserve, begun in 2004, is replenished with each new vintage. Dosage is modest at up to 4 grams per litre.

The range consists of the full-bodied Latitude from clay parcels in the southern part of Vertus, with about 40 per cent reserve wines, the racy Longitude, from vineyards in Cramant, Avize, Oger and Vertus, also with some 40 per cent reserves and Rosé de Saignée, made from Vertus Pinot Noir and Pinot Gris. In the vintage range, Les Chemins d'Avize, from two plots in Avize, is rich in aromatic energy and texture, and framed by spicy oak notes and an almost surprisingly soft acidity. Terre de Vertus Premier Cru Non dosé, from the northern part of Vertus, is expressively vivacious, biscuity, leesy-nutty and bone dry. I haven't tasted Vieille Vigne du Levant, but it is rated as one of Cramant's best cuvées. Average annual production is 150,000 bottles and most cuvées are also available in magnums. Each bottle carries a laser code with the disgorgement date, and the base year used in each wine is printed directly on the glass.

Champagne Jacques Lassaigne

Montgueux

www.montgueux.com

Be careful which Lassaigne you wish for, since there are apparently no fewer than 28 Lassaignes in the tiny village of Montgueux, to the west of Troyes and some, but not all, make Champagne. The Lassaigne here is Emmanuel, who has raised the 3.5-hectare domaine to great heights since he took over the running of the property from his father, Jacques, in 1999. Height is the operative word because the conical, south-facing chalk hill of Montgueux, based on ancient Turonian chalk, conceals a secret that has the big houses farther north fighting for a slice of the action. Relatively recently planted in the 1950s and 1960s, Montgueux' growers bottle less than a quarter of its Chardonnay, referred to by the late Daniel Thibault as 'the Montrachet of Champagne' for its richness. Locals talk of 'meursette', a Meursault-like character.

Since his solo first vintage in 2002, Lassaigne makes only Chardonnay-based *blanc de blancs*, buying in up to 2.5 hectares from neighbouring vineyards (hence *négociant-manipulant*). His vines are in one steep east- and south-east-facing block and, working organically, he uses no herbicides or other chemicals and rolls the grass flat between the rows. Yields are kept low by judicious pruning and lack of fertilizer. After pressing by Coquard press, he relies on spontaneous fermentation and uses a yeast culture from organic vineyards for the second fermentation. Each of the eight plots is vinified separately in a mixture of oak barrel and stainless steel. Malolactic fermentation is routinely carried out. Disgorgement is by hand and there is no fining, filtration or dosage. A low pressure mousse is created at some 4 to 4.5 bar.

By allowing the terroir to speak for itself, Emmanuel makes Champagnes of vinosity, citrusy freshness and balance. La Colline Inspirée, with its distinctively oaky character, is creamy-textured and Burgundian in style, while the single vineyard Le Cotet Blanc de Blancs Extra Brut NV, part-fermented in oak, part in tank, made from estate-grown fruit from old, south-facing vines, is impressively exotic, spicy, fine-textured and dry. There is a one-off three-pack of 2012 Champagnes, Soprano, Alto and Tenor, aged and bottled separately in 2013, 2014 and 2015, and a nutty Clos Saint-Sophie, vinified in Savagnin-cured oak and burgundy and Cognac barrels, not to mention a still Coteaux Champenois, Haut Revers du Chutat, a Coteaux Blanc and Rouge and a Pinot-dominant mousseux, Les Papilles Insolites. Annual production is 50,000 bottles.

Champagne AR Lenoble

Damery, Vallée de la Marne

champagne-arlenoble.com

Champagne names tend to take their name from the founder but not so the family-owned estate of AR Lenoble. Joseph Graser fled the Germans during the Franco-Prussian War, walking from his native region of Alsace to Épernay. After his sudden death at the age of 44, his son, Armand-Raphael, stepped into his shoes and developed his own business as a wine broker. After the First World War, he started to produce Champagne under the name AR Lenoble, combining his initials with '*le noble*' to add aristocratic lustre. Armand-Raphael's son Joseph took over on his death in 1947 and in 1973 it was taken over in turn by his grandson, Jean-Marie Malassagne who, with his wife, Colette, added 10 hectares of Chardonnay from Chouilly and 6 hectares of Pinot Noir from Bisseuil.

In 1993, their daughter Anne, then 28, left her job at L'Oréal to join Jean-Marie, while their son Antoine came on board for his first vintage in 1996. Motivated by reducing yields to make wines of character based on Chouilly and Bisseuil, they set about changing the vineyard management. A grass cover crop between the vines and ploughing for maximum nutrition was introduced and they became the second house in Champagne to be awarded HVE certification, for cutting out chemical fertilizers, weedkiller and pesticides. The vineyards were enhanced with hedgerows, orchards, embankments, trees and low walls and 70,000 bees were introduced in 2013 to the vineyards in Chouilly.

Pressing is carried out by Coquard press in Damery, with only the cuvée used. Parcels from 18 hectares in Chouilly, Bisseuil and Damery are fermented in barriques, foudres, stainless steel and enamel-lined tanks with malolactic fermentation blocked when freshness requires it. A perpetual reserve, kept in 5,000-litre oak, 250-litre barriques and stainless steel, was started in 2001; one reserve is Chardonnay-based, the other a blend of Chardonnay and Pinot Noir. Since 2010, they have also built up reserves in magnums, using some 45,000 out of a total of 100,000 magnums to blend with the latest harvest for additional precision and freshness. As much as 45–50 per cent reserve wine is used in the NV Champagnes and dosage is low. Antoine and Anne also produce the tiny single vineyard Les Aventures, a multi-vintage blend from 0.5 hectares in Chouilly.

The Intense 'mag' 14 NV is partially oak-fermented for a refreshingly dry, elegant mousse containing a fraction of reserve wines in magnum. The Grand Cru Blanc de Blancs Chouilly 'mag' 14 NV has a similar fraction of reserve wines and is seductively brioche-like in a wine of serious finesse. With barrel-fermentation and low dosage, the vinous Rosé

'Terroirs' NV from Chouilly and Bisseuil is delicately strawberry ripple-like. Best of the bunch are a stylish Grand Cru Blanc de Blancs Chouilly Vintage, 10 per cent barrel-fermented, displaying evolved toasty aromas and a nutty, fine-textured mousse, and the gloriously seductive Prestige Collection Gentilhomme Grand Cru Blanc de Blancs Chouilly.

Moët & Chandon

Épernay

www.moet.com

When the economist E.F.Schumacher wrote *Small is Beautiful*, he may not have reckoned with the sheer magnitude of Moët & Chandon, which is surely the most glaring exception to such a rule. While many might baulk at the notion that such an industry giant could be considered beautiful, 'bigger is better' could be Moët's motto. As Charles Curtis says in his book, *Vintage Champagne*: 'Moët & Chandon is the house of superlatives: the largest production, the most extensive vineyard holding, the longest cellars, a bottling line that operates at terrifying speed.'

Given Moët's immensity, it can be easy to forget that it started as a family company and remained that way for more than 200 years. Founded in 1743 in Épernay by Claude Moët, it was taken to the next level by his grandson, Jean-Rémy Moët, who became mayor of Épernay in 1792 at the height of revolutionary fervour. His great coup was to make the most of his friendship with Napoleon Bonaparte, who made him Chevalier of the Légion d'Honneur in 1814. The name was changed to Moët & Chandon following the marriage of his daughter to Pierre Gabriel Chandon de Briailles. Moët Impérial, which first appeared in 1869, was named in honour of the friendship between Jean Rémy and the French emperor.

After the First World War, the ailing firm was placed on an even keel by the whisky-drinking visionary and showman Comte Robert-Jean de Vogüé. De Vogüé launched Dom Pérignon in 1935 and expanded exports. He bought Ruinart, Veuve Clicquot, Lanson and Pommery and created new sparkling wine ventures in Europe, Argentina, California and Australia. After the acquisition of Christian Dior, Moët was to become part of the vast LVMH luxury goods empire and is now the world's most popular Champagne brand.

Moët owns 1,200 hectares, including 600 hectares in *grand cru* and 200 hectares in *premier cru*, providing a quarter of its needs. Pinot Noir accounts for 35–40 per cent, Meunier 33 per cent and the balance is Chardonnay. With access to grapes from some 240 villages throughout the region, the blending options for Impérial at Moët's ultra-modern Montaigu winery are mind-boggling. Benoît Gouez, chef de cave since 2005, is the master blender. Vinification is in stainless steel, protection from oxidation and malolactic fermentation contribute to a light, crowd-pleasing style for the non-vintage brut Impérial, which makes up the lion's share of production. Since 2005, dosage has come down from 13 grams per litre to 7–8 grams per litre and DIAM Mytik cork has been used on vintage cuvées since 2006.

Until 1996, Moët was making vintage rosé only but since introducing Rosé Impérial, it has become the market leader in rosé Champagne, which accounts for one in five bottles produced. Two sites produce the 40–50 red wines needed for the blend, one in Épernay, the other in the Côte des Bar. Thermovinification was introduced for the red wine proportion in the Rosé Impérial (13 per cent) in the 1970s. The red for the vintage rosé (9 per cent) is mostly from Aÿ Pinot Noir, macerated burgundy style. Vintage cuvées account for 5 per cent of production which, now called Grand Vintage, are excellent, ageworthy Champagnes, with the late-released Grand Collection great value. After Dom Pérignon was floated off as a brand in its own right, Moët filled the vacuum with MCIII, a delicious, Pinot Noir-dominant non-vintage Champagne with a high proportion of reserve wines.

Champagne Bruno Paillard

Reims

www.champagnebrunopaillard.com

Bruno Paillard Champagne started from scratch in 1981, making it by some distance the youngest of the big houses. Born in Reims in 1953 to an old family of brokers and vignerons from Bouzy, Bruno Paillard became a young broker in 1975, so he knew where the bodies were buried when the time came for him to accumulate his own stocks of Champagne. Nurturing greater ambitions, he famously sold his beloved vintage 1966 Jaguar Mark 2 in 1981 for 50,000 Francs (around £5,000 then), borrowing money from the bank to buy grapes and renting winery space to process them.

He has since acquired vineyards in Oger, Le Mesnil, Bouzy, Ambonnay, Festigny in the Marne and Les Riceys in the Aube, bringing his tally of managed vineyards to 34.2 hectares, over half it *grand cru*.

These comprise over two-thirds of what he needs to give him control over the harvest date and the ability to practise the kind of meticulous vineyard work he wants for all 112 parcels spread over 35 different *crus*. Alice, Bruno's daughter, joined the company in 2007 and is now effectively in charge, along with her father. As the jewel of the Paillard family, Champagne Bruno Paillard is run privately and separately from Lanson-BCC, of which Bruno is president.

Bruno Paillard produces its own organic compost, using compost tea in the vineyards, which are certified HVE3. In 1983, Bruno became the first to display the disgorgement date on the back label of his Champagnes, along with the grape blend. Only the juice from the first pressing, the cuvée, is used, which, with a good proportion of Chardonnay, gives a generally higher level of acidity than many Champagnes. In the cellar, the must is divided between tanks or barrels, according to origin, grape variety and parcel. Fermentation is in open tanks or small oak barrels, malolactic fermentation is between 80–100 per cent and dosage is low.

Having previously declared himself not a fan of zero dosage Champagnes, Bruno Paillard released Dosage: Zéro in 2018 after experimenting with a sugar-free Champagne as a result of the twin benefits of global warming and the accumulation of reserve wines. More than half is barrel-fermented, and pressure at 4.5 bar is low, resulting in one of the best zero dosages in the business, a gloriously harmonious Champagne with a mouthwatering freshness combining with a melt-in-the mouth texture before exploding on a bone dry, saline note.

With a high proportion of reserve wines, the multi-vintage Première Cuvée Extra Brut is a classic, elegantly textured blend of the three Champagne varieties, showing bright fruit and a nutty oxidative note. Nec Plus Ultra, the prestige cuvée made only in the best years (1990, 1995, 1996, 1999, 2002, 2003, 2004 and 2008) is an intense, crystalline Champagne, fermented in small oak barrels, with 12 years spent ageing, a dosage of 3 grams per litre and a three-year rest and recuperation period in Paillard's ultra-modern temperature and humidity-controlled facility on the outskirts of Reims.

Champagne Palmer & Co.

Reims

www.champagnepalmer.fr

Established in 1947 by seven grower families, the origins of the Palmer name appear to be lost in time, although it has been suggested by Tom

Stevenson and Essi Avellan that when they were at a loss as to what to call this *coopérative-manipulant*, the owners resorted to Huntley & Palmer biscuits. Apocryphal or not, Château Palmer in Bordeaux was not amused, but following the dispatch of a case of Champagne Palmer & Co, objections melted away.

Palmer's 350 members own some 220 hectares of *premier* and *grand cru* vineyards in the Montagne de Reims. Most of the vineyards are located in the cool, north-facing *grands crus* of Mailly and Verzenay and north-eastern *premiers crus* of Trépail and Villers-Marmery. They also own around 100 hectares in the Côte de Sézanne, Côte des Bar and Marne Valley. Chef de cave Xavier Berdin, a Reims University graduate taken on by Jean-Claude Colson in 2003, works with a winemaking team of Rémi Vervier, Liliane Vignon, Odile Munier and Noémie Martin. Palmer is part of the VDC certification.

Selected for their structure and ageing potential, Palmer's reserve wines, built up over 40 years, are key to the Palmer style, with 35 per cent reserve wine added to the full-flavoured yet elegant non-vintage Brut Réserve, aged on the lees for at least four years. In the excellent vintage range, the *blanc de blancs* is an exceptional, creamy, white burgundy-style wine with bubbles, given six to eight years on lees. Magnums and larger format bottles spend ten years or more on the lees. The rare Amazone de Palmer combines reserve wines only, currently a blend of the 2002, 2004, 2005 and 2006 vintages, with dosage from a 25-year-old perpetual reserve of Chardonnay.

Palmer is big on large formats, whose second fermentation takes place in the bottle. Rare older vintages are occasionally sold as museum releases. As yet, Palmer doesn't put the disgorgement date on the back label but because of 'the growing transparency expectation from consumer,' they are moving towards doing so. Annual production is 800,000 bottles, while member growers sell off around one million bottles of their own.

Champagne Perrier-Jouët Belle Époque

Épernay

www.perrier-jouet.com

Founded in the Year of the Comet, 1811, in Épernay by Pierre Nicolas-Marie Perrier, uncle of Joseph Perrier, the firm became Perrier-Jouët when, soon after marrying, Pierre added the surname of his wife, Rose-Adélaïde Jouët, to the partnership. It was his son Charles who built the brand by supplying Queen Victoria, Napoleon III, King Leopold of Belgium and the actress Sarah Bernhardt, who reputedly enjoyed a bath in it. The 1846 Perrier-Jouët was, very likely, the first Champagne without dosage, following an order for it by London merchants Burne, Turner and Co.

In 1902, Art Nouveau pioneer Emile Gallé created the iconic enamelled Japanese white anemone design for four prototype magnums of Perrier-Jouët Belle Époque. Perhaps they got lost in the 14 kilometres of cellars because they didn't see the light of day until 60 years later when the forgotten magnums were discovered by cellarmaster André Bavaret. Belle Époque's first vintage was 1964, a 90 per cent Chardonnay blend, launched in 1969 as Cuvée Belle Époque at Duke Ellington's seventieth birthday party at Maxim's in Paris.

Perrier-Jouët has 65 hectares of its own vineyards, 55 hectares of it *grand cru*, accounting for roughly a third of its requirements, with 40 hectares in the Côte des Blancs *grands crus* of Cramant and Avize, and Pinot Noir from Montagne de Reims' Mailly, Verzy and Verzenay and the Vallée's *grand cru* of Aÿ and *premier cru* of Dizy. Belle Époque is blended from Perrier-Jouët's best *crus*, fermented in stainless steel, and undergoes malolactic fermentation, with a slightly lower sugar addition of 22 grams per litre at tirage and 8 grams per litre dosage after six years on the lees, for an approachably soft-textured style. There is also a Belle Époque Rosé and a tiny quantity of Belle Époque Blanc de Blancs, first produced in 1993.

Following acquisition by Pernod-Ricard, Perrier-Jouët has gradually moved to more sustainable viticulture, reducing its carbon footprint. In 2014 trees were planted and beehives installed in the vineyards and in 2015 a pheromonal control through sexual confusion was introduced to combat moths. On 15 January 2021, Hervé Deschamps, Perrier-Jouët's seventh cellarmaster, handed the keys of the Eden Cellar to Séverine Frerson, who became the company's first female chef de cave.

Champagne Joseph Perrier

Châlons-en-Champagne

www.josephperrier.fr

Until the foundation of his company in 1825, Joseph Perrier worked with his father, François-Alexandre, as a Champagne merchant based in Châlons-en-Champagne, which had substantial vineyards in pre-phylloxera days. Joseph Perrier located an old *relais de poste* (staging post) backing onto Gallo-Roman *crayères* dug into the hill of Fagnières on the left bank of the River Marne. He extended them to provide the 3 kilometres of galleries, all on the same level and still in operation today. After his death in 1870, the house passed to Paul Pithois and is run today by the Pithois family. Benjamin Fourmon, the sixth generation, who took over in 2019 from his father Jean-Claude Fourmon, is actively involved in vineyard development with cheffe de cave, Nathalie Laplaige, a karate expert and saxophonist, who previously worked at Nicolas Feuillatte, De Castellane and Jean-Louis Malard.

Joseph Perrier's south-facing vineyards on the right bank of the Marne are mostly planted to Pinot Noir, notably in Cumières, particularly the *lieu-dits* in La Côte à Bras, whose eponymous vintage cuvée, a single vineyard *blanc de noirs* brut nature, is truly special, combining freshness and savouriness in equal measure. There are 2 hectares of Chardonnay there, and Pinot Noir in neighbouring Hautvillers and Damery. Further west they have Meunier and a little Chardonnay in organic vineyards in Verneuil. Farmed sustainably for two decades and now certified HVE3 and Viticulture Durable en Champagne (VDC), their 23 hectares of vineyards provide about a quarter of their requirements. The rest come from long term contracts in the Côte des Blancs, the Montagne de Reims and around Vitry-le François.

Over the last two decades, dosage and sulphur have been reduced, and two brut nature cuvées have been introduced in the last 12 years. Both traditional and pneumatic presses are used, the *taille* being retained as *vin clair* and used if required. No oak is used. The non-vintage style is light and refreshing with a dosage of around 7 grams per litre for the three non-vintage brut wines and normally 5 grams per litre for the vintage. The term Cuvée Royale has been used since 1892 to celebrate supplying Queen Victoria and Edward VII. The prestige Cuvée Joséphine is named for the daughter of Joseph Perrier. The date of disgorgement is mentioned on the single vineyard Blanc de Noirs from the Côte à Bras in Cumières and the Cuvée Royale NV Brut Nature and will feature on the 2012 vintage label with the rest of the range to follow suit.

Champagne Pierre Péters

Le Mesnil-sur-Oger
www.champagne-peters.com

Following Gaspar Péters' marriage to a Miss Doué, who conveniently came with a few hectares of vineyards in Le Mesnil, the domaine was founded in 1846. However, it was not until 1944 that Pierre Péters, grandson of the Luxembourgeois founder, launched the first vintage, under his own name. Pierre's grandson Rodolphe spent the first 12 years of his working life outside the business, making his mark when he suggested to his father that he sacrifice the entirety of his reserve wines going back to 1988 to upgrade the average quality of the blend. His father accepted his view and thus began the perpetual reserve which was to become the backbone of the Cuvée de Réserve.

The first principle Rodolphe learnt from his father was to allow the terroir to express itself. The second was that the best winemaker adapts to the varying conditions of terroir and vintage. Since Rodolphe came on board as chef de cave in 2007, the Pierre Péters non-vintage has been based on 50 per cent of the latest vintage plus 50 per cent of the perpetual reserve, stored 45 per cent in stainless steel, 35 per cent in concrete and 20 per cent in 45-hectolitre Stockinger casks. Vinification is in stainless steel and the wine remains on its gross lees in order to capture as much autolytic character as possible.

Pierre Péters Champagnes are made from its own grapes, grown in 16 hectares of east-facing Chardonnay in Le Mesnil-sur-Oger, Oger, Cramant and Avize and 2.5 hectares in the Cote de Sézanne, with 1.5 hectares sold to a négociant. The inner sanctum is Les Chétillons in Le Mesnil, with three plots of over 45-year-old vines, each vinified separately and then blended. Rodolphe likes to characterize Le Mesnil as austere, Avize as full-bodied and rich with ripe citrus flavours, Oger as showing white flowers, orange blossom and pear and Cramant as sweet spices with a creamy minerality.

The Cuvée de Réserve Blanc de Blancs is fresh and chalky, a touch of sweetness streaked with mouthwatering freshness; the Grande Réserve Blanc de Blancs, aged an extra year on the lees, is a vivacious blend with appley aromatics and Chablis-like vinosity. Vintage wines start with L'Esprit Blanc de Blancs which aims to embody the spirit of Le Mesnil, Avize, Cramant and Oger, hinting at biscuit, pear and a praline-like nuttiness. Both from Le Mesnil, Les Montjolys (Holy Hill) is gloriously aromatic, its vinosity underpinned by a filigree texture and salty dry finish, while Les Chétillons, is austere with citrus zest and saline minerality and has great ageing potential.

Three non-vintage cuvées complete an outstanding range. Réserve Oubliée is a multi-vintage blend of the best of the three perpetual reserves: smoky, tangy and toasty with a melting honeycomb texture. L'Etonnant Monsieur Victor, Edition Mk 12, whose playful labels reproduce famous paintings redrawn by Rodolphe's son, Victor, represents the best multi-vintage blend: toasty, richly spicy, sumptuously vinous and saltily dry. As for the Montrachet-like Cuvée Héritage, with its seductive layers of flavour and texture, this is a unique creation of 1,500 bottles that takes wines of each of the four generations of the family, Camille, Pierre, François and Rodolphe: a blend of one third of 2010, for freshness, and two-thirds from 18 vintages in bottle, the oldest, 1921.

Champagne Philipponnat

Mareuil-sur-Aÿ

www.philipponnat.com

Philipponnat was founded in Mareuil-sur-Aÿ in 1910 by Pierre and Auguste Philipponnat. After a miserable time under the ailing Marie-Brizard, it was purchased in 1997 by Bruno Paillard on behalf of BCC (Boizel Chanoine Champagne), following which the arrival of Charles Philipponnat in 2000 heralded a return to glory days. Pinot Noir is king, representing two thirds of the house's 20 hectares of *premier* and *grand cru* vineyards in the outstanding communes of Aÿ, Mareuil and Avenay. The house character lies in harnessing the grape's power and fruit without sacrificing freshness or relying on oxidative winemaking techniques.

The winery is located just a stone's throw away from the 5.83-hectare Clos des Goisses vineyard, the oldest and steepest walled vineyard in Champagne. The first bottling in around 1900, called Grand vin des Goisses, was made by the Bouché family, cousins of the Philipponnats and owner of the vineyard at the time. Philipponnat has owned the vineyard since 1935 and, in 1959, renamed the wine Clos des Goisses. Planted to 70 per cent Pinot Noir and 30 per cent Chardonnay, it's the region's warmest terroir, with no shade from sunrise to sunset covering the south-facing, wind-protected chalk hillside looking towards the Canal of the Marne River.

Clos des Goisses is blended from fourteen separate plots, allowing Philipponnat the flexibility to select and blend Pinot Noir for opulence and power and Chardonnay for an incisive stab of mineral freshness. Since 2011, a majority has been oak-fermented (apart from the 2013 which is 47 per cent) and in the case of the 2015, 2016 and 2019, fermentation was 100 per cent in oak. The wine stays on the lees for eight years, with a dosage of 4 grams per litre, remaining in the cellar post-disgorgement for at least a year. In 2007, the first rosé, the 1999 Clos des Goisses Juste Rosé, was launched. Always complex, rich and powerful, its late-disgorged iterations, LV (long vieillissement), show remarkable complexity and balance.

Since Charles Philipponnat's arrival, the range has grown in stature. A proportion of the wines are vinified and aged in oak and malolactic fermentation is generally avoided. Ageing is from three to eleven years and dosage low at around 4 grams per litre compared to 13 grams per litre when Charles arrived. The use of perpetual reserves, which are kept in oak barrels, is one of the hallmarks of the house. The Royale Reserve Brut, Grand Blanc, Blanc de Noirs, Cuvée 1522 extra brut, Cuvée 1522 Rosé, Mareuil Extra Brut and Clos des Goisses Juste Rosé are consistently, deliciously full-flavoured Champagnes. Since 1996, back labels have displayed the disgorgement date.

Champagne Pol Roger

Épernay

www.polroger.com

Just as Pol Roger occupies a special place in the affections of the British, so Britain fills a unique place in the coffers of the elite Champagne house. Thanks to a long-standing association that began with Winston Churchill's first order in 1908, Pol Roger uses his name for its 1 rue Winston Churchill Épernay address. The label destined for the UK used to be framed with a thin black line in homage to the great man. In 1975, a decade after his death, Pol Roger created Cuvée Sir Winston Churchill. Launched at Blenheim Palace in 1984, the aim was to make a traditional Pinot Noir-based, *grand cru* Champagne in the style Churchill loved: robust, full-bodied and relatively mature.

The company was founded in 1849 by Aÿ-born Pol Roger when he was not even eighteen. Initially called simply Roger, the name was only changed by his sons Maurice and Georges to honour the founder after his death in 1899. At 4 a.m. on 23 February the following year, the cellar collapsed, creating a huge sinkhole and burying 500 casks of wine and over one-and-a-half million bottles. Pol Roger was first issued with the British Royal Warrant in 1877 (re-awarded in 2004). The company was then run by Christian de Billy and Jean Pol-Roger, their grandsons, joined later by Christian Pol-Roger. Today, Laurent d'Harcourt rules the roost, becoming managing director in 2013 on Patrice Noyelle's retirement. The family is still involved, with Bastien Collard, the first member of the sixth generation, joining in 2020; Hubert de Billy was the first of the fifth generation to come along, in 1988.

Until 1955, Pol Roger was a négociant only, but thanks in large part to Christian de Billy and Jean Pol-Roger, it built its holding step by step to its present-day 92 hectares, which supply more than 50 per cent of its needs. Pol's vineyards are mainly located in the most famous subregions of Montagne de Reims, Côte des Blancs and Vallée de la Marne. New opportunities have allowed the company to source a growing number of *grand* and *premier cru* grapes for its fine Blanc de Blancs Vintage and immensely rich Cuvée Sir Winston Churchill without compromising the flagship non-vintage Réserve Brut, which represents around three-quarters of average annual production of some 1.8 million bottles.

Dominique Petit was chef de cave from 1999 until 2018, when he handed the baton to Damien Cambres. The wines are double cold-settled for a bright, fruity quality and fermented in stainless steel with malolactic fermentation routinely carried out. At 9.5°C, Pol's nearly 9 kilometres of cellars are just a little colder than the cellars of most other houses, bringing a Dorian Gray-like deceleration to the ageing process. Pol Roger also continues to riddle a large part of production by hand. With some 20–25 per cent of reserve wines held in tank in Pol's cellars, the Réserve Brut, one of the most consistently fresh and elegant non-vintage cuvées on the market, is kept for 42–54 months on the lees, vintage cuvées are kept for six to seven years and Sir Winston Churchill for eight to nine years.

At the behest of the previous managing director, Patrice Noyelle, Pol Roger started an ambitious programme of renovating the cellars between 2000 and 2013. The investment in a large number of small stainless steel tanks has enabled Pol to vinify increasingly by parcel. In a more recent major investment, the latest plans involve building on four levels over 15,000 square metres, keeping the facilities in the centre of Épernay so as to be able to continue to perform all cellar functions under one large roof. During the refit of the cellars in 2018, nearly 100 bottles, dating from between 1893 and 1898, were retrieved from the cellar that collapsed in 1900. In 2019, they were declared extraordinary by those lucky enough to be given a taste of the antiquities. Intriguingly, it appears that there may be more bottles yet to be unearthed.

Champagne Rare

Reims

www.rare-champagne.com

Floating off Rare in 2018 as a brand in its own right was the elegant solution dreamed up by parent company EPI as to how to hold on to the talents of one of Champagne's winemaking greats, Régis Camus, while giving full rein to the respective cellarmasters of Charles and Piper-Heidsieck. The first vintage of Piper-Heidsieck Rare was made in 1976, a miraculous drought year saved by deep-rooted old vines mainly from Trépail Chardonnay and Verzenay Pinot Noir. Since then, only nine vintages of Rare have been launched, 1979, 1985, 1988, 1990, 1998, 1999, 2002, 2006 and 2008; and two of Rare Rosé: 2007 and 2008.

Although always a blend of 70 per cent Chardonnay and 30 per cent Pinot Noir, the proportion of each *cru* that goes into Rare varies. Five per cent comes from the house's own vineyards, the remaining 95 per cent from loyal growers. Unusually, the Chardonnay is mainly from Montagne de Reims *premiers crus* for their citrusy vivacity, while Avize, Chouilly and Le Mesnil *grands crus* add backbone. The Pinot Noir is from Montagne de Reims. No oak is used in the fermentation and all the wines undergo a full malolactic fermentation. Recent iterations include the 2006, like a nutty white burgundy underpinned by a dry, saline minerality; the exceptional 2002, whose superb richness of texture is shot through with steely zest; and 1998, only produced in magnums, which is sweet with mocha-like notes and explosive flavours of dried fruits.

Having found that it was the rosés that tasted best in the torrid vintage of 2003, Régis Camus decided to make a 2007 vintage rosé despite a challenging season. Made from 56 per cent Chardonnay and 44 per cent Pinot Noir, it's a wine with a crunchy berry-like freshness and rich raspberry and black cherry mousse. 'I recently had it with Peking duck,' recalls Camus, 'and my only regret was the duck was too small.' Making its debut at a swanky Parisian party in 2019, the 2008 Rare Rosé, a blend of 70 per cent Chardonnay and 30 per cent Pinot Noir, does justice to a great vintage, with a floral fragrance, buoyed by a raspberries and cream mousse. The 2008 Rare is its equal; subtly savoury and nutty, it has a leesy and saline character reminiscent of a white burgundy.

Champagne André Robert

Le Mesnil-sur-Oger, Côte des Blancs

www.champagne-andre-robert.com

The estate was founded in the 1960s, when André Robert established the business in the heart of the village, although the Robert family have been vine growers since the 1800s. This Côtes des Blancs family domaine has 6.5 hectares in Le Mesnil, including the prestigious Les Chétillons, Les Vaucherots and Les Coullemets du Midi, and 14.58 hectares dotted around 53 parcels in Cuis, Étréchy, Oger, Vertus and the Vitrayat. The estate is run by the fifth generation, Claire Robert, who joined her father Bertrand in 2013, and her winemaker husband Jean-Baptiste.

Half of the production is sold to négociants; the other half, based around Chardonnay, is fermented two-thirds in oak, with the rest in stainless steel, with the steely precision gained from blocking the malolactic fermentation. Viticulture is sustainable, with ploughing in the vineyards, and they now have Haute Valeur Environnementale (HVE) certification. Among their wines, the Les Jardins du Mesnil Blanc de Blancs Grand Cru Extra Brut NV is pure *grand cru* Le Mesnil fruit vinified about half in stainless steel and half in oak, aged for some ten months before maturing on its lees for six years with a lowish dosage.

The vintage Terre du Mesnil Blanc de Blancs Grand Cru is a blend of plots in Le Mesnil, vinified and aged for ten months in small, mature oak casks that spends some six to eight years on the lees in bottle before disgorgement with a slightly higher dosage of 6–7 grams per litre. The bright, intensely flavoured, citrusy 2008 stands out. There is also a Collection d'Auteur range, with very low dosage and nearly 20 years on the lees.

Champagne Louis Roederer

Reims

www.louis-roederer.com

Founded in Reims in 1776 by Pierre-Joseph Dubois, Louis Roederer has been in the same family since 1800. Louis Roederer took over from his uncle in 1833 and decided to buy vineyards instead of grapes. In 1876, Tsar Alexander II commissioned the first 'prestige cuvée' from his favourite house, which at that time was already making 2.5 million bottles. His order resulted in Cristal, bottled in flat-bottomed clear glass, which is how it remains today, albeit shrouded in light-resistant orange cellophane. In the late nineteenth and early twentieth centuries, the visionary Léon Olry Roederer shrewdly acquired vineyards in the Côte des Blancs, Montagne de Reims and Vallée de la Marne, with a view to linking the best plots with Cristal. Taking over after her husband's death in 1932, the indefatigable Camille Olry-Roederer continued where he left off.

Roederer remains an independent family house, run by Frédéric Rouzaud, the seventh generation of the family and great-grandson of Camille Olry-Roederer. Jean-Baptiste Lécaillon arrived in 1989 and, as chef de cave since 1999, is also in charge of Roederer's portfolio of estates in Europe and California, while Champagne Deutz (see page 155) is run independently. Roederer today owns 242 hectares, 53 per cent are planted to Pinot Noir, 41 per cent to Chardonnay and 6 per cent to Meunier; most are *grand* and *premier cru*. Seventy-four hectares are in the Côte des Blancs, 82 hectares are in Vallée de la Marne, 70 hectares are in Montagne de Reims, 5 hectares are in Vitry-le-François and 11 hectares are in Vallée de l'Ardre. Vintage cuvées come from Roederer's own sustainably farmed vineyards, around half of which are certified organic. Since 2000, when it stopped using herbicides, its vineyards have been in transition to biodynamic viticulture. Brut Nature has been biodynamically farmed since 2006, Cristal Rosé from 2007 and, since 2012, Cristal itself.

Yield control is one of the most important factors, with severe pruning and debudding, if necessary, for a limited number of buds and green harvesting, again where necessary. 'It's very much Côte de Nuits-style viticulture,' says Lécaillon, 'low-yielding, calculated by vine, crop-thinning, shorter pruning technique, vineyards planted at 10,000 vines per hectare instead of 8,000 vines, 8–10 bunches per vine, to reduce growth per vine for more concentration and phenolic ripeness.' The Pinot Noir is massal selection with small bunches and small berries. Unique among négociants, Roederer has its own nursery in the village of Bouleuse. This gives it the freedom to experiment with low-vigour clones and varieties it believes will help meet the challenges of this century, not least climate change. Lécaillon is also working with Petit Meslier, Arbanne and Pinot Gris massal selections.

After picking ripe, on tasting, the grapes are pressed oxidatively in Avize, for Chardonnay, and in Aÿ and Verzenay for Pinot Noir, which is more gently and protectively pressed. All 410 plots are vinified separately in a cellar that houses 450 tanks and 9,000-litre oak vats. In a good year such as 2008, fermentation can be up to 40 per cent spontaneous, which Lécaillon increasingly favours for the first fermentation. 'The juice is the food for the yeast, so yeasts must be healthy. They must have enough food but not too much. It's the Mediterranean diet,' says Lécaillon. Thanks to picking ripe, Lécaillon can afford to avoid malolactic fermentation when possible: 'Ripeness and natural acidity are the keys to freshness. Malolactic fermentation is salt and pepper for me,' he says. 'It's a question of adding more, or less, roundness.' Roederer has decreased from 6 atmospheres of pressure to 5, the bigger the format, the lower the pressure.

Using a small quantity of oak-aged Cristal reserve wine, Roederer's elegant non-vintage Brut Premier, the only cuvée made from bought in fruit, is fermented in stainless steel and dominated by Pinot Noir, using a good percentage of Roederer's reserve wines. From September 2021, Brut Premier has been upgraded to Collection 242, a new multi-vintage cuvée aimed above all at freshness. Named for the two-hundred-and-forty-second harvest since Roederer's establishment in 1776, the promising inaugural 242 cuvée is based on 56 per cent of the 2017 vintage, with 'a reservoir of freshness' in 34 per cent *reserve perpetuelle* and 10 per cent oak-aged reserve wines. Dosage is 8 grams per litre (1 gram per litre lower than Brut Premier), with a third undergoing malolactic fermentation.

From 45 parcels in seven *grands crus*, Cristal comes from vines with an average age of 45 years. Pushing the envelope, Vinothèque is a new chapter in Cristal history aiming at 'going beyond Cristal as we've known it while respecting the DNA of Cristal at the same time,' says Lécaillon. 'In-house, we call it the eternal youth programme.' The technique is to age the wine on the lees for eight years or so for maximum autolytic effect, then turn the bottle upside down for another five to six years to stop the process and disgorge with 7 grams per litre dosage with another seven to eight years post-disgorgement ageing; 'the "caress" years'. The 1995, 1996, 1999 and 2000, all based on this model, are remarkable Champagnes with an amazing textural richness and no loss of verve.

Champagne Roses de Jeanne

Celles-sur-Ource

www.champagne-rosesdejeanne.fr

Born into a winemaking family, Cédric Bouchard worked as a sommelier and *caviste* in Paris, before returning to Celles-sur-Ource in

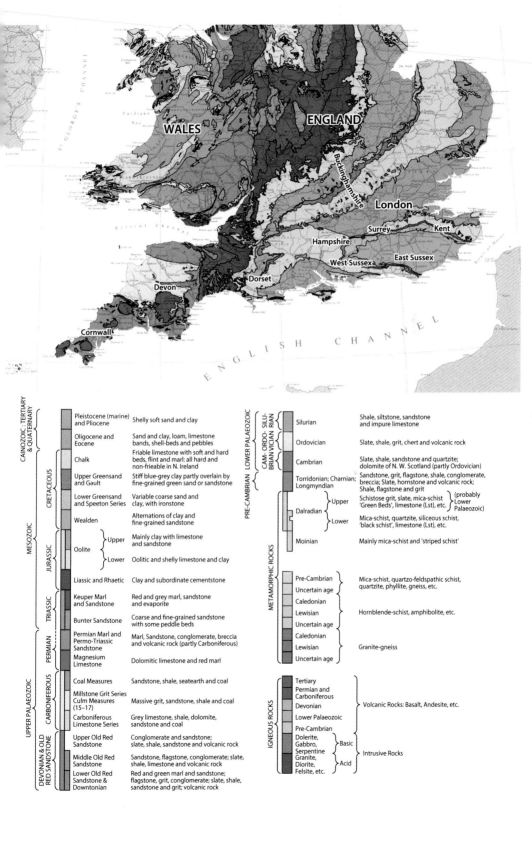

Map labels:

WALES

ENGLAND

London

Buckinghamshire

Surrey

Kent

Hampshire

West Sussex

East Sussex

Dorset

Devon

Cornwall

St GEORGE'S CHANNEL

Cardigan Bay

Bristol Channel

ENGLISH CHANNEL

Stratigraphic column legend:

Era/Group	Period/System	Unit	Description
CAINOZOIC : TERTIARY & QUATERNARY		Pleistocene (marine) and Pliocene	Shelly soft sand and clay
		Oligocene and Eocene	Sand and clay, loam, limestone bands, shell-beds and pebbles
MESOZOIC	CRETACEOUS	Chalk	Friable limestone with soft and hard beds, flint and marl: all hard and non-frieable in N. Ireland
		Upper Greensand and Gault	Stiff blue-grey clay partly overlain by fine-grained green sand or sandstone
		Lower Greensand and Speeton Series	Variable coarse sand and clay, with ironstone
		Wealden	Alternations of clay and fine-grained sandstone
	JURASSIC	Oolite — Upper	Mainly clay with limestone and sandstone
		Oolite — Lower	Oolitic and shelly limestone and clay
		Liassic and Rhaetic	Clay and subordinate cementstone
	TRIASSIC	Keuper Marl and Sandstone	Red and grey marl, sandstone and evaporite
		Bunter Sandstone	Coarse and fine-grained sandstone with some peddle beds
UPPER PALAEOZOIC	PERMIAN	Permian Marl and Permo-Triassic Sandstone	Marl, Sandstone, conglomerate, breccia and volcanic rock (partly Carboniferous)
		Magnesium Limestone	Dolomitic limestone and red marl
	CARBONIFEROUS	Coal Measures	Sandstone, shale, seatearth and coal
		Millstone Grit Series Culm Measures (15–17)	Massive grit, sandstone, shale and coal
		Carboniferous Limestone Series	Grey limestone, shale, dolomite, sandstone and coal
	DEVONIAN & OLD RED SANDSTONE	Upper Old Red Sandstone	Conglomerate and sandstone; slate, shale, sandstone and volcanic rock
		Middle Old Red Sandstone	Sandstone, flagstone, conglomerate; slate, shale, limestone and volcanic rock
		Lower Old Red Sandstone & Downtonian	Red and green marl and sandstone; flagstone, grit, conglomerate; slate, shale, sandstone and grit; volcanic rock

Group	Period/System	Unit	Description
PRE-CAMBRIAN / LOWER PALAEOZOIC	CAM- ORDO- SILU- BRIAN VICIAN RIAN	Silurian	Shale, siltstone, sandstone and impure limestone
		Ordovician	Slate, shale, grit, chert and volcanic rock
		Cambrian	Slate, shale, sandstone and quartzite; dolomite of N. W. Scotland (partly Ordovician)
		Torridonian; Charnian; Longmyndian	Sandstone, grit, flagstone, shale, conglomerate, breccia; Slate, hornstone and volcanic rock; Shale, flagstone and grit
		Dalradian — Upper	Schistose grit, slate, mica-schist 'Green Beds', limestone (Lst). etc. (probably Lower Palaeozoic)
		Dalradian — Lower	Mica-schist, quartzite, siliceous schist, 'black schist', limestone (Lst), etc.
		Moinian	Mainly mica-schist and 'striped schist'

METAMORPHIC ROCKS

Pre-Cambrian	Mica-schist, quartzo-feldspathic schist, quartzite, phyllite, gneiss, etc.
Uncertain age	
Caledonian	
Lewisian	Hornblende-schist, amphibolite, etc.
Uncertain age	
Caledonian	
Lewisian	Granite-gneiss
Uncertain age	

IGNEOUS ROCKS

Tertiary	
Permian and Carboniferous	
Devonian	Volcanic Rocks: Basalt, Andesite, etc.
Lower Palaeozoic	
Pre-Cambrian	
Dolerite, Gabbro, Serpentine — Basic	Intrusive Rocks
Granite, Diorite, Felsite, etc. — Acid	

Previous page: The geology of the south of England, showing the abundance of chalk, greensand, Wealden and other soil types ideal for growing the classic Champagne varieties.

Above: The view across the Derwent River from Moorilla Estate's restaurant in Hobart, Tasmania.

Below: Looking out across the Yarra Valley from the terrace at Coldstream Hills, Yarra Valley, Victoria, Australia.

Above: Extremes of light and marked day to night temperature differences contribute to the cool climate style of Quartz Reef in Bendigo, Central Otago, New Zealand.

Below: Sheep act as lawnmowers to keep the grass down in winter at Nyetimber's Tillington Vineyard, West Sussex, England.

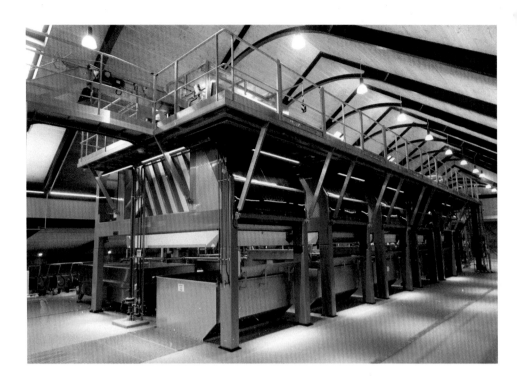

Above: This battery of six Coquard PAI tilted plate presses at Nyetimber, West Sussex, England, can be loaded from 15 kilo crates in just 20 minutes.

Below: A great English oak tree presides over Chapel Down's vineyards in Kent, England.

Left: Peter Hall with his Bengal cat Toto at his 1827 farmstead, Breaky Bottom, in East Sussex, England.

Below: Gold metallized bottles of Jay-Z's Armand de Brignac Champagne lying in *pupitres* in Champagne Cattier's cellars in Chigny-les-Roses, Champagne.

Above: The shape of the Charles Heidsieck bottle is taken from Crayère No. 9 in Charles Heidsieck's cellars in Reims, Champagne, France.

Right: This oval German oak barrel in the cellars of Emrich-Schönleber in the Nahe valley, Germany, is specially reserved for its Sekt (sparkling wine).

Above: Gut Hermannsberg's modern cellar with the *Grosses Gewächs* (*grand cru*) vineyard of the Hermannsberg behind it in the Nahe Valley, Germany.

Left: Traditional wine cellar artefacts in Asolo Prosecco Superiore DOCG in the province of Treviso, Northern Italy.

Above: A traditional lift for moving baskets of Cava in the cellars of Codorníu, Sant Sadurní d'Anoia, Alt Penedès, Spain.

Below: In the vineyards of the Takeda Winery in Japan's northerly prefecture of Yamagata, vineyards are routinely covered by a blanket of snow in winter.

2000 to the single hectare of north-facing vines, Les Ursules, inherited from his father. A purist from the start, he decided to craft each of his Champagnes from a single vineyard, a single vintage and a single variety (mainly Pinot Noir, although there is also a 100 per cent Chardonnay and 100 per cent Pinot Blanc cuvée). Bouchard increased his holdings by combining his micro-sized assortment of parcels with 1.37 hectares of vines previously owned by his father. He dramatically reduced yields to an average of around 25 hectolitres per hectare, resulting in wines of great vinosity and exceptional concentration. He works biodynamically but is not interested in certification.

Since 2012, Bouchard has been based at new premises in nearby Landreville. Each wine is made only from juice from the first pressing, tank-aged to avoid any suspicion of oxidation and fermented using indigenous yeasts. He avoids chaptalizing, fining, filtering or cold stabilizing. Cédric doesn't like Champagnes that are aggressively fizzy, so he aims for a relatively low 4.25 atmospheres of pressure (using just 17 grams per litre at tirage) and bottle-ages for a minimum time with zero dosage. Believing that bubbles 'get in the way', he prefers to carafe the wines to remove some of the carbon dioxide.

Although his father's holdings were originally bottled under the Inflorescence label, all his cuvées have been labelled Roses de Jeanne since 2014, named for his grandmother Janika. After suffering a stroke in the same year, Cédric has become even more intensely focused. Production of his seven wines is tiny, at just 15,000 bottles. Four wines, Côte de Val Vilaine, Côte de Béchalin, Les Ursules and Presles are *blancs de noirs* made from Pinot Noir. Le Creux d'Enfer is a foot-crushed *saignée* rosé, made from three rows of Pinot Noir, and the two *blanc de blancs*, La Haute-Lemblé and La Bolorée, are made from Chardonnay and Pinot Blanc respectively. Together with a couple of partners, he has launched the excellent restaurant Le Garde Champêtre in Gyé-sur-Seine.

Champagne Ruinart

Reims

www.ruinart.com

'In the name of God and the Saint Virgin shall this book be commenced', wrote the cloth merchant Nicolas Ruinart in the first account book, opened on 1 September 1729. The foundation of the first Champagne house, by the nephew of the Benedictine monk Dom Ruinart, followed Louis XV's decree of 25 May 1728 permitting the transportation of

Champagne in baskets containing 50 or 100 bottles. Acquired in 1768 by Claude Ruinart, the subterranean medieval *crayères* under the Butte Saint-Nicaise in Reims, with their constant, natural temperature of 11°C, became integral to the condition of Ruinart's Champagnes, and with 8 kilometres of cellars underground, they remain so today.

In 1764, Ruinart was the first to commercialize a rosé Champagne, then called Oeil de Perdrix, long before it became a favourite of the Empress Josephine, King Charles X of France, the American President Andrew Jackson and the Russian market in the 1860s. After the Second World War, Gérard Ruinart passed the ownership to his Chardonnay-loving cousin Bertrand Mure, famous for liking his Champagne 'from 9 a.m. until 9 a.m. the next day'. In 1963, the firm was acquired by Moët & Chandon and the wines today have been made by Reims-born Frédéric Panaïotis since he took over from Jean-Philippe Moulin in 2007.

While the fruit-driven R de Ruinart, which accounts for half of production, is a three-way blend, the house's reputation is largely based on Chardonnay, thanks to its non-vintage *blanc de blancs* and the fact that Dom Ruinart is the only *blanc de blancs* prestige cuvée in the Moët Hennessy portfolio. In a style that's essentially gently reductive in order to maintain the Ruinart hallmark of freshness Panaïotis craves, fermentation in stainless steel is followed by malolactic fermentation 'for that amazing mouthfeel', with three years of ageing for the bright, bite-into-a-ripe-peach style of the non-vintage *blanc de blancs*. The blend includes some 25–30 per cent reserve wines and dosage has been gradually reduced to around 7 grams per litre for the *blanc de blancs* and 8 grams per litre for the rosé.

First released with the 1959 vintage, Dom Ruinart Blanc de Blancs is pure Chardonnay, typically three-quarters from Cramant, Avize, Chouilly and Le Mesnil and a quarter, for its zesty freshness, from Sillery in the Montagne de Reims, where Ruinart owns around 20 hectares. Ageing is on cork, rather than crown cap, following a switch from the 2010 vintage, and dosage is low at 4–5.5 grams per litre. There is less Montagne Chardonnay than usual in the fiftieth anniversary 2009 Dom Ruinart Blanc de Blancs, whose freshness and complexity shine through after a decade of ageing. Dom Ruinart Rosé is in essence a Côte des Blancs Chardonnay with the addition of 15–20 per cent Aÿ Pinot Noir vinified as a red wine. In 2019, Ruinart unveiled a lightweight 'skin' made from sustainably produced recyclable paper for its clear glass bottle.

Salon Champagne

Le Mesnil sur Oger

www.champagne-salon.fr

Given the hierarchy of aristocracy within Champagne, Salon is a relative upstart, founded in 1905 by Eugène-Aimé Salon, the son of a champenois cart-maker, who started his working life as a furrier's messenger boy in Paris. Developed from pure Chardonnay vineyards in the chalky soils of Le Mesnil, Salon is declared as a vintage only in years which its president, Didier Depond, deems exceptional. Thanks to its uncompromising focus on quality, Salon, a *vin de garde* with an exceptional spine of acidity and a mineral quality bordering on the saline, often outclasses, and outprices, most of its luxury peers.

Eugène-Aimé chose east-facing *grand cru* sites in the *mi-coteaux*, the middle of the slopes, to create a Champagne from a single grape, a single *grand cru* and a single vintage. In 1911, he bought the single-hectare plot now known as Le Jardin de Salon, forming an association of 15 growers whose 20 parcels, including Le Jardin, are spread over 10 hectares. Its reputation was made in the 1920s at Maxim's in Paris, the 'temple of Champagne', where it was sold exclusively until the 1950s. 'You can just imagine him in his gleaming Hispano Suiza J12,' says Corney & Barrow's Rebecca Palmer, 'treading the vineyards in his shiny city shoes in pursuit of the finest plots, the most favourable gradient, the purest chalk.' Indeed you can.

Didier Depond, the son of a wine grower in Tours in the Loire Valley, joined Laurent-Perrier 20 years ago after being inspired by its charismatic owner, Bernard de Nonancourt. The 2004 vintage was his twentieth in charge of Salon and its sister house Delamotte. The wine is fermented in stainless steel with strict control over yield. 'Selection, a rigorous selection of quality, is the key word,' according to Depond. The time it spends on its lees, ten years in its Le Mesnil cellars, is testimony to the longevity of Salon and the building block of its iconic status. 'It's like burgundy with bubbles,' says Depond.

Salon produces 60,000 bottles (only 42,000 in 2004), a relatively small number compared to the usual prestige cuvée suspects. After the 2004 vintage, a sculpted beauty of floral fragrance, saline freshness and brioche-like complexity, close to the outstanding 2002 vintage, the 2006 is a current favourite of Depond. '1996 was a Schwarzenegger, good, showy, yes, but hardly elegant, while the 2006 is the opposite, like

Audrey Hepburn, supremely elegant.' He holds a small library stock of vintages going back to (two bottles of) the great 1928 vintage. I'll be walking on the moon before I get to taste one of those.

Jacques Selosse

Avize

www.selosse-lesavises.com

Sinatra's 'I did it my way' could be Anselme Selosse's anthem and, like Ol' Blue Eyes' crooning or not, there's no sitting on the fence. As Peter Liem puts it, 'no winemaker is more revered by his followers or ma-ligned by his detractors than Anselme Selosse'. What's all the fuss about? In essence, Selosse is an iconoclast, not for the sake of being contro-versial; he has gone against the grain by questioning the conventional wisdom in a region conditioned and often hidebound by tradition. By interrogating this and that practice every step of the way, he is looked up to as one of the most inspiring figures of the grower movement. He also commands prices for his wines to make the average Champagne house go green – and I don't mean environmentally.

Selosse's father, Jacques, bought vineyards in Avize in 1947 and started bottling his own wines from 1964. The young Anselme had a tough childhood thanks to a stern mother, a weight issue and a skin problem. An outsider who was obsessed with how things work, he went to boarding school at the age of 12 and studied viticulture in Beaune from 1969–73, an experience that opened his eyes to burgundy-style winemaking and terroir. He spent time in the Spanish wine regions of Penedès, Rioja and Jerez, returning in 1974 to take over the running of the 4-hectare domaine. Now expanded to 8.3 hectares, the domaine has vineyards in Avize, Cramant, Oger, Le Mesnil-sur-Oger, Aÿ, Mareuil-sur-Aÿ and Ambonnay. Selosse's son, Guillaume, has worked with his father since 2011 and is now in charge.

Influenced by Taoism, in essence living in harmony with the uni-verse, Selosse focuses on the cycles of nature in the vineyard. Believing that maturity is the apotheosis of the organic, he picks riper than the norm, resulting in multi-dimensional Champagnes of exceptional vin-osity. After abandoning herbicides and nitrogen supplementation, he stopped filtration and introduced oak fermentation along with indig-enous yeasts and his own selected yeasts (Levures Selosse), even at tir-age. Vinifying parcel by parcel, he is not afraid to let his wines age in barrel for lengthy periods even, in some cases, leaving space to allow a protective layer of sherry-like *flor* yeast to develop. It's this risk-taking that has led some to criticize his wines for being excessively oxidative, even volatile or over-oaky.

The range starts with Initial and V.O. (Version Originale), *blanc de blancs* blends of three vintages from Avize, Cramant and Oger, the V.O. from higher slopes with poorer soils. The Selosse Rosé blends two or three successive years of Avize Chardonnay with 6–8 per cent of red Pinot Noir, from Francis Egly. Substance, from two Avize vineyards, is drawn from a 'solera reserve' started in 1986. From 1991, he has used 22 per cent of the reserve for blending, replenishing it each year with the latest vintage. The Blanc de Blancs Millésimé comes from two sites in Avize and spends 12 years on the lees for bottles and 14 for magnums.

More recently, Selosse has produced a collection of single-vineyard Champagnes from six specific mini-plots, or *lieux-dits*: Aÿ – La Côte Faron; Mareuil-sur-Aÿ – Sous le Mont; Ambonnay – Le Bout de Clos; Avize – Les Chantereines; Cramant – Chemin de Châlons; and Le Mesnil-sur-Oger – Les Carelles. These spend between 6 and 12 years on the lees and dosage is low, varying from zero to 2.2 grams per litre. This single-vineyard collection provides perfect examples of Champagnes that express their distinctive terroir. Doubtless both admirers and detractors will be scrutinizing the direction in which Guillaume takes the domaine with considerable interest.

Champagne Taittinger

Reims

www.taittinger.com

Originally called Jacques Fourneaux after its establishment in 1734, the company was bought in 1932 by Pierre Taittinger, a cavalry officer during the First World War, and became Taittinger Mailly et Cie. Pierre fell in love with the Château de la Marquetterie, which in 1915 housed the HQ of General Joffre, deriving its name from growing alternating plots of black and white grapes. In 1933 the firm was transferred from Mailly to this thirteenth-century home of the Comtes de Champagnes. Pierre Taittinger had eight children and so, as it later turned out, eight factions. In the post-Second World War period Pierre's sons François and Jean purchased more prime vineyards, concentrating on refining the quality of their wines.

On taking control in 1942, François moved Taittinger to Place Saint-Nicaise, where the Roman chalk cellars rise to 20 metres at the apex of a hollow pyramid. In 1960, after François was tragically killed in a car accident aged 39, Jean went on to become mayor of Reims and Claude became the company president, from 1960–2005. In 2005, Pierre Taittinger's 45 descendants voted to sell their shares to Starwood Capital Group for €2.4 billion, but Jean's son Pierre-Emmanuel bought the house back a year later for €660 million, to be joined by his daughter Vitalie, and son Clovis. Today, the Reims-based house is renowned for its Chardonnay-dominant wines, one of the reasons for the elegance and finesse of the house style.

Taittinger owns 288 hectares of prime vineyards, buying grapes from around 300 growers for its annual six million bottle production. Four out of five are non-vintage Brut Réserve and the rest is split between Vintage, Prélude, Les Folies de la Marquetterie, Prestige Rosé and the prestige cuvée, Comtes de Champagne (007's Champagne of choice in Casino Royale). In 80 per cent of the vineyards, no herbicides are used. The most famous are in the Côte des Blancs and those surrounding Château de la Marquetterie. There is high quality Pinot Noir too in Les Riceys and Essoyes in the Aube. Pneumatic presses are used in the Côte des Blancs and a traditional Coquard press at Château de la Marquetterie.

The style of the house, based on Chardonnay, is lightness, freshness and drinkability. The Brut Réserve NV is consistently engagingly fresh and elegant. Aged for four to five years on its lees, and with 9 grams per litre dosage, Prélude, a blend of 50 per cent Chardonnay and 50 per cent Pinot Noir from *grand cru* vineyards, including Avize and Le Mesnil sur Oger for the Chardonnay, and Mailly and Ambonnay for the Pinot Noir, is a wine with an explosive mousse and delightful minerality. The Château de la Marquetterie, made since 2002 and only from domaine grown fruit, is one of Taittinger's most memorably elegant styles.

Made only in exceptional vintages, the first of which was 1952, Comtes de Champagne is a pure Chardonnay prestige cuvée with a small part fermented in oak and only the first pressing used from fruit sourced from Avize, Le Mesnil-sur-Oger, Oger, Chouilly and Cramant. The wine spends ten years on its lees, ending up effortlessly elegant and long-lived, with a delightful toastiness, almost Puligny-like on occasion, and not a hair out of place. Comtes de Champagne Rosé, made from fruit from Bouzy and Ambonnay, is rich and delicious with serious staying power.

The anglophile Pierre-Emmanuel was the first to break ground in England, with the announcement in 2017 that Taittinger was to plant 40 hectares of Chardonnay, Pinot Noir and Meunier at 80 metres above sea level in chalk and loam soil on south-facing farmland at Stone Stile near Canterbury in Kent to produce English bubbles. Coincidentally, his father, Jean Taittinger twinned Canterbury with Reims when he was mayor of Reims (1959–77). The estate is called Domaine Evremond after the epicurean Charles de Saint-Évremond, somewhat ironic given that Charles II's friend was none too keen on the new sparkling phenomenon of Restoration London.

Champagne Tarlant

Oeuilly

www.tarlant.com

Twelve kilometres west of Épernay at Oeuilly, on the left bank of the Marne, the Tarlant family have been making still wines from their own grapes since 1687, becoming Coteaux Champenois in 1974, and have produced Champagne since the beginning of the AOC in 1928. Today, the children of Micheline and Jean-Mary Tarlant, Benoît and Mélanie Tarlant, are the twelfth generation to be running the estate, which consists of 14 hectares of vineyards planted in Oeuilly, Celles-lès-Condé, Boursault and Saint-Agnan. Their traditional Champagnes follow the prescriptions of parents and grandparents, all without dosage 'in order to preserve the real taste of Champagne,' says Mélanie Tarlant.

The Tarlants grow all seven permitted grape varieties in different soils and microclimates. They grow 35 per cent Pinot Noir with 30 per cent Chardonnay, 30 per cent Meunier and 5 per cent of the traditional varieties, Arbanne, Petit Meslier, Pinot Blanc and Fromenteau. Based on 31 *lieux-dits*, the vineyards benefit from slopes and proximity to the River Marne and the vines are on average 40 years old. They work sustainably, eschewing chemical sprays and working towards organic certification with a view to highlighting their Marne Valley terroir, prioritizing biodiversity and the microbial life of the soil.

The grapes are picked when deemed fully ripe and two Coquard presses are used for gentle pressing, extracting the cuvée, to be vinified with native yeasts, in burgundy barrels. Each parcel is vinified separately to highlight the terroir expression of the single-vineyard Champagnes and to enable them to blend for Zero and Rosé Zero. Clarification, filtration and malolactic fermentation are avoided. Ageing on the lees is anything from 5 to 20 years. An interest in Georgian wine led to Benoît's first vinification in clay amphora in 2011, Argilité, based on grapes grown on Lutetian limestone from the *lieu-dit* Notre Dame.

To allow Meunier to express itself in its most favoured soils, La Vigne d'Or is based on the grape planted in clay–limestone Sparnacian soils. La Vigne d'Antan is an expression of ungrafted Chardonnay grown in silica-sand soil, while La Vigne Royale aims to show the character of Pinot Noir planted on south-facing limestone. Last, but a long way from least, Cuvée Louis Tarlant is a hugely characterful, richly toasty, intense 50:50 Pinot Noir–Chardonnay brut nature, the most recent iteration combining the 2002 and 2003 vintages, from the Les Crayons *lieu-dit* in Tarlant's oldest vineyard planted on Campanian chalk. Since 1999, the back label has shown origin, tirage and disgorgement dates and more recently an added QR code gives access to all necessary technical information. Production is 10,000 cases annually.

Champagne Vazart-Coquart

Chouilly

www.champagnevazartcoquart.com

Champagne Vazart-Coquart was founded by Louis and Marie Vazart-Coquart and developed by their son Jacques before Jacques' son Jean-Pierre took over the running of the estate in 1995. He joined the Club Trésors de Champagne at the same time and is a member of the 'Les Mains du Terroir' grouping. With 30 vineyards in 11 hectares of *grand cru* in Chouilly on the Côte des Blancs, Jean-Pierre is the third largest landowner in Chouilly behind Moët & Chandon and Louis Roederer. A perpetual reserve started in 1982 is topped up routinely with 40 per cent of the new vintage's wines. Jean-Pierre's wines are made in stainless steel and, since 2016, have not automatically gone through malolactic fermentation. He is also trialling a cuvée fermented in amphora, which bears the name TC (terre cuite), followed by the vintage.

Jean-Pierre was one of the first in Champagne to gain HVE certification and thanks to modest yields derived from sustainable viticulture (the estate is in conversion to organic status), he achieves good concentration, complexity and intensity in the wines, which show the freshness of Côte des Blancs Chardonnay with, on occasion, a floral note and a more rounded texture than, say, Le Mesnil, yet without any loss of minerality. He harvested his first organic grapes in 2020 and the wines will come on stream in 2025–6.

The non-vintage Brut Réserve *grand cru* Chouilly contains 35 per cent reserve wine including 25 per cent of the perpetual reserve and 7 grams per litre dosage. The non-vintage Extra Brut Réserve *grand cru* Chouilly, with 30 per cent from the reserve begun in 1982, spends 42 months on the lees with a lower dosage at 2.5 grams per litre. The Millésime Spécial Club 2012 *blanc de blancs grand cru* Chouilly, with 3.5 grams per litre, is effectively a prestige cuvée, spending 7.5 years on the lees and sealed with a cork and clip for minute oxygen ingress and excellent vinosity. Sixty per cent of Jean-Pierre's Cuvée 82/13 *blanc de blancs grand cru* Chouilly non-vintage, with a dosage of 1.5 grams per litre, comes from a perpetual reserve containing no fewer than 32 vintages, indicating the first and latest vintages included in the cuvée. It's a standout for its fabulous toastiness, explosively intense mousse and wonderful mineral finish.

Veuve Clicquot

Reims

www.veuveclicquot.com

After taking over the reins of the company founded by Philippe Clicquot in 1772, when her husband, François, died in 1805, the formidable Barbe-Nicole Clicquot Ponsardin, then aged 27, showed herself from the start to be a woman of ambition and imagination. With the 1811 vintage, she became the first to sell Veuve Clicquot in Russia, in 1814, through her sales director Louis Bohne, after the Napoleonic blockade. In 1810, she took on the talented chef de cave, Antoine Müller, and together they secretly devised the system of remuage, using pupitres, that was eventually to become standard practice as a way of removing the sediment.

Veuve Clicquot today owns 393 hectares of vineyards, mainly in *grand cru* and *premier cru* sites. The vineyards are farmed sustainably without the use of herbicides. Fermentation is in stainless steel and malolactic fermentation is part of the house style, but 10 per cent is blocked in the 2018 Grande Dame vintage to maintain a degree of freshness. In 2008, when Dominique Demarville took over from the legendary Jacques Péters as chef de cave, he continued the practice of building up reserve wines begun in 1988. He left to join Laurent-Perrier in 2020, and today his successor, the Swiss-born Didier Mariotti, has 300–400 reserve wines kept in separate in stainless steel vats to call on for the making of the Brut Yellow Label, which accounts for some 90 per cent of production.

Veuve Clicquot vintage and its rosé counterpart are often the best value in the line-up even if La Grande Dame is designed to be the house's ultimate expression. When launched in 1972 to celebrate the company's bicentenary, with the first vintage, 1962, Pinot Noir hovered at not much more than 50 per cent of the blend. Dominique Demarville decided to gradually increase the proportion from the 2008 vintage to upwards of 90 per cent. He brought the Pinot Noir up to 92 per cent of the blend, didn't declare 2009, which was better for Chardonnay, and in the silkily fine-textured 2012 vintage, La Grande Dame contains 90 per cent Pinot Noir and 10 per cent Chardonnay.

The Pinot Noir comes from the house's historic *grand cru* vineyards: Verzy, Verzenay, Bouzy and Ambonnay in the Montagne de Reims and from Aÿ in the Vallée de la Marne. The Chardonnay is from Le Mesnil, Oger and Avize in the Côte des Blancs with a dosage of 6 grams per litre. Using Pinot Noir grapes from the northerly *grands crus* of Verzy and Verzenay, the aim with La Grande Dame is to keep freshness, elegance and longevity. As distinct from Veuve Clicquot vintage, oak is not used for La Grande Dame.

Champagne Veuve Fourny et Fils

Blancs-Coteaux

www.champagne-veuve-fourny.com

While cynics might consider the name Veuve to be a marketing plus in Champagne, this Vertus estate changed its name to Veuve A Fourny in the 1950s after the death of Albert Fourny. When his daughter-in-law, Monique Fourny, also widowed, passed the baton to her two sons Charles-Henry in 1992 and Emmanuel in 1993, it became Veuve Fourny pure and simple. A négociant-manipulant since 1979 when it started to buy in grapes from family and friends, Veuve Fourny is essentially a family enterprise, with a substantial holding of 12 hectares in the *premier cru* village of Vertus in the southern Côte des Blancs.

Veuve Fourny's holdings supply around 50 per cent of their needs. With some 76 different parcels of sunlit east-, south- and south-east-facing chalky terroir on the hillside slopes of Monts Ferrés near the border with Le Mesnil, the family also has the advantage of vineyards with an average age of over 45 years grafted though massal selection by the brothers' grandfather Albert in the 1930s. They are committed to sustainable viticulture with a combination of grassing and cultivation adapted to their varied soils, some of which are ploughed.

When the brothers took over the running of the estate, the stamp-sized 0.29-hectare *monocru* of Faubourg de l'Abbaye Notre Dame was to become the focus of their terroir aspirations and the first for which small oak casks were used, along with ten years ageing. The different parcels are vinified separately in a mix of tanks and wood, using only the cuvée, and oak is now used for the full range. The wines are kept for long periods on the lees in bottle for a combination of body, minerality and finesse. Dosage is low.

Both the non-vintage Blanc de Blancs Extra-Brut Premier Cru, with 25 per cent oak and the drier, more complex all-tank-fermented vintage Blanc de Blancs 'Monts de Vertus' Extra-Brut Premier Cru, offer excellent value, while the dual-vintage Cuvée 'R' Extra-Brut Premier Cru made from old vines and vinified in wood, spends four years on lees and is malty, rich and complex. If the non-vintage Brut Nature Blanc de Blancs Vertus 1er Cru is for purists, count me in as a purist. This blend of three vintages is selected typically from old vines from the chalky Mont Ferrés terroir. Twenty-five per cent is vinified in barrel and 20 per cent reserve wines are added for a wine of exceptional aromatic purity and texture, finishing bone dry.

After nine years on the lees, the Clos Faubourg Notre-Dame 2006 Blanc de Blancs Extra Brut Vertus 1er Cru, entirely vinified in oak, is exceptional. Spending four years on its lees is a silky barrel-fermented vintage Rosé Vinothèque Extra Brut Vertus 1er Cru and, relatively new to the range thanks to the purchase of this plot in 2009, the vinous Rosé Les Monts de Vertus is made from a 0.22-hectare Pinot Noir plot, Les Rougesmonts.

Champagne Vilmart

Rilly-la-Montagne

www.champagnevilmart.fr

Since the estate was founded by Désiré Vilmart in 1890, five generations of the family have been ploughing their own furrow, 11 hectares of furrow to be precise, over just 13 parcels in Rilly-La-Montagne and Villers-Allerand. Producing their own Champagnes in the late nineteenth century, the modern incarnation began with Désiré Vilmart's grandson-in-law, René Champs, who took over in 1963 and, more recently, his son Laurent, who joined his father in 1989 and has run the estate since 1995. What singles out Laurent's Champagnes is meticulous attention to detail. Unusually for a property in the Montagne de

Reims, Vilmart's holdings are Chardonnay dominant with 60 per cent Chardonnay and 40 per cent Pinot Noir. The average age of the vines is 35 years and the oldest, at 60 years old, are reserved for the Coeur de Cuvée and Blanc de Blancs Champagnes.

Having obtained HVE and VDC certification, Laurent follows the principles of the Ampelos charter, which excludes the use of chemical fertilizer, herbicides and insecticides. The grapes are pressed by traditional Coquard press before settling by gravity and the juice is then transferred to oak barrels and foudres for vinification. This provides a textural quality which, combined with the high proportion of Chardonnay, creates a pristine purity and structure in the absence of malolactic fermentation. The non-vintage wines spend three to four years, the vintage five to eight years on the lees. After the 'entry level' non-vintage Grande Réserve, the non-vintage Grand Cellier *premier cru*, with 70 per cent Chardonnay and 30 per cent Pinot Noir, is a step up the quality ladder thanks to fermentation in large oak casks and the addition of 50 per cent reserve wines.

The vintage Grand Cellier d'Or *premier cru*, using four-fifths old vine Chardonnay from the single *lieu-dit* Les Blanches Voies in Rilly-la-Montagne, is vinified in older 228-litre barrels with up to six years ageing and 7 grams per litre dosage for a delicious, appley Champagne underpinned by lean, crisp acidity. The prestige cuvée, aptly named Coeur de Cuvée, is 80 per cent Chardonnay, 20 per cent Pinot Noir from 60-year-old vines, fermented from a 'super-cuvée' of 1,400 litres from the pressing and aged for 10 months in barrique. The syle is rich and vinous, with nutty burgundian notes and great longevity. Anyone who gets their hands on a bottle of the 2008 vintage is in for a treat.

Champagne Vouette & Sorbée

Buxières-Sur-Arce

www.vouette-et-sorbee.com

The charming names of Vouette and Sorbée belong to two *lieux-dits* that Bertrand Gautherot inherited from his father in his 5 hectares of biodynamic-certified Pinot Noir and Chardonnay vineyards. Growing up on a traditional mixed farm, Gautherot returned to the family estate in 1993 after working as a luxury goods designer for Dior and Chanel. Starting out by farming conventionally, selling his grapes, like so many from the Aube, to Champagne houses in the north, he became inspired by Jérôme Prévost, Anselme Selosse and Pierre Larmandier, gradually converting to biodynamic viticulture and becoming Demeter certified in 1998. He bottled his first Champagne in 2001.

On a slope behind the family's house, the south-facing Vouette, with Kimmeridgian limestone at the bottom, Portlandian at the top, was recently replanted from Pinot Noir to Chardonnay. Sorbée, planted to Pinot Noir and originally Gamay, is a south-west-facing plateau of Portlandian limestone; his very individual Saignée de Sorbée comes from here. In addition to Vouette and Sorbée, he has four more *lieux-dits*: Biaunes, 0.6 hectares of mostly Pinot Noir, which shares the same mix of Kimmeridgian and Portlandian limestone soils but faces west; Tirmy, a west-facing vineyard of upwards of 30-year-old Pinot Noir; Fonnet, mostly Pinot Noir, located in a small, enclosed valley of Kimmeridgian clay soils; and Chatel, a rocky, limestone site planted to Pinot Noir and located in the neighbouring village of Ville-sur-Arce.

Strict pruning ensures that yields are small and the wines concentrated. Bertrand harvests the grapes as ripe as possible, presses by traditional wooden Coquard and ferments with natural yeasts in oak barrels without chaptalization or filtration. Riddling is done by hand before disgorgement *à la volée*. All his Champagnes benefit from a couple of years bottle age after being disgorged without dosage. There is no *liqueur d'expédition* on his complex, long-aged Extrait. Bertrand also works with a perpetual reserve and has two 40-hectolitre barrels, one for Chardonnay, the other for Pinot Noir. He uses up to 5 per cent of the 'solera' in the pure Pinot Noir Fidèle. Textures, made from Pinot Blanc grown in Fonnet, is aged in both barrel and amphora. Average production is about 40,000 bottles per year.

THE REST OF FRANCE

If you're a thousand miles from Champagne and making fizz, the physical distance and perhaps the relative novelty can give you a certain clarity of vision, thought and ambition. Conversely, it can be less easy to see the bottle for the bubbles when you're oppressed by the weight of tradition and blinded by the white light of Champagne. Perhaps it's not that surprising then that the production of much French fizz is so often an afterthought reflected in the quality – or lack of it – of the grapes selected for the privilege.

That isn't to say there aren't pockets of excellence in many of the aspiring regions. In the Languedoc, Limoux has a proud tradition going back to medieval times and the same goes for Clairette de Die from the Rhône. Saumur in the Loire benefits from the natural advantages of cool, limestone (tuffeau) cellars in which to mature its sparkling wines and has a handful of good producers. North of Champagne, Alsace has the climate and the varieties for making some truly delicious fizz. And since crémant came into being as a unifying brand, there's more of an identity to French fizz, which can offer a diverse palette of affordable bubbles.

Crémant was originally the Champagne term for a soft, creamy style of fizz made at lower pressure than the norm. In return for their agreement not to use the term *méthode champenoise*, a deal was struck with French (and EU) producers outside Champagne, giving them the exclusive right to use the term crémant for their new fizz appellations. It is allowed in the EU (Commission Reg 2019/33 art 53) for any traditional method sparkling wine with a protected geographical indication (GI), and even if from outside the EU provided the wine is made from grapes that are manually harvested and destemmed.

Since the creation of the Crémant Federation in 1982, France now has eight crémant appellations: Alsace, Jura, Savoie, Loire, Bourgogne, Bordeaux, Limoux and Die. Between them, they cover an area of some 11,720 hectares with around 6,000 producers involved. Grapes must be manually harvested and wines produced at a volume of no more than 100 litres for 150 kilograms of grapes. Minimum atmospheres of pressure vary from 3.5 to 4 and ageing on the lees must conform to the EU nine month minimum, although it can be longer.

Alsace

In addition to the Champagne grapes plus Auxerrois and Riesling, Alsace producers use a lot of Pinot Blanc, whose neutral aromas and good acidity suit the style. Thanks to the Vosges mountains and a northerly latitude similar to Champagne's Aube region, Alsace vineyards have the altitude and climate for fizz together with a patchwork of varied soils. By adapting grape variety to soils, exposures and microclimates, the best producers can take advantage of a long growing season to achieve the desired ripeness and give themselves a multiplicity of blending options.

Loire Valley

In addition to Crémant de Loire and the new (2018) Prestige de Loire, the Loire Valley has a number of sparkling wine appellations: Anjou, Mountlouis, Saumur, Touraine and Vouvray. Vouvray and Saumur are

The crémant rulebook

Crémant	Permitted grape varieties	Pressure minimum	Ageing (besides EU 9 month minimum)	Vineyard area (ha)*	AOC date
Crémant d'Alsace	Pinot Blanc, Pinot Gris, Pinot Noir, Auxerrois, Chardonnay, Riesling	4 atm.		3,900	1976
Crémant de Bordeaux	Semillon, Sauvignon Blanc, Sauvignon Gris, Muscadelle, Ugni Blanc, Colombard, Cabernet Franc, Cabernet Sauvignon, Carmenère, Merlot, Malbec, Petit Verdot	3.5 atm.		910	1990
Crémant de Bourgogne	Pinot Noir, Pinot Gris, Pinot Blanc, Chardonnay, Sacy, Aligoté, Melon de Bourgogne, Gamay	4 atm.	Éminent: 2 years. Grand Éminent: 3 years.	2,860	1975
Crémant de Die	Clairette, Aligoté, Muscat à Petits Grains	3.5 atm.		30	1993
Crémant du Jura	Chardonnay, Pinot Noir, Trousseau, Savagnin, Pinot Gris, Poulsard	3.5 atm.		515	1995
Crémant de Limoux	Chardonnay, Chenin Blanc, Mauzac, Pinot Noir	4 atm.		820	1990
Crémant de Loire	Chenin Blanc, Cabernet Franc, Cabernet Sauvignon, Pineau d'Aunis, Pinot Noir, Chardonnay, Arbois, Grolleau Noir, Grolleau Gris, Orbois	4 atm.		2,630	1975
Crémant de Savoie	Jacquère, Altesse, Chardonnay, Pinot Noir, Gamay	4 atm.		57	2015

* From the 2018–2019 National Federation of Manufacturers and Mixers Crémant (FNPEC) press pack

the best-known and while Vouvray uses the high acid Chenin Blanc almost exclusively, Saumur can include Chardonnay, Sauvignon Blanc and red wine grapes such as Cabernet Franc, Pinot Noir and Gamay. Loire fizz can be up and down, but in the hands of a committed producer like Jacky Blot at Domaine de la Taille aux Loups or Vincent Carême, it can be thoroughly enjoyable.

Southern France

In southern France, there is something of a dichotomy between the traditional Blanquette de Limoux, which is based on the Mauzac grape, and the region's modern incarnation of Crémant de Limoux, which uses mainly Chardonnay and Chenin Blanc. Blanquette in its *méthode an-cestrale* form can make for a delicious drink. Gaillac also produces a *méthode ancestrale* brut and demi-sec from Mauzac, while its mousseux can also include the local Len de l'El and Ondenc. Clairette de Die is basically a sparking muscat that can be pleasantly sweet and grapey in *méthode ancestrale* form. I haven't tasted enough sparkling Bordeaux to be able to form an opinion.

Mountain wines

Jura and Savoie are the dark horses of crémant. Savoie uses the local Jacquère and Altesse varieties. Jura shows promise in its combination of Chardonnay and Pinot Noir with Trousseau and Savagnin, and for its rosé uses Pinot Noir and Poulsard.

Burgundy

My least favoured crémants are those from Burgundy. I have enjoyed the sparkling Crémants of Burgundy's Simmonet-Febvre, but I did one Burgundy négociant a favour by excluding their wines from this book. Time will tell whether the grandiose new designations of ageing, Éminent (minimum two years on the lees) and Grand Éminent (mini-mum three years) will make a difference.

Producers

Château de L'Aulée

Azay-Le-Rideau, Loire Valley

www.laulee.com

The Cordier family of Bordeaux built Château de l'Aulée and its cellars on the Indre, a tributary of the Loire, in 1856. The stately property was bought by Champagne Deutz in 1973, which renovated and replanted the vineyards to Chenin Blanc. In 2004, Marielle and Arnaud Henrion fell in love with the place and decided to give it a new lease of life, with biodiversity at the forefront of their approach, grassing between rows, ploughing, reducing sprays and installing beehives. Originally from Champagne, Marielle studied oenology in Reims and worked at Bollinger, Pommery and Bricout.

Chenin Blanc is planted on clay and flint soils, which Marielle feels brings finesse and freshness. In 2008, they took over 6.5 hectares of Cabernet Franc near Chinon for sparkling rosés, bringing their total vineyard area in production to 32 hectares. Marielle uses pneumatic presses and aims to protect against oxidation. Wines stay on lees for at least 18 to 24 months before disgorging and longer for the crémants.

While the Crémant Brut Zéro is peachy and ripe, it is shot through with classic Chenin acidity which makes for a thirst-quenchingly bone-dry style. Their Crémant Brut Classique shows lively freshness and a note of biscuity complexity balanced by freshness, and the Cuvée Intense is indeed intense, with a hint of apricot richness underpinned by a lively freshness. The disgorgement date is printed on the back label as well as a recommended consume-by date. Some 200,000 bottles are produced, of which 80 per cent is fizz.

Cave de Beblenheim

Beblenheim, Alsace

www.cave-beblenheim.com

The Cave de Beblenheim was established in 1952 and in the decades that followed, this cooperative grouped together 150 winegrowers owning a total of 500 hectares of vines spread mainly around the pretty Alsace villages of Beblenheim, Molsheim and Dorlisheim. Production of Crémant d'Alsace started in the 1980s, and with the arrival of Patrick Le Bastard, it developed new blends, including its highly regarded Crémant Sub Rosa. In 2020, the cave took on a new head winemaker, Corinne Perez, who has worked in Alsace since 2003. Corinne is especially focused on developing single varieties for Alsace crémant.

The Cave allocates some 140 hectares of vineyards to fizz, mainly on clay-limestone soils. With plenty of sunshine and protection from western rains in the Vosges hills' east- and south-east-facing vineyards, at between 150 and 400 metres above sea level, healthy grapes ripen gradually, with sprays kept to a minimum. Grapes are harvested by hand, whole bunches are pressed and only the cuvée and the next fraction are used for crémant. The must is fermented in stainless steel and malolactic fermentation is avoided where possible to maintain freshness and increase ageing potential. After blending and second fermentation, the wines remain on the lees for at least 12 months and up to 36–48 months for the top cuvées.

The range is made up of two entry-level cuvées, a white and a rosé (made from Pinot Noir) as well as single-varietal cuvées of Chardonnay, Blanc de Noirs and Pinot Blanc through to the top-of-the range cuvée, Sub Rosa. Both the non-vintage Blanc de Noirs Brut and the non-vintage Black Rose Rosé Brut are excellent, with all the freshness, complexity and finesse you could hope for. Overall, Beblenheim aims for freshness, varietal character and purity of fruit and succeeds. The sixth biggest producer in Alsace, its annual production of fizz is 1.8 million bottles.

Bouvet Ladubay

Saumur, Loire Valley
www.bouvet-ladubay.fr

Bouvet Ladubay was founded in 1851 by Etienne Bouvet and his wife Célestine Ladubé. In her dowry on their marriage in 1851, Célestine brought the Cave aux Moines, an ancient underground network of tunnels and caves, and changed the 'é' of her surname to 'ay', which she considered more elegant. It was bought in 1932 by Justin-Marcel Monmousseau, great-grandfather of the current incumbent, Juliette, taken over by his son Jean, in 1946, and in turn by Jean's son, Patrice, in 1972, reverting to family ownership in 2015 after periods of ownership by Taittinger and United Breweries.

Bouvet Ladubay is based in Saumur's Saint Hilaire Saint Florent, where it has recently invested in new production facilities at nearby Distré. It has never owned vineyards, but buys must or base wine to the tune of 42,000 hectolitres from 80 winegrowers between Touraine in the eastern Loire and Anjou in the centre. Bouvet works closely with its winegrowers, 70 per cent of whom have transitioned to HVE, Terra Vitis or organic certification, with the aim of reaching 100 per cent sustainable practices by 2023. Saumur is characterized by chalk and clay and the Saumur Brut appellation (created in 1957) overlaps part of Anjou where the soils are grey and black shale and clay.

Winemaking is a team effort, consisting of the company's president,

Patrice Monmousseau, his daughter Juliette, who joined the team in 2010, along with Vincent Herbreteau, cellar manager, and Grégory Fournier, head of production.

From a routine 9 per cent in the 1960s, potential alcohols now reach 11 per cent or more (11.5–12 per cent in 2020). The initial fermentation is non-oxidative, with pressing followed by ageing of the base wines in 0–2 year old barrels, 3–5 year old barrels and 6–9 year old for the Trésor, Instinct, Zéro and Ogmius cuvées in the Saumur Brut AOP. There is no malolactic fermentation and all wines are vintage (even, counterintuitively the non-vintage). Ageing varies from 12 months for the classic non-vintage Saumur Brut, to 18 months for Saphir Saumur Brut and up to 12 years for the vintage Ogmius Saumur. Dosage is wine of the same cuvée with sugar and *esprit de Cognac*.

Bouvet Ladubay's hallmark is its soft, rounded *blanc de blancs*. Chenin is used as the base for all the sparkling white wines, 100 per cent for the Saumur Brut, and 80–85 per cent with between 5 and 20 per cent Chardonnay for the rest of the *blanc de blancs* fizz. In contrast, the great value, crowdpleasing Saumur Brut Rosé is made from pure Cabernet Franc, with Cabernet Franc, Grolleau and Gamay used for the red sparkling wines. The overall aim is to capture the freshness and zesty acidity which the chalky terroir endows thanks to its sponge-like ability to absorb and retain water.

Vincent Carême

Vouvray, Loire Valley

www.vincentcareme.fr

Born in the Vouvray area to parents who ran a mixed farm comprising vineyards, cereals and vegetables, Vincent Carême has, in a relatively short space of time, become one of the leading vignerons in the revival of Vouvray. After trainee stints in Champagne, Anjou, Alsace, Thailand and South Africa (where he met his future wife, Tania), he set up his own winery beginning, in the inauspicious vintage of 1999, with a few hectares of rented vines at the same time as he was teaching at the Lycée Agricole. The wines were initially sold as Domaine de la Haute Borne after the eponymous lieu dit of La Haute Borne on the plateau.

Seduced by the pet nats from Christian Chaussard and Nicolas Renard, he decided to have a go at pet nat in his first vintage. Although relatively unknown at the time, the style was starting to gain traction thanks to the natural wine new wave. He started organic production in

2003 and today he and Tania have 18 hectares of organic vineyards based on Chenin Blanc, half of which is sparkling wine. For the Vouvray Brut, which comes from 20–30 year old vines, a natural fermentation in tank is stopped at 20 grams per litre of residual sugar and, after tirage, bottles spend at least 18 months on the lees in the naturally cool limestone cellars before being disgorged without dosage. Vincent makes 30,000 bottles.

The 2018 Plaisir Ancestral comes from 40-year-old, low-yielding Chenin vines grown on clay and flint soils with limestone subsoils and is picked by hand, then bottled during the first fermentation at 18 grams per litre, with no added yeast. Smelling of sweet apples and honey, it has more weight, richness and depth than the younger Brut and, with no added sugar or yeasts at tirage, it is a beautiful drop whose ripe stone fruit flavours are cut by the trenchant acidity of the Chenin grape. The pet nat process is not officially recognized by the Vouvray appellation 'but we are working on it,' says Vincent. After 18 to 24 months, the wine is disgorged with no dosage and 20,000 bottles are made.

Dopff & Irion

Riquewihr, Alsace

www.dopff-irion.com

René Dopff, a member of the Alsace-Lorraine brigade of the Free French Forces during the Second World War, joined forces with the widow Irion to found Dopff & Irion, acquiring Riquewihr's historic château, originally built in 1549 and owned by the Princes of Württemberg. Placing the emphasis on quality, reducing yields and modernizing the labels, he had a big influence on the vineyards of Alsace, above all pioneering crémants after the creation of the appellation in 1976. He claims to be the first in Alsace to associate a particular grape variety with specific terroirs.

Merging with the Cave de Pfaffenheim in 1998, Dopff & Irion today cultivate 27 hectares around Riquewihr, a relatively large estate in the context of the fragmented structure of Alsace's vineyards, where some 60 per cent of producers farm less than a hectare. They rely on 50 growers for the balance of their production, while a further 100 growers supply the Pfaffenheim cooperative. In a vast mosaic of soils and subsoils, their soils are mainly limestone and chalky-clay. To the west of Riquewihr, the Vosges mountains minimize the oceanic influence, while to the north, the Schoenenbourg ridge offers protection from cold north winds, so the climate lends itself to a slow ripening of the grapes.

The wines stay on the lees for between 15 and 18 months; five years in the case of the Pinot Gris. Dosage is around 10 grams per litre except for Extra Brut Zero Dosage. No white wines, still or sparkling, undergo malolactic fermentation, as they aim to preserve the natural aromatic qualities of the grape variety. The impressive Cuvée Prestige Elégance Brut is ripe without being sweet, the mousse nicely textured and balanced; there's a crisp, dry, citrusy Extra Brut Zero Dosage, the fine Egérie Chardonnay Brut, and the Brut Rosé is excellent thanks to a fleshy strawberryish fruitiness. Annual production is 300,000 bottles.

Domaine Dopff au Moulin

Riquewihr, Alsace

www.dopff-au-moulin.fr

Bubbles have been in the Dopff family blood ever since Etienne-Arnaud Dopff's great-grandfather Gustave-Julien came across the *méthode champenoise* at the Universal Exposition in Paris in 1900. Back in Riquewihr, when Alsace was part of Germany, he imported grape must from Champagne to make fizz and, after trial and error, he found that grapes of the Pinot family grown in Alsace's sandy soils with stones and chalk gave the best results. The Dopff family split in two after the Second World War, with only Dopff au Moulin remaining in private family ownership. Julien Dopff's son Julien-Pierre was instrumental in the creation of the Syndicat des Crémants d'Alsace and the Fédération Nationale des Producteurs et Élaborateurs de Crémants. Since joining the estate in 1998, his grandson Etienne-Arnaud Dopff, and his wife Marlène, have redefined the terroir and the processes. Yields have been cut, dosage reduced, fewer sulphites are used and quality has improved.

The Dopff family own 70 hectares spread between Hunawihr and Colmar, with the majority of the parcels around Riquewihr, which sits at 300 metres in the foothills of the Vosges. Twenty hectares are dedicated to fizz, topped up by the purchase of around 80 hectares of grapes, half of which are devoted to sparkling wine. Sparkling wine production totals 600,000 bottles. The soils are mostly sandy and stony, with chalk in Colmar, and heavier soils in Riquewihr. The estate has been HVE certified since 2019 and is moving towards organic conversion.

Montpellier-trained Pascal Batot began experimenting with oak fermentation on a Chardonnay–Pinot Noir cuvée in the 2016 vintage. Most crémants remain on the lees for at least 24 months. In 2012 Dopff made its first Chardonnay bubbles with no added sulphites. They also trialled a Vin Orange made from Gewurztraminer and, in 2020, released a limited edition crémant, Solera, a multi-vintage Chardonnay with no added sulphites. The whole range is well made, but I would pick out the Chardonnay Brut Nature, which shows light yeasty notes in a textured mousse with pleasingly crisp apple flavours, and the pure Pinot Noir Cuvée Blanc de Noirs for its appealing red berry mousse and subtle complexity. Somewhat teasingly, they only put the name Dopff on the label, which could lead to confusion with Dopff & Irion, but the depiction of a windmill, reprised on the cork, gives the game away.

Domaine Fernand Engel

Rorschwihr, Alsace

www.fernand-engel.fr

After the Second World War, Fernand and Elisa Engel moved to a farm belonging to their ancestors in Rorschwihr and planted vines. Their son Bernard joined Fernand in 1970 and today, three generations run the business, Bernard and his wife Danielle, their daughter Sandrine and her husband Xavier and, since 2015, their daughter Amélie. Graduating from Toulouse in 1995, Xavier became the winemaker in the following year. The biggest organic family winery in Alsace (Ecocert certified organic 1997–8), Fernand Engel work 65 hectares of vineyards, which are divided into 180 parcels scattered among the eight villages of Mittelwhir, Bergheim, Rorschwihr, Rodern, Saint-Hippolyte, Orschwiller, Kinztheim and Saint Pierre.

Domaine Engel started making Crémant d'Alsace in 1984, planting Chardonnay and Pinot Noir between 1995 and 2000 in red calcareous soils on marls with limestone which, thanks to excellent water retention during warm, dry summers, brings good ripeness and acidity. The plots are a geological jigsaw made up of a mix of limestone and marly-clay limestone soils (Rorschwihr and Bergheim), with granite, gneiss and calcareous sandstone in the other villages. Adapting grape variety to a diverse mix of soils, exposures and microclimates, gives the domaine a multitude of blending options.

They aim to harvest late to bring in the grapes ripe at around 12 per cent potential alcohol. At pressing, they separate the fraction as to 70 per cent cuvée, with the 30 per cent *taille* not used. The first fermentation is stopped at around 11 per cent alcohol and the base wines kept on the lees to increase body and roundness. A perpetual reserve is planned. Crémant Trilogie, made since 2007, is an unusual wine which undergoes a triple fermentation, including two *prises de mousse* with 18 months on the lees after each fermentation in bottle and no dosage. They are planning to print the date of disgorgement on the back label.

Langlois-Chateau

Saumur, Loire Valley

www.langlois-chateau.fr

If you're going to make sparkling wine, then you could do worse than have Champagne Bollinger as your boss. Perhaps the greatest benefit is access to the Bollinger savoir-faire, with Big Brother Bolly always there to keep you on your toes. So it is with Langlois-Chateau. The name derives from Jeanne Chateau who, in 1912, along with her husband Edouard Langlois, took over the enterprise founded as Maison Delandes in 1885. The Jacques Bollinger Family Group acquired a majority stake in 1973, and from the early 1980s the decision was made to produce only Crémant de Loire, with the ambitious but simple aim of producing the best Loire fizz.

The winemaking is overseen by Jean François Liegeois, an Alsace native who joined Langlois-Chateau in 2005. In 2008 François Régis de Fougeroux became managing director. Langlois-Chateau owns 95 hectares, with 51 hectares in Saumur, 11 hectares in Saumur-Champigny and 33 hectares in Sancerre, and buys in some 500 tonnes of grapes. In a transition of part of the vineyard to organic, 30 hectares (19 in Saumur and 11 in Saumur-Champigny) were certified organic in 2020. With a temperate-oceanic climate, the terroir is clay chalky soils in Saumur and silica chalky soils in Saumur-Champigny. The selection of grapes, largely Chenin Blanc, but also Chardonnay, Cabernet Franc and Pinot Noir, is based on five different soil types with separate vinification by grape variety and soil type.

After a gentle pressing of 160 kilograms to 100 litres of juice and separation of the first pressing, traditional method fermentation takes place in the company's naturally cool tuffeau cellars. The wines are held in bottle for at least two years for the classic cuvée and four years or longer for the four-grape Quadrille, then held in the cellar for at least three months after disgorgement. The style is fresh and elegant, with ageing lending classic buttery and yeasty characters, and a style and quality not a million miles from that of one Champagne Bollinger.

Domaine de la Taille aux Loups

Montlouis sur Loire, Loire Valley

www.jackyblot.fr

Domaine de la Taille aux Loups was established by Jacky Blot, a former wine broker, in the late 1980s, when he purchased 5 hectares of 55- to 70-year old vines in Montlouis-sur Loire on the southern bank of the Loire opposite Vouvray. Working organically since 1988, his aim is for quality based on low yields, ploughing and avoiding herbicides and, in the cellar, avoiding chaptalization and working with natural yeasts. Working with his son, Jean-Philippe, the 'maestro of Montlouis' believes that sugar distorts the purity of which Chenin Blanc is capable. He also works with barrel-fermentation *à la bourgogne*, using old oak to avoid importing the flavours of new oak.

Including Clos Mosny, bought in 2011, the vineyard area today covers 55 hectares of Chenin Blanc, of which some 15 hectares are devoted to Triple Zéro, which Jacky likes to call 'the ancestor of pet nat'. In 1993, Jacky set out to make a fizz with no chaptalization, no topping up at tirage and no dosage, hence Triple Zéro. To begin with, hardly anyone took any interest 'so eventually we ended up drinking it ourselves,' he says. With hindsight and almost 30 years of experience and hard work, Jacky has fine-tuned the quality to remove any traces of fermentation and cidery aromas.

The grapes used for Triple Zéro come from Taille aux Loup's organic clay–flint on limestone vineyard in Montlouis-sur-Loire. Yields from his massal selection of old vines are less than 40 hectolitres per hectare, helping to ensure full ripeness. Only the first pressing is kept for Triple Zéro, whose inviting perfume leads to an appetizing purity. Jacky purchases 80 new barrels a year for his complement of 1,000 casks and the juice is moved by gravity into these old Burgundian oak barrels where a lengthy fermentation using native yeasts begins in the domaine's cool cellars. Gaining in complexity, the wine is disgorged some 30 months later. Since 2012, Jacky has kept back some stocks of older vintages of Triple Zéro for late disgorgement and they are astonishingly good, especially the rich and complex 2008 Triple Zéro Millésimé, disgorged in 2018. Total annual production is 60–80,000 bottles.

Domaine André et Mireille Tissot

Montigny-les-Arsures, Jura

www.stephane-tissot.com

There are three domaines in the Jura bearing the Tissot name and all roads lead back to Maurice Tissot, a mixed farmer in Montigny-les-Arsures, who had six children. After his return from the Algerian war in 1962, one of Maurice's sons, André, married Mireille and created the family estate of Domaine André et Mireille Tissot. It has been run since the early 1990s by their son Stéphane, with his wife Bénédicte, who work the vineyards sustainably. In 1999 he switched to organic production and in 2003 the estate was certified biodynamic with Demeter.

The estate is made up of 50 hectares with a multitude of cuvées in crémant, red and white, each aiming to express a particular terroir. Soils are a mixture of heavy clayey marls that 'bring structure and reduction' and calcareous soils that bring 'tension and minerality'. The cool Jurassic climate helps with both optimum ripeness and in maintaining freshness. Crémants began with the 1989 vintage. In 2005 Stéphane started making crémants with longer ageing on the lees, notably a *blanc de blancs élevé en fûts*, BBF, made from an oak-aged base wine, and Crémant Indigène, which is based on a straw wine must.

Chardonnay and Pinot Noir are handpicked and whole bunch pressed in pneumatic presses. The BBF and *blanc de noirs* crémants are fermented exclusively in barrels for complexity and depth. BBF is a blend of 80 per cent wine from the previous year that has been aged and fermented in used barrels for 12 months with 20 per cent of the new vintage. The Indigène and Classic Crémant cuvées are made with a blend of half of the wine fermented in vats and half in barrel to obtain structure and complexity while retaining their fruity side. The rosé is mostly tank-fermented for freshness. No crémant receives any dosage and the use of sulphur is minimal. Ageing of wines on the lees varies from 14 to 48 months depending on the wine. Yearly production is 60,000 bottles, which represents a third of total production.

8

GERMANY

Krug, Heidsieck, Bollinger, Deutz, Taittinger, Roederer and Mumm were all of course German or from German families associated with bubbles. So one might wonder how different the story of German sparkling wine could have been had they not all strayed to Champagne in the early nineteenth century to find fame, or at least fortune. As it was, Georg Kessler, who worked for Madame Clicquot at the start of the nineteenth century, returned from Champagne to his home city of Esslingen in 1826 to found the Sekt firm of GC Kessler. At the Leipzig Fair in 1850, his successor Carl Weiss first presented the new brand Kessler Cabinet – Germany's oldest known sparkling wine brand.

Why Sekt? Shakespeare's German translators turned Falstaff's sack (Sherry) into 'Sect'. The story goes that, in the year before Georg Kessler founded his firm, the German actor Ludwig Devrient (1784–1832), who played Falstaff, was in his favourite restaurant Lutter & Wegener, when he ordered a glass of wine: 'Bringe er mit Sekt, Schurke' ('bring me a cup of sack, rascal'). Whether Devrient meant Sherry or sparkling wine history does not record, but either way, the put-upon waiter brought him a glass of his usual fizz and the association of sparkling wine and Sekt stuck.

The German sparkling wine industry got off on the right footing in the nineteenth century. From the 1850s to the turn of the century, 11–12 million bottles were being made annually. Brands were marketed similarly to Champagne and the English crown princess Alice, Queen Victoria's daughter, visited the Kupferberg Cellars in Mainz in 1870. However, it didn't stop the German Chancellor, Otto von Bismarck, from declaring: 'my patriotism stops short of my stomach'. A victim of its own success, Sekt had a tax slapped on it in 1902, the Flottensteuer, which helped to build Kaiser Wilhelm II's navy. By 1909, the sliding 'Banderole tax' and VAT amounting to 55 per cent of the bottle price, combined with the loss to the French of Lorraine, the source of much quality base wine, put paid to the industry until after the Second World War.

The 1960s saw the beginning of a revival and rapid expansion with giant *sektfabriken* producing tank-fermented fizz. But Sekt is not a protected term and producers can, and did, import grapes, juice, or wine to make cheap fizz, labelled according to minimum standards with no protected designation of origin. While the base wines were initially from Germany, the pressures of competitive pricing soon meant sourcing the cheapest within Europe. Quality was the first to go, although the wine remained popular within Germany.

From 1986 all Deutscher Sekt had to be made from German wine, while from 1988 the law enabled producers to hold Sekt in their cellars untaxed. These two regulations kickstarted the move to quality and a legal framework for premium German Sekt b.A. and Winzersekt. German Sekt b.A. is quality sparkling wine from a protected designation of origin wine region, while Winzersekt must be from single estates, with extended lees ageing.

By the new millennium, the big brands of Rotkäppchen-Mumm, Henkell-Söhnlein, and Schloss Wachenheim were producing 575 million tank-method bottles a year, more sparkling wine than all of Champagne, but much of it was mediocre sweet and sour fizz made from a blend of wines from various European countries. Although there are some 2,000 producers today, the new pioneers of quality fizz, a tiny proportion of the vast sparkling wine industry, are small producers making bottle-fermented sparkling wines, mostly brut and extra brut, either from Riesling or the classic Champagne varieties.

The positive development of high-end Sekt has been fuelled by increasing consumer interest in the €10–€15 per bottle price category thanks to quality producers such as von Buhl and Griesel and a growing awareness that achieving higher quality depends on precisely crafted base wines. The reduction of sulphite additions pioneered by Matthieu Kaufmann at von Buhl (now in a fizz project with Christmann) has also been stylistically significant. In 2020, the VDP, the association of top German estates, raised the bar by applying its high quality standards to sparkling wines, stipulating a minimum of 24 months on the lees for vintage Sekts (VDP. SEKT) and 36 months for prestige cuvées (VDP.SEKT.PRESTIGE®).

Germany's flagship grape, Riesling, is capable of producing a fizz that retains the variety's fragrance and vitality, developing a more Champagne-like complexity after the yeasts go to work on it in the bottle. The challenge of climate change is giving Riesling producers pause for thought with cool regions like the Mosel and Nahe showing signs of warming up and speeding up evaporation rates. Chardonnay and Pinot Noir are not insulated against climate change either, but there's no doubting the quality of the many excellent new sparkling wines, vintage, non-vintage and rosé, now being made from blends of the Champagne varieties. Regional crémant too, bottle-fermented with a minimum of nine months on the lees, hand-picked and whole-bunch pressed, is looking promising.

Producers

Wein- & Sektgut Bamberger

Meddersheim, Nahe

www.weingut-bamberger.de

On the western outskirts of the charming village of Meddersheim, close to the meandering Nahe River, Heiko and his wife Ute specialize in traditional method fizz. Theirs is a substantial range made from 15 hectares of vineyards, but their reputation is largely based around the fizz they make from both Riesling and Pinot (Noir and Blanc) grapes, even though it accounts only for some 20 per cent of their production. That's why they refer to themselves as 'bubblemakers'. 'We focus on the grape varieties, so I think that Riesling Sekt has to taste like a Riesling, with bubbles, as well as making a fizz from Pinot Noir and Blanc.'

Heiko's grandfather had always delivered his Riesling to the Meddersheim cooperative. But in 1968, his father, Karl-Kurt, decided to switch the mixed farm to vineyards, expanding to 5–6 hectares and bottling his own wine. In 1984, when Heiko was 15, his father took him to Champagne to learn the ropes. His father believed that Riesling, as the Nahe's signature variety, should be the mainstay of his fizz production (today it's over 50 per cent). Not only was it a known quantity, but companies like Henkell paid top dollar for Nahe Riesling for its acidity. After studying at Geisenheim, Heiko joined his father in 1993 at a time when 85 per cent of production was in sweeter wines, compared with 90 per cent dry today. The vineyards were restored and Riesling, Pinot Noir and Pinot Blanc were planted.

With a harvest more than a week later than Bad Kreuznach and three weeks later than Pfalz, colder days and nights bring the desired aromatic character and freshness over a longer ripening period. Even with climate change, the age of the vines, which are mostly over 30 years old with deep roots, means they can cope with hot, dry days in the red sandstone soils, Rotliegende. The colder years this century have been 2008, 2010, 2012 and 2014, while 2007, 2009, 2011, 2013, 2015, 2018 and 2019 were warmer, and 2016 and 2017 somewhere in between. They have been certified for three years as Fair and Green, a sustainable system. Grapes are picked by hand and they are giving the wines longer on the lees. In late 2019, they still had some 2009 vintage undisgorged.

Riesling is fermented in stainless steel, while up to 20 per cent German oak fermentation, using 1,200-litre Stückfass and 500-litre tonneaux, is used for Pinot. Some reserve wines are kept in barrel as up to 15 per cent can be used for vintage fizz; they are toying with using it in non-vintage fizz too. Since 2015, dosage has come down from 10–12 grams per litre to 8 grams per litre and lower thanks to increased ripeness and a demand for drier styles. They are also starting to put the date of disgorgement on the label in response to demand.

The entry level Bamberger Riesling Brut is an appealing appley textured fizz that benefits from a year or two's post-disgorgement ageing. Their Pinot Rosé Sekt Brut, a blend of Pinot Noir and Blanc, smells of summer berries and refreshes with a vivid, strawberry mousse and dry cranberry aftertaste. A selection of the best grapes, the Riesling S Brut combines savoury nutty and brioche aromas with textural finesse and vivacity. Bamberger's Riesling Brut Nature is mouthwateringly dry and stylishly gastronomic, while the Riesling 25 Brut Nature Jubiläum, with six years on the lees, completes the picture.

Sekthaus BurkhardtSchür

Bürgstadt am Main, Franken

www.burkhardtschuer.de

Laura Burkhardt and Sebastian Schür have no qualms in admitting that Champagne is their model and for that purpose, they only source Chardonnay, Pinot Noir and Meunier. With no vineyards of their own, their raw material comes from wine growers, friends and Sebastian Schür's brother Marcus. After founding Sekthaus Burkhardt Schür in the Franken town of Bürgstadt am Main, Sebastian and Laura, both Geisenheim graduates, produced their first sparkling wine, a *blanc de noirs* Brut Nature made from Pinot Noir, in 2012.

As vineyard manager at Rudolf Fürst from 2006, Sebastian Schür's experience dovetails with that of Laura Burkhardt, who worked at Vinaturel, an organic and biodynamic wine specialist. They know and talk to all of their suppliers, who are happy to grow the grapes as directed by them for the desired result of healthy quality. Pinot Noir is grown on sandstone and weathered gneiss in Bürgstadt and Glottertal. Schwarzriesling (Meunier), added in 2013, is planted on muschelkalk limestone in the Württemberg's Taubertal and also red sandstone and muschelkalk in the Baden part of Würrtemberg. The Chardonnay, from Sebastian's brother Marcus, enabled them to complement the range. It is grown on white loess volcanic soils and muschelkalk in Oberrotweil am Kaiserstuhl in Sebastian's native Baden.

The current range of five sparkling wines is made in the cellar of Paul and Sebastian Fürst. The Pinot Noir base wine is gently pressed before a spontaneous fermentation takes place in used oak barrels of 2,400 litres, with the Chardonnay fermented in barrique. After the *prise de mousse*, the wines remain in storage on their yeast lees for over 60 months in their historic red sandstone cellar in Bürgstadt am Main. Most of the sparkling wines undergo malolactic fermentation. Five thousand bottles a year are made.

VDP.Weingut Emrich-Schönleber

Monzingen, Nahe

www.emrich-schoenleber.de

When Goethe came to the St Rochus Festival in Bingen 200 years ago, as he sat at a table with local VIPs, he was introduced to the lightness and drinkability of the Monzingen Riesling. Two centuries on, Werner Schönleber and his son Frank uphold the tradition for elegantly crafted Riesling. Wines are made from the estate's 5.5 hectares of blue slate and quartzite Halenberg and 4 hectares of red slate and gravel Frühlingsplätzchen sitting cheek by jowl at altitudes of 160–250 metres close to the nearby Soonwald Forest in the western Nahe. Thanks to thermal winds, ridden by falcons and buzzards, and cooling night-time breezes, the vineyards enjoy a relatively cool climate.

Twenty-five years ago, a third of production was sweet wines, whereas that's just 10 per cent today, with 85 per cent of production from Riesling, mostly dry and sparkling. The rest is Pinot Gris and Pinot Blanc. In 1994, they joined the VDP. Today, Werner's son Frank runs the estate while Werner spends his time in the vineyard on most days. 'We don't kiss every morning,' says Werner with a twinkle in his eye, but it's clear that even if they don't see eye to eye on every little detail, there is great respect between father and son.

Riesling is made in stainless steel and big oak vats. After fifty years, Werner has seen a tendency for summers to begin earlier, with more vintages with hot days over 30°C. Picking is two weeks earlier these days and tends to be earlier than most in the Nahe, which is good for the excellent sparkling Riesling that they make. The Monzingen NV Nahe Riesling Brut is kept on the lees for 24 months and, with 8 grams per litre dosage, is delightfully aromatic with a mouthwateringly dry, lime-zesty quality.

Geils Sekt- und Weingut

Bermersheim, Rheinhessen

www.geils.de

Located in the historical centre of Bermersheim, in south-western Rheinhessen, Geils has been family-run for over 200 years. Originally from Flörsheim-Dalsheim, Rudolf Geil's father was already producing and bottling wines in the 1930s and selling them to his local customers. Rudolf's first vintage was at the end of the 1970s. After he and Birgit married in 1986, they moved to Birgit's home town of Bermersheim and started producing dry wines from Pinot Blanc and Pinot Gris. The reputation of fizz began to improve in the 1980s and they took advantage of the mobile bottling plant that called by for tirage and disgorgement.

Today they have 14 hectares of vineyards in Bermersheim,

Flörsheim-Dalsheim and Gundersheim, partly in the single vineyard of the 100-hectare Höllenbrand, which has a high proportion of loess and limestone in the soils. There has been a more recent planting of Pinot Noir with burgundian clones and they are adding 1–2 hectares of Chardonnay and Meunier for sparkling wine. The winery is managed by Birgit, Rudolf and their son Florian. Working side by side, father and son focus on the Pinot varieties because they like what they give to sparkling wines.

All fruit is harvested by hand and the *mittelstück*, or cuvée, is gently pressed before slow fermentation in small barrels. With lengthy maturation on the lees, the result is distinctive Rheinhessen sparkling wines that bear their own signature. The vintage *blanc de noirs* Brut, with three years on the lees, is creamy, balanced and refreshingly dry, while the Brut Rosé, a blend of Pinot Noir and Meunier, is fragrantly floral with a hint of biscuit and attractively balanced berry fruit flavours. Best of the bunch is the excellent Pinot 3 brut, with fine textured biscuit and brioche notes.

Gut Hermannsberg

Niederhausen, Nahe

www.gut-hermannsberg.de

The grand Prussian spread eagle with a crown sitting on its head is a clue to the origins of this large Nahe estate, amplified by the small print beneath the brand name telling us that this was 'vormals königlich-preussische Weinbaudomäne', or, once upon a time, a royal Prussian state property. Founded in 1902 on the site of an old copper mine, Gut Hermannsberg is located on the steep, rugged hillsides of the Nahe Valley overlooking the Nahe River and beyond it the pretty village of Oberhausen.

Its three major vineyard sites, Hermannsberg, Kupfergrube (copper mine) and Steinberg were created by blasting the volcanic terrain and shaping it into south-facing terraced hillsides suitable for planting Riesling at high density, which began in 1905. The first vintage of Hermannsberg was 1907 and it was a founding member of the VDP in 1910. Since 2009, the estate has been run by Jens Reidel and his wife Christine Dinse and the wines made by the talented winemaker Karsten Peter. The estate's 30 hectares of vineyard, cultivated sustainably, are all classified as Grosse Lage. Six of the seven vineyard sites have shallow and stony volcanic soils, while the Hermannsberg itself is the exception with slate bedrock and a shallow layer of loess.

Sparkling wine started as a hobby in 2013 with Riesling, Chardonnay and Weissburgunder fruit mainly from Bad Kreuznach contract growers and leased vineyards, but fizz has since become more serious. Apart from a refreshingly crisp non-vintage Riesling Sekt Brut and a bright, creamy non-vintage Blanc de Blancs, Karsten Peter has created 880 bottles of a 2013 Kupfergrube Extra Brut fizz. After a first fermentation with natural yeasts and five years on the lees, the wine was disgorged with no added dosage in order to maintain terroir expression. Nearly 500 bottles of 2013 Schlossböckelheimer Kupergrube Extra Brut were knocked down at the Nahe wine auction for €62.50 and, with an almost Champagne-like complexity and mineral dryness, the 2014 is arguably even more delicious.

Sekthaus Raumland

Flörsheim-Dalsheim, Rheinhessen

www.raumland.de

In the centre of the featureless Rheinhessen town of Flörsheim-Dalsheim sits an anonymous box of a building with the name Raumland affixed to it. Flörsheim-Dalsheim was a centre of furniture manufacture in its heyday, so it would only be fair to assume that Raumland is the Furniture Village of Rheinhessen. Indeed the distinctive, yellow neo-Palladian villa opposite was home to the Merkel family, whose business empire made furniture for railway stations along the Bingen-Köln railway line. Raumland however, which owns both properties, is in fact the producer of one of Germany's top sparkling wines. The fact that Volker Raumland collects antique furniture is the surreal icing on the cake.

Volker Raumland is from a family winery owned by his parents, Willi and Hedi, in Bockenheim at the border of Rheinhessen and Pfalz. Their typically mixed agricultural enterprise was left to his brother Wilfried to run while the more academic Volker enrolled at Geisenheim, where he joined a Sektprojekt. It was not a popular choice at the time because of the association of sparkling wine with downmarket producers Rotkäppchen and Henkell. Nonetheless, when the project winner was the 100 litres of 1981 Müller-Thurgau Volker had taken from his grandfather's cellar and turned to fizz, this was the catalyst that gave him the confidence to set up his own sparkling wine business.

In 1986, he bought a truck, installed it with fizz-producing equipment, placed an advert in the papers and was soon travelling around Germany, Austria and even the Loire Valley to meet demand. At a

Stuttgart wine festival, he met and then married Heide-Rose in 1988. They bought the Merkel house and found a large, abandoned wine cellar on four stories, three of them below ground, in Mölsheim, 4 kilometres away. Initially too big, the business has grown to such an extent, including contract winemaking, that today, the cellar now bulges with one million bottles. The mobile bottling kept going until 2012, when they decided to park the truck.

Raumland has 16 hectares in Rheinhessen and Pfalz, including sites in Bockenheim, Hohen-Sülzen and Mölsheim, 10 hectares of which are for fizz, with 40 per cent Pinot Noir, 40 per cent Chardonnay and the remaining 20 per cent in Riesling, Pinot Blanc and Meunier. Volker stresses that his aim is not to copy Champagne, because the vineyards, the soils and the climate are all so different. The soils are mainly terrafosca, muschelkalk and algenkalk. The region is on a similar latitude to Burgundy and rainfall is sufficient but not excessive because they are in the rain shadow of the Donnersberg Mountains, which also protect the vineyards from hail. Nights are cool and days are warm, which is ideal for acidity retention. Since 2002, Raumland has been certified organic but it is not written on the label.

In 1997, Raumland took on the young champenoise, Carole Lefebvre, who taught them how to press different fractions and introduced picking for lower sugar levels and lower alcohol levels. Today, the 4,000-kilogram Willmes pneumatic press produces the first 2,050 kilogram cuvée while the *taille* is used for Sekt and sold. Raumland also introduced a minimum bottle-ageing period of 4.5 years to bring the toasty flavours that create a more 'Champagne-like' style. The date of disgorgement is printed on the neck label. In 2012, they took on a Japanese cellar master, Kazuyuki Kaise, a perfectionist who studied winemaking at Geisenheim and became a cooper as well.

At the Mölsheim facility, Volker Raumland devised the 'berry-spa' technique learnt from Ca' del Bosco in Franciacorta and adapted a salad washing machine to wash 95 per cent of the grapes, the remaining 5 per cent of grapes with very ripe, thinner skins requiring greater care. All the wines undergo malolactic fermentation and the dosage is set at a maximum of 6 grams per litre. Production is 100,000 bottles a year. Apart from the rosé, Raumland are vintage specialists. They also started putting aside reserve wines in 2018 to carry out trials for continuity after the fashion of non-vintage Champagne. Raumland even has a reserve cuvée with vintages going back to 1991, their thirtieth anniversary flagship wine and the birth year of Marie-Luise who, like her sister Katharina and mother Heide-Rose, is actively involved in the business.

A vintage Riesling brut combining citrusy tang with briochey notes speaks of its German origins while the rest of the range is focused on the Champagne varieties. A savoury, saline *blanc de blancs* Brut is followed by two cuvées named after the Raumland daughters, Cuvée Katharina brut nature, which is complex, creamy-textured and nutty and Cuvée Marie-Luise brut, a pure Pinot Noir with vinosity and an expansive, finely textured mousse. The Rosé Prestige brut, made by the *saignée* method is sumptuously rich in berry fruit flavours with a satisfyingly dry raspberry-ish mousse, while Triumvirat Grande Cuvée brut is the house's crowning glory, biscuity and full-flavoured, with nutty–almondy notes and great ageing potential. Traditional method producers still represent only 2–3 per cent of the market for German sparkling wines, but quality is improving enormously. As evidence of that progress, Raumland has been accepted as the first fizz-only winery in the VDP.

Volker and daughter Katharina Raumland

9

ITALY

Italy is the world's biggest producer of sparkling wine and boasts the highest number of fizz appellations. The lion's share of Italian bubbles is down to the Prosecco phenomenon. From little more than a standing start at the beginning of the new millennium, Prosecco production today stands at some 600 million bottles of fizz, roughly double the quantity of Champagne. Prosecco shows no signs of waning in popularity, and needless to say, the recent introduction of Prosecco DOC Rosé offers a fresh opportunity to 'add value', as marketers say. Yet while Prosecco is the giant, big in Italy does not necessarily mean best.

Franciacorta in Lombardy is regarded by many as Italy's top sparkling wine region. But Trentino's hill country and cool, northerly climate can be its equal. Alta Langa too is making sparkling wines of crystalline purity and freshness thanks to its location in the foothills of the Alps and newbie enthusiasm. While Prosecco and Lambrusco made by the tank method allow economies of scale, the success of the three top quality fizz regions, Alta Langa, Franciacorta and Trentino, is built on the Champagne grapes and the traditional method. Native grape varieties still dominate numerically. Prosecco's Glera grape apart, from Veneto, Turbiana (aka Trebbiano di Soave), the Durella grape as used in Durello, and Wildbacher, whose origins are in Styria, Austria, can be good. Pignoletto, with its high acidity, is capable of making attractive fizz in the Colli Bolognesi.

Even Asti, with an eye on Prosecco, is trying its hand with a drier style. Asti Secco, created in 2017, is as yet a blip among the 85 million bottles of sweet Asti Spumante and Moscato d'Asti produced. But there are always new discoveries to be made. The traditional method wines of

Oltrepò Pavese south of the River Po in Lombardy are not well-known but show potential, with altitudes higher than those of Franciacorta. Other regions producing credible fizz include Liguria, Campania, Tuscany, Alto Adige, Marche, Puglia and Sicily.

ALTA LANGA

The best sites in Italy's north-western province of Piemonte are historically planted to the likes of Nebbiolo, Barbera, Moscato and Braccheto. Yet, with a competitive eye on Franciacorta and Trentodoc, Piemonte's wine producers have effectively said 'anything they can do we can do better'. With a view to finding the best places to grow Chardonnay and Pinot Noir, the traditional method sparkling wine project was started in 1990 and an experimental 50 hectares planted. The Consorzio Alta Langa was founded in 2001 with seven founding members: Banfi Vigna Regali, Giulio Cocchi, Fontanafredda, Gancia, Martini & Rossi, Enrico Serafino and Tosti. DOC status was awarded the following year, and in 2011 Alta Langa was promoted to DOCG.

The production area is limited to vineyards located at least 250 metres above sea level in the 146 villages in the high hills of Alessandria, Asti and Cuneo south of the Tanaro River, which winds from east to west. The climate is typically temperate continental with average summer temperatures of 2°C lower than the Bassa Langa (the heart of red wine production), and strong Apennine influences. Cooler temperatures at high altitude allow the vines to avoid summer heat spikes and help to delay the harvest for up to two weeks, depending on the vintage. In the region's Serravallian soils, stratified sediments of marl and sandstone are cemented by the presence of limestone, which is well suited to viticulture for sparkling wines.

Pinot Noir tends to be the main variety, thereby distinguishing it from Trentodoc and Franciacorta. The region also has Nebbiolo. It may not yet be part of the Alta Langa DOCG, but a number of producers are trying it out, in part or in whole, in their rosé blends. With the freshness and tang Nebbiolo can bring to a fizz, it could catch on. For the Alta Langa DOCG, all sparkling wines, white or rosé, are vintage-dated, and must spend a minimum of 24 months on the lees or, in the case of riserva, 30 months. For such a young region, the results are immensely encouraging, with wonderful sparkling wines of aromatic intensity, crystalline purity and vivid freshness.

Producers

Coppo Srl

Canelli, Asti

www.coppo.it

Canelli, where the Coppo family is based, is regarded as the birthplace of Italian spumante. It was here in the 1800s that Moscato Champagne, as it was then called, first underwent a secondary fermentation in bottle. In 1892, when Coppo was founded by the meticulous, uncompromising Piero Coppo, Canelli was a major market for Piedmontese grapes. After the Second World War, two major floods caused the family to move to Via Alba. Piero Coppo's son Luigi was a modernizing influence and in the 1970s and 1980s, his four sons Piero, Gianni, Paolo and Roberto, reduced yields, introducing manual harvesting and trials with French oak barriques. From 1984, they began blending Chardonnay and Pinot Noir for the impressively wrought Riserva Coppo and richly textured Piero Coppo fizz.

The estate extends over more than 50 hectares between Alba and Asti, owned or rented and managed by Coppo. The heart of the vineyards, with their sedimentary marine origins and mineral-rich soils, is in Monferrato, where Coppo grows Moscato Bianco and, for the Metodo Classico Riserva Coppo, Pinot Noir and Chardonnay. Using organic manure, pheromones to combat insects and planting cover crops, their viticultural methods follow organic and biodynamic principles, although they are not certified. Some 9 hectares in the Alta Langa are devoted to sparkling wines in a total production of 420,000 bottles.

Fermentation is in barrique, followed by nine months ageing before tirage and secondary fermentation. Bottles are aged in the Underground Cathedrals – a Unesco World Heritage site – which were expanded in the nineteenth century to over 5,000 square metres and 40 metres in depth. At a constant 12–14°C, the calcareous tufo of Canelli is ideally suited to slow bottle-ageing. Historical evidence of the winemaking process can be seen today in the presses, filtration systems, vats and barrels. Indeed, it would be remiss if you're in the area not to enjoy a stroll with Luigi along the corridor of spumante, out through the ancient wood and cast iron door into the garden of the art nouveau villa bought by Piero in 1913, the year he was married to Clelia Pennone.

Azienda Agricola Deltetto S.S.A.

Canale, Cuneo, Piemonte

www.deltetto.com

Family winemakers since 1953, the estate was founded by Carlo 'Carlin' Deltetto who, with his wife Catterina, established the winery in Canale in the heart of Roero, producing Nebbiolo and Barbera. After Carlin's son, Antonio, graduated from Alba wine school in 1977, he added Arneis and Favorita and classic method fizz was made, initially from Nebbiolo and Arneis. Pinot Noir and Chardonnay were planted in 1997 and a first lot of 1,200 bottles of fizz was made. Today, Antonio runs the business with Carlo, Cristina and Claudia. Its 25 hectares are mostly located around Canale with new investments in the Alta Langa hills for the DOCG Alta Langa. Characterized by its Rocche, sandstone canyons rich in gorges, spires and steep peaks, Roero has a mineral-rich, alluvial soil of shells, fossils and sandstone originating in the Pliocene era.

Deltetto has been certified organic since 2017. Antonio uses cover crops for improving the soil structure and protecting it from erosion. Green manure from local farms provides organic matter and helps maintain the natural balance of the soil. Harvesting is done by hand. In the cellar, there is minimal use of sulphur and clarification of the must is with plant products. Antonio produces three wines, an outstanding Alta Langa Brut, which came top in a 2020 *Decanter* magazine tasting of 96 Italian sparkling wines, a distinctive Spumante VSQ rosé called N, Rosé de Noirs, and an accomplished Blanc de Blancs Riserva made from pure Chardonnay. In future the Rosé will be made entirely from Nebbiolo and there will be a Blanc de Noirs Riserva with extended lees-ageing. Annual production is 180,000 bottles.

Az. Agr. Germano Ettore di Germano

Serralunga d'Alba, Cuneo

www.ettoregermano.com

When Francesco Germano started growing grapes in the Barolo hills back in 1856, he could hardly have imagined that his great-grandson Sergio would be making sparkling Alta Langa and sparkling Nebbiolo in the twenty-first century. It was Sergio's father, Ettore, who renovated the vineyards in the 1960s, selecting vines for small bunches and disease resistance, selling the grapes and gradually acquiring small plots of land around Serralunga, notably in the *crus* of Cerretta, Prapo', Lazzarito and Vignarionda. The winery was officially established in 1975 with just a few hundred bottles sold to private customers and friends. A decade later, Sergio returned after graduating from Alba wine school to work with his father, and by 1993, all the grapes produced were being vinified and bottled by the estate. In 1998 the first Chardonnay and Riesling vineyards were planted in Cigliè, rising to a height of almost 550 metres with soils of glacial deposits and marls.

It was followed from 2001 by further plantings of Chardonnay and Pinot Noir along with Nascetta, and 0.7 hectares of Chardonnay and Riesling in the hamlet of Montiglio. In conversion to organic, most of the vineyard work is manual with natural fertilizer, pheromones to ward off pests and no herbicides. The grapes are hand harvested and gently whole bunch pressed with fermentation of just over half in stainless steel and the rest in 500-litre, low-toast barrels. After bâtonnage and second fermentation, the wine remains on the lees for at least 30 months. The Alta Langa DOCG, a wine with subtle fragrance and attractive richness of flavour, is textured and tangy. Production runs to 23,000 bottles. Pressed and fermented in stainless steel and staying on the lees for around 18 months, the Rosanna sparkling VSQ Rosè, first made in 2009, is an appetizingly food-friendly, pure Nebbiolo sparkler. Annual production is 15,000 bottles.

Gancia

Canelli, Asti

www.gancia.com

Gancia began in Piemonte in the mid-eighteenth century in the shape of Carlo Gancia. Visiting Champagne in the revolutionary Spring of Nations year of 1848 to learn the *méthode champenoise*, Carlo is believed to have cut his sparkling winemaking teeth at Piper-Heidsieck. On his return in 1850, he and his brother Edoardo founded Fratelli Gancia in Turin's Chivasso commune using the local Moscato Bianco to make 'champagne'. After trial and error, he succeeded in 1865 in creating the 'first Italian sparkling wine', then called Moscato champagne, or Italian champagne. In 1895, after Carlo's son, Camillo introduced Federico Martinotti's tank method (before the tank method Eugène Charmat patented in 1907), production soared tenfold to three million bottles.

With its historic link to the hills around Asti and Canelli, Gancia today (motto: 'Gancia, drink beauty') is very much the Made in Italy brand. Following three strict rules – freshness, structure and attention to detail – Casa Gancia relies on its contracts with some 150 growers to source grapes from areas as diverse as Alta Langa and Asti. A Marmonier press is used to gently separate 60 per cent of the must from 100 kilograms of grapes used for its traditional method wines. After fermentation in stainless steel and oak barriques, with no malolactic fermentation, the wines spend a minimum of 36 months on lees for Alta Langa DOCG and a minimum 24 months for Asti Classic Method, with the date of disgorgement printed on the back label. The dosage at 5–8 grams per litre is a secret recipe.

Sparkling wines make up more than two-thirds of production, with Charmat method for its Asti, Prosecco, its three-grape Pinot di Pinot and Brachetto; and traditional method for its Alta Langa range and Classic Asti. The Alta Langa DOCG Pas Dosé and the Alta Langa DOCG Brut, based on 70 per cent Pinot Noir and 30 per cent Chardonnay, spend 36 months on the lees, as does the new all-Pinot Noir Alta Langa DOCG Rosé. The Alta Langa DOCG Riserva spends 60 months and the Alta Langa DOCG Riserva Brut 120 months. Unique to the range is the opulent Classic Method Asti à la Carlo Gancia, with 5,000 bottles made, only in exceptional vintages. In 2011, Gancia was acquired by the Russian entrepreneur Roustam Tariko. The management remains Italian but the Vallarina Gancia family are no longer involved. With Gancia vermouths and specialities like Fernet, Americano, Bitters and still wines, total production is around thirty million bottles.

Azienda Agricola Roberto Garbarino

Neviglie, Cuneo, Piemonte

www.robertogarbarino.it

In 2013, the Champagne-loving Roberto Garbarino produced his first Alta Langa DOCG. As sparkling wine stories go, that makes him a relative newcomer, having only moved to the area in 2001 after graduating from Turin's Faculty of Agricultural Science. After returning from a stint in New Zealand in 2010 to set up his own winery, in 2012 he acquired a nineteenth-century farmhouse, including vineyards, in the commune of Neviglie 'with the aim of producing high quality bubbles in a land of important reds'. The cellar was completed in 2013.

On a hillside facing south-west at 450 metres, Roberto's steep vineyards, with their calcareous-clayey and sandy soils are located directly west of Alba. Covering 6.5 hectares, with vines on average 25 years old, there are 2 hectares of Alta Langa, 4 hectares of Moscato and 0.5 hectares of Dolcetto. A single hectare of Alta Langa Pinot Noir, planted in 2012, faces east at 550 metres. The grapes are grown organically, with systemic sprays used sparingly, environmental conditions permitting. Winters tend to be mild and summers cool with considerable day to night temperature fluctuations.

Without the albatross of tradition round his neck, Roberto has the freedom to be his own man. After manual harvesting, gentle pressing and fermentation, the wine remains on its lees over winter before tirage. Both his Alta Langa extra brut and Alta Langa Rosé brut nature are well-made sparklers, the former a wine of genuine aromatic complexity combining nutty notes from 32–40 months on the lees, the latter strikingly fresh with a bone dry, soft-textured summer pudding fruit mousse. He produces around 20,000 bottles, of which 8,000 are Alta Langa, with plans to add to the range with a *blanc de blancs* and a *blanc de noirs*.

Azienda Agricola Ghione Anna

Canelli, Asti

www.ghionewine.com

Founded in 1850, and set in the hills around Canelli, part of the Vineyards and Landscape of Piedmont UNESCO World Heritage Site, Ghione is family-run with fourth generation Anna Ghione at the helm, assisted in the winemaking by her husband, oenologist Marco Pippione. Fizz comes largely in the shape of sweetly fragrant Moscato d'Asti Canelli. As lovers of bubbles however, Ghione also produce two spumante wines made from international varieties. Its spumante brut *blanc de blancs*, Monblanc, is a Charmat method Chardonnay while the Alta Langa DOCG spumante brut, La Reine, is made by the classic method from pure Pinot Noir.

Certified SQNPI (Italian System of Quality Integrated Production), Ghiona Anna owns 12 hectares of vineyards between Monferrato and Langhe at an average altitude of 450 metres above sea level, mostly south-facing and composed of calcareous marl and limestone. For its classic method fizz, grapes grown in the higher hills above Canelli are gently pressed and stainless steel fermented, remaining on the fine lees until spring before a second fermentation and a minimum of 30 months on lees. The La Reine Alta Langa brut is an impressive fizz whose ripe peachy fruit is complemented by a savoury, tangy acidity.

The low-alcohol Moscato d'Asti *sottozona* Canelli is a well-executed example of the delicately sweet, perfumed style. Annual production runs to 70,000 bottles.

Az. Agricola Marcalberto S.S.A.
Santo Stefano Belbo, Cuneo
www.marcalberto.it

Named for the brothers Marco and Alberto who now run the company, Marcalberto was founded by Piero Cane. Piero was already an established winemaker when he produced his first bottles of sparkling wine in 1993 in Santo Stefano Belbo, birthplace of the famous Italian writer Cesare Pavese, in the Langhe. It was his ambition, continued by his two sons, to make sparkling wines exclusively from Chardonnay and Pinot Noir, using the traditional method. Marco and Alberto expanded production to its current tally of 50,000 bottles from its 6 hectares of vineyards in Calosso, Cossano Belbo, Santo Stefano Belbo and Loazzolo. Vineyards of marl and chalk sit at 300 and 650 metres above sea level.

In the cellar of the family's nineteenth century stone and tufo house, fermentation is in used oak barrels and stainless steel and the wines stay in cask for around seven to eight months with weekly bâtonnage over some four months. Neither filtered nor clarified, the wine is bottle-aged for at least 24 months. The Millesimato extra brut is a terrific Pinot-led fizz with expansive mousse, excellent flavour and structure and the zero dosage Blancdeblancs Metodo Classico rich and appetizingly dry. Both their Nature Metodo Classico and Sansannée Metodo Classico are well-balanced sparklers while the Rosé Metodo Classico stands out for its delicious cherry and raspberry fruit flavours and textural finesse.

Enrico Serafino S.r.l. Azienda Vitivinicola
Canale, Cuneo
www.enricoserafino.it

In 1878, the 23-year-old Enrico Serafino moved to Canale in the Roero, beginning traditional method sparkling wine production in the same underground cellar used today. After the First World War, both the Sparkling Metodo Classico Asti Champagne and Gran Spumante Regina were exported around the world. In 1928, Pope Pius XI acknowledged the commitment to social values of the founder's son, Luigi, by conferring on him the Croce di Cavaliere dell'Ordine di San Silvestro. For long passed down from father to son, Enrico Serafino was acquired by the modernizing Barbero Group in 1989, joined the Alta Langhe project in 1994, and changed hands when it was bought by the Campari Group in 2003 and finally, by the American Krause Gentile Family in 2015. Today the winery owns 14 hectares in the Langhe and 11 hectares in Roero, with grower partnerships in a further 35 hectares between Langhe, Roero and Monferrato.

At 500 metres above sea level, the La Soprana Estate in Cerretto Langhe is particularly suited to Pinot Noir and Chardonnay and the organically poor marls of the Langhe help to keep yields low, resulting in *metodo classico* fizz that's austere and refreshingly dry. After manual harvesting and sorting, the gently pressed juice is fermented in stainless steel. Grapes for the Alta Langa Rosé de Saignée are destemmed, chilled and left for two to four hours in an inert nitrogen environment. After the first fermentation, the wines remain in contact with the lees and are given a periodic bâtonnage until tirage and second fermentation. They remain on the lees in Serafino's historic underground cellars for 36 months, extended to up to 144 months for the vivacious Zero 140 Pas Dosé with its ripe orchard fruitiness and hints of nuttiness. The Alta Langa winery is the first in the region to get VIVA Sustainable Viticulture Certification.

Vite Colte

Barolo, Cuneo

www.vitecolte.it

With 300 hectares of vineyard in prime Barolo real estate, the 180 winegrowers who belong to Vite Colte contribute a proportion of their own estate to the Alta Langa sparkling wine project, which is overseen by vineyard manager Daniele Eberle and winemaker Bruno Cordero. While already making sparkling Brachetto d'Acqui, Moscato d'Asti and Moscato Passito, Vite Colte released their first traditional method 2016 Alta Langa DOCG in February 2020. Some 15,000 bottles of spumante are made from Pinot Noir and Chardonnay grown in vineyards at 500 and 600 metres above sea level. There is also a Charmat method Piemonte Chardonnay brut Vallerenza and Piemonte Pinot Noir extra brut Molinera DOC.

Manual harvesting is followed by gentle pressing, and after fermentation the wine rests on the lees until the following spring, when the Pinot Noir and Chardonnay are blended for tirage. After 30 months of bottle ageing, the wine is riddled, disgorged and a dosage of 6 grams per litre added, followed by a further few months maturation. If the 2016 Vite Colte Alta Langa DOCG, an 80 per cent Pinot Noir and 20 per cent Chardonnay blend, is anything to go by, this is a promising start for the quality-conscious Vite Colte project. From the 2017 vintage, the wine is called Cinquecento to reflect the altitude of the vineyard selection.

TRENTINO

Credit for the origins of Trentino's sparkling wines lies with Giulio Ferrari, who founded Ferrari in 1902 when Trentino still belonged to the Austro-Hungarian empire. Ferrari studied at the Imperial Regia Scuola Agraria in San Michele all'Adige before learning how to make wine sparkle in Épernay. Only 830 cases had been made when he sold the winery 50 years later to the Lunelli family, but the Lunellis have since become Trentino's biggest producer of sparkling wine, with more than half the region's bubbles Ferrari-shaped.

Between the Dolomite Mountains and Lake Garda, the region, accorded DOC status in 1993 and then DOCG two years later, is well situated for making traditional method fizz, especially since it adopted the Champagne grapes, Chardonnay principally, at some 26 per cent of the surface under vine, along with Pinot Noir, Meunier and a dash of Pinot Blanc. The Istituto Trento DOC, founded by producers in 1984, has 55 members. In June 2007, Trentodoc became the trademarked name for its sparkling wines.

Vineyards are rich in calcareous rocks and mineral salts with a high silica content and at 200–800 metres benefit from pure Alpine air, warm days and cool nights, with day to night fluctuations in temperature and winds off the Ora del Garda lake contributing to a natural freshness, aromatic intensity and flavour. On Trento's steep hillsides, often trellised with the traditional pergola system for optimum sun exposure and pruning, much of the viticulture is done by hand including the harvesting of the grapes.

Bottle-ageing varies from 15 months for non-vintage wines, to 24 months for vintage and 36 months for riserva which, since 2015, can also include rosé. These are legal minima and the best producers age their fizz for considerably longer. Sensibly, non-vintage fizz must by law show the year of disgorgement on the back label. From the region's 55 producers covering 10,000 hectares of vineyards, production of sparking wines from 800 hectares is of some nine million bottles, with Ferrari and the two big cooperatives, Altemasi (Cavit), and Rotari, the major players. Eight in ten bottles are drunk in Italy.

Wines vary in style from a refreshingly effervescent fruit in citrusy and sometimes more tropical vein to the toasty delights of wines aged on the lees like Champagne. Both styles are valid and quality is generally high at reasonable prices. Could it be that Ferrari's big beast status has held Trentodoc's development back? Perhaps. There is also the rarely stated issue of the Trentodoc name, which may play well in Italy, but to English ears, sounds just a bit plodding compared to, say, Franciacorta or Prosecco.

Producers

Cesarini Sforza Spumanti

Trento

www.cesarinisforza.it

Lamberto Cesarini Sforza founded the Cesarini Sforza Winery with Giuseppe Andreaus and a few of his friends in 1974. Chardonnay and Pinot Noir were selected from a mosaic of local vineyards at altitudes between 300 and 600 metres in the Alta Valle di Cembra. Vineyards are in Meano and Cortesano, in the Sorni and the Pressano hills as well as above the city of Trento and in the Besagno Hills. The first Cesarini Sforza sparkling wine was made in 1976, followed in 1985 by a classic method rosé made from Pinot Noir grown in the hillside vineyards of the Valle di Cembra. The following year saw the first Aquila Reale Riserva, made from Chardonnay grown in well-drained, calcareous, loamy, sandy soils in Maso Sette Fontane in the Adige Valley.

The grapes are harvested by hand and, overseen by Giorgia Brugnara, Cesarini Sforza's winemaker, whole bunch soft pressed and stainless steel fermented before bottle-ageing from between 24 months for the Brut and Brut Rosé to 48 months for the 1673 range. The Brut is impressive and both the 1673 Riserva Extra Brut Trentodoc and its Rosé counterpart are appealing sparklers, refreshingly dry, with savoury characters brought on by lees-ageing. The flagship Aquila Reale Riserva is fermented in oak casks and aged for 90 months on the lees, endowing this wine with notes of toasty oak and nuttiness before dissolving on the tongue in a satisfyingly dry, classy finish. Cesarini Sforza was acquired by the La Vis cooperative in 2001 and is owned today by the giant Cavit cooperative.

Cantina Endrizzi

Trento

www.endrizzi.it

Cantina Endrizzi, founded in 1885 in San Michele all'Adige in the Trentino hills, is run by the charming Paolo and Christine Endrici, together with Lisa Maria and Daniele, the fourth and fifth generation of the family respectively. Endrici is the family name, Endrizzi the brand. Based on principles of being 'good, clean and fair', Endrizzi's vineyards are cultivated sustainably, without chemical fertilizers, in the cool Dolomite microclimate. Co-founders of the Istituto Trento DOC in 1984, the Endricis invested in the 1980s in the sloping, terraced vineyard of Pian di Castello, one of the few in Trentino with an authentic *clos* structure, at an altitude of around 400 metres above sea level. Planted with Épernay clones of Chardonnay and Pinot Noir selected more than 30 years ago, Pian di Castello's soil is formed mainly from sedimentary dolomite rock, which helps keep yields low.

The first fermentation of the wine is carried out partially in French and Hungarian barriques and partially in stainless steel followed by bâtonnage. The Trentodocs are left to mature on the lees for between 24 and 84 months, with a minimum of dosage. The pale onion skin Piancastello Rosé Riserva Trentodoc is clean and fresh with a lively mousse of berry fruitiness, the Piancastello Riserva Trentodoc appetizingly soft and creamy-textured and finely balanced between ripe fruit and savoury dryness. In 2020, a limited edition of a new zero dosage fizz, Piancastello Zero, was launched. Best of all, with 84 months of ageing, the Masetto Privé Riserva Trentodoc shows a mature nuttiness of aroma and burgundy-style vinosity. In total, Endrizzi produces 600,000 bottles from its two estates in Trentino and Tuscany, of which Trentodoc sparkling wines account for 55,000 bottles.

Ferrari Trento

Trento

www.ferraritrento.com

To call Ferrari the Rolls-Royce of Italian sparkling wine is to confirm its exalted status while distinguishing it from its four-wheeled namesake. Ferrari Trento is a family company owned by the Lunelli family and unrelated to the automobile even if Ferrari toasts Ferrari after Formula One victories and neither would be icons without the appropriate levels of atmospheric pressure in bottle and tyre respectively. The Lunelli family came into the picture in 1952 when Bruno Lunelli acquired the company from Giulio Ferrari, who had seen the potential of Trentino's mountain vineyards for world-class fizz, founding the firm in 1902 when Trento still belonged to the Austro-Hungarian Empire.

Today, the company is run by a quartet of engaging cousins, Marcello, Matteo, Alessandro and Camilla, who work with the experienced cellar-master, Ruben Larentis, who has been with Ferrari since 1986. Ferrari Trento owns 100 hectares of chalky, stony, mountain vineyards varying between 400 and 700 metres above sea level, crucial for natural acidity. All estate vineyards are certified organic and Ferrari is proud of the Biodiversity Friend certification awarded by the Worldwide Biodiversity Association. Grapes bought from 500 hectares of vineyards owned by 600 families supply 80–85 per cent of the rest of its needs. The wines are put together from 80 separate batches for a production of some 5.5 million bottles, with 20 million bottles lying in storage in their cool, underground cellars.

The entry level Classic line, in Brut, Rosé and Demi-Sec, is a reliable, affordable fizz, followed by the great value Maximum line aimed at the restaurant sector, in Blanc de Blancs, Rosé and Demi-Sec. A step up in class, the excellent Perlé range consists of the Blanc de Blancs, Bianco Riserva, Rosé Riserva, Nero Riserva and a new all Chardonnay, multi-vintage Perlé Zero, launched in 2017. The reserve line embraces Riserva Lunelli made from oak-fermented Chardonnay, the complex, Giulio Ferrari Riserva del Fondatore, Giulio Ferrari Rosé and Giulio Ferrari Collezione (the latter, from 1995, 1997 and 2001, bottle-aged for more than 18 years). If you buy the 12-litre bottle in the big format Gran Cuvée line, you may find a Lunelli family member helping you do the heavy lifting and pouring. If not, take a table at their Michelin-star restaurant, worth it just for the opportunity to inspect the stunning sixteenth century Villa Margon.

FRANCIACORTA

Although Franciacorta fizz is a relatively recent phenomenon dating from 1961 when the first sparkling wine was made by Franco Ziliani, Berlucchi's winemaker, its historical vine growing roots date back to Roman times and thereafter from the winemaking monastic foundations of the Middle Ages. When, in 1570, a Brescian doctor, Girolamo Conforti, published the *Libellus de vino mordaci*, he describes the wines as 'mordacious', or effervescent. The name Franciacorta is taken from the Latin *francae curtes*, the courts exempted from paying customs duties thanks to their efforts in land reclamation and tilling. By the start of the nineteenth century, the Napoleonic land registry included 1,000 hectares of vineyards and nearly another 1,000 hectares of mixed agriculture including vines. It was one of the first regions to achieve DOC status, in 1967, and in 1995, it was elevated to DOCG.

Today, Franciacorta is positioning itself as Italy's top region for sparkling wine, even if Trentino and Alta Langa might beg to differ. The focus is on quality sparkling wines that will behave well at the dinner table. Made by the *metodo classico*, mainly from Chardonnay, it includes Pinot Noir and Pinot Blanc (or, to give them their Italian due, Pinot Nero and Pinot Bianco), and more recently, the indigenous Erbamat, a late ripener with higher acidity and lower sugar, reintroduced in 2017 (with a maximum of 10 per cent permitted for all Franciacorta except Satèn, see below) to add freshness in the face of climate change. A leader in sustainability, with 70 per cent of its vineyards organic, Franciacorta is working with Padua University to find ways of capturing carbon dioxide in its soils.

With vineyards on hilly slopes south of Lake Iseo, one of the region's special features is its sponge-like, ancient glacial and red clay–iron soils which are capable of retaining humidity in hot weather. These glacial soils of moderate depth, good drainage and medium to high water reserves are diverse. In fact, six specific vineyard terroirs have been identified. Winters are relatively mild and summers not excessively hot, with cooling breezes that blow along the Valcamonica corridor and notable daily temperature differentials. Franciacorta is relatively small, with just 2,900 hectares, producing some 17.4 million bottles in 2018. That's just three for every hundred bottles of Prosecco.

Dosage tends to be low and zero dosage often suits Franciacorta's natural generosity of fruit. Alcohol levels are moderate, which makes the wines elegant partners for food. Aside from non-vintage, rosé, vintage and riserva (riserva must spend at least 60 months on the lees), Franciacorta has its own unique category, known as Satèn. The term was created by Bellavista's winemaker Mattia Vezzola, apparently thanks to his admiration from afar of a stylish lady in Venice. It denotes a silkier-textured 'more feminine' style of Franciacorta brut fizz made from white grapes at a pressure lower than five atmospheres, an Italian answer to what used to be crémant in Champagne.

Producers

1701 srl società Agricola

Cazzago San Martino, Brescia

www.1701franciacorta.it

If you were to call the 1701 winery run by brother and sister team Federico and Silvia Stefini a fusion of innovation and tradition, you might not be far off. The eighteenth century Villa Bettoni, Cazzago San Martino, next to the cluniac church of Santa Giulia, is home to the 'brolo' vineyard, a sunny 4-hectare parcel of vines framed by eleventh century walls, while viticulture and vinification techniques are very much of the twenty-first century. The 1701 name refers to the date of the first vinification of the 'Brolo' vineyard.

In 2012, Silvia and Federico decided to renovate the historic winery belonging to the family of Count Bettoni Cazzago, following organic and biodynamic viticultural principles. They avoid chemical sprays or insecticides and instead use biodynamic preparations: quartz silica for attracting sunlight, and the stimulating homeopathic effects of plants including nettle, camomile, achillea and valerian. In 2015 the winery was certified organic and in July 2016 it became the first (and only) Franciacorta winery to obtain biodynamic Demeter certification. 1701 is also a member of the Renaissance des Appellations and the Vi.Te. associations.

Silvia and Federico cultivate 10 hectares, eight of Chardonnay and two of Pinot Noir in Cazzago San Martino in the heart of a region whose soils are rich in sand and loam, with exceptional drainage, while proximity to Lake Iseo mitigates temperatures during both summer and winter. The wines are fermented with natural yeasts in stainless steel, concrete tanks, amphoras and barriques before spending a minimum of 24 to 30 months on the lees. No dosage is added. Sixty thousand bottles are produced annually, and the focus is on sparkling wines, with five in the range, including a pet nat style frizzante, a *sur lie* refermented with the Chardonnay must, and there's also a still Chardonnay.

This is a quality range of sparkling wines, led by the pure Chardonnay 1701 Satèn Vintage, a full-flavoured, nicely textured wine whose fruit richness is balanced by an attractive savoury quality and fine dry finish. Also excellent is the vintage 1701 Rosé Nature, a pure Pinot Noir-based rosé whose floral and berry fragrance is complemented by lees-aged complexity and a crunchy berry-like tang. The non-vintage 1701 Brut

Nature is commendably dry and gently effervescent, while the lightly cloudy 1701 Sullerba Non Dosato should appeal to pet nat lovers.

Bellavista

Erbusco, Brescia

www.terramoretti.it / www.bellavistawine.it

If the shoulder of the bottle were adorned with the letter K, you might almost mistake it for Krug, but the embossed B and oval-shaped label stands of course for Bellavista. Beauty is in the eye of the beholder at Bellavista, whose name comes from the hamlet of Bellavista, so called because of its scenic views over the majestic landscape of Franciacorta. In 1977, wealthy businessman Vittorio Moretti decided to build a winery and home here after buying up small plots of land from 30 different owners. Today, Bellavista is owned by the umbrella group Terra Moretti.

Production has gradually increased over time and, thanks to the accumulation of a mosaic of over 100 plots in 10 municipalities, the estate has grown from only 3.5 hectares to its current size of almost 200 hectares with as many as 64 different types of soil in Franciacorta's six terrains. Overseen by Moretti's daughter, Francesca, the winemaking team is managed by the experienced Mattia Vezzola, who has been with Bellavista since 1981. After a long, soft pressing of the grapes, fermentation is in stainless steel with roughly one-third in older oak 228-litre casks.

Satèn is the most delicate style, made from pure Chardonnay grown in higher altitude vineyards with a slow maturation in small oak barrels and then four years on the lees for a pleasing melon-like richness supported by a vivacious freshness. Alma, blended from Chardonnay, Pinot Noir and Pinot Blanc, plus reserve wines, also fermented in oak, is a gastronomic style thanks to a degree of grip and vinosity. Four years on the lees for the Rosé, a 60 per cent Chardonnay, 40 per cent Pinot Noir blend, is reflected in a wine with delicious summer pudding fruit mousse and satisfyingly savoury tang.

Dedicated to the famous Milan opera house, Teatro alla Scala Brut comprises the top selections of Chardonnay and Pinot Noir for a generously peachy yet elegant style underpinned by toasty, leesy notes and real finesse. The prestige cuvée, Vittorio Moretti, incorporates the best selections of Chardonnay and Pinot Noir, fermented in oak casks followed by extensive ageing, resulting in a wine of generosity and purity, tempered by a creamy texture and a long-lasting tangy dryness. The year of disgorgement is indicated on the back label and annual production is 1.5 million bottles.

Guido Berlucchi & C S.p.a

Corte Franca, Brescia

www.berlucchi.it

Franciacorta's biggest producer, Berlucchi, claims to be the first Franciacorta classic method fizz. It came about following a meeting in 1955 between Guido Berlucchi, a chip off the wealthy Lana de' Terzi family block, and Franco Ziliani, a young winemaking graduate from the Alba Wine School. Berlucchi was looking for a technician to stabilize his Pinot del Castello, while Ziliani saw the potential for his own wine project in the Franciacorta terroir. Berlucchi's underground cellars, built in 1680 by the Conti Lana de' Terzi family, were the icing on *la torta*.

After renovating the traditional winery and following six years of trials, the first 3,000 bottles of Pinot di Franciacorta were produced in 1961. Flushed with the success of this first classic method fizz, Guido Berlucchi expanded production, creating Max Rosé, the first Italian classic method sparkling rosé, for a family friend, the Milanese antiquarian Max Imbert. Rapid expansion meant Berlucchi leaving Franciacorta for pastures new in Lombardy from which to source its grapes, but Franco Ziliani's children persuaded their father to return to Franciacorta in 1999 and bought the company from him in 2017.

Guido Berlucchi today owns 115 hectares of vineyards in the Borgonato area and draws grapes from a further 400 hectares. With a firm commitment to sustainability, precision viticulture determines the moment to start the harvest, when hand-picked bunches of Chardonnay and Pinot Noir are placed in 18-kilogram boxes and separated at pressing by variety, vineyard and analytical characteristics. Eight Coquard PAI presses create four selections of juices. The first fermentation is in stainless steel, while for base wines destined for the top of the range fizz, 300 second-use barrels are used. One-hundred-and-fifty base wines remain in stainless steel or oak before blending and tirage in the historic subterranean cellars at Palazzo Lana.

Above the dependable entry level Cuvée Imperiale range, things become more interesting with the '61 range featuring Brut, Satèn and Rosé aged for at least 24 months. The centrepiece is the impressive '61 Nature vintage range of Brut, Rosé and Blanc de Blancs, all three spending five years on the lees, and, with no dosage, textured, mouthwateringly dry and savoury. Also impressive is the distinctive white Pinot Noir Palazzo Lana Extrême, produced only in the best vintages, which spends ten years on the lees for a wonderfully mature, toastily complex fizz with an appetizing, grapefruit-zesty dryness.

Ca' del Bosco

Erbusco, Brescia

www.cadelbosco.com

The Ca' del Bosco story is a relatively recent one, beginning in the mid 1960s when Annamaria Clementi Zanella bought a cottage on an Erbusco hilltop, known as Ca' del bosc because it was surrounded by dense chestnut woods. The first vineyard was planted in 1968 in the year after Franciacorta received DOC status and the first products were still wines. After a trip to Champagne, Annamaria's son Maurizio was so inspired that he resolved to exploit the potential of Franciacorta's terroir to make a wine to match Champagne.

The first sparkling wine was made in 1976. Three years later, when Maurizio took on André Dubois as cellar master, quality improved dramatically. Today, Ca' del Bosco's 248 hectares are certified organic. The average age of the vines is over 20 and the vines must be at least 15 years old to qualify for the eight cuvées. The exposure of the vineyards is important for the optimum ripeness sought by Maurizio Zanella, who has continued to manage the vineyards and renovate the cellar following acquisition by the Santa Margherita group. Maintaining sustainability and fastidious detail in the cellar are essential to Maurizio, who calls his winemaking the *metodo* Ca' del Bosco.

After meticulous selection, cold storage and gentle pressing, the pampered grapes have undergone a 'berry spa' since 2008 in order to keep sulphur to a minimum and cleanse any impurities and spray residues. The grapes bobble their way through three soaking vats, initially a minute and a half's pre-wash, followed by a two-minute full wash then a minute's citric acid rinse before a luxurious blow-dry that removes 98 per cent of the water. Vinification of each vineyard is carried out separately and the eight cuvées are blended after seven months ageing. Ageing on the lees is long, followed by bottling without sulphur dioxide.

At the top of the range, both the Annamaria Clementi and its Rosé counterpart are among Italy's finest sparkling wines, the former almost Meursault like, but with bubbles, showing the fruit concentration and serious vinosity of low yields with just a hint of spicy oak, the latter fragrantly strawberryish with toasty notes and an exuberant, red berry fruit mousse. No less impressive are the enticingly complex smoky-toasty undertones of the savoury and bone dry Vintage Collection Dosage Zéro and Zéro Noir, while the Satèn Millesimato is notable for the delicacy of its clean, dry style.

Azienda Agricola Ferghettina di Gatti Roberto

Franciacorta

www.ferghettina.it

Roberto Gatti's work with Bellavista convinced him that Franciacorta's gentle, sunny slopes made it the ideal spot for fizz. In 1990, he and his wife Andreina took on 4 hectares in Erbusco, building a winery and starting with a red and a white in 1991, closely followed by their first Franciacorta sparkling brut. Assisted by their children Laura and Matteo, both oenology graduates, Ferghettina today manages 200 hectares in 11 municipalities. One-hundred hectares of Chardonnay and Pinot Noir grapes are selected from 55 vineyards for a sparkling wine range that now stands at 500,000 bottles. The wines have been certified organic since 2017. Work on a new three-storey headquarters with fantastic panoramic views was completed in 2005. In order to expand capacity, improve vinification and to extend the time of lees-ageing in the bottle, a winery extension was completed in 2018, to include a charming tasting room that receives visitors in style.

You can hardly miss the sparkling wines of Ferghettina because its Satèn, Milledì and Rosé come in the distinctive square-based bottle whose flat sides are designed to allow maximum surface contact between the yeasts and the wine in the bottle as it ages. In case these don't fit your wine rack, they make four other wines, a Franciacorta Brut, Extra Brut, Riserva 33 and Eronero that will. After hand-picking, each parcel is vinified separately to create 90 different blending wines. Franciacorta Brut, 'the soul of the company' has been made from day one. In addition, the rich, exotically flavoured *blanc de blancs* Satèn is made in a creamy, softer style. Franciacorta Milledì, also Chardonnay-based, is more mineral, while the elegantly dry, raspberryish Rosé is pure Pinot Noir. Franciacorta Rosé Eronero is made only in hot years from a selection from two vineyards and the Extra Brut is based on grapes from the oldest vineyards and the company's reserves. The Riserva 33 is a 'blend of blends', comprising a third of the base wine for Satèn, Milledì and Extra Brut.

Barone Pizzini

Provaglio d'Iseo, Brescia

www.baronepizzini.it

Barone Pizzini's dates from 1870, and its first Franciacorta was made in 1971. On sites noted for their glacial deposits, the vineyards cover 54 hectares at 200 metres above sea level divided into 29 parcels in the municipalities of Provaglio d'Iseo, Corte Franca, Capriolo and Passirano. Work towards organic certification began in 2001. The winemaking team at Barone Pizzini is committed to chemical-free farming and grass between the rows helps promote the microbial life of the soil. Under the stewardship of Silvano Brescianini, Barone Pizzini is aiming to encourage the return of the ancient, local, late-ripening Erbamat grape, referred to by the Brescian agronomist Agostino Gallo in 1564.

Grapes are hand harvested and each parcel vinified separately in stainless steel tanks and barrels. After fermentation and blending, bottle-ageing varies from 18 to 60 or more months according to the cuvée. The range consists of two non-vintage Franciacorta (Animante and Golf 1927), three vintage Franciacorta (Satèn, Rosé and brut nature, called Naturae) and a riserva (Bagnadore). Most wines do not go through malolactic fermentation, to keep the style refreshingly crisp and pure.

Low or no dosage suits the Pizzini style, notably in the vintage Franciacorta Bagnadore Dosaggio Zero Riserva, a 60 per cent Chardonnay 40 per cent Pinot Noir blend that's biscuity with a tangy mousse of pristine fruit purity and the equally impressive non-vintage zero dosage Animante L.A. Franciacorta, a bright, lightly toasty blend of 84 per cent Chardonnay, 12 per cent Pinot Noir and 4 per cent Pinot Blanc, aged 60 months on lees. The Pinot Noir-based Rosé Franciacorta extra brut is also good and the Perlugo Dosaggio Zero Metodo Classico VSQ is a distinctive, classic method biodynamic fizz made from the Verdicchio grape grown in Barone Pizzini's vineyards in the Marche. Some 300,000 bottles are produced annually.

CONEGLIANO VALDOBBIADENE PROSECCO SUPERIORE DOCG

If the wines of a region are to be judged on the scenic beauty of its landscape, then Prosecco Superiore Conegliano Valdobbiadene DOCG, an area of some 8,000 hectares in the rolling, wooded hills of north-east Italy's Venetian hinterland, would lord it over Champagne every time. A mosaic of steep, east-west slopes forming wave upon wave of verdant, narrow terraces, or hogbacks (*ciglioni*), recedes towards the dramatic backdrop of the Dolomites 100 kilometres to the north. The landscape is interconnected by a patchwork of vineyard parcels whose woodlands, hedges and small villages provide a unique ecological network. Recognized as a protected UNESCO World Heritage Site in 2019, protection of the rural landscape and local traditions is guaranteed by the rules of the Conegliano Valdobbiadene Prosecco Superiore DOCG.

While wine production in the area, with its history of aristocrat-owned farms, summer residences and sharecropping, dates back to the late Middle Ages, the modern story of Prosecco fizz begins in 1876. Italy's first winemaking school, the Istituto Enologico G.B. Cerletti, was founded in Conegliano in this year by the scientist Carpenè Malvolti. Malvolti taught growers how to optimize their viticulture, using the Bellussera technique of training the vines on the area's steep slopes. The system, invented by the Bellussi brothers in an attempt to defeat downy mildew, consists of a structure where 4-metre high poles are linked by iron cables arranged in rays. Each pole supports four vines positioned at 2.5 metres from the ground and from each vine, cordons grow inclined upwards and diagonally to the row, forming a system of rays.

At the same time, Federico Martinotti came up with a sparkling winemaking prototype in Valdobbiadene, allowing refermentation of the base wines in *autoclavi* (large pressurized tanks). In 1969 Conegliano and Valdobbiadene achieved DOC status, elevated in 2009 to DOCG.

Three oases of superior quality stand out from common or garden Prosecco: the DOCG area of Conegliano and Valdobbiadene, linked together as the 15 communes of Conegliano Valdobbiadene Prosecco Superiore DOCG (ConVal), and the smaller sub-region of Asolo Prosecco Superiore DOCG in the west of the zone. The three DOCGs account for around 100 million bottles, one in six of all Prosecco. The Conegliano area is based on clayey, often reddish, ancient soils of alluvial and glacial origin rich in calcium carbonate, yielding wines with fruity aromas and rich structure. Valdobbiadene's steep slope soils are based on water-retentive marl as well as glacial moraines and sandstone, characters that tend to produce floral aromas and finesse in the wines.

Between the two towns, largely to the north, the soils of the steep, south-orientated hills are based on shallow conglomerates. Thanks to altitudes that vary between 100 and 500 metres, the vine is as much influenced by elevation, exposure and aspect as soil.

The main grape variety is Glera, a delicate, fragrant variety with a tendency to become angular and austere. Formerly known as Prosecco, it was changed to Glera in a cunning wheeze that allowed the denomination to call itself Prosecco (thanks to the discovery of a small village called Prosecco near Trieste) to prevent potential rivals from copying it. Because of systematic co-planting with other local varieties, up to 15 per cent of the traditional varieties, Verdiso, Bianchetta Trevigiana, Perera and Glera Lunga, are allowed; Verdiso for a degree of salinity, Perera for its fragrance and Bianchetta Trevigiana for softness of texture. Pinot Bianco, Pinot Grigio, Pinot Nero and Chardonnay are allowed but little used.

After harvesting, a maximum of 700 litres per tonne of free-run juice is permitted. Once the base wines are blended, the second fermentation takes place in *autoclavi* over 30 to 90 days. In 2019, a new category of *sui lieviti*, the vivacious, artisanal pet nat style of brut nature Prosecco, formerly *col fondo*, was added to the appellation. There is also a Frizzante (semi-sparkling) and even a Tranquillo (still) category. Along with trials with metodo classico and a growing trend towards drier, more food-friendly wines, the creation of the artisanal, cloudy *sui lieviti* Prosecco, is paying dividends. The trend towards lower sugar levels was recognized by the creation of the Extra Brut category (0–6 grams per litre) and is increasingly common with Rive Prosecco.

Vineyards lying on the most precipitous slopes, known as *rive*, denote an expression of the distinctive nature of soil, exposure and microclimate. To qualify as one of 43 Rive, grapes must come from one of 12 designated communes or 31 hamlets. The maximum yield is 13 tonnes per hectare compared to 13.5 tonnes per hectare for the ConVal DOCG, harvesting must be by hand and the wine, which can only be spumante, must state the vintage. The pinnacle of the Rive expression is Cartizze, where 100 growers share 108 hectares of vineyards in an amphitheatre of limestone-rich oceanic soils on the steepest hillsides of San Pietro di Barbozza, Santo Stefano and Saccol in Valdobbiadene. From the dialect term *gardiz* (the reed mat on which late-ripening grapes are dried), Cartizze is traditionally on the floral, sweeter side.

ASOLO PROSECCO SUPERIORE DOCG

The term *asolare*, a localized form of *dolce far niente* (the joy of doing as little as possible), was coined for the walled, hilltop town of Asolo by the medieval poet, Pietro Bembo. The Victorian poet Robert Browning called it 'the most beautiful spot I ever was privileged to see', naming his final collection of poetry (published in 1889, the year of his death) *Asolando* after the walled town. Asolo's historic Montello hills are based on red earth over conglomerates of calcareous cobblestones, porphyry and granite kneaded with clay from the Piave river and the erosion of the Alps. Asolo belongs to the I Borghi più belli d'Italia club, an association of the most beautiful medieval and renaissance fortified towns and cities (or *borghi*) in Italy.

Glera vines in Asolo Prosecco Superiore DOCG

With fewer than 2,000 hectares, Asolo Prosecco Superiore DOCG produced some 18.7 million bottles in 2020 (in 2013 there were just over a million). Thanks to lower yields and higher dry extract, Asolo Prosecco owes its superior quality to an understanding of the terroir and an attractively mouthwatering dryness. The traditional style of Asolo Prosecco Sui Lieviti DOCG Spumante (*sur lie*) is fermented naturally in the bottle, using wild yeasts. Because the lees remain in the bottle, the effect is to produce authentic, often cloudy, sparkling wines, which must be brut nature. While regular Prosecco is generally drunk as an aperitif because of its higher residual sugar, *sui lieviti* wines tend to go better with food.

Producers

Adami

Colbertaldo di Vidor, Treviso

www.adamispumanti.it

Adami was founded in Treviso's Alta Marca area in 1920 by Abele Adami, when he bought his first vineyard, Vigneto Giardino (at that time Riva Zardin), a beautiful natural amphitheatre, from Count Balbi Valier. Invited in 1933 to the wine fair, Mostra mercato dei vini tipici d'Italia, in Siena, he showed the Riva Giardino Asciutto as Valdobbiadene's first single vineyard wine. Until 1983 the wines were either still or *col fondo*, while all production today is sparkling, mostly *metodo Martinotti* plus a smaller percentage *col fondo*. Abele's son Adriano expanded production, and from 1980 the third generation, Franco and Armando Adami, both winemakers, took over the management of the estate. Fabrizio and Claudio Adami, the fourth generation, came on board in 2019.

The grapes are sourced from some 50 hectares, mainly within Valdobbiadene, Colbertaldo and Farra di Soligo, roughly 13 hectares from Adami's estate vineyards on steep slopes, and the balance from long-term contracts. On shallow soils over chalky bedrock, the vineyards benefit from natural air-conditioning from the Venice lagoon to the south and the protective shield of the Dolomites to the north. Production of some 82,000 bottles comprises one Prosecco Treviso, three Valdobbiadene Superiore and three Valdobbiadene Superiore from micro areas (Cartizze) and single vineyards such as Rive di Colbertaldo and Rive di Farra di Soligo. The unfiltered base wine stays on the lees in stainless steel for at least three months before the second fermentation which takes place over 30–45 days in stainless steel pressure tanks. The month and year are mentioned on the back label. To ensure freshness, complexity and bright fruit, the operation is repeated up to 100 times throughout the year. The results are impressive, with refreshing sparkling wines of presence and personality.

L'Antica Quercia

Scomigo di Conegliano, Treviso

www.anticaquercia.it

L'Antica Quercia, owned by Claudio Francavilla, is an estate of 30 hectares in the Scomigo hills north of Conegliano, with olive and pomegranate trees as well as 21 hectares of vineyards, principally of Glera. The climate is temperate and the vineyards are refreshed by a breeze that blows from the Belluno Dolomites to the north. The grapes have been grown organically since 2007 in a vineyard rich in limestone and rocky clay soils. Grapes are harvested by hand and whole bunch pressed before ageing on the lees over the winter and are Charmat method fermented. The resulting L'Antica Quercia Rive di Scomigo is an elegant style with off-dry cream soda and pear-like flavours and a frothing, zesty mousse that leaves a trace of saltiness on the tongue. In the delicately yeasty Conegliano Valdobbiadene Prosecco Superiore DOCG Brut Nature Sui Lieviti Ancestrale, the fermentation is stopped at around 25–30 grams per litre and bottled in the spring for the second fermentation.

Bepin De Eto

San Pietro di Feletto, Treviso

www.bepindeeto.it

The Ceschin family winery is run by Giuseppina, Cristina and Silvia, the three daughters of Ettore Ceschin, who inherited the Conegliano hills winery from his father Giuseppe. Giuseppe's strong resemblance to his grandfather Nicoletto, the founder, resulted in the locals giving him the name of Bepin de Eto, a name he subsequently bestowed upon the winery he founded in 1965. Production is from vineyards at 270 metres on the slopes of the Dolomite foothills. After a brief ageing on the lees, dosage varies from 15 grams per litre for the extra dry to 3 grams per litre for the extra brut Conegliano Valdobbiadene Prosecco Superiore DOCG Rive di Rua di Feletto. With its eye-catching packaging, this wine shows an alluring floral and fresh pear fragrance and fresh, almost bone-dry mousse. All three wines are attractively elegant.

Cantine Umberto Bortolotti

Valdobbiadene, Treviso

www.bortolotti.com

Emerging from the Second World War, a small group of pioneering

winemakers, among them Umberto Bortolotti, decided to start producing sparkling wine, basing their vision on the success of Carpenè
Malvolti in Conegliano and the new style of lightly sweet sparkling
fizz made from the Prosecco grape and other local varieties. Bortolotti
founded the company in 1947, moving to the winery's current location in 1954. His son Bruno now buys grapes and base wines from 22
local growers, managing around 60 hectares mainly from the hamlets of
Guia, San Stefano, San Pietro di Barbozza, San Vito and San Giovanni
(mainly for Cartizze) in Valdobbiadene. A regular supply also comes
from the Col San Martino area, from Rolle di Cison and from Santa
Maria di Feletto. The soils consist of mainly clay, sandstone, marl and
limestone, while altitudes vary from 245 to 360 metres above sea level.

After fermentation in stainless steel, the wines are stored, clarified and
kept at 10°C until February of the year after the harvest, when tirage
takes place. In the 'long Charmat method', wines remain from four to
twelve months on the lees and for between one and three months after
bottling for ageing potential. Apart from the Valdobbiadene DOCG
extra dry '47', which shows typical off-dry fruit, the Valdobbiadene
DOCG Rive Di Rolle Vigneto Piai Alto is an attractive drop, while
Valdobbiadene DOCG brut Vigneto Altena and Valdobbiadene DOCG
Rive di San Stefano Brut Vigneto Montagnole are both single vineyard
wines expressing the personality of an appetizingly dry Prosecco, refreshing enough to be drunk with food.

Bottega

Bibano di Godega di Sant'Urbano, Treviso

www.bottegaspa.com

Originally farmed by tenant farmers for the Counts of Collalto, the
modern foundations of Bottega lie in the grappa distillery developed
by Aldo Bottega in the 1950s and 1960s and continued by his children
Sandro, Barbara and Stefano. A winery was added to the distillery in
1992 and Il Vino dei Poeti Prosecco Spumante was created. In 2007
Distilleria Bottega moved to Bibano di Godega di Sant' Urbano, north
of Venice, where the seventeenth-century farmhouse sits among 10
hectares of vineyards. Guglielmo Pasqualin is the winemaker. Bottega
also manages wineries in Valgatara, Verona and Montalcino. While the
Valdobbiadene Prosecco Superiore DOCG extra dry Il Vino Dei Poeti
is on the sweet side, its delicate fresh apple and pear perfume and refreshing bubbles make it palatable enough.

Azienda Agricola Case Paolin di Pozzobon Fratelli Soc. Agr. Sempl.

Volpago del Montello, Treviso

www.casepaolin.it

Home to the sharecroppers who used to farm the surrounding land, the historic wooden cellar of Case Paolin stands in the shadow of its three arches. Today, Case Paolin is owned by the Pozzobon family, father Emilio and his three sons, winemakers Adelino and the technically minded Mirco, who graduated in oenology from the University of Padua in the 1990s, and their older brother Diego, who manages the vineyards. Certified organic in 2012, the 15-hectare estate produces mainly Prosecco from low yields whose ratio of skins to juice brings texture and structure. Vineyards are based on the grey stones of the Belvedere plain and the iron-rich red soils of the Montello hill.

From 30-year-old vines, Case Paolin's Col Fondo Asolo Prosecco Superiore DOCG undergoes a first fermentation in stainless steel after 15–18 hours skin contact, using wild yeast, and a second fermentation in the bottle, producing a slightly cloudy, textured fizz that's leesy and refreshingly dry. Verging on the off-dry, the Asolo Prosecco Superiore DOCG Brut shows pleasant fresh apple and pear aromatics and a juicy textured mousse with commendable freshness. There's also a new Asolo Prosecco Superiore DOCG Extra Brut, Pietra Fine. Bubbles don't have it all their own way. The San Carlo Montello e Colli Asolani DOC is a stylishly oaked blend of Cabernet Sauvignon, Cabernet Franc and Merlot.

Az. Agr. Conte Collalto

Susegana, Treviso

www.cantine-collalto.it

Collalto calls its fizz 'aristocratic', which is justifiable given the pedigree of its owner, Princess Isabella Collalto de Croÿ. With her children Emmanuel and Violette, Isabella has managed 164 hectares of vineyards and the winery in the Prosecco Superiore DOCG since 2007. Including the Wildbacher grape introduced by Count Antonio Rambaldo in the eighteenth century, 100 hectares are devoted to Collalto Prosecco Superiore. After gentle pressing and fermentation in stainless steel, the wine stays on its lees for three to six months before the Martinotti method induces the all-important fizz, spending a further eight months on the lees before being bottled at 4.5 atmospheres of pressure. The resulting Conegliano Valdobbiadene Prosecco Superiore DOCG Brut Rive di Collalto Isabella is a crowd-pleasing fizz, only just off-dry, and so retaining the freshness of the grape and finishing with a clean, crisp flourish.

Le Colture

S. Stefano di Valdobbiadene, Treviso

www.lecolture.com

Cesare Ruggeri started to produce sparkling wine in the small village of Santo Stefano di Valdobbiadene in 1983 although his family has been involved in viticulture in the area since the 1950s. Today, Cesare's three children, Silvia, Alberto and Veronica, run 40 hectares of vineyards split between 16 properties lying in the Valdobbiadene and Conegliano areas, as well as Montello to the West. They are particularly proud of their Cartizze, 'our gold', as Veronica calls it, producing some 1,700 cases of this fragrant, medium-sweet sparkling wine. The Valdobbiadene Superiore di Cartizze DOCG Dry shows energetic medium-sweet peach and honeyed fruit tempered by juicy balancing acidity.

Nino Franco Spumanti SRL

Valdobbiadene, Treviso

www.ninofranco.it

Cantine Franco was founded in Valdobbiadene in 1919 by Antonio Franco, expanded by his son Nino, and turned on its head by Primo who, after graduating from Conegliano, modernized the winery. Until the 1970s, the Prosecco was *col fondo* but then a switch was made to the Charmat method. From the start of the 1990s, Primo, who took charge in 1982, experimented with new planting techniques and the use of old clones, all the while maintaining a close relationship with local grape producers. In this endeavour, Primo is assisted by his wife Annalisa and daughter Silvia.

Nino Franco owns and rents three vineyards in Valdobbiadene: the 2.4-hectare Grave di Stecca, which is on mainly chalky soils and produces Grave di Stecca; San Floriano, where Vigneto della Riva di San Floriano is based on chalk, stones and clay soils; and the clay soil Col del Vent, where Nodi is produced. In the cellar, Glera is fermented in stainless steel tanks by the Charmat method, producing some one million bottles in both brut and dry versions. While the fresh and attractively perfumed Rustico and appetizingly dry Nino Franco Brut offer good value, Grave di Stecca and Nodi Brut are intensely fragrant, softly textured and poised and the Vigneto della Riva di San Floriano Brut is well-balanced, tangy and dry.

Conte Loredan Gasparini di Palla Giancarlo

Volpago del Montello, Treviso

www.loredangasparini.it

Readers of a certain age may remember a delicious red called Venegazzù. It was, and still is, a Bordeaux-style blend from Loredan Gasparini, whose estate extends to some 60 hectares on the slopes of the Asolo and Montello hills north of Venice. The estate was founded in the 1930s by Count Piero Loredan, who planted Cabernet Sauvignon, Cabernet Franc, Merlot and Malbec and in 1951, the first Venegazzù red was made. In 1973, the property was bought by the present owner, Giancarlo Palla. The company works over 23 hectares, almost totally dedicated to Asolo Prosecco Superiore DOCG.

While the winery's flagship wines remain its two red blends, the recent Prosecco boom has seen it develop Asolo Prosecco Superiore DOCG. The Loredan Gasparini extra dry, Cuvée Indigena, shows attractive aromatics with some complexity behind the fruit, which is ripe in stone fruit flavours and richly textured with an off-dry honeyed finish. The Loredan Gasparini Monti Asolo Prosecco Superiore DOCG, a wine of exceptional finesse, displays an intense nutty aroma from, unusually, traditional method fermentation, with a rich and creamy textured mousse and a fine biscuity flavour shot through with fresh acidity.

Mani Sagge

San Pietro di Feletto, Treviso

www.manisagge.com

To the north-west of Conegliano in San Pietro di Feletto, Marco Cescon runs the scenic Tenuta Mani Sagge, started by his great-grandfather with vineyards replanted in 1985. The Palladian-style Pink House was built in 1820, and remains a strong focal point for vineyard walks, wine tastings and the panoramic view from the terraces that are part and parcel of an enjoyable visitor experience. The extra brut here is made by the 'long Charmat method' to bring out the flavour, and they also make a classic method brut using natural yeasts. The Conegliano Valdobbiadene Prosecco Superiore DOCG extra brut Audace, in its bell-bottomed bottle, is fresh and floral with an appley, salty dryness; a Prosecco superiore demanding sheep's cheese.

La Marca

Oderzo, Treviso
www.lamarca.it

Founded in 1968, La Marca is one of a number of cooperatives that saved winemaking when the region was on its knees after the war. It is a huge collection of cooperatives with eight wineries all located in the province of Treviso, linking some 5,000 winegrowers who tend around 15,000 hectares of vineyards. Territoriality, cooperation and sustainability are the company's stated values. Of its five brands, La Marca is of a reasonable commercial standard. Its Conegliano Valdobbiadene Prosecco Superiore DOCG Millage Extra Dry NV is made in a pleasant style with noticeably off-dry fruitiness on the palate, bisected by a clean streak of freshness.

Martignago Vignaioli

Maser, Treviso
www.martignago.wine

At the foot of the Asolo hills in the small town of Maser, Cantina Martignago's family vineyards cover 8 hectares, of which roughly two-thirds are planted to Glera, with some Cabernet and Merlot. Martignago belongs to FIVI, the Italian Federation of Independent Winegrowers and is moving towards a goal of sustainable vineyards. Production is 60,000 bottles, the rest of the wine being sold to big companies. They welcome small tours and will organize a wine tasting with lunch or dinner at a local restaurant.

The Martignago Asolo Prosecco Superiore DOCG Extra Brut, made from 50-year-old vines harvested with half a degree more ripeness than the normal 9.5–10 per cent, displays fresh peachy fruit and citrusy acidity. Its Col Fondo shows a good yeasty nose and biscuity dry fruit with a Champagne-like complexity and gastronomic mineral dryness. With 10 grams per litre, the Asolo Prosecco Superiore DOCG Brut is pleasantly approachable with balanced peachy off-dry fruit, while the Asolo Prosecco Superiore DOCG Extra Dry is spicy and less obviously sweet than some in the style. A vinous Spumante Rosato is made here too, from a blend of 50 per cent Schiava and 50 per cent Cabernet Sauvignon, as well as a good Cabernet Merlot Montello Rosso.

Masottina

Castello Roganzuolo, Treviso

www.masottina.it

Masottina was founded in 1946 in the Treviso foothills by Epifanio Dal Bianco, with 5 hectares. Today, the wines are created from the 280 hectares of vineyards, with 74 hectares in Ogliano, run by the Dal Bianco family. With around 500 hectares of hills, Ogliano itself is one of the most important hubs of wine production in this historic area. At altitudes ranging from 60 to 170 metres, the soils are based on glacial deposits. Wind, sunlight and day to night differences in temperature are important factors; grassing, green manure and organic fertilization return nutrients to the land. The Dal Bianco family started Rive production from 2009, producing two Rive di Ogliano, R.D.O. Levante made from a single clos-like vineyard of 1.2 hectares and R.D.O. Ponente, from a vineyard of 1.75 hectares. The former is appetizingly off-dry, the latter refreshingly dry. The winery located in Ogliano houses the cellar with an underground complex extending down for 20 metres, split over three different levels and based on gravity-flow. The preferred style, and biggest part of production, is Brut Prosecco.

Soc. Ad. Siro Merotto

Farra di Soligo, Treviso

www.siromerotto.it

Siro Merotto is run by Mirko and Nicola Merotto, continuing the work of their father Siro and their grandfather Giovanni, who founded the company in 1960. The estate vineyards are located in the Col San Martino hills in Sanvigili and Rive Alte between Farra di Soligo and Vidor, whose steep slopes range from 150 to 450 metres above sea level. The work in the steep, free-draining vineyards is labour intensive, with operations including pruning and harvesting done by hand. Yields range from 9 to 12 kilograms per vine. After fermentation, the base wines spend time on the lees for the right balance of acidity, minerality and structure. Their Rive di Col san Martino is nicely concentrated, showing attractive orchard fruit ripeness and a gentle-textured mousse with a mouthwateringly dry finish.

Mongarda

Col San Martino, Treviso

www.mongarda.it

A young graduate of the wine school at Conegliano, Martino Tormena took over this small, family-owned estate in Mongarda from his father Bruno in 2011. Poor, rocky limestone soils on steep slopes characterize the 10 hectares of vineyards, cultivated sustainably and spread between the villages of Col San Martino, Farra di Soligo and Valdobbiadene. The Glera grape here is often co-planted, and co-fermented, with the local Perera, Verdiso and Bianchetta grapes. Martino is working towards organic certification and soft presses whole bunches for his Charmat method fizz. Total production from the south-facing San Gallo, east-facing Rive Alte vineyard and south-east-facing Mongarda vineyard is 50,000 bottles, including a fragrant, winey Valdobbiadene Prosecco Superiore DOCG Brut Vigneto San Gallo, a pet nat-style Colli Trevigiani IGT and a bone-dry Metodo Classico Extra Brut.

Montesel

Colfosco, Treviso

monteselvini.it

This family winery, now in the third generation, is run by husband and wife Renzo and Vania Montesel. With their son, Davide, they produce three Prosecco Superiore DOCG wines and some frizzante. Located on the main hill in Colfosco in the southern part of the DOCG area, their small estate is one of the warmest sites in the region. Family management allows them to follow each production step by step, from the vineyard all the way through to marketing and retail. In addition to their Millesimato, their two most interesting wines are Vigna del Paradiso Extra Dry and Riva Dei Fiori Brut – both Prosecco Superiore DOCG Rive di Colfosco.

Ruggeri & C. S.p.A.

Valdobbiadene, Treviso

www.ruggeri.it

The Bisol family have been making wine in the Valdobbiadene region since Eliseo Bisol owned a small winery in Santo Stefano in the mid-nineteenth century. In 1950, Ruggeri was founded by Giustino Bisol with his cousin, whose surname, Ruggeri, distinguished it from the Bisol family winery. From 1989 to 2017 it was run by Giustino's son, Paolo Bisol, becoming part of the German fizz behemoth Rotkäppchen-Mumm Sektkellereien in 2017, but its Valdobbiadene Prosecco Superiore DOCG fizz continues to be made by Paolo and his granddaughter Isabella.

Ruggeri sources its grapes, including the indigenous Bianchetta, Perera and Verdiso, from the 'Golden Triangle', the hilly area, that is, delineated by the hamlets of Santo Stefano, San Pietro di Barbozza and Saccol. Working with growers, Ruggeri has the biggest production of the prestigious Cartizze, the south-facing area whose fossil-rich limestone, clay and sandstone soils are said to express the best of the delicate floral fragrance of the Glera grape. Ruggeri's Valdobbiadene Prosecco Superiore di Cartizze Brut DOCG achieves that, a fragrant fizz of unusual finesse thanks to a zesty, dry twist on the finish.

Ruggeri prides itself on the number of century-old Glera vines it controls, so much so that it has established a training programme to help local growers develop a deeper understanding of pruning techniques, disease prevention and sustainability. Thanks to the quality of the 2014 vintage, Ruggeri decided to push the envelope by setting aside the grapes from a small plot of 80- to 100-year-old vines. After the first fermentation, it was placed in an autoclave in the spring of 2015, and following the second fermentation, the Cinqueanni Brut was left undisturbed for 46 months and topped up with just 2 grams per litre dosage.

Scandolera

Colbertaldo di Vidor, Treviso

www.scandolera.it

Scandolera manages 22 hectares of vineyards with different microclimatic and geological characteristics in steep, mostly south-facing vineyard plots of marl, sandstone and chalky conglomerates scattered throughout the sub-region of Conegliano Valdobbiadene. Mostly focused on the domestic market, the family work the vineyards sustainably and produce two non-vintage fizzes from Glera, the better being the Costa d'Oro Brut, which shows an appealing pear-like fruitiness with a persistent prickle on the tongue and delicately dry finish. Visitors are offered a guided tour on a 'cognitive and sensorial journey', starting in the vineyards, heading into the winery, and ending with a tasting.

Valdellövo

Susegana, Treviso

www.valdellovo.com

The 10 hectares of the Valdellövo winery are located at Collalto di Susegana in the south-eastern hills between Conegliano and Valdobbiadene. Owned by Benedetto and Clotilde Ricci, the vineyards, cultivated sustainably without herbicides and with 'green' fertilizer to contribute to biodiversity, comprise some 2 hectares of 60-year-old mixed vines of Glera, Verdiso and Bianchetta, while another 8 hectares are planted from a massal selection. Their Conegliano Valdobbiadene Prosecco Superiore DOCG AnnoZero Extra Dry is a sweet-and-sour, tangy blend of 90 per cent Glera, with 10 per cent Bianchetta and Verdiso.

Val d'Oca

Valdobbiadene, Treviso

www.valdoca.com

The Group Cantina Produttori di Valdobbiadene Val d'Oca is a cooperative established in 1952, comprising 600 growers covering almost 1,000 hectares of vineyards. As well as satellite-mapping, training, technical consultancy and selection of the best *crus*, this go-ahead co-op has undertaken a number of initiatives in the vineyard and cellar. All grapes are hand-picked and some 90 per cent of its 15,000 tonne production is from Glera for Valdobbiadene Prosecco Superiore DOCG and Prosecco DOC. Its Val d'Oca Valdobbiadene Prosecco Superiore DOCG Brut Rive di San Pietro di Barbozza is pleasantly fresh and floral, the off-dry fruit balanced at 10 grams per litre. Val d'Oca is proud of its sustainability record which includes obtaining the VIVA certification in 2020.

Le Vigne di Alice

Vittorio Veneto, Treviso

www.levignedialice.it

In the eyes of Cinzia Canzian, 'la vita è una bollicina' (life is a bubble), a phrase coined as a modern carpe diem and due to the fact that she can't conceive of a life without bubbles (and let's face it, who can?). Indeed, starting out as a wine producer in 2005, she has always produced only sparkling wines, including those made in Prosecco's typical Charmat method, as well as classic and ancestral method fizz. Born in an *osteria*, and surrounded at an early age by the smells of her grandfather's

Prosecco *sur lie* (he told her 'just by smelling you can understand if a wine's good or bad'), you might say that Cinzia was born to the bubble. After she started working in her husband's winery, she grasped the nettle of setting up on her own 'amid a million reasons why not to' after an inspirational meeting with Pietro Pellegrini, her Italian distributor.

In the north-east of Conegliano Valdobbiadene, Le Vigne di Alice benefits from a temperate climate thanks to the natural barrier of the Belluno Dolomites to the north and the relative proximity of the Adriatic to the south. Hillside slopes of free-draining soils on a marine platform of rocks eroded by glaciers and composed of alluvial deposits ensure maximum solar radiation and significant day to night temperature differences, while a healthy breeze brings ventilation to the vines. Eschewing herbicides, fungicides and pesticides, Cinzia grows a natural cover crop, using composted manure and organic preparations. Woodland is preserved to encourage biodiversity and in 2020, she set up a bee colony.

In the cellar, ambient yeasts are used for the first fermentation of the semi-sparkling and sparkling wines. Her zero dosage Alice .G Valdobbiadene Prosecco Superiore is a complex expression of Prosecco with an elegant, underlying nuttiness and salty, dry finish. Also without dosage, the slightly cloudy, bone dry P.S. Integrale Metodo Ancestrale brut is a gastronomic fizz, while Doro Nature Brut Valdobbiadene Prosecco Superiore DOCG Millesimato and Alice Extra Dry Conegliano Valdobbiadene Prosecco Superiore with their gently off-dry apple and pear mousse, are closer to the Prosecco archetype. As far from common or garden Prosecco rosé as you'll get, Osé Nature Rosé Brut Nature Vino Spumante, a blend of Refrontolo and Carpesica, is quite the discovery. Cinzia puts the date of disgorgement on the back label, feeling it helps consumers understand the wine and the style better.

Villa Sandi S.P.A.

Crocetta del Montello, Treviso

www.villasandi.it / www.lagioiosa.it

Nestled at the foot of the Marca Trevigiana hills, in the heart of the Prosecco area, Villa Sandi is a Palladian-style villa dating back to 1622 and the HQ of the company. Owned and run by the Moretti Polegato family, Villa Sandi owns 160 hectares of vineyards and relies on long-term contracts with growers. Villa Sandi also owns the La Rivetta Estate covering 1.5 hectares in the Cartizze area between the hamlets of Santo Stefano and San Pietro di Barbozza in Valdobbiadene. The accent is on freshness and, with exports to over 110 countries, the 30-label-strong range, including still wines and grappa, is vast, varying from average to good at the top. Typical is the Villa Sandi Valdobbiadene Prosecco Superiore DOCG Brut, not too sweet, but off-dry with a pleasantly fresh apple and pear fruitiness. The tongue-twisting La Gioiosa brand also belongs to Villa Sandi. Whole bunches for the vintage Prosecco Superiore are gently pressed and the base wine kept in tank until its second fermentation by Charmat method. La Gioiosa Valdobbiadene Prosecco Superiore DOCG Brut is a crowd-pleasing fizz with off-dry pear flavours and a cleansing twist on the finish.

LAMBRUSCO

Despite its notoriety as an industrial fizz of dubious quality, Lambrusco too has its vivacious, foaming red highlights, particularly with the native Lambrusco di Sorbara grape, but also with the Lambrusco Grasparossa and Lambrusco Marani varieties. Some producers here are even using the traditional method.

Producers

Cantine Cavicchioli

San Prospero, Modena

www.cavicchioli.it

Cavicchioli pinpoint 6 April 1928 as the precise date on which Umberto Cavicchioli transformed his workshop in Modena's village of San Prospero into a cellar to found Lambrusco Cavicchioli. Expansion followed after the Second World War under his sons, Umberto, Franco, Romano and Piergiorgio. New *autoclavi* were acquired in 1962 for Charmat method production and a separate production facility was built a short Lambretta-ride of six kilometres away in Cristo di Sorbara. The business was sold to GIV in 2010, but continuity is maintained by Piergiorgio's son, Sandro, a Conegliano wine school graduate.

The vineyards, some 100 hectares of fertile sandy, mixed soils on spur-pruned, double curtain trellis in the DOC area between the Secchia and Panaro rivers, remain in family ownership. The fruit used solely for Cavicchioli bottlings is processed in the Cristo di Sorbara winery. Cavicchioli oversees the production process for the grapes from its partners' vineyards, resulting in production of around 20 million bottles, much of it *vino da pasto*, cheap and cheerful everyday wine, that is.

Cavicchioli's quality fizz is made by Charmat, which revolutionized Lambrusco production in the 1960s, and the *metodo classico*. Sandro uses two processes for Charmat, in both of which the grapes are mechanically harvested and destemmed before fermentation. One involves early picking and a 48- to 72-hour pre-fermentation maceration, the second a maceration up to 4–5 per cent alcohol. For *metodo classico*, grapes are hand-picked and after cold storage pressed by pneumatic Wilmes presses before batches are split for fermentation according to sugar and acidity levels.

Both the floral, spicy Col Sassoro Lambrusco Grasparossa di Castelvetro DOC Secco and the frothy Vigna del Cristo Lambrusco di Sorbara DOC Secco make excellent aperitif or food wines with their drier than expected black cherry fruitiness. The star of the show is the Rosé del Cristo Lambrusco di Sorbara DOC Rosato Spumante Brut Metodo Classico, an onion skin rosé that's subtly floral with vivacity in its crunchy berry-like fruit and creamy-textured mousse.

Cantina Paltrinieri

Sorbara, Modena

www.cantinapaltrinieri.it

Paltrinieri is a family-run winery, founded by Achille Paltrinieri, who started producing the first bottles of Lambrusco di Sorbara in 1926. It's been run by Alberto and Barbara since 1996, when Alberto took over from his parents, Gianfranco and Pierina. In 1998, Alberto used the Sorbara name to distinguish his pale, light-coloured Lambrusco from the dark and largely sweet stuff for which Lambrusco was, and arguably still is, known. The turning point was the 2008 creation of its Leclisse, a dry, fresh, pink frizzante made from a selection of pure Sorbara grapes that has found popularity with a younger audience.

Paltrinieri owns 17 hectares of vineyards in the Il Cristo area of Sorbara, a fertile strip of land in the lower part of Modena between the Po Valley's Secchia and Panaro rivers. Some 180,000 bottles with eight different labels are produced from their plantings of Lambrusco di Sorbara and Lambrusco Salamino. Five of the wines are sparkling frizzante made by the Charmat method (Leclisse, Sant'Agata, Piria, Solco, Bianco), one is refermented in the bottle (Radice), and there are two spumante, a *metodo classico* (Grosso) and a 12-months Charmat (La Riserva).

The Grosso Lambrusco di Modena DOC Metodo Classico, combines rhubarb and cherry fruit to good effect with a light complexing smokiness and a vinous fruitiness that finishes on a food-friendly, laser-edged dry note. Awarded the Gambero Rosso's highest accolade, Tre Bicchieri, in 2010, the quirky semi-dry Solco is strawberryishly sweet and meatily dry and made from pure Salamino, Leclisse was awarded Tre Bicchieri in 2010 and in 2016–2019, while Radice won the accolade in 2013 and 2015.

Of the five pure Sorbara wines, the Sant' Agata Lambrusco di Sorbara comes on with an initial sour cherry-like freshness and finishes with a superdry, mouthwatering twist, while the cranberry-like bite of the Piria Lambrusco di Sorbara makes it a perfect gastronomic red. Most interesting of all, Paltrinieri's Radice, Lambrusco di Sorbara DOC Vino Frizzante Secco is a pet nat style, refermented in the bottle, whose vivacious fizz, veering from subtle fruit sweetness to tangy dryness, gives the lie to the image of Lambrusco as a bland wine. Paltrinieri's artist labels are stunning.

10

CENTRAL AND EASTERN EUROPE

Before the nineteenth century, Ottoman rule across much of this vast region had stifled the wine industry, though wine did hang on in the Christian community, and among rural peasants. It was a little different in Austro-Hungary and the Habsburg empire, which did not fall under the Ottomans. The nineteenth century was the starting point for serious efforts with sparkling wine in Central and Eastern Europe.

AUSTRIA

Although Austria boasts a 180-year tradition of producing sparkling wine, starting with Robert Schlumberger, who took the traditional method back from Champagne to Vienna in 1842, it has only recently covered itself with sparkling wine glory. The vast majority of its fizz has long been of simple, cheap wines made for domestic consumption. In the 1970s, only companies with a trade licence to produce sparkling wines were permitted to do so, until Gerald Malat, who started producing sparkling wine in 1976, successfully went to the Supreme Court for the right to produce sparkling wine without the need for a trade licence.

Since then, there has been a trickle of producers in the vanguard of Austria's new wave, making quality fizz from both the Champagne grapes and the native varieties of Grüner Veltliner, Welschriesling and Pinot Blanc. Steininger and Szigeti were among the early adopters of the new era of quality Austrian fizz following the 1985 wine scandal and the country now has over 100 producers of sparkling wine based in most of the country's wine regions.

Since 2015, Austria has moved up from basic Austrian Sekt with a set of three classifications based on Sekt g.U., an abbreviation of *geschützte Ursprungsbezeichnung* (PDO), identifiable by a red and white banderole on the capsule. Austrian Sekt Klassik is from a protected designation of origin made by tank or transfer method with an ageing requirement of at least nine months on the lees. Austrian Sekt Reserve must be from hand-harvested grapes from just one of Austria's wine regions, made as brut, extra brut, or brut nature by the traditional method and aged for at least 18 months on the lees. Austrian Sekt Grosse Reserve, also made from hand-harvested grapes pressed by pneumatic or basket press, with a juice extraction rate of 50 per cent and made only as brut, extra brut, or brut nature, must come from a single commune or vineyard and spend at least 30 months on the lees.

Producers

Weingut Bründlmayer

Langenlois

www.bruendlmayer.at

Dating back to 1581, Bründlmayer today is not only one of the oldest, but also one of the most modern cellars in Austria. Willi Bründlmayer Senior, born 1916, switched from traditional mixed farming to full wine production, and his son, Willi Junior, a University of Vienna graduate, entered the family business in the late seventies. The estate has since experimented with different sustainable regimes in the vineyard, culminating in certification of the entire estate by the organic farming control body, LACON, AT-BIO-402, in 2015. Apart from a focus on turning Grüner Veltliner from a quaffer into a serious white and an increased use of barrels from native wood, the love of Willi and his French wife, Edwige, for Champagne, led him to create Bründlmayer Brut, the estate's first traditional method wine, in 1989.

The Bründlmayer family's 90 hectares of vineyards lie on the hills around Langenlois, 70 kilometres west of Vienna. Normally in the first weeks of September (although as early as the twentieth of August in recent vintages), the grapes best suited to the Sekt base wines are selected for their freshness. Hand-harvested and gently whole-bunch pressed, after fermentation in stainless steel, the base wines generally undergo malolactic fermentation. In the case of the brut, extra brut and *blanc de blancs*, a part is racked into Austrian oak barrels with a proportion of the lees. After bottling, the wine remains on the lees for 20–36 months, sometimes longer.

There are currently four reserve and two grosse reserve bottle-fermented, hand riddled Sekts. The Brut Reserve is a star, with seductive, toasty characters and a trenchant, sumptuously flavoured mousse. The bone-dry Extra Brut Reserve has a refreshing summer aperitif style. A blend of Pinot Noir, Zweigelt and Saint Laurent, the Brut Rosé Reserve is charmingly floral and strawberry fruity, while the Blanc de Blancs Extra Brut Reserve shows real depth of leesy flavour and saline dryness. The Blanc de Blancs Brut Nature, with little sulphur dioxide, forms one part of the Langenlois Grosse Reserve duo. The partner here is a 100 per cent Pinot Noir Blanc de Noirs Extra Brut with chalky, refined elements.

Weingut Loimer

Langenlois

www.loimer.at

A Vienna Klosterneuburg graduate, Fred Loimer took over the Langenlois estate from his parents in 1997, moving to its current location in Kamptal two years later. The new cellar was built in 2000 and the old one restored. After winning Falstaff's Winemaker of the Year in 2002, Loimer changed to biodynamic viticulture in 2006, gaining organic/respekt-BIODYN certification in 2009. In 1991 he made his first foray into fizz with a *blanc de noirs* made from Pinot Noir. He had what he calls 'an on and off' relationship with fizz until going into sparkling wine production in 2013.

Austria's climate is cool, that of Langenlois in particular, thanks to a cooling influence from the north and west. The fruit comes from Loimer's 70 hectares of vineyards owned and leased in Langenlois in Kamptal and 10 hectares (leased) in Gumpoldskirchen in the Thermenregion. The whole gamut of Austrian varieties is used to make Loimer's fizz: Zweigelt, Pinot Noir, Pinot Blanc, Pinot Gris, Chardonnay, Grüner Veltliner and Saint Laurent. Working with his German cellarmaster David Döring, Loimer gives the base wines lees contact of 6–12 months after fermentation in stainless steel and oak cask followed by malolactic fermentation. At disgorgement, dosage is at a low 2–3 grams per litre for the extra brut and brut rosé with no dosage on the *blanc de blancs* brut nature.

The results are sparkling wines of distinctive personality, elegant with good natural energy and distinctly refreshing. You feel that Mozart himself would have approved of the Brut Reserve, a full-flavoured fizz with a balanced, creamy mousse whose flavours mingle notes of lees-aged nuttiness with salted caramel, and the non-vintage Extra Brut Reserve, with its aged scents of nuttiness delivering flavour with a vivacious mousse in a refreshing counterpoint to a long, savoury finish. Also good are the elegantly balanced, effortlessly dry non-vintage Brut Rosé Reserve and savoury, toasty, dry Langenlois Blanc de Blancs brut. From the autumn of 2021, there will be a Gumpoldskirchen *blanc de noirs* made from pure Pinot Noir grown on calcareous gravel soils with heavy clay sediments.

Weingut Malat

Furth bei Göttweig

www.malat.at

Established in 1722, the estate, which sits below the Stift Göttweig Abbey in the Kremstal, has been in the Malat family ever since. Gerald Malat took over the reins of the company from his father in 1974 and started to produce sparkling wine in 1976. After completing his business studies in Krems, tenth generation Michael Malat graduated from the University of Vienna and worked in Austria, France, California, Argentina and New Zealand before returning to the family winery full time, taking over from his father in 2008.

Malat owns 45 hectares, producing wines from organically farmed estate grapes only. The Chardonnay, Pinot Noir, Pinot Blanc and Pinot Gris for the sparkling wines are planted close to the River Danube, where the calcareous soils help to enhance the vibrant Malat style. The grapes are picked manually and pressed with 50 per cent extracted from the four tonnes. The brut nature and brut rosé, fermented in stainless steel, undergo malolactic fermentation in cooler years with high acidity such as 2014, 2016 and 2020 but not in the warmer vintages of 2015, 2017, 2018 and 2019. The wines remain for at least 40 months in the bottle.

The vintage Malat Brut Rosé Reserve displays an elegantly dry, raspberries and cream mousse combining the fruity and the savoury; the Brut Nature Reserve is nicely balanced and uncompromisingly bone dry. The full-flavoured and refreshingly dry Blanc de Blancs Grosse Reserve is naturally fermented in used 500-litre oak barrels, staying in contact with the lees in the bottle for at least 60 months. All are vintage and brut nature and Malat also now mentions the date of disgorgement on the back label. Annual production of the sparkling wines is around 20,000 bottles.

BULGARIA

Bulgaria doesn't appear to have a long history with sparkling wine as its industry was affected by both Ottoman rule and the fact that prior to the Second World War its holdings were tiny and rural. Post-war nationalization didn't initially prioritize sparkling production, though the state-owned Magura winery was set up in 1967 near Vidin specifically to produce bottle-fermented sparklers in this cooler zone. Bottles are aged in the bat gallery in the 15-million-year-old Magura cave where palaeolithic cave art can be seen above the ranks of maturing bottles. There are records of the Chirpan sparkling wine factory being set up in 1982 with state support from the USSR. Whole-bunch pressed Mavrud was often used as the base wine here. Modern-era sparklers are led by Miroglio, but others worthy of note include the tiny Borovitza with its handcrafted batches of sparkling Mavrud and even orange sparkling; Logodaj, who have successfully developed quality sparklers from the difficult-to-ripen broad-leafed Melnik and, most recently, Midalidare has impressed with its sparkling range additions.

Producers

Edoardo Miroglio Wine Cellar
Nova Zagora

www.emiroglio-wine.com

When Caroline Gilby MW first visited Edoardo Miroglio's winery soon after it opened, it made quite an impression. 'The cellar spiralled down into a small hill rather like the inside of the snail shell. I knew they were serious about their sparkling wine when I spotted the separate tiny tanks for each batch, all watched over by the scrupulously competent Desislava 'Desi' Baicheva who gives every impression of pursuing perfection.' A Plovdiv graduate, Desislava is the winemaker in an East-meets-West team of consultant Donato Lanati and production manager and agronomist Alberto La Rosa.

Instead of impulse-buying, like many did in the early 2000s, once it became possible for private wineries to acquire land, Miroglio, which owns Tenuta Carretta in Piemonte, searched widely across the Thracian valley before settling on Elenovo. Pinot Noir was a focus in all styles because of Edoardo's love of burgundy and for the relatively cool continental climate, with its notable diurnal temperature differences. Champagne clones were planted, while local grapes, especially Mavrud, a focus for the winery today, arrived later. Edoardo's son Franco took over the management in 2008.

The winery has 150 hectares and 20 clones and varieties, and La Rosa admits that the changing climate is bringing new challenges, including using judicious irrigation from the winery's own reservoir and managing leaf cover. There is a Coquard press for gentle pressing, up to 52 per cent free-run juice, the only fraction used for fermentation in stainless steel. The four main wines are single vintage and undergo at least 36 months on lees, with a few special batches aged for ten years and more. If Southern Bulgaria is not an obvious destination for great sparkling wine, Miroglio's track record belies this, making fine, precise and pure wines. The Brut Rosé shows delicate wild strawberry fruit and beautiful integration of fruit, acidity and autolytic character while the Brut Blanc de Blanc is an elegant, gently creamy and refined pure Chardonnay.

HUNGARY

The cradle of Hungarian sparkling wine was Pozsony (now Bratislava) where, so the story goes, on returning from Napoleon's campaigns in Russia, Johann Evangelist Hubert settled and started to make sparkling wine. The company that became Hubert was actually founded in 1825 by Mihály Schönburger and János Fischer, winning best Hungarian sparkling in 1842. The Hubert brand today is part of Henkell. The first sparkling producer on the Pest side of Budapest was founded in 1852 and domestic sparkling production took off later in the nineteenth century. József Törley, who moved to Champagne and worked for Delbeck, saw potential in the deep cellars of Budafok (part of Budapest), moving there in 1882. Guided by French specialists and equipment, he was the first to introduce freezing technology for disgorging. Fruit came from the cool rolling limestone hills of Etyek region – still the origin for Törley's best bottle-fermented wines.

By the First World War sparkling wine was being made in 23 regions, but two world wars, the Treaty of Trianon and economic crises caused closures and stagnation. A nationalized Törley restarted in 1951, as the only sparkling wine factory in the country. Hungarovin took over in 1973, adding François Frères to its labels in 1982 and becoming part of Henkell in 1992. By 2019, 21 million bottles of fizz were being produced in a multi-storey winery, largely in tank, though with some decent bottle-fermented wines under the François brand. With its high acidity and relative neutrality, the potential of Furmint has now been recognized for Hungarian fizz (known as *pezsgő*). It was almost certainly pioneered by Chateau Vincent in the 1990s, but adopted widely in Tokaj since 2010, largely thanks to the efforts of Demeter-Zoltán who not only demonstrated that quality sparkling was possible in Tokaj (it must be bottle-fermented by law), but also lobbied to remove onerous taxes and licences, thus allowing small wineries to join the new sparkling wave.

Producers
Kreinbacher Birtok
Somlóvásárhely
www.kreinbacher.hu
Rooms and restaurant: kreinbacher.accenthotels.com/

As you drive across the Hungarian plains, the dramatic, extinct volcano of Somló (Nagy-Somló in full) suddenly comes into view. Hungarians like to describe it as the place God forgot his hat for the shape of the basalt cap rising from the fields. It's Hungary's second smallest region, where the vineyards sit on degraded volcanic and sedimentary soils, overlooked by dramatic basalt pillars. The region has long been famous for firm, mineral-rich wines, among them Juhfark, renowned as wedding night wines to guarantee an heir.

The unrealized potential of the region brought József Kreinbacher to buy his first vineyards here in 2002. After the founder's devotion to Champagne and some early picked grapes prompted the idea of fizz, Christian Forget from Champagne Paul Bara was invited in 2009 to help the winery team, which made Kreinbacher's first fizz in 2011. Micro-vinifications on the local grape varieties showed that, sourced from cooler plots and picked at the right moment, Furmint showed a similar sugar to acid ratio to Chardonnay along with refined and relatively neutral aromas that would allow autolysis to add complexity.

The winery has 48 hectares under cultivation, certified organic since 2010, and buys from another 20 to 40 hectares of vineyards hand harvested by the Kreinbacher team. In 2011 the statement winery and boutique hotel were also completed (Kreinbacher's other business is construction). Kreinbacher installed Coquard presses and mostly only uses cuvée juice with hyper-oxidation carried out to remove any unripe polyphenols, followed by reductive winemaking. Fermentation is in stainless steel and all the wines go through malolactic fermentation. The winery keeps up to 50 base wines by variety and plot. Lees ageing is at least 18 months, moving up to two years for the Prestige Brut and three to six years for magnums. Experiments with oak and reserve wines are ongoing.

In less than a decade since its first release, Kreinbacher has already built a reputation as one of Hungary's best and most consistent sparkling wine producers. The backbone of Furmint is unique and characterful with vivid, mouthwatering acidity, while Chardonnay adds another dimension of refinement. Across the range, the wines always show beautifully integrated autolytic notes, refined fruit and fine, lingering bubbles without coarseness.

MOLDOVA

As many historic records were destroyed in the Soviet era, it's hard to track down much early history in Moldova. There are a few mentions of 'champagne' in Southern Bessarabia, and it's reported that Prince Paravichini made 'an extremely pure champagne', probably from the Iaidzhi variety, in Akkerman in 1825. Karl Tardan, son of the founder of the Swiss Chabag colony, won medals for eight wines, including one effervescent, at the first agricultural exhibition in Chişinău in 1847. Famously, Henri Roederer founded what became the Odessa Sparkling Wine Factory in 1896, initially making traditional method wines, but switching to tank production by 1952. A newspaper report in Sovetskaya Moldaviya in 1952 shows the Moldovan Soviet Socialist Republic (MSSR) meeting 168 per cent of its 'champagne' production targets.

Research into using the mining tunnels at Cricova near the capital Chişinău for maturation of classic sparkling wine began in 1947, with approval granted in 1951. During this era every third bottle of sparkling wine sold in Russia came from MSSR, probably much from Cricova. Today this subterranean city, with its street names such as Strada Pinot and Strada Riesling and traffic lights, contains 120 kilometres of tunnels at a more or less constant temperature of 12°C. Production is around six million bottles with over half a million bottles of traditional method, which are hand-riddled by a team of six women who pass the role on through their families. Cricova also houses the private cellars of Hermann Göring and Vladimir Putin (no connection intended).

Producers

Château Purcari

Purcari Village, Stefan Voda

www.purcari.wine

Purcari is the name of a village in the southern part of Moldova, close to the Black Sea, west of the Ukraine border and the Dniester River. Château Purcari is its historic winery, just south of the village, the first specialized winery in Bessarabia, thanks to a special decree issued by Emperor of Russia Nicholas I in 1827. The winery first left its mark at the Paris Exhibition in 1878, winning the Gold Medal in a blind tasting competition, for their Negru de Purcari, a blend of Cabernet Sauvignon, Saperavi and Rară Neagră.

Best known for quality still wines, with a particular focus on using local Viorica, Rară Neagră and Fetească Neagră grapes, sparkling wines are a relatively recent phenomenon for Purcari. After Château Purcari replanted 250 hectares of vineyards at the turn of the century and modernized the old winery, their first fizz was their Cuvée de Purcari, made in 2016. With 130 hectares dedicated to sparkling wines, the vineyard soils are mostly clay-based, which, tending to be cooler and water-retentive, give good reserves of humidity, a particularly important feature of its terroir in dry summers. Some 50 kilometres away from the Black Sea, Purcari also benefits from its moderating maritime influence, which contributes to mild winters and summers.

Grapes are hand-harvested and pressed by pneumatic Bucher press with only the first fraction used for sparkling wines. The juice is fermented in stainless steel and oak with some cuvées undergoing malolactic fermentation. After tirage, the wines are aged on the lees for between 12 and 36 months. In addition to traditional sparkling blends based on Chardonnay and Pinot Noir, indigenous grapes such as Fetească Albă are pressed into service, literally, for experimental editions. Total annual production is some 300,000 bottles. Bottles are labelled with their disgorgement date.

SLOVENIA AND CROATIA

Sparkling history in Slovenia dates back to 1852 with the first traditional method sparkling made in Radgona (today in Austria). The tradition was continued by Radgonske Gorice on the Slovenian side of the border with its recent 'untouched by light' launch a notable step forward in quality. Penina is the generic term for sparkling wine for both tank and bottle-fermentation and today there are around 100 producers. Local grapes often play a role, such as Rebula in Brda where Medot uses a majority of the variety, or in Movia's dramatic Puro – which is undisgorged, so opened at point of service in a bowl of water. Furmint (aka Šipon) is proving its merits in Podravje while in the south-eastern Posavje, local grapes with high acidity like Rumeni Plavec, Kraljevina and Žametovka are proving valuable additions (possibly the best Žametovka is from the tiny Domaine Slapšak).

Croatia has two main areas for sparkling wine production. West of the capital city of Zagreb, Plešivica is the leading region, where vineyards in the Plešivica hills, at 300–400 metres altitude, are home to the Korak, Griffin and Tomac wineries. Tomac began sparkling wine production on an experimental basis in 1990, increasing to 80 per cent of their total output today with the help of the agronomist Franjo Jambrović. East of the Istrian coastal town of Poreč, Đordan Peršurić started producing sparkling wines from the local Malvazija Istarska and Teran varieties in the early 1990s under the Misal brand, since when his daughters Katarina and Ana have maintained continuity. Meneghetti in Istria also makes a traditional method fizz. North of Zagreb, the Štampar winery produces good fizz at Štrigova.

Producers

Bjana
Biljana, Slovenia
www.bjana.si

Miran Sirk grew up with winemaking in his blood thanks to his father and uncle. His enthusiasm was bolstered by visiting Champagne while studying in Ljubljana in 1986. He also inherited a ruined mansion, bought by his great-grandfather after the First World War, and a single hectare of vines in the village of Biljana (Bjana in the local dialect). The Dorišče mansion dates back to 1205 and its 800-year-old cellar is the oldest in Slovenia's stunningly beautiful Brda region, where Alpine and Mediterranean influences meet. In his first 17 years after graduating, Miran spent all the spare money he made from working for a hotel and casino group on vineyards and the cellar, until he could afford to leave. After making his first 500 bottles in 1990, he pioneered the idea of brut sparkling wine at a time when fizzy Slovenian *penina* was typically sec or demi-sec and used for toasts and celebrations.

For Miran, making wine in a drier style leaves nowhere to hide poor quality grapes. He went on to pioneer Slovenian Brut Rosé, a Cuvée Prestige and zero dosage sparkling. He and his wife Petra now own 7.5 hectares of Chardonnay, Pinot Noir and the local Rebula (Ribolla Gialla), admitting that the heat of the Mediterranean summer is a growing problem. Bjana's plots, on poor, stony, well-drained soil called flysch, are mostly on north- and north-east-facing slopes (meaning 3–4 hours less sun each day) and Miran has also increased yields to around 10 to 12 tonnes per hectare to get the desired level of ripeness, with moderate alcohol and good freshness. Picking is done in the morning and usually begins in early August.

The hand-sorted grapes go into a pneumatic press and each variety is vinified separately as the blend varies each year. Fermentation starts in steel, apart from Cuvée Prestige which is part-fermented and aged for seven months in used French oak. Lees ageing ranges from around two years for Brut, up to 48 months (and more) for Cuvée Prestige. Dosage (where used) is made with a sweet late harvest wine from the estate. The style is one of elegance, precision and purity, with a unique local identity thanks to the Rebula. Whether it's the intensity and finesse of Cuvée Prestige or the refined, delicately red-fruited vibrant Brut Rosé, the integrated elegance of the Brut Zero or even just the well-made basic Brut with its apple, lemon and biscuit notes, Bjana is one of a handful of wineries in Slovenia where sparkling wine is the main focus. With 30 years under his belt, Miran is continuing to pioneer and improve his wines.

Dveri-Pax

Jarenina, Slovenia

www.dveri-pax.com

The archbishops of Salzburg gave this historic, 800-year-old property to the Benedictine order of Admont in 1139. For centuries, only disrupted in the twentieth century by Hitler's confiscation in the 1930s and nationalization by Yugoslavia after the Second World War, wine was the main commercial activity. After Slovenia's independence in 1991, the property was returned to the Benedictines who founded a new winery in 1997, releasing the first wines in 2002. The focus was always on quality over quantity, expressing the cool continental climate, with variety to the forefront, though increasingly single vineyards feature in the winery's best wines.

Danilo Flakus (winemaker and general manager) was the first employee of the fledgling winery in 2003, following years of experience at the state-owned Vinag in Maribor. In the face of the conservatism of its Benedictine owners, in 2008 Danilo had to make his first 4,000 bottles of sparkling wine in secret. After a year on lees, he presented a bottle to the winery director and the rest, as they say, is modern history. The winery now owns 73 hectares in three areas. Furmint grows close to the hilltop town of Jeruzalem where the grapes for sparkling wine come from sandy soils with some clay. Chardonnay and Pinot Noir come from a clay-based dedicated vineyard at Kapela.

After transport in refrigerated trucks, sorting and gentle pressing, the free-run juice and up to 5 per cent press wine is used. Furmint is only fermented in steel while both large casks and steel tanks are used for the other varieties. Reserve wines may be added to the non-vintage wines and there is no malolactic fermentation. Lees ageing is at least 24 months for DP Furmint and DP Brut Rosé and up to 6 years for DP Brut, followed by dosage of around 6–10 grams per litre. In a clean, well balanced and fresh style, the DP Brut Rosé shows appealing gentle fruitiness while DP Brut is more serious, with complex autolytic character and a zesty, precise finish. The single vintage DP Furmint has impressed over multiple vintages with varietal expression of quince and apple blossom and vivid citrus and mineral undertones.

Vino Gross

Podlehnik, Slovenia

www.vinogross.com

Michael and Maria Gross are the heart and soul of Vino Gross. Michael is from a family of winemakers in Austria (Weingut Gross in Südsteiermark) and his family bought a plot of land in Haloze – Štajerska Slovenija – in 2005. On seeing the land for the first time, Michael realized its incredible potential and knew he wanted to make wine here – which he did for the first time in 2011. Maria's first vintage was 2013, and she felt the same way, falling in love with the region and giving up her career as a teacher to move to Gorca.

The 13 hectares of vines grow at around 350 to 400 metres, in steep, terraced vineyards in south-facing basins. The slopes are as steep as 65 per cent and can only be worked by hand; the vines root deep into the limy marl below sparse topsoil. Ideal for aromatic development, Alpine and Adriatic influences bring typically mild but occasionally hot days with notably cooler nights. The winery's first release was 2011 and Michael admits that working with Furmint was new to them, so they made several research trips to Tokaj. Their philosophy is to focus on the vineyard first and to work with what the vintage gives them, so in years when Furmint is less ripe, it makes good raw material for sparkling.

Their first attempt at fizz came in 2013. Furmint undergoes gentle whole-bunch pressing with no sulphur dioxide and the free-run juice only undergoes spontaneous fermentation, with a year on lees in large oak casks and natural malolactic fermentation. Lees ageing is for at least five years, often more, and there's no dosage. Michael's idea is to focus on vintage, variety and the region. Only the 2013 had been released at the time of writing, but it has made quite a splash with a beautifully pure Furmint expression of quince and apple blossom, overlaid with a touch of biscuit and the grape's typical vibrant acid lift. If Vino Gross's excellent still wines are any guide, Michael and Maria's sparkling Furmint is one to watch.

Klet Penin Istenič

Bizeljsko, Slovenia

www.istenic.com

In the 1960s, long before fizz was a twinkle in the Slovenian eye, Miha Istenič's father Janez juggled a dual career as both goalkeeper for the national team and winemaker at one of Yugoslavia's state cellars. The die was cast when he won a scholarship to study in Champagne. On his return, he realized that his father-in-law's vineyard, which produced wines with 'distinct freshness' had similarities to the high-acid grapes of Champagne. He used the football savings he'd squirreled away to buy land and equipment, becoming the first private producer of bottle-fermented sparkling wine in Slovenia. The year 1968 saw the birth of his first wine and his daughter, both christened Barbara.

The winery has 5 hectares in production, buying from certified sustainable vineyards only in some vintages. Their best plot at Drenovec is on well-drained soils over fractured Triassic and Miocene dolomite and limestone, at around 170 to 350 metres altitude. On the Croatian border, the climate is continental with strong diurnal temperature variation. Climate change is managed by early picking and the use of a native grape called Rumeni Plavec, which has notable acidity and gives a note of real local distinction. With pneumatic pressed free-run juice only, largely non-oxidative winemaking aims for freshness with long-lasting bubbles. Base wines are aged on lees for 7–9 months before bottling, with 20 per cent aged in used oak. Malolactic fermentation is avoided except for the no-added sulphite wine.

Istenič makes 10 styles with ageing for 18, 36 and 60 months. Overall the wines always show an undertone of bright crisp acidity: Barbara sec is the commercial entry-level wine, gently off-dry with crisp green apple and touch of biscuit. A blend of 60 per cent Chardonnay, 30 per cent Rumeni Plavec and 10 per cent Pinot Noir, the flagship No. 1 Brut (a reference to Janez's football shirt number) adds more complexity from three years on lees, with lemon zest, toasty notes and poached pear. Gourmet Rosé is pure free-run Pinot Noir giving elegant, bright red fruit. Prestige Extra Brut is only made in the best years from the best fruit and long ageing on lees adds yet more depth and complexity, plus great keeping potential.

Misal

Visnjan, Croatia

www.misal.hr

In the late 1980s Đordan Peršurić embarked on his first sparkling wine as part of a research project, which eventually led to the production of the first hundred bottles in the early 1990s. The Peršurić family has five centuries of tradition as wine growers and winemakers. Returning to his family home in the small village of Pršurići, near Poreč, alongside his father, Đordan Peršurić started producing sparkling wines from the local varieties Malvazija Istarska and Teran in the early 1990s, creating the Misal brand.

Until 2000, production remained a family hobby, but the new millennium brought about a new perspective, which saw an expansion of the production and manufacturing facilities. After graduating from college, his daughters Katarina and Ana joined the family enterprise, first of all managing the winemaking and marketing and taking over the winery after their father died in 2015. The family's 5 hectares are on deep red soils just 500 metres from the winery, which was built in 1999, and 15 kilometres east of the Adriatic as the crow flies. The Misal Blanc de Noirs Brut Prirodno Pjenušave Vino is an expressive fizz with light biscuity notes and a fine-textured mousse full of opulent, stonefruit flavours. With a range of 11 sparkling wines, annual production has gradually increased to around 40,000 bottles.

SWITZERLAND

In the canton of Neuchâtel, not far from the border with France, where Jurassic limestone dominates, the first Swiss sparkling wines were made in 1811. Two traditional houses still exist here today. Mauler & Cie operates from a former Benedictine abbey (an offshoot of the famous Cluny Abbey) in the remote Val de Travers and lets its top cuvées mature on the lees for up to five years. Bouvier Frères in Boudry can boast that its founder comes from the same family as Jacqueline Lee Bouvier Kennedy Onassis. Both houses are known for classic, fresh sparklers with a comparatively low dosage. The recent boom in the innovative Swiss fizz scene is largely down to Champagne-loving Swiss winemakers giving their fizz longer lees-ageing and lower dosage. Mainly made from Pinot Noir and Chardonnay, wines containing established Swiss varieties such as R Noiseling (Zurich region) or Petite Arvine (Valais) are becoming increasingly noteworthy. Top producers include Henri Cruchon (Echichens, Waadt), Clos de Tsampéhro (Flanthey, Wallis), Mauler & Cie (Môtiers, Neuenburg), Domaine La Colombe (Féchy, Waadt), Weingut Familie Hansruedi Adank (Fläsch, Graubünden) and Weingut Besson-Strasser (Uhwiesen, Zürich).

11

SOUTH AFRICA – CAP CLASSIQUE

South Africa has an enviable record of historical data going all the way back to Jan van Riebeek, who was on hand to record the first Cape wine harvest on 2 February 1659. Less enviable was the Grand Mousseux Vin Doux, a sweet carbonated job created at the Stellenbosch Farmers Winery in 1929 and a market leader until a handful of pioneers tried their hand at something more serious. In the absence of Pinot Noir or Chardonnay, Simonsig's Frans Malan created his and the country's maiden bottle-fermented sparkling wine in 1971 from Chenin Blanc. Accounting for nearly a third of South Africa's vineyards, Chenin Blanc was well-suited to the method, with fresh acidity when harvested early, producing a low alcohol base wine. Clairette Blanche was used occasionally for its low alcohol base wines too.

In 1980, Achim von Arnim, the cellarmaster at Boschendal Estate, created its first experimental Cap Classique, an unconventional cuvée from Cape Riesling and a blend of red varieties, giving it at least three years on the lees. Boschendal Brut 1986 was the first fizz made exclusively from Chardonnay and Pinot Noir and Von Arnim established his own specialist sparkling wine cellar, Cabrière, whose first vintage, named Pierre Jourdan, was 1984. At the time, vines illegally imported as Chardonnay turned out to be Auxerrois, but Cabrière had some genuine Chardonnay. In 1984 the Grier family saw the maiden vintage of their Chenin Blanc and Pinotage blend, resulting from their association with French bubble master, Jean-Louis Denois.

Thanks to growing consumer enthusiasm and increased plantings of Chardonnay and Pinot Noir, momentum for bottle-fermented bubbly made from the classic Champagne varieties grew. Initially, the wines were referred to as *méthode champenoise*, but once the champenois outlawed the term for use elsewhere, a new name had to be found. In 1988, Johan Malan organized the seminal group tasting that led to the formation, in 1992, of the Cap Classique Producers Association (CPPA). The CCPA adopted the name Methode Cap Classique to replace *méthode champenoise*. Malan was the first chairman of the initial 14-member body which, by 2021 had grown to 93 members. CONSOL glass produced a bottle suitable for Cap Classique, one that's still used today.

Producers of Cap Classique are scattered across the Cape winelands, where the three main soil types are Table Mountain sandstone, decomposed granite, slate and shale, as well as some alluvial soils in valley floors. Around 160 kilometres north-east of Cape Town, Robertson is an important source of fruit for makers of bubbly. This might seem surprising, given its inland location with very hot summer days. Soils are one key: the ancient shale and limestone produces wines with high acid and low pH, ideal for Cap Classique. Diurnal temperatures are another. While a daytime 30°C isn't unusual in January, it can fall to 15°C in the evening thanks to the cooling breeze which blows up from the mouth of the River Breede at the Indian Ocean, some 70 kilometres away.

While there are no restrictions where Cap Classique may be produced nor stipulations regarding varieties, the CCPA recommends Chardonnay, Pinot Noir and Meunier. Chenin Blanc and Pinotage are also often used. More eclectic choices are Sauvignon Blanc, Cabernet Franc and Shiraz. Red Cap Classique from Shiraz, made in the same way as Australian sparkling Shiraz, has been tried, while the latest variety to be put to the test is Colombard from heritage vines. In the cellar, whole bunch pressing is recommended. Rules do state the minimum time on the lees prior to disgorgement. From the 2021 vintage, the minimum was raised to 12 from 9 months and a minimum of 3 bars of pressure is required. Stricter new laws under discussion include prescribed varieties, whole bunch audit, separate fractions, a minimum 36 months on the lees, declaration of date of bottling and disgorgement and a ten-point quality charter.

In the light of increasing temperatures, both maximum and minimum, and the growing frequency of hot days, producers are paying attention to row direction to create shade in the fruit zone and night harvesting, when it's much cooler, the grapes fresher, the pickers happier. Cellar techniques include eschewing malolactic fermentation to retain what high, natural malic acidity there is, and longer lees ageing to allow for less dosage. In the broader picture, new vineyard sites and new varieties are being examined to counteract the potentially damaging effects of climate change. Cooler areas being explored include Elgin, Darling, Hemel-en-Aarde, parts of Stellenbosch and, further afield, Plettenberg Bay along the Cape South Coast. Altitude and hillside slopes as well as access to secure, established water sources are important features. Counterintuitively, it remains of the utmost importance for Cap Classique producers that the wines capture the taste of sunshine.

Consumers have close to 380 Cap Classique labels to choose from and it remains the fastest growing category, doubling every 4.5 years. Production for 2019–20 stood at 10.2 million bottles and sales mirror production. By far the majority of these, 7.5 million bottles, are made by the big seven (Graham Beck, Boschendal, KWV, Pongrácz, Simonsig, House of Krone and Villiera) with around 200 others accounting for the balance. Other specialist Cap Classique producers it was not possible to profile below include: Ambeloui, Bon Courage, Charles Fox Cap Classique Wines, Dainty Bess, Domaine des Dieux, Genevieve Methode Cap Classique, Haute Cabrière, Huis van Chevallierie, Le Lude, Matthew Krone Wines, Newstead Lund, Paul René, Saltare, Steenberg, Tanzanite and The House of GM&Ahrens.

Producers

Graham Beck (Wine Estate)

Robertson

www.grahambeck.com

From a successful home renovation business, Cape-Town born Graham Beck ventured into the coal mining business in Kwazulu-Natal. His love of horses and racing saw him establish successful stud operations throughout the world, a passion pursued by his son Antony, who's overseen the business since his father's death in 2010. Beck's entrepreneurial spirit next led him to purchase the farm called Madeba, near the town of Robertson, in 1983. A terrible flood two years earlier had devastated the farm, but Graham spent the next two years establishing the vineyards in the limestone soils of Robertson. He was joined in 1990 by the highly experienced Pieter Ferreira, and together they designed a dedicated Cap Classique cellar to fit in with its surroundings. It was built and ready to receive the maiden vintage in 1991. As Graham Beck became associated with, in his words, 'bubblies', they stopped making still wine after 2014.

The greatest challenge was gaining recognition for fizz in Robertson. Robertson soils have the highest incidence of rich limestone deposits along with the classic Red Karoo profile with the same limestone. These soils, Robertson's climatic conditions and precision viticulture are particularly favourable for the production of quality Cap Classique. Irrigation is required in all the vineyards due to low annual rainfall (the yearly average is 180 millimetres). Fruit is drawn from the Robertson farm's 140 hectares of vineyards, planted to a broad selection of Chardonnay and Pinot Noir clones. Another quarter is drawn from seven other areas where they manage the vineyards. Robertson's sunshine, high incidence of limestone and a marked diurnal temperature range, have seen its potential realized.

'Attention to detail is key', says Pieter Ferreira. Manual selection and picking starts at dawn with night-harvesting starting from 2021. Whole bunches are pressed, with the cuvée normally only used for the vintage and prestige cuvées. Fermentation is in stainless steel with a large part of Chardonnay barrel-fermented in 205-litre Champagne barrels. Malolactic fermentation is not encouraged. A perpetual reserve for the non-vintage range promotes consistency and continuity of the house style with 6 to 12 per cent reserve wine added. Non-vintage wines spend an average of 18 months on the lees, with four years for vintage and five or more years for prestige cuvée. Current production is 1.8 million bottles, split 85 per cent non-vintage to 15 per cent vintage and prestige cuvée. The vintage range carries the year of harvesting, a lot number of tirage bottling and the date of disgorgement appears on the back label.

Texturally rich with a creamy mousse, the Graham Beck Brut NV is a bright fizz with zesty, limey notes, underlaid by quiet leesy tones and tangy acidity. Mainly Pinot Noir, the pale pink vintage Graham Beck Pinot Noir Rosé is fragrant with red fruit and spiced with biscuity complexity. Drawn from the best Chardonnay, with 48 months ageing, the vintage Graham Beck Blanc de Blancs displays nutty tones and a creamy texture underpinned by subtle citrus, finishing dry. The vintage Graham Beck Ultra Brut spends 60 months on the lees, resulting in a fizz of lemony, oyster shell character and clean-cut, savoury bone-dry finish. Also aged for 60 months, the pure Chardonnay, vintage Graham Beck Cuvée Clive is a sleek, ageworthy prestige cuvée sharing refined citrus and toasty notes. The multi-regional Graham Beck Rosé NV is creamy, rounded and dry while two medium sweet yet fresh sparklers, Graham Beck Bliss Nectar NV and Graham Beck Bliss Nectar Rosé NV, complete the range.

Colmant Cap Classique and Champagne

Franschhoek

www.colmant.co.za

Born in 1965 in the French-speaking part of Belgium, Jean-Philippe (JP) grew up in a culture of wine and Champagne. Feeling the need for a new challenge after running his own stone manufacturing company for 11 years, Jean-Philippe purchased a 5-hectare smallholding in Franschhoek, emigrating with his family in 2002, and establishing Chardonnay and Pinot Noir vineyards in 2005. Colmant became one of South Africa's earliest wineries dedicated to the exclusive production of Cap Classique, with the first vintage produced the following year. A self-taught winemaker, Jean-Philippe visited Champagne, met Cap Classique makers and in 2019 was joined by the experienced bubbly winemaker, Paul Gerber.

Over half the Chardonnay is grown on the 3-hectare home farm vineyards, whose sandy- to clay-dominant soils bring vivacity and freshness. The balance of Chardonnay comes from Robertson on a mix of sandy alluvial clay and small areas of chalk, with a special shale site in Bonnievale. Pinot Noir is drawn from five farms located in Franschhoek, Robertson and cool climate Elgin. Co-managed vineyards cover 7–9 hectares with a total harvest of 83–85 tonnes. Whole bunches go through pneumatic press for the first, second and third juice fractions. Primary fermentation is mainly in stainless steel with no malolactic fermentation, while some 10 per cent of Chardonnay is barrel-fermented in second- to fifth-fill oak. Depending on style, the wines remain on lees for between 12 and 45 months and, after disgorgement, the wines are kept for three to six months before release. It is planned to add date of tirage and disgorgement on the back label. Total production across all six wines is 60,000 bottles.

The entry level Brut Plaisir NV based on Pinot Noir and Chardonnay is a light, vivacious blend with delicate pear flavours and crisp, just dry finish, while the Brut Rosé NV, with 24 months on the lees, is a fizz of red-fruit fragrance, creamy mousse and gentle freshness. The refined citrus, nutty flavours and stone-fruit characters in Colmant's Sec

Reserve NV are lifted by 20 per cent reserve wine and two years on lees. Colmant's partially barrel-fermented Brut Reserve NV, its signature blend, reflects the house style of elegance, harmony and freshness. The pure Chardonnay Blanc de Blancs NV, with 45 months on lees, displays complex, nutty tones and an elegantly textured creaminess, and the new Absolu Zero Dosage NV, after seven years on lees, is a complex, rich pure Chardonnay combining lees-derived biscuity tones with a refreshing salinity.

Pieter Ferreira Cap Classique

Franschhoek

www.pieterferreiramcc.co.za

Pieter 'Mr Bubbles' Ferreira has been instrumental in driving improvement for, and enthusiasm in, Cap Classique since he was first involved with making the style in 1984. For the past 30 years, he has been cellarmaster at Graham Beck Wine Estate and was due to retire in 2020 at 60, but when retirement age at Graham Beck was extended to 65, his wife, Ann, stepped in to take temporary charge of Pieter's long-anticipated retirement project. The fruit for Ferreira is sourced from growers in Darling, Elgin, Durbanville, Slanghoek Valley, Napier and Robertson, whose diverse soils of limestone, decomposing granite and Table Mountain sandstone contribute different flavours, textures and aromatics.

The parcels of Chardonnay and Pinot Noir are taken to Graham Beck in Robertson, where the Pinot Noir bunches are given a brief period of colour extraction before pressing. The whole bunches are pressed by pneumatic PERA press with only the cuvée used. Chardonnay is fermented in three neutral Champagne barrels, the balance in stainless steel. The individual components are left on the lees for three months after fermentation, followed by bottle-fermentation in the cellar for six years, before being riddled and disgorged with a low dosage.

Production is just 2,500 bottles in each of three styles. The maiden vintage in 2012, a seamlessly elegant, complex and classically dry Blanc de Blancs from Chardonnay, was Cap Classique of the Year in the *Platter's Wine Guide* after its launch in 2019. Released in early 2020, the delicately pink and floral Rosé made from Pinot Noir, displays a fine red fruit fragrance and gentle, creamy mousse. These two varietal Cap Classiques represent the best selections of each variety in the vintage with brightness, tension and complexity the defining features. The Brut, with four years on lees and Chardonnay from Robertson and Darling, Pinot Noir from Elgin, shows delicate, pure fruit with invigorating acidity. Dates of tirage and disgorgement are printed on the back label.

Pongrácz

Stellenbosch

www.pongracz.co.za

Desiderius Pongrácz, a Hungarian count, pursued a career in viticulture in his home country. After joining the cavalry, he was captured by the Russians on Hungary's surrender at the end of the Second World War, spending a decade in a labour camp in Siberia before returning to Hungary. Escaping from the chaos of the 1956 uprising, he secured positions as a farm manager first in Namibia, then in the Stellenbosch winelands, and was appointed Chief Viticultural Adviser at Distillers Corporation in 1973 (Distell today). Pongrácz had a major influence on the introduction and propagation of premium grape varieties but, alas, died in a tragic accident at the age of 61 while transporting Chardonnay to Uitkyk Estate. Launched in 1990, the Cap Classique that honours his name became the biggest selling Cape bottle-fermented sparkling wine, helping this fledgling category to become better known by South African wine lovers.

Drawing fruit from a range of climatic zones and diverse soils, winemaker Transkei-born Andiswa Maphelela has many building blocks of Chardonnay and Pinot Noir from which to create her blends. She works closely with viticulturist Isabel Teubes, sourcing some 1,500 tonnes from premium vineyards in the cooler parts of Stellenbosch, Elgin and Darling. The grapes are hand-harvested in the early morning and whole bunch-pressed with only the cuvée used for the base wine blend. Fermentation proceeds in stainless steel. Vintage wines are blends of the best vineyards and microclimates. Time on the lees – the Pongrácz range has its own individual bottle mould – varies from 15 to 60 months for the flagship Desiderius Pongrácz.

Pongrácz Brut, a 60 per cent Pinot Noir and 40 per cent Chardonnay blend, is a balanced fizz with a rich, creamy texture and a rounded finish. From Robertson and Elgin, the Chardonnay for the Pongrácz Blanc de Blancs shows characterful yet unshowy nutty, creamy aromas, finishing balanced and dry. For the 60 per cent Pinot Noir, 40 per cent Chardonnay blend, the Pongrácz Rosé's *saignée* method provides a pearly-pink strawberries and cream fizz. The sweet of tooth may enjoy the honeyed though uncloying Pongrácz Noble Nectar, while five years on the lees for the top of the range Desiderius Pongrácz imbues this elegant 70 per cent Chardonnay, 30 per cent Pinot Noir blend with complex, evolved spiced citrus and nut characters, a creamy texture and a resolutely dry finish.

Silverthorn Wines

Robertson

www.silverthornwines.co.za

The Loubsers' decision to specialize in Cap Classique stems from John's student days, when, through a selection of styles students had to learn about, and nurture, John drew Cap Classique from names placed in a hat. Following a visit to Champagne in 1995, Cap Classique was a natural choice when the Loubsers decided to make their own wine after Karen and John took over the family farm close to the Breede River in 1999. The first vintage, 2004, was a *blanc de blancs*, The Green Man, followed by a rosé, The Genie, and two years later, the prestige cuvée, Jewel Box. Apart from an annual bottling for the Cape Winemakers Guild named Big Dog, the range only grew in 2020 with the release of an unusual acacia-fermented Cap Classique, River Dragon, made from 36-year-old Colombard vines.

Silverthorn owns 3.24 hectares of vineyards bearing Chardonnay, Colombard and Shiraz. Old vine Pinot Noir is bought from a grower, and Chardonnay and Shiraz are also purchased when home-grown fruit is insufficient. Robertson's ancient shale and limestone ensure perfect freshness for Cap Classique, helped by low rainfall and irrigation via the Zandrift irrigation system. Along with cooling afternoons and nights thanks to the influence of the Indian Ocean, the deep, well-established roots of the vines, which are between 22 and 39 years old, help provide a buffer against dry conditions.

Harvest is in January, before the hottest month of the year. Grapes are whole bunch pressed in a pneumatic press and juice extraction low at 530 litres per tonne. After fermentation, the wine is treated reductively. Chardonnay and Colombard are barrel-fermented in 500-litre French oak and acacia oak respectively. The barrel-fermented Chardonnay is used in both The Green Man (10 per cent) and Jewel Box (70 per cent) while Colombard for River Dragon is 100 per cent barrel-fermented. The Jewel Box portion is kept in a perpetual reserve dating back five years. Annual production is 30,000 to 40,000 bottles.

In youth, the wines are tight, slowly revealing more complex characters over time. The Green Man Blanc de Blancs, named after an ancient mythical figure, with up to 33 months on the lees, mingles nutty, leesy aromatic characters, enhanced by a dainty, persistent mousse. Shiraz works well in the Genie Rosé with aromas and flavours of Turkish delight and spice. Jewel Box is a 70 per cent Chardonnay, 30 per cent Pinot Noir prestige cuvée, combining opulence and complexity after at least 42 months ageing, for toasty notes with tangy red fruit enriching the creamy mousse. River Dragon is distinctively different, a refreshing aperitif-style fizz with the fragrance of wild herbs and spice.

Simonsig Estate

Koelenhof, Stellenbosch

www.simonsig.co.za

Simonsig Estate and the Malan family were the pioneers of Cap Classique in 1971, the same year in which Frans Malan co-founded the Stellenbosch Wine Route with Spatz Sperling of Delheim and Neil Joubert of Spier. Exploding bottles and loss of wine as well as the lack of racks for riddling were among the many teething problems Malan had to overcome. After a local carpenter created 'a spider with four legs' for the riddling, second-hand pupitres were subsequently imported. Production was only every other year until 1978, when Kaapse Vonkel, Afrikaans for Cape Sparkle, began to be produced annually. In 1981, Johan Malan joined his father in the cellar. By 1987, the Kaapse Vonkel blend became Pinot Noir and Chardonnay and, ten years later, the introduction of Meunier made it the first Cap Classique to include all three main Champagne varieties.

Simonsig's 200 hectares under vine include 38 hectares of Chardonnay, 21 hectares of Pinot Noir and 2 hectares of Meunier. Chardonnay and Pinot Noir are also bought in from long-term growers. Simonsig's home vineyard soils are mainly weathered shale, containing high levels of clay, which acts like a sponge to soak up the winter rain, which is released slowly during the long, dry summers. Heavier, dark red soils for Pinot Noir provide fruitier, fuller-bodied cuvées, working well in the rosé, while cooler areas such as Elgin and Darling add different flavour profiles. Early harvesting is needed for Meunier to retain acidity and in 2020, a small-volume cuvée was made from the locally rare Pinot Blanc.

Vinification proceeds via whole bunch pressing in Bucher pneumatic presses, with the cuvée and *taille*, totalling 620 litres per tonne, extracted. Only the first 350 litres are pressed off for the prestige Cuvée Royale. The first fermentation is in stainless steel, while Chardonnay, barrel-fermented since 1996, remains in older barriques for four to five months with some bâtonnage. Malolactic fermentation is avoided. All Simonsig's Cap Classiques are vintage wines with the date of disgorgement printed on the cork. Malan is not trying to copy Champagne, but rather, to reflect the Cape terroir: a combination of sunshine, a unique maritime climate and among the oldest wine growing soils in the world.

Cuvée Royale, made from Stellenbosch Chardonnay, is tight, bone-dry and bright, with gentle biscuity complexity. Richer in style, oak adds an extra dimension to Kaapse Vonkel, which develops a warm bread note with age, while brisk acidity ensures freshness. Kaapse Vonkel Brut Rosé is a pale salmon pink Pinot Noir and pinotage blend with generous summer red berry flavours infused with a mouthwateringly dry, creamy mousse. Made only in the best vintages, Cuvée Royale Blanc de Blancs spends five years on the lees. Two demi-sec Kaapse Vonkels, Kaapse Vonkel Satin Nectar and Kaapse Vonkel Satin Nectar Rosé, complete the set.

Villiera Wines

Keukenhof

www.villiera.com

Having made still wines since purchasing this Stellenbosch farm from the wine producer, Helmut Ratz, in 1983, the Grier family wanted to add an extra dimension in order to stand out from the crowd. A meeting between Villiera's winemaker, Jeff Grier, and Jean-Louis Denois, resulted in an agreement for Villiera to produce Tradition de Charles de Fère, the Cape version of Jean-Louis' Charles de Fère Limoux brand. With access to French savoir-faire in return for a royalty, Villiera set up with a press from Jean-Louis' home town, Cumières in Champagne, for bottle-fermented fizz in time for the first vintage in 1984. The first to produce a sparkling wine in every category, rosé, *blanc de blancs*, brut natural, light and prestige cuvée, Villiera's reputation has grown over the years.

A family business, Villiera's vineyards cover 180 hectares with soils that are duplex in structure, predominantly sandy with underlying clay and gravel, with some supplementary irrigation required due to the dry summers. Around 500 tonnes of fruit is also drawn from neighbours. After hand-harvesting before full ripeness, the grapes are whole bunch pressed and the cuvée and *taille* separated. Thirty per cent of the Prestige Cuvée is fermented in used oak. Non-vintage wines spend on average 18 months on the lees. A 70 per cent Chardonnay, 30 per cent Pinot Noir blend, the Tradition Brut NV, an accessible wine with ripe aromas and generous creamy, brioche interest, was the first Cap Classique produced by Villiera in 1984.

Uniquely South African, the Villiera Tradition Rosé Brut NV blends 35 per cent Pinot Noir, 30 per cent Chardonnay, 30 per cent Pinotage and 5 per cent Meunier for rich red fruit flavours with a biscuity, umami note. A refreshingly featherlight Starlight Brut NV, at 9.5 per cent, shows racy sparkle and delicate citrusy leesy notes. The pure Chardonnay *blanc de blancs*, Villiera Brut Natural Vintage, aged for three years, with no dosage, is pure and bone-dry, its leesy aromas and breadth of flavour complemented by a toasty richness. Villiera's Monro Brut, an impressive Stellenbosch prestige cuvée of 58 per cent Chardonnay, 30 per cent Pinot Noir and 12 per cent Meunier, aged for five years, is rich, leesy and complex in a mature Champagne-like mould. A new super-premium fizz in the pipeline, made from *tête de cuvée* only, is fermented in a large Pithos amphora and will remain on the lees for seven years. Annual production totals around 600,000 bottles across the range.

12

SPAIN AND PORTUGAL

SPAIN

Cava (the word means 'cellar') is the traditional method Spanish sparkling wine mainly produced in Catalonia's Penedès region. The traditional Cava grape triumvirate consists of Macabeo, Xarel·lo and Parellada. Xarel·lo has character and flavour and the greatest potential for quality and Macabeo good acidity, while Parellada, although inclined to be neutral, can bring aroma to a wine, and much can be done with altitude, older vines, massal selection and low yields. The grapes are generally harvested ripe, resulting in a soft-textured fizz with unique Mediterranean aromas and flavours.

Most wineries are located in Sant Sadurní d'Anoia, the so-called Capital of Cava. To confuse the issue, small quantities of Cava have also been produced in other Catalan regions, such as Conca de Barberà and Costers del Segre, as well as the Spanish regions of Aragón, Euskadi (Basque Country), Extremadura, La Rioja, Navarra, and Valencia. In the face of criticism of this dispersal of the Cava DO, which of course makes it harder for producers to claim any terroir identity for it, new rules require from 2022 that Cava made outside Catalonia is limited to the Valle del Ebro, essentially Rioja's Alto Ebro and Valle del Cierzo, from Levante west of Valencia and, in Spain's far west Badajoz province, from Viñedos de Almendralejo.

The claim for the first Spanish sparkling wine belongs to Antoni Galo Comas who entered his fizz in a Madrid competition in the mid-eighteenth century. The first to produce a bottle-fermented sparkling wine from local Penedès varieties was Josep Raventós, who was from a family already steeped in wine for 300 years. The introduction of temperature controlled stainless steel in the 1960s endowed Cava with the necessary freshness and fruitiness to appeal to modern palates outside the traditional market of Spain. The Cava DO dates from 1986, about the same time that it started to be produced on an industrial scale as an easy-drinking, inoffensive fizz with low prices to match.

In 1984, Codorníu took the controversial step of incorporating Chardonnay and Pinot Noir from its Raimat estate, much to the ire of traditionalists. If the Champagne varieties have diluted the traditional Spanish character of Cava, as some have suggested, that's to underestimate the transformative power of terroir. Chardonnay and Pinot Noir have brought a new dimension of quality and style to the party. Nonetheless, the pendulum has swung back again, with some of the best, traditionally minded Spanish fizz producers keen to show that world-class sparkling wines can indeed be made from native varieties.

In 2020, there were 370 wineries and 6,800 vineyard growers covering 38,000 hectares of vineyards. In terms of plantings 81.5 per cent are the three native varieties, Macabeo (13,800 hectares), Xarel·lo (9,600 hectares) and Parelleda (7,500 hectares). The remaining 18.5 per cent are Chardonnay (3,000 hectares), Garnacha (1,670 hectares), Trepat (1,170 hectares), Pinot Noir (870 hectares), Subirat Parent (225 hectares) and Monastrell (50 hectares). In 2018, of the 245 million bottles of Cava produced (of which 165 million were exported), just under five million were Cava de Paraje and Gran Reserva. These figures do not include production by the two new premium groups, Clàssic Penedès and Corpinnat, that have decoupled from Cava in the wake of what they see as Cava's distant relationship with quality and its image problem.

In 2012 Raventós i Blanc shocked Penedès when it announced its decision to leave the Cava DO for the small geographical area of Conca Del Riu Anoia. Pepe Raventós claimed that Cava had shot itself in the foot by paying bottom dollar for grapes and selling at low prices and he was determined to show how good Cava could be if there was a commitment to viticultural traditions and the uniqueness of location. By 2014, other Cava wine producers had left the DO and formed the Clàssic Penedès group. Clàssic Penedès requires 100 per cent organic production and is limited to the Penedès DO. It tightened the regulations to a minimum of 15 months for ageing on the lees and required the date of disgorgement to be stated on the label. The group comprises 18 members with Albet i Noya, Colet and Loxarel among the most prominent.

Cava de Paraje Calificado

Stung by the departure of Raventós i Blanc and the new Clàssic Penedès group, the Cava Regulatory Board launched a counter-offensive, Cava de Paraje Calificado, in June 2016. Paraje doesn't quite equate to France's terroir but it's related in the sense that it's about uniqueness of location, whether a single vineyard or other distinctive part of the Penedès. Cava de Paraje Calificado wines come from a diverse range of soils: saulò (sandy granite), llicorella (slate), calcareous, clay or loam, in Penedès' varied topography of Mediterranean-influenced, mountainous landscapes. It's restricted to vintage wines only in brut styles or drier, with maximum yields limited to 48 hectolitres per hectare and it must spend at least 36 months ageing in bottle. There is an approval process for the location, a tasting requirement for both base and finished wines and a somewhat meaningless vine-age requirement of 10 years. The term can only be claimed by companies vinifying 85 per cent or more of their base wines. Any Paraje vineyard must be wholly owned by the company and have been separately fermented for at least three harvests. The wine cannot be acidified and must have a natural finished acidity level of 5.5 grams per litre of tartaric acidity (the minimum for Cava is 5 grams per litre). The first set of Cave de Paraje sites was declared in 2017.

Initially, top Cava producers such as Recaredo and Gramona welcomed the new scheme, although only 33 producers qualified thanks to Cava de Paraje's 85 per cent rule (see box on Cava de Paraje, above). Codorníu also backed it, having launched its Ars Collecta single vineyard series of Finca La Pleta (Chardonnay), 2007 Finca El Tros Nous (Pinot Noir) and Finca La Fideuera (Xarel·lo). Pepe Raventós called it sticking plaster. By 2018, a disillusioned breakaway group of premium Cava producers formed Corpinnat (heart of the Penedès in local dialect). The first members, Gramona, Llopart, Nadal, Recaredo, Sabaté i Coca and Torelló, have since been joined by Huget-Can Feixes, Julia Bernet and Mas Candí. The new group established a set of quality guidelines including requirements for hand-harvested organic grapes (with up to 10 per cent international grapes permitted), paying top dollar for grapes (70 cents a kilo by 2021), only purchasing a maximum of 25 per cent of grapes, and longer ageing times.

Playing catchup, the Cava DO announced after two years of deliberation a new zoning and sub-zoning classification system in July 2020 aimed at improving quality. Cavas with over nine months ageing are called Cava de Guarda. Cava de Guarda Superior is the term for those with over 18 months ageing (previously 15 months), encompassing Reserva, Gran Reserva (30 months) and Paraje Calificado (36 months). There are also three new tiers to the Cava DO. The first tier is defined by large climatic and geographical features, leading to the delimitation of four separate zones. The second zoning level is for sub-zones defined by specific climatic and other characteristics. The third level is the Paraje Calificado itself. Too little too late? Doubtless this long overdue reform is a step in the right direction but whether it will reunite the disparate forces of Spanish sparkling wine remains to be seen.

Producers

Can Sala

Sant Quinti de Mediona

www.vinsfamiliaferrer.com

The Ferrer family can trace its winegrowing history back to 1616, when the first Ferrers arrived in La Freixenada. The name gave birth to the Freixenet brand, founded in 1914. Wholly owned by Vins Familia Ferrer, who own 43 per cent of Freixenet, Can Sala is produced in a cellar built in 1895. Run by Jose Ferrer alongside Freixenet's technical director, Josep Bujan, the project, only producing Cava de Paraje with long ageing, began with the 2004 vintage. The 250-hectare estate, Jose's mother's home, is in Mediona, the highest part of the Penedès Region, at 400 metres, with some vineyards as high as 700 metres. The cool climate allows for a longer growing season with freshness bringing vitality to the sparkling wines.

In the winery, Can Sala uses a traditional vertical wooden press dating from 1895. Only 50 per cent of the cuvée, the first pressing, is used. All operations are carried out by gravity without the use of pumps or filters. The second fermentation is carried out under natural cork and the riddling and disgorgement processes are by hand. The Vinyes de Can Sala Cava Brut Nature, a blend of 50 per cent Parellada and 50 per cent Xarelo·lo with a minimum of five years' ageing on the lees, is an alluring fizz with vanilla and paprika spice notes underpinned by a mouthwatering freshness. Annual production is 6,000 bottles. Also a blend of 50 per cent Parellada, 50 per cent Xarelo·lo, but with a minimum of ten years' ageing on the lees, Can Sala Cava Brut Nature smells sweetly of grilled nuts and ginger spice with a light sherried whiff and a lively mousse, with flavours of toasted almond and dried fruits. The 2008 vintage was the winner of the Global Sparkling Wine Masters Award 2020. Annual production is 12,000 bottles.

Codorníu

Sant Sadurní d'Anoia, Barcelona

www.codorniu.com

Codorníu traces its origins back to 1551 and a document mentioning Jaume Codorníu's vineyards and winemaking equipment in Sant Sadurní d'Anoia. The union of Anna, Codorníu's heiress, and Miquel Raventós in 1659, brought two wine dynasties together, but the 'modern era' began in 1872 with Josep Raventós, the first to produce a traditional method fizz from Xarel·lo, Macabeo and Parellada. Arthur O'Connor became the company's first Global Winemaker Director in 2006 and Bruno Colomer joined Codorníu as head winemaker in 2008. The own-label side of the business was dropped and the premium element reinforced with the introduction of the single vineyard Gran Reserva and more recently the Cava de Paraje and Ars Collecta ranges. Reflecting a move up in quality, annual production has been downsized from 40 million to 26 million bottles.

Codorníu's Cavas are made from its 2,500 hectares of vineyards, which supply half of its needs. A technical pioneer in the introduction of new pressing processes, Codorníu also introduced the first Cava containing international varieties. With 70 per cent Chardonnay, Anna de Codorníu has really helped to up the ante for quality at the value level. In 2001, the first rosé Cava made with Pinot Noir appeared and the first *blanc de noirs* using Pinot Noir appeared in 2008. Codorníu uses high-tech satellites to map its vineyards, provides anti-frost protection with a sprinkler system and uses pheromones in the fight against insect damage. After picking, the grapes are gently pressed, with vineyards and varieties fermented separately for the base wine. Following the second fermentation, the wine is aged for between 9 and 12 months for the fresh and fruity Clásico style, up to 18 months for Reserva and at least 30 months for Gran Reserva.

Codorníu was among the first to produce Cava de Paraje after its introduction, with three single variety wines that spend up to 48 months or longer on the lees. The commendable Ars Collecta range comprises the emblematic Jaume Codorníu; three Gran Reservas (Blanc de Blancs, Blanc de Noirs and Rosé Brut); three estate cavas from certified locations – La Fideuera, El Tros Nou and La Pleta; and 457, a blend of all three certified terroirs, taking its name in 2008 from the number of Codorníu harvests since records began in 1551. The Ars Collecta Codorníu El Tros Nou Pinot Noir Paraje Qualificat is a complex, mature Cava showing toasty notes with an intensely flavoured mousse and elegant lemony acidity. None of the Ars Collecta range undergoes malolactic fermentation.

Colet

Pacs del Penedès, Barcelona

www.colet.cat

Colet is a family winemaker that has been working the same vineyards since 1783. After graduating in 1992, Sergi Colet worked his first vintage at Gramona, then, with his father, established a small winery making 12,000 bottles. He prefers to call himself vigneron rather than winemaker. 'I'm not a cook. I prefer to let the wines express the terroir, the grape variety, the weather.' Colet is a member of Clàssic Penedès, making sparkling wines only from its 24 hectares of north-east facing vineyards in Penedès. Rich in magnesium with chalky deposits and clay, the soils and big day to night temperature swings help impart the desired texture and freshness to their wines. As well as the classic Penedès varieties, they also use Moscatel, Chardonnay, Gewürztraminer, Riesling, Pinot Noir, Merlot and Moneu. They are 100 per cent organic and produce only reserva and vintage.

After machine harvesting at night and pressing by a Vaslin plate press for the first fraction of 55 per cent, 90 per cent of the first fermentation is carried out in stainless steel and 10 per cent in eggs (Nomblot). No malolactic fermentation is done: 'we have to protect all the acidity; we are in Spain,' says Sergi. Bottle ageing varies from 18–60 months and dosage ranges from 0 to 6 grams per litre. Colet's Tradicional extra brut, a blend of Xarel·lo, Macabeo and Parellada, with its veneer of light toast, has an energetic, lively mousse that's mouthwateringly savoury. Its Gran Cuvée Rosé, Clàssic Penedès Traditional Method, a blend of Merlot and Pinot Noir, is appealing too with a juicy cranberryish mousse and bell pepper sweetness etched with dry acidity. And the Colet Gran Cuvée Extra Brut, Traditional Method, two-thirds Chardonnay with one-third Macabeo and Xarel·lo, makes for a pleasing, pineappley aperitif style. Overall, the style is creamy, clean, fresh and elegant. The disgorgement date is printed on the label; annual production is 100,000 bottles.

Freixenet

Sant Sadurní d'Anoia

www.freixenet.com

Given that Freixenet took its name in 1914 for the youngest of the Ferrers, Pedro, nicknamed 'el Freixenet', the diminutive one, it is somewhat ironic that Freixenet today is the world's largest traditional method sparkling wine company. By joining forces with the multinational fizz giant Henkell in 2018, the Catalan leviathan managed to sell 99.3 million bottles in 2020, almost 10 per cent of the world's bubbles, with operations in France, California and Mexico. Freixenet is best known for its iconic (I use the word advisedly) Cordon Negro, a consistently fruity Cava presented in the evocative frosted black bottle. It followed Carta Nevada, its flagship brand in the distinctive white frosted bottle, which was developed in 1941 by Dolores Ferrer, who, after the loss of Pedro Ferrer and his elder son during the Spanish Civil War, ran the company in the grand tradition of bubbles widows with her elder daughter Pilar.

Grupo Freixenet owns a comparatively modest 123 hectares of vineyards next to the nearly 60 million kilos of grapes supplied by some 600–800 wine growers. In the 1970s, Freixenet introduced pneumatic presses for a more gentle pressing of the grapes. It was also the first to ferment in large, temperature-controlled stainless-steel tanks. Under the stewardship of long-term technical director, Manel Quintana, Freixenet's ground-breaking robotic technology allows it to use modified gyropalettes, taking a mere hour for the riddling process. It uses its own special recipe dosage liqueur kept in chestnut barrels and maintained over many years in a solera system. Freixenet continues to develop new wines in the premium sector as well as novelty products, aimed at a younger audience, such as Ice and Ice Rosé (2016), Prosecco (2017) and Italian Rosé (2018). After the launch of a Monastrell–Xarel·lo blend, and a pure Trepat *blanc de noirs* in 1996, its traditional Cava Cuvée D.S. (for Dolores Sala) was followed by two non-traditional prestige cuvées, a non-vintage Cava Elyssia Gran Cuvée and Cava Elyssia Pinot Noir.

Gramona

Sant Sadurní d'Anoia, Barcelona

www.gramona.com

The Gramona family has been working the land continuously since the mid-nineteenth century. They believe that on their land in the

Anoia and Bitlles river basins near Sant Sadurní d'Anoia, it is possible to produce world-class sparkling wines based largely on the native Xarel·lo. Indeed, Gramona think of Xarel·lo as their DNA. It's a belief reinforced by the results, which are among the very best in the region. Gramona today is run by the fifth generation Jaume Gramona, a restless Dijon-trained oenologist, and the analytical marketing man Xavier.

In 1850, Josep Batlle managed vineyards and made wine for a family. His son Pau, who sold wine to French sparkling wine producers, set up his own winery, Celler Batlle in 1861, and bought the Xarel·lo vineyards worked by his father. Gramona was established when his daughter, Pilar, married Bartolomé Gramona. Gramona's Champan de Cava was released in 1921. After the Second World War, a new era began under the stewardship of the two brothers, Bartomeu and Josep Lluis, who pioneered sparkling wine destined for long ageing with the first Gramona III Lustros, created in 1951 and released in 1961.

Gramona is located in the Alt Penedés region, 30 kilometres south of Barcelona, where the climate is typically Mediterranean, with hot, dry summers and mild winters. Their 119 hectares (70 hectares of vineyards and 49 hectares of forest and crops), located on hillsides in the higher part of San Sadurní d'Anoia, are protected during harsher winters by the rocky Montserrat mountain to the north. Characterized by the presence of calcareous *têtes de poupées*, the soils are clay- and calcareous-loam, with a few areas of alluvial soils found near the Anoia River and slate soils closer to Montserrat. The winery, built in 2001 on the 22.5 hectares Font de Jui site, uses geothermal energy, the first to do so in Spain.

In 2016, after hiring Claude Bourguignon as its consultant, Gramona converted to biodynamics and is certified with Demeter. Gramona created the Aliances per la Terra association in 2015. All members are 100 per cent biodynamic, making it the only Spanish association to belong to Biodyvin. Gramona has long-term contracts with its growers, and between them Gramona and its growers cover some 350 hectares of vineyards. The average yield in the past few years has been between 6,000 and 8,000 kilograms per hectare. The association sells Gramona between 700 and 1,200 tonnes per year depending on the vintage.

Age of vine, grape variety and the balance of acidity and maturity at harvest all provide a broad palette of flavours and tones for Jaume Gramona to work with. After the first fermentation, with natural yeasts, natural cork is used for all of its sparkling wines aged over five years as well as for the Argent range. The wines are hand-riddled and disgorged. The dosage for Imperial, aged for 60 or more months on the lees, is a fortified wine aged in a system of soleras and criaderas made up of old casks containing some century-old 'mother' sediments. III Lustros, Celler Batlle and Enoteca are aged for 7, 10 and at least 12 years while the Colección de Arte spends 15 years in the cellar.

Perhaps the two standout wines in an impressive range are the III Lustros Brut Nature and Celler Batlle, the former fine-textured with engaging firm, buttery characters and with toasty undertones, the latter intense with lemon thyme and verbena notes, followed by creamily rich yet savoury bubbles in a finely woven texture. While there's no doubting the quality of the enticingly fragrant and appetizingly dry Argent Rosé Brut Nature, the Pinot Noir Brut Rosé, La Cuvée Brut, Imperial Brut and Argent Brut Nature are not diminished by comparison. Having left the DO to join the Corpinnat group in 2019, Gramona's sparkling wines will no longer be called Cava, Cave de Paraje or Gran Reserva. Average annual production is 700,000 bottles of sparkling wine and 500,000 of still wine.

Juvé & Camps

Sant Sadurní d'Anoia, Barcelona

www.juveycamps.com

With a production of 2.7 million bottles of still and sparkling wine a year, it's hard not to be impressed by a commitment to quality that's seen the Juvé & Camps family enterprise survive and prosper since Joan Juvé Mir ventured into the wine business in 1796. Following his marriage to Teresa Camps Ferrer, his grandson, Joan Juvé Baqués, released the first sparkling wine under the Juvé brand in 1921. A pioneer of Gran Reserva, it produced the first such cuvée back in 1972. Today, some 40 per cent of all Juvé & Camps fizz is Gran Reserva cava and the founder's great grand-daughter, Meritxell Juvé Vaello, an oenology, viticulture and wine marketing graduate, runs the company with the same commitment to quality.

The Juvé & Camps family owns an estate of over 450 hectares in Penedès, 271 of which are planted to vines. Their vineyards are situated in three locations. With the Casa Vella, Can Torres and Can Rius properties, Espiells comprises 200 hectares at 180 to 245 metres above sea level with calcareous-clay soils and a sheltered Mediterranean microclimate.

At 220 metres, the deep calcareous soils of the 17-hectare La Cuscona are ideally suited to Macabeo, while in the highlands of Mediona, at 500 to 750 metres, the Can Massana, Alzinetes, El Prat, Mas Pagès and Can Soler vineyards provide good conditions for Parellada thanks to significant changes between day and night-time temperatures. Juvé & Camps' wines are all made from organic grapes, mostly from their own estate. They work with free-run juice only and grape varieties are vinified separately.

In the 1970s, friends were so impressed with the family fizz, a brut nature aged for three years, that they decided to expand production for sale, so much so that the Reserva de la Familia Cava Gran Reserva Brut Nature has become the winery's flagship cava. There is no sense of austerity from zero dosage in this fine wine, a blend of Macabeo, Xarel·lo and Parellada, aged for 36 months. Equally smart is another zero dosage blend, the La Capella Cava de Paraje Calificado Brut Nature which, made from pure Xarel·lo, shows fine toasty development and nutty complexity in a savoury whole. Along with the well-balanced and refreshingly dry Milesimé Cava Reserva Brut and the Essential Cava Reserva Brut, the Blanc de Noirs Cava Brut (from Pinot Noir) and Gran Reserva Cava Brut are also impressive.

Loxarel

Vilobí del Penedès, Barcelona

loxarel.com

In 1985, at the age of 16, Josep Mitjans broke with the family tradition of making only bulk wines and made his first 1,000 bottles of sparkling wine. After studying winemaking, he converted the business to the production of sparkling wine and in 1987 registered the Loxarel brand which was to focus on Xarel·lo. The estate uses only its own grapes, sourced from 20 hectares in Vilobí del Penedès, the location of the Mitjans cellar and home, plus 15 hectares more in Pla de Manlleu, the property of Mitjans' wife Teresa Nin, on slopes varying between 500 and 800 metres in altitude.

Vineyards are planted at a density of 3,000 vines per hectare. In keeping with its biodynamic status, Loxarel uses a flock of sheep to 'green prune' the leaves and applies cow horn manure, silica and nettle. Loxarel left the Cava DO to join the DO Penedès (later Clàssic Penedès). In 2011, Loxarel started a range of natural wines, made without added sulfites, based on minimal intervention in the winery. In the following year, it introduced amphorae with the aim of recreating a centuries-old tradition. The first wine to be fermented in 720-litre amphorae was the 2013 Xarel·lo.

The classic method Refugi (5,000 bottles) is an intense, seriously savoury brut nature reserva vinified part in stainless steel, part in new French oak hogsheads and aged for at least 32 months. Cent Nou 109 (1,000 bottles), a powerfully smoky and concentrated brut nature gran reserva, spends more than 109 months on the lees. The grapes for both are grown on stony clay–chalk, the Xarel·lo at 250 metres, and the Chardonnay at 700 metres. The exhilarating, vibrantly cranberryish pet nat 5,000-bottle A Pèl Ancestral (250 metres) is vinified in 1,000 litre amphorae, and the 3,000-bottle Barba-Roja (600 metres) in 720-litre amphorae. Both are aged for at least nine months.

Raventós i Blanc

Sant Sadurní d'Anoia, Barcelona

www.raventos.com

Tracing its family history back to five years after Christopher Columbus discovered America, the estate's first modern phase began with Josep Raventós Fatjó, who visited Champagne in 1872 to learn how to make Champagne method fizz. That same year he made 3,000 bottles of the first traditional method Xarel·lo fizz and, after selecting the best vines from native varieties, the first Xarel·lo, Macabeo and Parellada blend was pioneered in 1888 by his son, Manuel Raventós Domènech.

On leaving Codorníu with a golden handshake in the form of a sculpture in gold of a bottling machine, Josep Maria Raventós i Blanc's lofty ambition in founding Raventós i Blanc was to make the best possible fizz from his 50 hectares of vineyards. He was joined in 2001 by his grandson, Pepe, who decided to leave the DO Cava in 2012. The fact that he's referred to as a maverick should not be taken in any negative sense. On the contrary, leaving to plough a furrow of his own shows an independence of spirit that has imbued this Catalan winery with its commitment to making sparkling wines from a specific terroir using only local grape varieties. After five years in New York, he returned to the family domaine in 2016.

Located among olive, almond, fig trees, a lake and woods, the estate is an agricultural entity of 100 hectares with vineyards of water-retentive, marine fossil-rich, calcareous soils whose terraces date from the 16 million year-old Penedès depression. The influence of the

Mediterranean provides a microclimate of mild winters and hot, dry summers, while a cool Pyrenean climate helps bring about a long, slow ripening for optimum acidity. Plant cover and animals provide organic matter, plant-based treatments reduce the use of sulphur and copper sulphate and natural predators and pheromonal sexual confusion treatments help to limit grapevine moth damage. The winery was certified organic by CCPAE (Consell Català de la Producció Agrària Ecològica) in 2009 and biodynamic by Demeter in 2013. Depending on the vintage, Raventós i Blanc buys between 15 and 20 per cent of its grapes from growers, all of whom work organically. Each year, 500,000 bottles of fizz are made.

Overall, this is an impressive range, of a high standard, showing style and personality. The *blanc de blancs* shows a lightness of touch and mouthwatering savouriness and the pure Xarel·lo Manuel Raventós Negra has fine textural complexity and depth with toasty, persistent bubbles. Both the De La Finca, from Vinya dels Fòssils and Textures de Pedra Blanc de Negres are fine-textured drops of fizz, whose silky mousse is streaked with refreshing acidity, while De Nit Rosé, based on Monastrell, aka Mourvèdre, shows restrained berry fruit supported by toasty, melt-in-the-mouth bubbles.

Independently of Raventós i Blanc, Pepe Raventós set up Vins Pepe Raventós, a garage project based on his vision of a natural wine project in Penedès. Inspired by Pierre Overnoy and Frank Cornelissen, he started working three different plots that were fermented separately and naturally in the garage of the Mas del Serral: Del Mas Vineyard, Del Noguer Vineyard and Terrasses del Serral Vineyard. The vineyards comprising local old Xarel·lo and Bastard Negre were restored and wines are made in stainless steel and amphora with skin contact, wild yeasts and spontaneous fermentation, and without additives. Since 2015, a limited production of Bastard Negre from Terrasses del Serral vineyard and Xarel·lo from Ancestral Vinya del Mas and Vinya del Noguer has been made.

Recaredo Mata Casanovas

Sant Sadurní d'Anoia

www.recaredo.com

If the Recaredo name sounds like a rodeo in rural Mexico, it is in fact the nickname given to Recaredo Mata Figueres, the father of founder Josep Mata Capellades, who was born in Sant Sadurní d'Anoia in 1878 to a family of craft potters. His son, Josep Mata Capellades was a travel-ling disgorger who, in 1924, decided to cultivate his own vineyards and build a cellar under his house to start his own long-aged, brut nature sparkling wines using Penedès varieties fermented in oak barrels. His work was continued by his sons, Josep and Antoni Mata Casanovas, while today, it's his grandson Ton Mata who heads up the family winery.

Production comes only from the estate's 80 hectares of biodyna-mic vineyards based mainly in the 25 kilometres around Sant Sadurní d'Anoia in the Corpinnat territory, a natural area of mainly calcareous soils and landscapes, broken up by ravines, forests and hills and domin-ated by the Montserrat Mountain. The vineyards are dry farmed and planted only with local varieties, notably Xarel·lo, which accounts for 60 per cent of production. A cover crop helps keeps the soil friable, regulates water retention and drainage and fosters biodiversity. Based on low, albeit variable, yields, some 250,000–280,000 bottles are produced annually.

Since leaving the Cava DO in 2019, the entire range is vintage and made in brut nature style under the Corpinnat umbrella. Fermented with native yeasts, the wines are aged for at least 30 months, using nat-ural cork closures. Bottles are hand-riddled and disgorged. Since dis-gorgement is based on demand, the wines remain on the lees for as long as possible and the precise number of months spent on the lees and the date of disgorgement are printed on the label. In 2010, Recaredo be-came the first in the Penedès region to obtain biodynamic certification.

The range comprises Terrers, Serral del Vell estate, Subtil, Reserva Particular, Turó d'en Mota and Intens Rosat. The spicy, sour lemony fresh Terrers, usually a blend of Xarel·lo, Macabeo and Parellada, is made from a select mosaic of Recaredo's vineyards and aged for at least 30 months. Serral del Vell brut nature, from the Serral Del Vell es-tate is made from a blend of Xarel·lo and Macabeo grown on the pla-teau's gently sloping terraces and aged for at least 65 months for a richly full-flavoured fizz with a fine-textured mousse and delightfully savoury, nutty notes. The Intens Rosat is a sparkling rosé blend of Monastrell and Garnatxa (Grenache) with a minimum of 50 months on the lees.

With his sons Josep and Antoni, Josep Mata Capellades created the Reserva Particular de Recaredo in 1962 with the aim of achieving the deli-cacy and the complexity of an aged fizz without sacrificing freshness. Made with Xarel·lo and Macabeo from old vines on three Recaredo estates, the Reserva Particular de Recaredo Brut Nature, a blend of 60 per cent

Macabeo and 40 per cent Xarel·lo aged for 129 months on the lees with no dosage, has an intriguing woodsmoke and Amontillado sherry-like bouquet and is equally distinctive in its oxidative, smoky dried fruits and herb taste. Last and certainly not least, Turó d'en Mota is a limited production (3,000–4,000 bottles) of Xarel·lo from the eponymous 0.97-hectare north-east facing vineyard planted in 1940, aged for at least 12 years.

Vardon Kennett

Sant Joan de Mediona, Barcelona

www.vardonkennett.com

Until recently, Torres hadn't made a sparkling wine in Spain, which some may find surprising given that the famous Spanish wine dynasty has Catalonia coursing through its veins. Familia Torres had been making a sparkling Pinot Noir in Chile since 1986 but it was access to Pinot Noir, Chardonnay and Xarel·lo vineyards at altitude that led Torres to decide to make Vardon Kennett. An unlikely Spanish sparkling wine brand name perhaps, but Daniel Vardon Kennett was a British seafarer (1781–1835) who fell in love with a Catalan pubilla (the eldest daughter who would inherit in the absence of a son) and came to live in the Penedès. Kennett was the former owner of the winery in Sant Joan de Mediona where Torres makes its fizz and is buried there in an eleventh-century Romanesque chapel.

After two years of trials led to the conclusion that working with high-altitude vineyards was a prerequisite for elegance and freshness, Torres decided to work with its 14 hectares of vineyards in Tremp in the pre-Pyrenees at 900 metres. Planted to Chardonnay, Pinot Noir and Xarel·lo, the soils are shallow, formed in glaciers from quaternary deposits of limestone gravels with a texture that's rich in silts, sands and stones providing good drainage and moderate water retention capacity. A pruning and fertilization check is carried out in winter with a couple of tillings every year. Frequent hail episodes have necessitated the installation of protective nets. Yields are low at around 4,000–5,000 kilograms per hectare.

Vardon Kennett is made by Mireia Torres and Anna Velázquez. The grapes are picked manually at 10.5 per cent potential alcohol and transferred in cold storage to the winery where they are pressed by pneumatic press. Working with different yeasts in the first fermentation, roughly 10–15 per cent of the wine is fermented in second-use French oak barrels while a proportion of the wine undergoes malolactic fermentation depending on the year. Ageing is at least 30 months but in practice much more (72 months). Dosage is around 3 grams per litre. The project is still in its infancy but with its ripe stone fruit flavours complemented by a complex, nutty mousse and refreshingly dry, lemony-crisp finish, the future for Vardon Kennett Cuvée Esplendor looks promising.

Vilarnau

Sant Sadurní d'Anoia, Barcelona

www.vilarnau.es

The first Cava labelled Vilarnau was created in 1949, when the owners first sold a Cava made from grapes grown for centuries on the Can Petit i Les Planes de Vilarnau estate in d'Espiells. Today, the top-of-the-range Cava bears the name of the fourteenth century Albert de Vilarnau, whose family settled in Penedès in the twelfth century. Vilarnau joined the González Byass family of wineries in 1982 and has been certified organic since 2016. Located close to Barcelona, the clean lines of the new artisan winery, designed by architect Luis González, combine glass, oak and running water to emphasize its organic Mediterranean identity.

Protected from cold Pyrenean winds, the 20-hectare Can Petit i les Planes de Vilarnau estate, at 250 metres altitude, is bordered to the south by the Serralada Litoral (the Coastal Range) while to the east the vines are open to the Mediterranean, 30 kilometres away. The soils, alluvial in origin, consist of layers of lime and clay. Chardonnay and Pinot Noir are the cornerstone varieties along with Macabeo and Xarel·lo. Some 80 hectares of organic vineyards are looked after by long-term contract growers, with Parellada mainly from Penedès Superior, and Macabeo and Xarel·lo from the central areas of Penedès.

Vilarnau aims for minimum oxidation to preserve aroma, and works at low temperatures, chilling the grapes, fermenting with cryo-yeasts and preserving the wines with the carbon dioxide generated during the first fermentation. Starting with the entry-level Barcelona Cava Brut Reserva wines in their colourful Gaudi sleeve livery, the range moves up a gear with the refreshingly tangy Vilarnau Brut Reserva, the moreishly strawberryish Brut Reserva Organic Rosé Delicat Cava Reserva and the creamy-textured, appetizingly dry Brut Nature Reserva. At the top of the pyramid, with more than 50 months on the lees, there is Albert de Vilarnau Chardonnay–Pinot Noir and the 100 per cent Xarel·lo Albert de Vilarnau Fermentado en Castaño, 50 per cent of which is fermented in chestnut barrels in the Penedès farmhouse tradition.

PORTUGAL

Even though the production of sparkling wine in Portugal increased by a whopping 324 per cent in the first decade of the twenty-first century (against a trend of decreasing total production), the category still accounts for less than 1 per cent of all wine produced in the country. Bairrada, the home of well-known producers such as Luis Pato, Quinta das Bágeiras, Campolargo, Filipa Pato & William Wouters and Caves Aliança, stands out for both quality and volume, accounting for roughly 62 per cent of the country's fizz. It has also attracted renowned producers from other regions, most notably Dirk Niepoort, eager to add Bairrada bubbles to their ranges.

Bairrada's trademarks – indigenous varieties, chalky soils and Atlantic influence – translate into wines with fine mineral backbone and delicious salinity. Although Champagne varieties gained some ground in the 1970s and 1980s, the focus has consistently remained on indigenous grapes, namely Baga, Arinto, and Bical. While most producers refrain from extended bottle ageing, seeking that fresh and mineral profile, there are also good examples with marked autolytic character and richness of texture.

Other DOCs worthy of mention are Dão, Távora-Varosa and Península de Setúbal. The Douro is also increasing its share of fizz, having gone from a virtually non-existent output in the early 2000s to over 2,000 hectolitres in 2009–10. Sparkling production in Minho, of Vinho Verde fame, remains surprisingly low, even if the potential of the region's Alvarinho grape has been proven by producers such as Soalheiro and Niepoort. Beyond Bairrada, established still wine producers and new wave names across all Portuguese regions are increasingly looking to add fizz to their ranges, with the traditional method and *méthode ancestrale*, respectively, the preferred methods of production.

At the lowest level of the Portuguese sparkling pyramid, *espumoso* is the term used for wines injected with carbon dioxide. Next up, Vinho Qualidade Produzido em Região Determinada (VQPRD), is a generic classification for sparkling wine made in the traditional, Charmat or transfer method, anywhere in Portugal. Then comes Vinho Frisante de Qualidade Produzido em Região Determinada (VFQPRD), a regional sparkling wine made in the traditional, Charmat or transfer method in one of the following DOCs: Douro, Ribatejo, Minho, Alentejo or Estremadura. At the apex of the pyramid, Vinho Espumante de Qualidade Produzido em

Região Determinada (VEQPRD) is the quality certification given only to wines produced in the Bairrada DOC, following the traditional method and with the indication of the harvest year.

Producers

Filipa Pato & William Wouters

F.Pato – Vinhos Unip., Lda.

Óis do Bairro, Anadia

www.patowouters.com

Filipa Pato is the daughter of Bairrada legend Luis Pato and her husband is Belgian sommelier extraordinaire William Wouters. Her technical expertise and knowledge of the traditions and terroir of Bairrada, combined with his tasting acumen and international outlook have led the pair to produce some of Portugal's most sought-after wines. This dream team created their venture 20 years ago and their wines now feature in the world's best wine lists.

Sparkling wine started as a way of using grapes from vineyards not yet ready for the production of still wines. The couple have introduced biodynamic practices across all vineyards, both their own and those under contract, and are not afraid to wait for ripeness. The first fizz was the 3B Rosé (Baga and Bical from Bairrada). A 3B Blanc de Blancs followed, blending Cerceal, Bical and Maria Gomes; the trademark acidity of each contributes structure and aromatic vibrancy. Both wines have zero dosage and spend nine months on the lees prior to disgorgement.

The grapes for fizz are harvested from late August to early September at a maximum potential alcohol of 12 per cent. The couple believe that the purity of a base wine is essential for texture and complexity, so the base wines are fermented spontaneously, unfined, unfiltered and undergo a light sulphur regime. These are effectively traditional method 'natural' bubbles. This low-intervention approach, unorthodox in the context of Bairrada's institutionalized production, is perhaps the main reason why they don't submit their wines for DOC approval. Not that they need to.

The estate's commitment to sustainable viticulture and the strict use of local grapes, against the ongoing trend among Bairrada producers to introduce Champagne varieties and Touriga Nacional, has set them apart and allowed them to build a faithful international following for the 50,000 bottles produced annually. With 90 per cent sold on export, that's not enough to meet demand. Their fizzes, say Filipa and William, are wines they like to drink: fresh, saline, structured, but retaining lively, fresh aromas. They do not follow stylistic scripts, and are arguably making the sparkling wines that best represent the essence of Bairrada.

Soalheiro

Alvaredo

www.soalheiro.com

Soalheiro is a family-run business that relies on a close-knit group of associated growers to produce its wine range. Specializing in Alvarinho and pioneering sustainable viticulture in Vinho Verde's subregion of Monção–Melgaço, Soalheiro was the first across Vinho Verde and the adjoining Spanish region of Rías Baixas to produce a single variety, traditional method, sparkling Alvarinho. The idea of adding bubbles to the range came to second generation Luis Cerdeira in 1995 when a nearby lab developed encapsulated yeasts that would allow a second fermentation with limited contact with the lees. The goal was to develop a style marked by Alvarinho's aromatic footprint and mineral backbone rather than by Champagne-like autolytic characters.

After initial teething issues, Alvarinho in the Minho terroir has shown its aptitude for sparkling production, developing a creamy mousse, velvety mouthfeel and great ageing potential, supported by its trademark minerality. Soalheiro's expertise is showcased in the four cuvées now in its sparkling range, corresponding to 80,000 out of the 700,000 bottles produced annually. The first two to be released were a Bruto and a Bruto Rosé, the latter, initially blended with some Touriga Nacional, now contains a small percentage of Pinot Noir too. In 2019, Soalheiro added Bruto Barrica, a brut with base wine partially fermented in wood, and Bruto Nature, produced without sulphites and released undisgorged.

Freshness and mineral drive are achieved through a balance between early harvest in lower altitude sites and later harvest in higher altitude plots, where acidity levels are maintained late into the growing season. Altitude has been key to handling the current and future impact of climate change, with recent new plantings at 1,100 metres above sea level. The base wines do not undergo malolactic fermentation and are neither fined nor filtered. With their textural and flavour complexity, the wines age for between 12 and 24 months in bottle prior to disgorgement (18 months prior to release to market for the Bruto Nature). Relentlessly committed to innovation, Soalheiro is now working on two pet nats. Because innovation and experimentation are key, some of the cuvées are not bottled under the Vinho Verde DOC, but rather with the Minho IG stamp, allowing for greater flexibility.

Vértice (Caves Transmontanas)

Alijó

www.dourovertice.pt

Established in 1989, Caves Transmontanas quickly turned heads by pioneering a style few thought possible from the Douro. It produces a range of traditional method fizz, labelled under the Vértice brand, with a faithful following for both its consistency and distinctive profile. Having pioneered not only a style but also a business model, Caves Transmontanas remains the DOC's single dedicated sparkling producer. It does not own vineyards but buys grapes from 40 growers with whom it works closely, giving it access to expressions of the same grapes from different terroirs and microclimates.

The project's story began when Schramsberg's Jack and Jamie Davies came to Portugal to investigate the potential for quality fizz. They eventually settled on the area surrounding Alijó, at the heart of Douro's Cima Corgo, the most prized of the valley's sub-regions, and a careful study of the most suitable grape varieties followed. Micro-vinifications of 25 varieties enabled them to shortlist Gouveio, Códega and Malvasia Fina, along with one red, Touriga Franca, for the best balance of acid retention and aromatic expression. A massal selection then expanded plantings of the selected grapes and Viosinho and Rabigato have since been added, as well as a small percentage (2 per cent of total plantings) of Chardonnay and Pinot Noir. It currently produces a pure Chardonnay and pure Pinot Noir cuvée in magnum, but only as a way of benchmarking the potential of the local terroir against international counterparts.

Vértice's range currently includes six cuvées with a total annual production of 100,000 bottles. When asked how he would define the house's style, Celso Pereira, winemaker and manager of Caves Transmontanas, said that minerality, freshness and ageing potential were key. The wines spend between two and ten years on the lees with clear autolytic markers across the range. The integration of autolytic aromas, along with the potential for further complexity with ageing are, according to Celso, the fundamental pillars of his work. Climate change, drought and growing competition are challenges that Caves Transmontanas, relying on years of specialized expertise, close relationships and competitive pricing, feels confident it can meet.

13

USA AND CANADA

ONCE UPON A TIME IN AMERICA

California is the hub of today's American sparkling wine industry, but wind the clock back to before Prohibition (1919–32) and it was the eastern states that dominated, particularly the Finger Lakes of upstate New York. Even after Prohibition, of the ten million bottles of American 'champagne' produced in the first four years after restrictions were lifted, nearly half came from New York and only 20 per cent from California, the rest coming from New Jersey, Michigan and Ohio. New York 'champagne' was based on blends of hybrid varieties, Catawba, Delaware and Elvira, with the addition of Dutchess, Isabella, Iona and Eumelan.

By the mid-nineteenth century, sparkling wine production was already sufficiently established in America for the British merchant T. G. Shaw, writing in 1864, to conclude: 'The most important vineyards are those of Ohio, Missouri and Indiana, but the most celebrated is in Cincinnati, where there are large vineyards, especially those belonging to Messrs. Longworth and Zimmermann, who have gained a high reputation for their sparkling Catawba.' Shaw damns the wine with faint praise by comparing it to Vouvray of a 'very coarse, common kind' but he was ahead of his time because he felt that 'California is better adapted for producing good wine, including champagne'.

Nicholas Longworth's successful Cincinnati legal practice allowed him to indulge in his passion for horticulture by planting vineyards on slopes (later named Mount Adams) overlooking the Ohio River, in 1813. He planted Catawba in 1825, but it wasn't until 1842, when a batch accidentally went through a second fermentation, that the resulting sparkling wine proved more attractive than the still. Soon rich enough to invest in making *méthode champenoise*, his attempt at bringing in champenois savoir-faire resulted in the first Frenchman drowning in the Ohio River and the second losing 42,000 out of 50,000 bottles in one season to burst bottles. Third time lucky, a Monsieur Fournier arrived in 1852 and by the mid-1850s, Longworth was producing 100,000 bottles a year.

'I shall not attempt to imitate any of the sparkling wines in Europe,' said Longworth, with commendable honesty. When he sent a case of his sparkling Catawba to Henry Wadsworth Longfellow, the poet wrote glowingly about 'a taste more divine, more dulcet, delicious and dreamy [than Champagne]'. As the American wine and food expert Darrell Corti points out: 'If the wine tasted good and was different smelling or tasting, it was probably liked since it was novel. The very different "American" taste must have appeared intriguing, not something to be dismissed as we would do.' He adds, 'There is probably also a diminution of the foxy character with bottle fermentation which made the Longworth wines interesting to Europeans.' Alas, black rot, powdery mildew and the subsequent American Civil War put paid to the enterprise and Longworth's vineyards were abandoned after he died in 1863.

The first New York 'champagne' was made in 1865 by Joseph Masson, who called his first fizz Sparkling Catawba. With his brother Jules, he made a cuvée in 1870, which, on being mistaken at a meeting of Pleasant Valley growers for a 'great champagne of the West' (i.e. California), adopted the Great Western Champagne name. For the next 50 years it was the most important sparkling wine brand in America. The other, Gold Seal, made by the Urbana Wine Company in Hammondsport, New York, was made by a succession of five French winemakers in over a century from the 1870s until after its purchase by Seagram in 1979 – and closure five years later.

Meanwhile, California was not sitting idly by. On his return from Champagne in 1857, Pierre Sainsevain set up a winery in San Jose for the production of bottle-fermented sparkling California, selling for $1 a bottle. Within a year, he was making 150,000 bottles. At the same time, Agoston Haraszthy, founder of Buena Vista in Sonoma, sent his son Arpad to learn the tricks of the fizz trade at De Venoge Champagne. After an inauspicious start thanks to the use of the Mission grape, Arpad was forced out in 1864, but the ship steadied and between 1866 and 1868, production trebled from 40,000 to 120,000 bottles. Arpad's own company, Arpad Haraszthy & Co., produced Eclipse, one of the most successful American sparkling wines of the 1870s.

In 1878, at the age of 19, Paul Masson left Burgundy for California, where he teamed up with Charles Lefranc, and subsequently Lefranc's daughter Louise, to establish the Paul Masson Champagne Company in 1892. For his many awards, Masson became known as the 'Champagne King of California'. At around the same time, the three Korbel brothers, who had planted vineyards in Sonoma's Russian River, were joined by a Czech immigrant, Franz Hazek, whose own sparkling wine brand, Grand Pacific, was later changed to the highly successful Korbel Sec. To this day, Korbel continues to make the innocuous Korbel Champagne.

The early promise of American fizz was snuffed out in the wake of Prohibition, the Great Depression and the Second World War. By the 1950s, pressure on price led to a downward spiral in quality as the traditional method was replaced by cheaper tank method fizz. Many wineries also made 'carbonated wine' to offer a sparkler, since fizz was considered the pinnacle of 'fancy' wine. Almaden, with its transfer method *blanc de blancs*, was the first of its type in California and was made to be an imitator of Taittinger's prestigious *blanc de blancs*, Comtes de Champagne. At the time, Almaden was making affordable wines of reasonable quality, 'just out of being a wealthy man's hobby,' says Darrell Corti.

One of the few producers to stick to the traditional method for sparkling wine was Martin Ray, who was 'flamboyant, vocal, outrageous, bombastic, imperious, opinionated, unreasonable', according to Roy Brady. After acquiring Paul Masson, Ray brought in Oliver Goulet as winemaker, and the 1955 vintage of his own pure Pinot Noir fizz, Madame Pinot, was highly rated at an otherwise depressing time for California fizz. The influential Russian immigrant, André Tchelistcheff's Beaulieu Vineyards also made some interesting examples, most notably a Pinot Noir-based rosé for the winery's fiftieth anniversary in 1958.

Sparkling wines like these inspired Jack and Jamie Davies, shareholders in one of Ray's ventures, to buy Schramsberg in 1965. When the Davieses acquired the house that Jacob Schram built, the Victorian des res came with 63 hectares of forested land, including abandoned vineyards and one and a half miles of caves in the Calistoga Hills excavated by Chinese labourers for wine storage. After embarking on a pioneering project to make world-class traditional method California fizz from the Champagne varieties, the strategic product placement of Schramsberg's Blanc de Blancs for President Nixon's 1972 'Toast to Peace' with China's

Premier Zhou Enlai secured Schramsberg's place in the fizz hall of fame and enhanced the growing reputation of California bubbles.

At the time, Hanns Kornell's Champagne Cellars in Napa Valley (closed in 1992) was the reference point for traditional method fizz, but over half of California's sparkling wine was Cold Duck. A German tradition of putting put all the parts of bottles left unemptied together at the end of an evening, called 'kalte ende', became corrupted to 'kalte ente', or Cold Duck. Perhaps this was the wine that caused Rénaud Poirier, dispatched to America by Moët & Chandon, to pronounce Californian sparkling wine 'imbuvable' (undrinkable). Recognizing the limits to growth of the Champagne region, Moët & Chandon's Robert-Jean de Vogüé was on a mission to expand into new destinations with suitable locations and markets. Moët plumped in 1973 for the exclusivity of a Napa Valley address as the right spot to produce *méthode champenoise* for domestic consumption.

Chandon's example was followed by other Champagne houses keen to sink their capital into California's new sparkling El Dorado. Piper-Heidsieck set up a joint venture with Rodney Strong in Sonoma in 1980. The following year, Maison Deutz (now Laetitia), with Beringer, pioneered the cold, breezy San Luis Obispo area. Champagne Pommery & Greno took over Scharffenberger's discreet redwood winery, later acquired (after Veuve Clicquot) by Louis Roederer, who themselves put down roots in Mendocino County's remote Anderson Valley in 1982. Domaine Mumm (later Mumm Napa) was established on Napa's Silverado Trail in 1984 in partnership with Seagram and, in 1987 in Napa County, Taittinger created its grandiose château, Domaine Carneros, in the image of its Château de la Marquetterie. Not to be left out, the Spanish giants piled in, Freixenet, with Gloria Ferrer, in Sonoma County in 1983, and Codorníu in 1989.

Roederer's Jean-Claude Rouzaud was aware that it wasn't simply enough to create *méthode champenoise* wines based on the Champagne grape varieties, stating: 'We cannot reproduce what we do in Champagne but in the right place we can produce good sparkling wine.' Dawnine Dyer, Domaine Chandon's first winemaker, recognized that 'there are aspects of climate and grape that inevitably create stylistic difference from Champagne'. The grapes often have thicker skins and bigger pips than their French counterparts. Grapes that would be ripe in Champagne at a typical picking level of 9.5 per cent potential alcohol, would not ripen enough in California, producing tart sparkling wines unbalanced by compensating doses of excessive sugar. If overripe, the danger is of heaviness and a loss of natural acidity. The solution to early problems of unripe, vegetal characters was, as the estate agents say, location, location, location.

Barry and Audrey Sterling found that solution when they stumbled upon Iron Horse in 1976 in a cool, fog-enveloped spot in Green Valley, Sonoma County. Jean-Claude Rouzaud instinctively found the answer in the northerly Anderson Valley, where aspects and altitudes help in day to night temperature differences. Wineries that started out in Napa have gradually changed vineyard sources to include cooler locations, in particular Carneros, Russian River Valley, Green Valley and Mendocino's Alexander Valley and Anderson Valley. Proximity to the Pacific Ocean brings cool, air-conditioning sea mists, and breezes blow through river valleys that run west to east, like the Petaluma Wind Gap, moderating temperatures that increase the further inland you go.

In tandem with anxieties over climate change, the search was on for cooler locations for a longer growing season. Opening up the canopy has paid dividends in achieving ripeness at lower potential alcohol levels and the retention of natural acidity. Careful picking and sorting, attention to pressing and refinements in the cellar with partial or no malolactic fermentation, blending across sub-regions and the use of reserve wines and length of time on the lees have all contributed to the overall improvement in the quality and intensity of California's sparkling wines. Not least, the training and experience of the winemakers has had a significant impact.

For a while, it seemed as though limits to growth in Champagne could be compensated for by burgeoning demand for California's homegrown fizz, but in the late 1990s, the bubble burst. The big, new, glossy, French-owned wineries found themselves operating at a fraction of capacity so they breached their own policy of making fizz for the domestic market by seeking new markets overseas. The ill wind of longer than anticipated lees ageing blew in a new generation of prestige cuveés such as Chandon's Etoile, Iron Horse's Brut LD, Mumm's DVX and Schramsberg's J Schram. Albeit distinctively different from Champagne in style, the quality of prestige cuvées such as Roederer Estate's Ermitage and Domaine Carneros' Le Rêve has probably even exceeded Jean-Claude Rouzaud's expectations.

Impressive as these achievements have been, a new generation of sparkling winemakers is starting to reshape the traditional idea of sparkling wine as a drink for special occasions only. Paula Kornell, the daughter of Hanns Kornell, is one who now makes her own fizz. A lot of wineries also contract out to facilities like Rack and Riddle where they can have wines custom made for them. Among other relative newcomers adding a new dimension to American fizz, names to watch include Caraccioli Cellars, Michael Cruse, Frank Family, Flaunt Wine Co., Inman Family Wines, Carboniste and Maitre de Chai, not forgetting a mushrooming of pet nat from the likes of Birichino, Blue Farm, Broc Cellars, Fathers & Daughters, Albatross Ridge, Purity Wine Scribe and Donkey & Goat.

Producers

Domaine Carneros

Napa

www.domainecarneros.com

Kudos to Claude Taittinger for naming Domaine Carneros after its location, with its cool-climate image, rather than succumbing to an ego-driven temptation to use the Taittinger Champagne name. He didn't need to, a point driven home forcibly when you see the imposing château modelled on Taittinger's Louis XV Château de la Marquetterie back home in Pierry. In keeping with all things American however, Domaine Carneros, 'an elegant pastiche', as Claude Taittinger put it himself, sits grandiosely atop a knoll with a panoramic vista taking in the rolling vineyards of Carneros. Quite the cellar door experience.

Intent on staking a future in the promising California wine industry, Claude Taittinger began his recce for the right soils for high quality American bubbles in the late 1970s. Recognizing that Carneros was producing excellent cool-climate Pinot Noir and Chardonnay, in 1982 he and his agents, Kobrand, jointly purchased a 40-hectare vineyard 'where the strong smell of the ocean mingles with the perfume of sequoia trees'. After recruiting Eileen Crane as founding winemaker for its 1987 vintage, the winery was officially launched in 1990. On Crane's retirement in 2020, Remi Cohen was put at the helm and the sparkling winemaking baton handed to Zak Miller.

Since 2020, Domaine Carneros' wines have been sourced exclusively from its six sustainably farmed estate vineyards, 165 hectares planted to 60 per cent Pinot Noir and 40 per cent Chardonnay, with a variety of French clones and California heritage field selections on drought-tolerant rootstocks. Carneros soils are predominately gravelly clay loam.

Trellising and vineyard management are geared to protect grapes from the heat of the afternoon sun. A slow, even ripening and bright acidity are encouraged by the marine-influenced climate, with its morning fog and breezy afternoons. In total, Domaine Carneros makes 11 sparkling wines which include a range of brut, rosé, *blanc de blancs* and *blanc de noirs* for some 60,000 cases of sparkling wine annually.

Minimal malolactic fermentation is practised in order to preserve acidity. Only one or two lots proceed with malolactic fermentation, and these are used as a blending component, for texture. After pneumatic pressing, the top cuts are used for sparkling wine, and the press wine sold off, before fermentation in stainless steel and glass. The wines are aged for at least three years with a range of dosage from 5 grams per litre to 25 grams per litre. The bright, cheerful, entry level Brut Traditional is vintage dated and aged for a minimum of three years. The tête de cuvée, Le Rêve Blanc de Blancs is aged for at least six years before release, and is one of America's best sparkling wines. Wines are held for at least three months post-disgorgement prior to release.

Chandon California

Yountville

www.chandon.com

In the land of the founding fathers, Robert-Jean de Vogüé was the founding father of the first Champagne-house-led sparkling outpost in the USA. After considering John Wright's industry report compiled for the Bank of America, Moët bought 324 hectares (now some 400 hectares) of Napa Valley real estate in 1973 for the production of traditional method fizz. Sites were chosen by Wright in Carneros, Mount Veeder and Yountville for a cool to temperate climate that could provide the right conditions for intensity, concentration and ripeness. With a range of altitudes, aspects and microclimates, a 'smorgasbord' of options for blending was the prerequisite for the estate's first winemakers, Dawnine Dyer and Edmond de Maudière. Planting began immediately and 1976 saw the first harvest.

Today, using fruit from 25 different vineyards, with some 20–25 per cent bought from cool climate grower–partners, blends are made from more than 60 base wines. Grapes are the classic Champagne varieties, Chardonnay and Pinot Noir with 4–5 per cent Meunier from Chandon's own vineyards. Sustainable farming practices are linked to biodiversity with reforestation projects leaving almost half the land undeveloped. More than 1,300 sheep graze before bud break and there are beehives among the vines. Water resources, energy use and carbon foot-print are monitored, resulting in Napa Green and California Sustainable Winegrowing Alliance (CSWA) certification.

Chandon's head of winemaking is Pauline Lhote, an Auboise, who graduated in oenology from Reims in 2005. After working at Moët & Chandon and Nicolas Feuillatte, she started a three-month intern-ship in Yountville in 2006, becoming chief winemaker ten years later at the age of just 34. Pinot Noir is the backbone of Chandon's wines, with Chardonnay adding crispness and delicacy to Pinot's body and red fruit nuances. Chandon's grapes were initially 100 per cent hand-picked, followed by night-time machine harvesting to capture aroma and freshness. Bucher membrane presses are used for two press fractions for Chardonnay and three for Pinot Noir.

Fermentation is mostly in stainless steel, with some barrel used for the By the Bay cuvée. Since 2016, typically 70–75 per cent malolactic fermentation is aimed for, depending on the vintage. After tasting 40 to 60 base wines over a week for the blends, reserve wines go into the non-vintage blends but not the vintage wines (even though 5 per cent is permitted in California). The Chandon Signature tier spends 12–15 months on the lees, the reserves three years, vintages four years and the Etoile range five years. After disgorgement, they rest for a minimum of three months in the cellar. Disgorgement dates are not routinely applied but the 45th Anniversary Cuvée and Blanc de Noirs Late Disgorged did have tirage and disgorging dates. In the future? 'This is something we are thinking about.'

Iron Horse Vineyards

Sebastopol

www.ironhorsevineyards.com

Motoring along Ross Station Road in Green Valley and thinking them-selves lost one fittingly cold and rainy day in 1976, Audrey and Barry Sterling suddenly found themselves in the midst of a rustic idyll where vineyards surrounded a dilapidated Victorian gothic house. The prop-erty, Iron Horse, named after a railroad stop that crossed the property in the 1890s, was rediscovered in 1970 by Rodney Strong, whose vineyard manager Forrest Tancer planted 22 hectares of Chardonnay and Pinot Noir. The Californian couple's ambition of making wine had begun when they lived in France in the late 1960s. They promptly made a deal with Strong to purchase the property. Green Valley was already on its way to American Viticultural Area (AVA) status, achieved in 1983. Their daughter Joy, an ex-ABC news journalist, became CEO in 2006, and her brother Laurence, director of operations. In March 2020, Aube-born Sofian Himeur took over the Iron Horse winemaking reins from David Munksgard, who is now winemaker emeritus.

Ten miles from the Pacific as the drone flies, Iron Horse benefits from a cool and foggy climate. With 65 hectares in 39 vineyard blocks planted to Pinot Noir and Chardonnay, its sandy loam Goldridge soils are especially suited to Pinot Noir. With its diverse habitats, Iron Horse is certified sustainable and started practising precision agriculture in 2005, with pruning, canopy management, irrigation and cover crops, and harvesting decisions determined on a block-by-block basis. After a dawn harvest and vineyard sorting, the grapes are pressed in a Defranceschi Champagne press, with the juice fermented in stainless steel and older French oak. Most sparkling blends are non-oxidative, but in 2017, Iron Horse started crafting a number of more oxidative small lot blends for barrel-fermentation with full malolactic fermentation. Cuvée Joy! which sees no barrel or malolactic fermentation, spends at least 12 years on the lees.

Iron Horse aims for 'about 8.1' atmospheres of pressure in the bottle. Dosage is low, its composition selected on taste from components including five barrel-fermented still wine Chardonnays and six Pinot Noirs, as well as sparkling wines *en tirage* going back to 1983. The end result is sparkling wines (19 in the range) that are fine and elegantly dry, reflecting in their crispness and delicacy of flavour their cool climate, oceanic origins. The Classic Vintage Brut is co-founder Audrey Sterling's favourite and she calls the shots on the dosage. The range culminates in the Brut LD, a prestige cuvée blend of 50 per cent Chardonnay and 50 per cent Pinot Noir whose lightly toasty, complex aromatic quality is revealed by the blend's seven years of lees-ageing. The date of disgorgement is stamped on the outside of each case. Average annual production of the sparkling range is 12,000 to 15,000 cases.

J Vineyards & Winery

Healdsburg

www.jwine.com

Founded as a dedicated sparkling wine house in 1986, J Vineyards & Winery began with a focus on finding the most ideal sites for crafting New World sparkling wine. Founder Judy Jordan, a lover of Champagne and a trained geologist, was convinced that Sonoma County, with its cool, foggy climate and wide diversity of soils, was perfect for producing world-class bubbly. The end result was 80 hectares planted across six sites focused almost entirely on the Russian River Valley, where the estate also sources fruit; the exception is the Annapolis Ridge Vineyard in the far north of the Sonoma Coast AVA. A diverse topography of mountains, valleys, plains and riverbeds with varying microclimates and soils contribute to J's ability to blend.

The Russian River Valley growing season is marked by clear, warm days moderated by Pacific coastal breezes, cool, misty fog and cold nights. The diurnal range allows fruit to develop ripe, mature flavour characteristics while maintaining bright acidity. One of its unique aspects is its Goldridge soils, a fine, well-draining, sandy loam found in pockets throughout the region. The generally acidic soils allow the roots of vines to burrow deep in search of moisture and nutrients.

Born in Carmel, J's Davis-trained head winemaker, Nicole Hitchcock, worked for E. & J. Gallo in Sonoma County, so when, in early 2015, Judy Jordan sold the winery to Gallo, Nicole continued where her predecessors, Melissa Stackhouse, George Bursick and founding winemaker Oded Shakked, left off. Chardonnay, Pinot Noir and Meunier are sorted by hand before whole-bunch pressing in two Coquard presses. The classic Champagne press cuts are taken, cuvée and *taille*, and kept separately. Stylistically, the base wines are bright, fresh, and reductive in style, except for a few select lots fermented in neutral French oak for the flagship Cuvée 20, created in 2006 for the twentieth anniversary.

The 12-wine sparkling collection is led by the refined citrus and brioche notes of the non-vintage Cuvée 20. The plush Pinot Noir-led red fruit flavours of the Brut Rosé offer a bit more body than the other sparkling wines, aiming to showcase Russian River Valley Pinot Noir along with Chardonnay for vibrancy. Other wines in the portfolio are the California Cuvée, Cuvée XB, Blanc de Noirs, Blanc de Blancs, Demi-Sec, Vintage Brut, Vintage Brut Rosé, Late Disgorged Brut, Cuvée 20 Magnum and Vintage Brut Magnum. Labels are screen-printed onto the bottle before filling, so tirage and disgorgement dates are not included.

Mumm Napa

Rutherford

www.mummnapa.com

In 1979, G. H. Mumm sent winemaker Guy Devaux on a recce, known as Project Lafayette, to find the best spot for growing the traditional Champagne varieties in the US. Devaux plumped for Napa Valley's Silverado Trail and by 1983 the first vintage of Mumm Napa was made. Devaux continued to manage the winery, taking on Greg Fowler, who had worked at Schramsberg, to be followed by the champenois Ludovic Dervin. Around the millennium, the company changed hands several times and, while now owned by Pernod-Ricard, it is run independently of its champenois sibling.

Early efforts were often on the unripe, green side because, as Greg Fowler admitted, 'we used to pick green because that's the way Champagne did it'. Gradually, like other Champagne houses that adapted to a warmer climate, winemakers and viticulturalists worked to solve the problem of picking the grapes riper while still managing to retain freshness. In Mumm Napa's case, this was achieved by sourcing a greater proportion of grapes from cool Carneros. Hand-picking in the cool pre-dawn and blending from a wide spread of growers led to a substantial improvement.

Mumm Napa's 44.5-hectare estate vineyard, Devaux Ranch, is planted to Pinot Noir, Chardonnay, Meunier and Pinot Gris. Ninety-five per cent of its supply comes from growers. Most grapes are sourced from Carneros and Oak Knoll, both of which are influenced by San Pablo Bay breezes. Cool nights help maintain natural acidity with Carneros Chardonnay showing citrus and green apple flavours while Oak Knoll, warmer with deeper soils, shows more in the golden apple, pear and apricot spectrum. Mumm Napa takes sustainability seriously and is Fish Friendly Farming and CSWA certified at Devaux Ranch, where bat, bluebird and owl boxes are happily occupied.

Born and raised in Napa, Tamra Lotz, a UC Davis graduate, returned to Mumm Napa in 2003 after a year's work experience overseas as assistant winemaker under Ludovic Dervin, and was named head winemaker in 2019. She uses membrane presses, keeping cuvée, *taille* and press fractions separate. Primary fermentation is carried out at cool temperatures, while select small lots fermented in barrel generally make it into the Mumm Napa DVX or Reserve wines. In its broad range of cuvées, Mumm Napa's focus is on bright, fresh, and enjoyable fruit-forward sparkling wines. In following traditional method techniques, it successfully brings out the ripe fruit expression of the Napa terroir. Annual production is around 250,000 cases.

Roederer Estate

Philo
roedererestate.com

When Jean-Claude Rouzaud scoured the California landscape in search of a terroir for making bubbles worthy of Roederer Champagne, he alighted on Mendocino's rugged, rural Anderson Valley, two-and-a-half hours north of San Francisco, for the influence of the Pacific Ocean in enabling a long, slow ripening season. As its first winemaker, Michel Salgues, pointed out soon after the establishment of the winery in 1981, 'we never have to fight to get fruit or intensity; instead we have to fight to get elegance'. Since its debut vintage in 1988, Roederer Estate has lived up to Rouzaud's vision of the Anderson Valley's potential.

Roederer originally bought 235 hectares of land, 137 hectares planted to vineyards over four ranches, two north of the town of Philo in the coolest part of the AVA and two smaller ones further inland near Boonville. Having to replant after the appearance of phylloxera in 1993 proved a boon. Instead of a single clone of Chardonnay and the Gamay that much of the initial planting turned out to be, more diverse clonal material was planted. Since then, the family has added new vineyards to reach a current total of 248 hectares of estate-grown vineyards spread over seven ranches in the Anderson Valley AVA.

Running atypically north-west, the Anderson Valley spans roughly 15 miles along the Navarro River and its numerous tributaries on the way out to the Pacific Ocean. Soils are alluvial loam and clay, while the average daily temperature, at just 11.5°C, is only one degree different from that of Champagne, with a diurnal range of up to 10°C during the growing season. The ocean fog that settles in the valley can act as a thermal blanket, allowing for gradual warming. Flowering to harvest is just a few days shorter than in Champagne. In the last decade, about a third of the estate fruit has been picked cool at night.

Roederer Estate's winemaker, Arnaud Weyrich, a Montpellier graduate, became chef de cave in 2003 on Michel Salgues' retirement. Weyrich uses pneumatic membrane presses, gently extracting only the first 125 gallons per tonne from a potential 185 gallons. The approach tends to be oxidative, while fermentation is mainly in stainless steel, occasionally in oak. Malolactic fermentation, initially not done, now is, in small proportions. The best wine of each vintage is set aside to be aged in oak casks for an average of four years and is used as reserve at blending, in approximately 12 per cent of multi-vintage wines and 4 per cent of vintage wines, while some is used for dosage.

Roederer Estate thinks of itself as the most French of the California sparkling wines and it probably is, although even the prestige cuvée, L'Ermitage has a fruit sweetness more in tune with the American than the European palate. It describes its non-vintage wines as multi-vintage. The wine spends a minimum of two years on the lees, L'Ermitage five years, and is aged for at least six months before release. The date of disgorgement is printed on the neck foils on all bottles as 'a useful tool for the trade and customers to understand the age of their bottle'. The range currently consists of two multi-vintage wines, Brut Multi-Vintage and Brut Rosé Multi-Vintage, and two prestige cuvées, L'Ermitage and L'Ermitage Rosé, conditions permitting, with an annual production of around 100,000 cases.

Schramsberg

Calistoga

www.schramsberg.com

A profile of Schramsberg beginning with the birth of Jacob Schram in 1826 in Pfeddersheim, near the Rhine River, would be a book in itself. A history of the estate founded in 1862 by Jacob and Annie Schram, including a visit by Robert Louis Stevenson in 1880, recorded in his book *The Silverado Squatters* (1883), would make a sequel. An account of the awards received and the state dinners at which Schramsberg has been served would require a third volume. For now though, let's skip to Volume Four, the achievements of the Davies family, the first to adopt the traditional method, using Chardonnay and Pinot Noir, to create the state's first *blanc de blancs* in 1965, followed by a *blanc de noirs* in 1967. Originally referred to as Napa Valley Champagne, the word champagne was removed from labels from the 1997 and 1998 vintages.

Today, their son Hugh Davies, a U.C. Davis graduate, continues that work. He joined the business in 1996 as part of the winemaking team that includes Sean Thompson, director of winemaking, and Jessica Koga, winemaker. Schramsberg has gradually moved closer to the coast and its 16°C water for its Chardonnay and Pinot Noir. It owns 8 hectares across Napa Carneros and Sonoma for sparkling wine, bringing in fruit from 90 hectares of Chardonnay and 100 hectares of Pinot Noir (plus 2 hectares of Flora, a Gewurztraminer–Semillon crossing, at Yountville), from leased or contracted vineyards in a variety of locations with considerable soil variations in the Sonoma Coast, Mendocino's Anderson Valley, Marin County and Carneros.

Grapes are hand-harvested at varying levels of ripeness to maximize blending options from some 300 base wines. The first pressings are separated into stainless steel tanks and mainly neutral barrels, with some barrels allowed to go through malolactic fermentation for creaminess of texture. Pressure is 8 atmospheres at disgorgement, dropping to six after, and four for the crémant. An innovative reserve wine barrel-ageing programme involves ageing small lots of wine for 10–15 years. Portions of J. Schram along with the vineyard designated blends and *blanc de blancs* are set aside to age in barrels each year. The disgorgement date is stamped on every case, and there is an electronic stamp marking the disgorgement date on the neck under the foil of every bottle. Eighty per cent of production is vintage-dated.

The pale, coppery gold Schramsberg Blanc de Noirs is one-third barrel-fermented, for balance and texture in a wine of stone fruit and tangy citrus flavours. The Schramsberg Blanc de Blancs combines fragrant clove with pink floral and vanilla notes and an elegantly textured dry finish. In its impressive top two sparkling wines, the J. Schram and Schramsberg Reserve, 40 per cent of the components are barrel-fermented. The excellent J. Schram Rosé is a smart, self-assured fizz whose strawberry shortcake note is complemented by a fine summer pudding mousse of elegant sweet-savoury richness. Some 2.7 million bottles are aged for between two and twenty years in the 34,000 square feet of Schramsberg's consistently cool hillside caves. And thereby hangs a tale.

CANADA

What first comes to mind when you think of Canadian sparkling wine? For many, Canada's USP is its sparkling Icewine, the first commercial example of which was produced by Magnotta in 1997. However, the country has shown that, despite the vagaries of climate, it is capable of producing elegant, balanced and above all full-flavoured fizz in a variety of styles from diverse terroirs stretching 5,800 kilometres from Nova Scotia in Atlantic Canada, across Ontario and Quebec all the way over to British Columbia on the Pacific.

In the 1950s, the chief chemist at Brights Wines, Adhemar de Chaunac, produced the world's first 7 per cent alcohol sparkling wine at the behest of the Liquor Control Board of Ontario (LCBO), which was looking for a low-alcohol wine. This created the 'pop wine' category, which eventually gave birth to Andres' *Vitis labrusca*-based Baby Duck, modelled on Portugal's carbon dioxide-injected Mateus Rosé. Baby Duck spawned a menagerie of taste-alike products such as Gimli Goose, Pink Flamingo, Baby Deer, Baby Bear, Little White Duck, Luv-a-Duck, Pussycat and Spaghetti-Duck for those uncertain as to the best food match. The category also included Fuddle-Duddle, a name based on the late Pierre Trudeau's use of unparliamentary language. The usual blend for Canadian fizz at the time was North American *Vitis labrusca* and French hybrids.

In 1955, the president of Chateau-Gai, Alexander Sampson, sent a consignment of his 'champagne' as a promotional gimmick to Paris. Feathers ruffled, the French appealed to the Canadian government, citing the terms of the Canada–France Trade Agreement Act of 1933, which protected the Champagne name. After a slew of legal actions, the EU's Wine Management Committee granted Ontario Icewine access to European member markets in a quid pro quo preventing Canadian winemakers from using traditional European appellation names. Today Canadian wineries are producing sparkling wines that no longer need the crutch of the Champagne name to define them, although in consumer minds the idea that anything that sparkles is Champagne lives on.

On a similar latitude to Oregon, Nova Scotia is Canada's new frontier of cool-climate fizz. No vineyard is more than 65 kilometres from open water, whether it be the Atlantic Ocean or the dramatic tidal Bay of Fundy that separates Nova Scotia from the province of New Brunswick. In an average year, the vines get 30–40 per cent more rain than in the wine regions of Ontario. L'Acadie, a hybrid crossing between Cascade and Seyve-Villard 14-287, is its signature grape. Soils range from silty, sandy and clay loams to more gravel-rich sandy loams and mineral-rich ancient seabeds. There are nine wineries producing fizz, two of which, Benjamin Bridge and Lightfoot & Wolfville, are profiled here; others to watch are L'Acadie Vineyards (Prestige Brut, Vintage Cuvée), Blomidon (Brut Réserve and Blanc de Blanc), Gaspereau (Cuvée Brut), and Domaine de Grand Pré (Champlain Brut).

In south-east Canada, Ontario's Niagara Peninsula, Lake Erie North Shore and Prince Edward County produce most of Canada's sparkling wines. The appellations share limestone bedrock and stony, sandy soils and a climate similar to Burgundy during the growing season while the

Great Lakes act as a moderating climatic influence. Nearly 100 local wineries produce at least one sparkling wine and several make sparkling Icewine using either Charmat or the traditional method. Vintners Quality Alliance (VQA) regulations state a wine needs at least one year on its lees to be vintage dated and nine months for non-vintage, although in practice most wineries age traditional method wines for two years or more.

Most wineries rely on Chardonnay and Pinot Noir. Sparkling Riesling is also made by both traditional and Charmat methods (Thirty Bench Wine Makers, Kew Vineyards, Vineland Estates, Back 10 Cellars). Two Sisters Winery produces a 100 per cent Cabernet Franc sparkler called Blanc de Franc, and 13th Street Winery is the first winery to produce a sparkling Gamay. Space permitting, we could have celebrated more Ontario producers but here are brief details on a few we wouldn't want to completely overlook. Trius (formerly Hillebrand), along with Inniskillin and Château des Charmes, has a history of traditional method fizz dating back to 1988. Stratus Vineyards' inaugural release in 2020 of a Canadian Artist Label series featuring six estate-grown Chardonnay sparklers aged for seven years was impressive. Huff Estate in Prince Edward County produces a fine Cuvée Peter F Huff traditional method sparkler. Brut nature traditional method fizz is becoming more popular (Stratus, Leaning Post, Hinterland). Tawse Winery has had success with its Quarry Road Rosé and Spark Laundry Road Blanc de Noirs, and Jackson-Triggs produces a top flight, traditional method wine, Entourage Grand Reserve, as well as a Charmat Reserve Moscato. Malivoire Winery produces two sparkling wines cheekily called Bisous Brut and Bisous Rosé.

With five separate designated viticultural areas, British Columbia stretches some 235 kilometres northwards from the Washington State border through the Okanagan Valley to Salmon Arm. The province's first sparkling wine made by the traditional method, Steller's Jay, was produced by Sumac Ridge in 1989, by the late Harry McWatters, a celebrated pioneer of Okanagan wine. Some British Columbia wineries specialize in fizz. Bella Wines in Naramata focus on single vineyard expressions of Chardonnay and Gamay Noir, using both traditional and ancestral methods and also produces pet nat and 'Trad-Nat' (the first vintage fermented dry, the next vintage added while still fermenting). Founded by the eccentric showman Stephen Cipes, Summerhill Pyramid Winery in the Okanagan matures its fizz in a four-storey high,

3,249-square-foot replica of Egypt's Cheops pyramid at Giza for the 'life-force energy the sacred geometry brings'. About one-third of the province's 320 wineries currently produce sparkling wine. Other notable British Columbia sparklers are Tantalus Old Vines Riesling Brut, Okanagan Crush Pad's Haywire The Bub and The Bub Rosé and Gray Monk's Odyssey.

Most of Quebec's 800 hectares of vines are winter-hardy hybrids to survive temperatures that can drop below -15°C. This daunting environment has not deterred some intrepid producers from making bottle-fermented sparkling wines, notably the organic and biodynamic producer Domaine Bergeville, which focuses on fizz, and Domaine St-Jacques. Other Quebec wineries making fizz include Le Cep d'Argent, on Lake Magog, operated by brothers François and Jean-Paul Scieur (originally from Champagne), which produces its Selection Blanc de Blancs cuvée and Selection Brut Nature from Seyval Blanc. At Vignoble Sainte-Pétronille, on the island of Orléans, Louis Denault makes a brut nature from Vandal-Cliche. Le Domaine des Brome's winemaker Léon Courville produces a brut from the St-Pépin hybrid variety labelled Muse, and L'Orpailleur produces a brut blend with Seyval Blanc and Vidal.

Producers

Angels Gate Winery and Kew Vineyards Estate Winery
Beamsville, Ontario

angelsgatewinery.com / kewvineyards.com

Angels Gate was established in 2000 on a 2-hectare site on the Niagara Escarpment and the Beamsville Bench subappellation. Originally owned and occupied by an order of Cistercian Nuns, hence the name Angels Gate, and the celestially-named Archangel fizz range, the company now owns 72 hectares, including the Mountainview Vineyard with Chardonnay planted in 1976, making it one of the oldest Chardonnay vineyards in Niagara. Angels Step Vineyard was established in 2007 and is organically certified. In 2008 the company purchased the Kew Vineyard, formerly home to the Kew family, and established for Riesling in the 1970s by the late Hermann Weis from the Mosel.

A complex mix of red, yellow and olive-coloured soils derived from the continuing erosion of the Niagara Escarpment has resulted in water-retentive soils with good sub-soil drainage. The combination of short slopes, high elevation and lake breezes helps moderate day and night temperatures. Heat tends to accumulate, beginning in May, accelerating during veraison and continuing warm, not cooling until well into October. The first sparkling wine made at Angels Gate was 200 bottles of Pinot Noir rosé 2007, followed in 2008 by the Chardonnay Blanc de Blancs and, soon after, the Blanc de Noirs. Next came Meunier in 2014 and Muscat in 2016 (for a Prosecco-style wine), with Riesling added to the portfolio in 2017.

Philip Dowell, an Australian, who emigrated to make the wines at Inniskillin, picks on flavour ripeness then whole bunch presses, retaining a small amount (5–15 per cent) of reserve wine, depending on the vintage to balance out the cuvées. After tirage in the spring, the wines are aged for at least 12 months. Dowell differentiates between Kew and Angels Gate by giving the base Chardonnay for Kew some barrel ageing. His wines across both portfolios are finely textured and flavourful with excellent persistence. Perhaps his best wine is the excellent Kew Amalia, while the medium-bodied Archangel Chardonnay Brut and Pinot Meunier Brut with 5 per cent Chardonnay are both, as it were, a revelation. Current production amount to 80,000 bottles.

Benjamin Bridge Winery

Wolfville, Nova Scotia

www.benjaminbridge.com

Given Nova Scotia's cool climate, Gerry McConnell, who made his fortune in mining, wisely decided to focus on sparkling wines, albeit with the not unambitious aim of emulating great Champagne. In 1999, he purchased a 20-hectare property, along with its 1845 Westcott family barn, and planted 4 hectares. He hired consultant Peter Gamble, the founding executive director of Ontario's Vintners Quality Alliance who, with his wife, Ann Sperling, had compiled climatic data identifying the potential for ripeness and natural acidity.

McConnell took on Raphaël Brisbois, a former chef de cave at Piper Heidsieck and, together with Gamble, the pair started experimenting with sparkling blends in 2002, using Pinot Noir, Chardonnay, Vidal and Nova Scotia's signature white grape L'Acadie. At a blind tasting in Toronto ten years on, pitting two of Benjamin Bridge's 2004 sparklers against David Léclapart's 2005 L'Apôtre Blanc de Blancs Champagne and Roederer Cristal 2004, Benjamin Bridge came in second. Today, McConnell and his daughters, Ashley and Devon, run Benjamin Bridge with a total of 25 hectares. Production is augmented by a network of neighbouring growers. The Gaspereau slopes provide drainage in the glacial sedimentary soils with alternating layers of sand and clay, explaining perhaps a note of salinity.

After Brisbois passed away in 2013, Jean-Benoît Deslauriers came on board, assisted by the champenois grower Pascal Agrapart. No yeast, sulphites or nutrients are added and no chaptalization is done. Since 2015, malolactic fermentation has become more frequent. Fermentation is in stainless steel, neutral French oak and, more recently, concrete eggs. Since 2019, the secondary fermentation is carried out with unaltered must and aged base wines. Five wines are produced annually, Vintage Brut, Vintage Rosé and Vintage Brut Reserve and an NV Brut and NV Rosé. After eight years on the lees, followed by an additional six years of post-disgorgement ageing, the Benjamin Bridge Blanc de Blancs is a tribute to patience, showcasing Nova Scotia's ability to produce long-lived fizz blessed with enduring youth.

Blue Mountain Vineyard and Cellars

Okanagan Falls, British Columbia
www.bluemountainwinery.com

'The primary reason for making sparkling wine,' confesses Ian Mavety, tongue only half in cheek, 'was not being able to afford to buy Champagne.' A drive of four and half hours (400 kilometres) to the east of Vancouver, Blue Mountain's 40-hectare vineyard lies above Vaseux Lake, sloping south to the dramatic McIntyre Bluff – a majestic wall of granitic gneiss – and to Vaseux Lake itself. A picture postcard for the Okanagan Valley, with its tasting room and large outdoor picnic area, Blue Mountain Estate was established by Ian and Jane Mavety in 1991. At the time, they were considered mavericks for focusing on making dry French-style wines while their neighbours were concentrating on off-dry German products.

The couple hired French oenologist and sparkling wine specialist Raphaël Brisbois to make their first still wines in 1991 and to create their fizz. Today the sparkling wine tradition has been embraced with enthusiasm and success by Ian and Jane's son Matt, whose first vintage as winemaker was in 2005, and daughter, Christie, who took over sales and marketing in 2008. Blue Mountain's vineyards form a single contiguous site with deep alluvial deposits and sands and a microclimate in which the intensity of sunshine and substantial diurnal temperature swings between day and night ensure good acid retention.

The estate-grown Pinot Noir and Chardonnay are hand-picked, sorted, whole-cluster pressed and racked from tank to barrel. Only the cuvée and first taille are retained and the must is handled oxidatively with fermentation in stainless steel and 500-litre French oak barrels, while vats are used primarily for reserve wines. Malolactic fermentation is blocked to preserve freshness. The Brut Rosé spends 30 months on the lees and Blanc de Blancs and Brut Reserve both spend 6.5 years. All wines are vintage-dated and annual production is 60,000 bottles. The harmonious Blue Mountain Brut shows tangy apple and citrus flavours with minerality from a soil structure derived from Ice Age glaciation. The Reserve is broader with leesy, red apple notes, while the Blanc de Blancs, with 6.5 years lees ageing, shows nutty, toasty notes and lingers on the tongue.

Cave Spring Vineyard

Beamsville, Ontario

www.cavespring.ca

Cave Spring Cellars, established in 1986 in the Niagara Peninsula's Beamsville Bench appellation, is owned by the Pennachetti family and its founding winemaker Angelo Pavan. The company's sparkling wines are produced from the 61-hectare vineyard, home to a confluence of particular conditions, from a slight western exposure and proximity to Lake Ontario, to its elevation and position at the foot of the steep Escarpment cliffs, unique to this particular stretch of the Beamsville Bench. The soils have slow-moving, heavily mineralized ground water springs that nourish the vines, and thanks to vigorous air movement throughout the year bringing protection from disease and frost, Cave Spring is blessed with healthy fruit and good late season ripening.

Since its first production of sparkling wine in 2002, the winery has focused on traditional method *blanc de blancs* made from Chardonnay. Chardonnay sites close to the steep cliffs of the Niagara Escarpment produce fine base wines thanks to reduced morning sun exposure and conditions allowing for a gradual ripening. Winemakers Angelo Pavan and Gabriel Demarco use a pneumatic press and neutral oak for fermentation and ageing of the base wine. The NV Blanc de Blancs is made every year, with up to 40 per cent fermented in neutral barriques and the remainder in tank, avoiding malolactic fermentation, balancing the steely acidity provided by the terroir with six months of lees contact. The wine is then aged for 30–36 months before disgorgement.

The top-of-the-line CSV Blanc de Blancs is vintage-dated in the best vintages; to date only the 2009, 2013, 2017 and 2018 have qualified. Since 2017, neutral barrel fermentation and ageing has also been introduced for a small percentage of the base wine in the NV Blanc de Blancs, with considerably more for the Vintage Blanc de Blancs CSV. They are experimenting with longer lees contact for their Vintage Riesling CSV Brut. Cave Spring sparklers are nuanced, precise and chiselled, with enough texture and weight to balance the acidity and carry the fruit and mineral nuances with persistence. They deliver a fine balance of steely minerality and richness, albeit fresh and elegant. Their power lies in a mineral underpinning and with time in the bottle, they develop and soften.

Henry of Pelham Family Estate

St. Catharines, Ontario

www.henryofpelham.com

Henry of Pelham's original owner was Nicholas Smith, whose son Henry (after whom the winery is named), built a coaching inn and tavern in 1842, which now serves as the winery's tasting room, wine store and restaurant. Henry had waggishly nicknamed himself, 'Henry of Pelham', after Henry Pelham, the British Prime Minister (1743–54), also recognizing Pelham Rd and Township. In addition to raising sheep, Henry operated a toll road and grew some of the first grapes to be planted in Canada. The property was purchased in 1982 by Paul Speck Senior, and the first vines planted in 1984, making them some of the oldest in the Niagara region.

Since Speck's premature death in 1993, the winery remains family owned and, certified sustainable in both winery and vineyard, is now run by Paul and his brothers Matthew and Daniel. With the main focus on Chardonnay and Pinot Noir, Lawrence Buhler, their winemaker since 2018, makes three traditional method sparkling wines and 23 table wines from 136 hectares of vineyards, all on the Short Hills Bench surrounding the winery. The vineyards have a deep blue clay with a loam–clay topsoil over limestone (the bedrock of the Niagara Escarpment), producing small crops with vivid acidity and an identifiable vein of minerality. They buy in another 136 hectares from local winegrowers.

The first experimental sparkling wine was made from Riesling in 1992. They produced their flagship sparkler, the much-awarded traditional method Cuvée Catharine, in 1998. Hand-picked estate Chardonnay and Pinot Noir are pressed with only the cuvée used for the base wine. The non-vintage Cuvée Catharine Brut is approximately 75 per cent Chardonnay with 25 per cent Pinot Noir, aged on the lees for two years. The signature Henry of Pelham style is exemplified by the delightful honey-tinged, barrel-fermented vintage Carte Blanche Blanc de Blancs, aged for five years, its exuberant fruit balanced by a toasty creaminess; while top marks go to the seductively aromatic, strawberryish non-vintage Cuvée Catharine Rosé Brut, a blend of 70–80 per cent Pinot Noir and 20–30 per cent Chardonnay. All in all, Henry of Pelham's fizz is consistently good from one vintage to the next.

Hinterland Wine Company

Hillier, Ontario

www.hinterlandwine.com

Even before they met, Jonas Newman and his partner Vasiliki (Vicki) Samaras both wanted to plant a vineyard. Jonas was a sommelier, Vicki studied botany at the University of Toronto and the couple planned their winery project while dating. On the lookout for limestone soils, they opted for Prince Edward County, a burgeoning new region where, in 2005, only seven vineyards had been planted, naming their winery Hinterland (the land behind Lake Ontario). Half of the 70-hectare estate consists of woods, wetlands and a pond, home to all manner of animals, including an aggressive beaver. The property is surrounded by the Bay of Quinte and Lake Ontario. 'Nothing is paved,' says Vicki, 'which makes watching visitors arrive in high heels quite interesting.'

When they found that the grapes at harvest were ripe with low sugar and high acidity, they decided on making fizz. In 2005, 6.5 hectares of Chardonnay and Pinot Noir was planted and 6 hectares planted with small amounts of Pinot Gris and Riesling for their Charmat wines. Soils are Hillier-Clay Loam, a shallow, free-draining alkaline glacial clay-loam with a smattering of granite. Prince Edward County has virtually the same summer temperature as the Niagara Peninsula but the northerly winds make it colder in autumn and winter, so they blanket the vines with geotextiles from November to April. Summers are consistently inconsistent and the growing season is short and intense with bud break in May and harvest in September. They pick the grapes two weeks later than their colleagues in Niagara but have never had to adjust sugar or acidity at time of harvest.

Hinterland's first traditional method sparkling wines were made in 2007. Three years later, the couple were producing Charmat method Whitecap Blanc and Borealis Rosé, made with purchased grapes. Using a pneumatic Willmes press, they take off the same fractions as in Champagne, fermenting in oak and using natural yeasts. A portion of each vintage is held back for later disgorgement. All wines, whether traditional method, Charmat or ancestral method, are vintage dated, and annual production averages 60,000 bottles. The winery's flagship Les Etoiles has floral notes and an elegance and finesse that belies the rustic nature of the operation. Without recourse to blending in reserve wine, other than for dosage and topping up, the portfolio shows consistent quality from vintage to vintage.

Lightfoot & Wolfville Vineyards

Wolfville, Nova Scotia

www.lightfootandwolfville.com

It may sound like a law firm but Lightfoot & Wolfville is in fact an artisanal winery in Nova Scotia's Annapolis Valley across the Bay of Fundy from the American coast at Maine. Built on land farmed by the Lightfoot family for eight generations, the winery operation was started by Michael and Jocelyn Lightfoot in 2009, when the couple planted their first vineyard after an extensive terroir study in consultation with Peter Gamble. They made their first sparkling wine in 2012 and released the first Lightfoot & Wolfville labels in 2015, opening their doors to the public two years later. From an initial 500 cases, production has grown to 12,000 cases, roughly half of it fizz.

This narrow stretch of land on the western edge of Nova Scotia is situated between two parallel mountain ranges along the shores of the Bay of Fundy. Proximity to the bay and the world's highest tides (up to 15.8 metres) create a unique growing environment for the production of distinctive cool-climate fizz. Lightfoot & Wolfville's 16 hectares of vines are planted on two sites along the shores of the Minas Basin, an inlet of the bay where hilly slopes extend the frost-free period and provide excellent exposure. Natural airflow and moderating saltwater breezes assist in slow ripening for a relatively low sugar content and are much needed when temperatures dip below freezing in winter.

A shared aspect of the terroir at both vineyard sites, which are certified organic through Ecocert Canada and biodynamic by Demeter Canada, is the rare Wolfville Formation Soil, which makes up just 3 per cent of the province's soil spectrum. The upper root horizon consists of glacial till with coarse sandy loam, while the deep root horizon's clay content provides good moisture retention. In addition to their own vineyards, they buy in grapes from a handful of like-minded local growers. Along with the three traditional Champagne varieties, Lightfoot & Wolfville use hybrids L'Acadie Blanc and Geisenheim-318, and cool-climate aromatic varieties such as Siegerrebe and Ortega for the entry-level fruit-driven Charmat fizzes they call, simply, Bubbly White & Bubbly Rosé.

Pressing is done in a Marzola basket press and both wild and cultured yeasts are used in fermentations in stainless steel and neutral oak. The traditional method fizz is made from Chardonnay, Meunier and Pinot Noir with extended lees ageing of three years or more. In more recent vintages, they have allowed more malolactic fermentation, partial and full, feeling it helps to balance the naturally high acidities and add texture. They also make a number of vintage-dependent experimental sparkling wines by the traditional and ancestral methods, as part of their Small-Lot series from varieties including Chenin Blanc, Scheurebe, Kékfrankos and Riesling. The Blanc de Blancs Brut is elegant and stylish with mouthwatering acidity and great persistence, the Extra Brut finely balanced and mouthfilling, while the pale pink Brut Rosé carries pomegranate and cranberry flavours across the tongue.

Sperling Vineyards

Kelowna, British Columbia

www.sperlingvineyards.com

In 1884, Giovanni and Lorenzo Casorzo reached the Okanagan Valley by pack horse over the Dewdney Trail, arriving at about the point where the modern Coquihalla Highway intersects the mountain range. They soon recognized that similarities in terrain and climate to their native Piemonte made this the ideal spot for fruit and vegetables. Since the start of grape growing in 1925, the 20-hectare East Kelowna Bench site east of Lake Okanagan has been planted and replanted several times, and the lessons of the previous crop have been applied with each new planting to find the ideal combination of slope and variety.

For Ann Sperling and her winemaking partner Peter Gamble, 2008 marked the first year of classic method sparkling production. The key draw to producing sparkling was a particular block of vines planted in the 1990s that consistently showed ripeness while retaining acidity and low potential alcohol levels. The only thing holding winemaker

Ann Sperling back was the variety, Pinot Blanc, but after tasting Cedric Bouchard's Roses de Jeanne La Bolorée Champagne, she was swayed. The most important lesson they have learned is that 30 months of lees-ageing is just the beginning. They prefer closer to 60 months.

With only half a hectare of organic vineyards used for sparkling wine production, each wine is made from a single block, single aspect and single vintage, including Sperling Reserve which is 80 per cent Pinot Noir and 20 per cent Chardonnay, produced from co-planted grapes. Hand-harvested whole bunches are pressed using a 2-tonne pneumatic press with the cuvée racked into stainless steel to ferment, some lots with non-aromatic yeast, others with native yeasts. The base wines sit in stainless steel barrels and small vats and may undergo some malolactic fermentation. They prefer no dosage but acknowledge that some customers like it.

Sperling Vineyards produces a Classic Method Brut Blanc de Blancs from 100 per cent Pinot Blanc and a Reserve Brut from 80 per cent Pinot Noir and 20 per cent Chardonnay. There is also a white and a red pet nat from aromatic varieties such as Perle de Csaba and Bacchus for the white and carbonic fermented Foch for the red. A 'celebrity sparkler', the Guy Lafleur 60 Brut Blanc de Blancs pays homage to the legendary Montreal Canadiens right winger who, in 1978, scored 60 goals. It is crisply dry, elegant and beautifully balanced after 60 months on the lees.

Township 7 Vineyards & Winery

Okanagan winery: Penticton, BC

Greater Vancouver winery: Langley, BC

township7.com

Township 7 takes its name from the late nineteenth century name of the historic community of south Langley. One of the first British Columbia wineries to make traditional method fizz, with its inaugural bottling of the 1999 seven stars, Township 7 was founded in greater Vancouver's Fraser Valley farming community by Gwen and Corey Coleman, who in 2004 added the Okanagan winery on the Naramata Bench. The two wineries were bought in 2006 by Mike Raffan, a former restaurateur, who sold the enterprise to Vancouver-based Ge Song, a Beijing-born entrepreneur, in 2014.

The wines are made by Mary McDermott, a transplanted Ontarian who moved to the Okanagan in 2014. Township 7 owns three estate vineyards for its fizz: the 2-hectare Langley estate in the Fraser Valley, the 2.8-hectare Naramata Bench site on the eastern side of Okanagan Lake and the 4.75-hectare Blue Terrace Vineyard in north Oliver. It also sources from several long-time growers. With microclimates varying from cool to temperate, and a mosaic of different soils, gradients and altitudes, each vineyard contributes different elements to the final blend.

Township 7 picks at night or early morning to ensure the grapes are cold when they arrive at the crush pad, where the juice is gently pressed, separated into fractions and mostly cool-fermented in stainless steel. The aromatic single vineyard viognier (seven stars Vega) and single vineyard Riesling (seven stars Rigel) are left on the lees for 12 months, the other cuvées for 18 to 60 months. Made from Chardonnay from the Hidden Terrace and estate Naramata Bench vineyards, seven stars Polaris is the founding cuvée of Township 7's sparkling wine range.

The brut rosé, seven stars Equinox, is a single-vineyard Pinot Noir sourced from Sperling Vineyards and for vintages from 2018 to 2020, from Stoneridge Vineyards in Okanagan Falls. Seven stars Sirius is the premium fizz, a single vineyard Chardonnay and Pinot Noir blend from the Langley vineyard that has spent 60 months on the lees. Overall, Township 7 sparkling wines show fine autolytic character expressed as toasty, minerally (almost saline) orchard fruit flavours carried on vibrant, lemony acidity with a creamy and silky texture. Bottling and disgorgement dates are printed on the label.

14
ASIA

JAPAN

The native grape that the Japanese claim as their own is the pink-skinned Koshu, whose ancestry includes a small proportion of the Davide hybrid. During the lengthy Edo Period (1603–1868), Koshu was much loved as an eating grape by the ruling Tokugawa shogunate. Adapted to the wine industry after two Japanese young guns were sent to Champagne in the late nineteenth century to learn the art of winemaking, Koshu languished in a backwater for decades until it was adopted, partly for sentimentally patriotic reasons, by a small number of pioneering wine producers, who were able to harness modern viticultural and winemaking techniques to produce a variety of dry, sweet, barrel-fermented and, as much to the point, sparkling styles.

Most Japanese Koshu is grown in Yamanashi, where it accounts for roughly a tenth of the prefecture's 4,000 hectares of vineyards. Among impressive producers, Château Lumière takes its fizz seriously, with six cuvées in the range, including the fresh, biscuity, creamy Lumière Bottle-fermented Sparkling Koshu, the leesy, Bollinger-esque Kakitsubata Traditional Sparkling Koshu Lumière NV, Sparkling Rosé (a blend of Cabernet Franc, Black Queen, Tannat and Merlot), Sparkling Orange Koshu, Sparkling Delaware and Sparkling Rouge. Katsunuma Jyozo Winery's traditional method, zero dosage Brilhante is subtle and vibrant, while Grace Wine excels, in this case using Chardonnay for its Akeno Blanc de Blancs, which was awarded Asia's first platinum medal at the Decanter World Wine Awards in 2016 and selected as one of the Top

10 wines of 2019 by Bloomberg. For its Serena Extra Brut, a blend of Hishiyama and Akeno grapes is used.

In neighbouring, cool climate Nagano Prefecture, Manns Komoro Winery produces a range of fizzes including its traditional method Solaris series: Shinshu Chardonnay Barrel Fermentation Méthode Traditionnelle, Shinshu Chardonnay Méthode Traditionnelle Brut and the popular Charmat method Kobo no Awa series. In Yamagata, in Japan's north-west, the talented winemaker Noriko Takeda makes some of Japan's finest fizz in the richly full-flavoured and toasty, zero dosage Domaine Takeda Cuvée Yoshiko, named in honour of Noriko's Champagne-loving mother. Her 2003 vintage achieved the distinction of being served at the thirty-fourth G8 Summit, in Toyako, Hokkaido, in 2008. On a more unusual note, her Sans Soufre Blanc uses the hybrid Delaware grape to make a vivacious ancestral method sparkler.

Bottling at Château Lumière

Based in Tochigi Prefecture, Coco Farm made its first sparkling wine, using the traditional method and Koshu grapes, in 1992. Served at the 2000 Okinawa G7 summit, it was also the first traditional method

Koshu fizz made in Japan. Coco now makes three sparkling wine lines, the first a pet nat made from Yamanashi Koshu and Yamagata Shokoshi (a red Japanese crossing), using natural yeasts, the second a traditional method fizz made from Riesling Lion in Tochigi. Since 2012, Coco Farm has been making traditional method fizz from Pinot Noir, Meunier and Chardonnay grown by the Kimura family in Yoichi on the Japan Sea coast of the northerly island of Hokkaido. The cold climate growing season temperatures resemble those of Champagne but even here, climate change may in the future mean having to prevent malolactic fermentation to preserve freshness.

CHINA

In China, sparkling wines barely account for 1 per cent of (grape) wine sales. Perhaps due to a traditional aversion to icy drinks, or a perception of the bubbles as more 'frothy' than 'effervescent', Chinese people used only to drink sparkling wine to project a modern image or to humour foreign guests. That narrative is changing, however, particularly with the younger generation, who are readily adopting Western lifestyles and tastes, with many returning to China with Western education and experiences. Many international players in the sparkling wine category are now positioning themselves for the uptick in the 'hockey stick' growth profile in China's demand for sparkling wine.

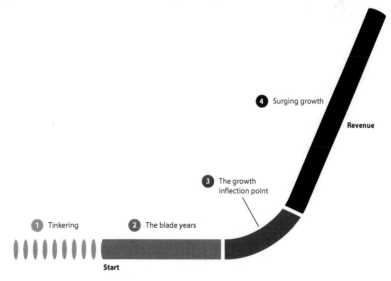

The four stages of hockey stick growth

Notable domestic producers today include COFCO Great Wall's Chateau Sungod in Hebei province, whose vintage Blanc de Blancs made in the traditional method has been served at state functions and the Beijing Olympics. Grace Vineyard, a family run boutique winery in Shanxi province produces the creative and acclaimed 'Angelina' range of sparkling wines, named after the owner's daughter, while Dynasty Fine Wines based in Tianjin, has opted for a sweeter, low alcohol (5% ABV) style, possibly to appeal to the preferred style for the Chinese palate, often referred to in consumer surveys. Tonhwa Winery in Jilin province makes a lightly sparkling sweet wine using the indigenous *Vitis amurensis*.

The most high profile sparkling wine producer in China is part of Chandon worldwide (itself part of the global LVMH superbrand), which has outposts covering 1,389 hectares of vineyards in Argentina, Brazil, California, Australia and India. With China's potential identified back in 1985 by a team of experts led by Philippe Coulon, Domaine Chandon China was established in 2013 in Ningxia province, the poster child wine region of modern China, situated at the foot of Helan Mountain in the central-north of the country. Chandon China is entirely focused on the domestic Chinese market. Apart from the classic brut styles associated with one of the world's most recognizable Champagne houses, Chandon China also produces innovative lines specifically geared to Chinese culture and preferences.

Chandon Me, a demi-sec sparkling wine that can be enjoyed at room temperature, emphasizes the delicate aromas and gentle sweetness of the wine, which would be more pronounced at room temperature. It also simplifies the serving requirement for a consumer base that still needs some persuasion, and encourages a more casual outlook to pouring bubbles, for example at picnics. This line of thinking has proved to be a huge success, and Chandon China followed up with Chandon Xi, a demi-sec sparkling red wine made from Pinot Noir, Syrah and Marselan, which plays to the auspicious red colour associated in China with celebrations, such as wedding banquets. If hockey stick growth for sparkling wine does occur in China, who knows what that could do to the supply of bubbles worldwide.

APPENDIX I: CHAMPAGNE PRODUCTION 2000–2020

Actual and permitted yields, stocks blocked and level of reserve held in Champagne 2000–2020.

Year	Maximum permitted yield set (kg/ha) that can be bottled and sold	Total maximum permitted yield including reserve (kg/ha)	Average yield achieved without the reserve (kg/ha)	Average level put into the reserve (kg/ha)	Maximum level that could be put in reserve (kg/ha)	Collective unblocking set (kg/ha)	Stocks blocked (buffer) in year to end July (million bottles)	Average level held in individual reserve (kg/ha)
2000	11,000	12,600	10,995	1,586	1,600	-	87	3,300
2001	11,000	11,000	10,988	0	0	-	120	4,500
2002	11,400	12,000	11,390	577	600	-	120	4,500
2003	11,400	11,400	8,256	0	0	-	133	4,900
2004	12,000	14,000	11,998	1,992	2,000	-	77	2,800
2005	11,500	13,000	11,499	1,492	1,500	1,000	101	3,600
2006	13,000	13,000	12,995	0	0	500	123	4,400
2007	12,400	15,500	12,274	1,966	3,100*	1,600	117	4,100
2008	12,400	15,500	12,310	1,918	3,100*	1,200	122	4,200
2009	9,700	14,000	9,695	2,580	4,300*	-	140	4,900
2010	10,500	12,000	10,423	478	1,500*	-	207	7,100
2011	12,500	13,600	10,491	2,774	3,100**	2,000	218	7,500

Continued overleaf

Year	Maximum permitted yield set (kg/ha) that can be bottled and sold	Total maximum permitted yield including reserve (kg/ha)	Average yield achieved without the reserve (kg/ha)	Average level put into the reserve (kg/ha)	Maximum level that could be put in reserve (kg/ha)	Collective unblocking set (kg/ha)	Stocks blocked (buffer) in year to end July (million bottles)	Average level held in individual reserve (kg/ha)
2012	11,000	12,000	9,071	138	1,000**	-	238	8,100
2013	10,500	13,100	9,989	2,019	3,100***	500	186	6,400
2014	11,000	13,200	10,099	1,455	3,100**	900	228	7,800
2015	10,500	13,100	9,979	620	3,000**	500	249	8,500
2016	10,800	12,800	9,026	138	3,100***	1,100	295	8 700
2017	10,800	13,400	9,723	334	3,100***	500	207	7,100
2018	10,800	15,500	10,796	1,564	4,700*		184	6,250
2019	10,200	13,300	10,108	148	3,100*		227	7,750
2020	8,000	15,500	7,995	289	7,500*	400	223	7,700

* providing the reserve doesn't exceed 8,000 kg/ha
** providing the reserve doesn't exceed 10,000 kg/ha
*** providing the reserve doesn't exceed 8,500 kg/ha
Table devised by Giles Fallowfield using CIVC statistics

APPENDIX II: CHAMPAGNE HARVEST DATES, MUSTS, TEMPERATURES AND GRAPE PRICES*

Harvest dates in Champagne

Year	Date	Year	Date
1995	18 September/2 October	2008	15/25 September
1996	16 September/1 October	2009	8/21 September
1997	12/25 September	2010	13/23 September
1998	10/26 September	2011	19 August/1 September
1999	15/23 September	2012	10/26 September
2000	11/25 September	2013	24 September/9 October
2001	22 September/2 October	2014	8/20 September
2002	12/26 September	2015	29 August/18 September
2003	21 August	2016	10/27 September
2004	20 September/2 October	2017	26 August/10 September
2005	09/22 September	2018	20 August/2 September
2006	07/25 September	2019	02/16 September
2007	23 August/7 September	2020	17/30 August

* Source: Comité Interprofessionnel du Vin de Champagne – Épernay

Musts in Champagne

Year	Potential alcohol (% vol)	Total acidity (H_2SO_4, grams per litre)
1995	9.4	9.0
1996	10.3	10.0
1997	10.2	8.4
1998	9.8	8.1
1999	10.0	6.3
2000	9.9	7.6
2001	8.5	8.6
2002	10.5	7.2
2003	10.6	5.8
2004	9.8	7.3
2005	9.9	7.0
2006	10.2	7.0
2007	9.4	8.6
2008	9.8	8.6
2009	10.3	7.5
2010	10.0	8.5
2011	9.4	7.4
2012	10.6	7.8
2013	9.9	8.5
2014	10.0	8.4
2015	10.5	6.9
2016	9.9	7.4
2017	10.2	7.8
2018	10.2	5.9
2019	10.6	6.9
2020	10.2	6.4

Average annual temperature in Champagne

Year	Average temperature
1995	11.08
1996	9.30
1997	10.76
1998	10.66
1999	11.33
2000	11.46
2001	10.89
2002	11.36
2003	11.22
2004	10.65
2005	11.00
2006	11.35
2007	11.33
2008	10.84
2009	11.06
2010	9.92
2011	11.84
2012	10.71
2013	10.14
2014	11.64
2015	12.30
2016	11.30
2017	12.00
2018	12.18
2019	12.10
2020	Not yet calculated

Grape prices

Year	Price (€/kg)
1995	3.39
1996	3.66
1997	3.66
1998	3.81
1999	3.89
2000*	4.00
2001**	4.13
2002	4.22
2003	4.39
2004	4.62
2005	4.65
2006	4.81
2007	5.11
2008	5.40
2009	5.25
2010	5.36
2011	5.6
2012	5.73
2013	5.8
2014	5.89
2015	5.89
2016	5.9
2017	6.0

* indicative price until 2000;
** average price from 2000

APPENDIX III: CHAMPAGNE VINTAGES

Vintages 2000–2020

2020 ***

The sixth August harvest since the millennium. A mild and humid winter. Hot, dry conditions, a low-yielding harvest producing concentrated base wines. Twenty-five per cent smaller than 2019.

2019 ****

Down 10 per cent on average on previous recent levels. Exceptional maturity and health in the grapes with balanced sugars and acidity levels. Early days but promising.

2018 ***

The fifth August harvest since the millennium. Consistently good weather, a hot summer and a huge crop, resulting in some degrading of acidity. Much hyped as vintage of the century, fleshy wines and good for clearing out the inferior 2017 reserves.

2017 *

A challenging vintage with hot, dry weather from May to July, with a warm, wet August, inducing rot and necessitating quick and selective picking. Meunier very ripe. The Aube fared better.

2016 **

A difficult vintage, 15 per cent down on average thanks to downy mildew.

After a wet May–July, concerns by mid-August had been partly mitigated by mainly sunny days and cool nights into September but ripening was inconsistent. The Aube was hit by spring frosts. Reserves important.

2015 ***

The fourth August harvest since the millennium, after a hot, dry growing season. A Pinot Noir year of opulent fruit with lowish acidity and freshness slightly compromised, so expectations of a great vintage not fully realized.

2014 ***

A large crop with rot in the Marne, with Meunier most affected, but saved in large part by good September weather.

2013 ****

Following a good summer, rain from 10 September brought rot and just took the edge of a potentially great vintage, nonetheless a cool growing season brought some excellent results.

2012 *****

This could turn out to be the vintage of the decade. Despite a challenging winter and spring, with frosts, coulure and millerandage at flowering, hail, sunburn and both powdery and downy mildew, the growing season was perfect from mid-July onwards. A smallish crop with above average sugars and acids produced a minor miracle: excellent, ageworthy wines.

2011 *

The third August harvest since the millennium and even earlier than that of 2003. Poor weather from the end of June resulted in rot in the Marne, and lots of rain meant that meticulous sorting was required to avoid unripeness. No Moët vintage for the second year running (last time that happened: 1967/1968).

2010 **

Testing conditions from mid-August when rain interrupted play, which resumed under sunny skies in September, but there was some botrytis, especially in the Marne, and selection at harvest, Chardonnay being superior to Pinot, was critical in an uneven vintage. No Moët vintage but Dom Pérignon managed an impressive wine.

2009 ****

A hot and dry summer until mid-August, some rain at the beginning of September, but healthy conditions by and large producing a very good vintage of good acidity and high quality, opulent wines that were broadly speaking more evolved than the more classic 2008s, although Moët and Ruinart prefer 2009.

2008 *****

Bright, dry conditions in spring, a cool middle growing season and a gloomy, overcast summer, but a fine September helped produce wines of natural precision, high acid freshness and vibrancy. A great vintage, albeit marginally better for black grapes, arguably vintage of the decade.

2007 ***

The second August harvest since the millennium. Like 2003, 2007 was an unusually early harvest, but this was because of exceptionally dry and warm conditions during flowering in April, bringing forward the vegetative cycle by around one month. Uneven ripeness, but a curate's egg, with freshness and some surprisingly good wines, e.g. Bollinger R.D., Dom Ruinart.

2006 ***

A cloudy, wet August, but sunny September resulted in a large crop of wines with richness and relatively low levels of acidity but overall sufficiently balanced to give a lot of pleasure; Taittinger Comtes de Champagne stands out.

2005 **

Heavy rain in early September slowed ripening and encouraged the spread of botrytis, but there was an abundant harvest, with some good, approachable wines, even if acidity is on the low side.

2004 ****

The first – and best – of three abundant years, 2004 was a very good year, with a hot, dry July ensuring healthy vines, a wet August followed by a dry and windy September and then a glorious Indian summer, with many excellent wines despite a large crop.

2003 **

The first heatwave harvest of the new millennium. Half of the 2003 crop was destroyed by spring frosts making it the smallest harvest since 1981. Picking starting on 25 August (21 August in the Aube), resulting in the earliest harvest since Champagne viticultural records began in 1822. Low acidity, so some houses didn't declare, notably Pol Roger, whereas Bollinger, Dom Pérignon, Krug, Philipponnat Clos des Goisses and Pommery Les Clos Pompadour did.

2002 *****

A warm, dry late summer–early autumn resulted in an extremely ripe vintage of opulent, luxurious, yet beautifully balanced, ageworthy wines with the requisite freshness, even if the acidity was lower than 1996 and 2008.

2001 (no stars)

In a cold, wet growing season, there was rot, but in an often dire vintage, probably the most forgettable of the first two decades of the millennium, the Côte des Blancs got off lightly.

2000***

More of a Chardonnay than a Pinot year, a warm growing season made for an average to good year of rich, fast-evolving wines.

Best of the post-Second World War twentieth century

Both 1995 and 1996 were good years, but 1996 is controversial, with excessive acidity in some wines. The three great vintages of the 1980s were 1982, 1985 and 1988. The 1970s also produced three great vintages, in 1973, 1975 and 1979. Exceptional vintages of the post-war era until then are: 1945, 1947, 1949, 1955, 1959, 1961, 1964.

APPENDIX IV: TRADITIONAL METHOD MINIMUM AGEING PERIODS

Classification	Minimum ageing (months)
Europe (EU)	9
Austria – Sekt	18
Austria – Sekt Grosse Reserve	30
Champagne (non-vintage)	12 (15 months before release)
Champagne (vintage)	36
Franciacorta	18
Franciacorta Rosé NV	24
Franciacorta Vintage Rosé	30
Franciacorta Riserva	60 (67 months before release)
Germany – VDP.Sekt	24
Germany – VDP.Sekt.Prestige	36
Trentodoc Brut	15
Trentodoc Millesimato	24
Trentodoc Riserva	36
Alta Langa Spumante and Rosato Spumante	30
Alta Langa Riserva	36
Cava de Guarda	9
Cava de Guarda Superior Reserva	18

Classification	Minimum ageing (months)
Cava de Guarda Superior Gran Reserva	30
Cava de Paraje Calificado	36
Clàssic Penedès	15
Corpinnat	18
Méthode Cap Classique (South Africa)	12

GLOSSARY

Adjuvant. A riddling agent facilitating remuage.

Autolysis. The breakdown of dead yeast cells created after the second fermentation in bottle.

Balthazar. A 12-litre bottle, the equivalent of 16 standard 75 centilitre. bottles. It can be and usually is transvasaged (see transfer method).

Bar. Atmosphere of pressure, generally 5–6 for traditional method fizz.

Pressure terms	
perlant	Up to 2.5 atmospheres
pétillant, frizzante	2.5–3.5 atmospheres
mousseux, spumante	3.5–6 atmospheres or more

Base wine. The wine of the first fermentation, normally the harvest year in most of a non-vintage fizz.

Biodynamic wine. Certified producers are subject to the vineyard management rule book based on the writings of Rudolf Steiner, in which plant, compost and mineral preparations replace chemical inputs and work is carried out according to lunar cycles and the biodynamic calendar. Certifying bodies include Demeter and Biodyvin.

Bottle size. The standard bottle size is 75 centilitres. By law Champagne has to be sold in the bottle in which it undergoes the secondary fermentation, but the transfer method can be used for quarter bottles, half-bottles (up to 20 per cent of annual production) and formats bigger than jeroboam.

Bottle sizes

Melchizedek or Midas — 30 litres (40 bottles)

Primat — 27 litres (36 bottles)

Sovereign — 26.25 litres (35 bottles)

Solomon — 18 litres (24 bottles)

Nebuchadnezzar — 15 litres (20 bottles)

Balthazar — 12 litres (16 bottles)

Salmanazar — 9 litres (12 bottles)

Methuselah — 6 litres (8 bottles)

Rehoboam — 4.5 litres (6 bottles)

Jeroboam — 3 litres (4 bottles)

Magnum — 1.5 litres (2 bottles)

Bottle — 0.75 litres

Half-bottle — 0.375 litres

Quarter bottle — 0.2 litres

Brut. Dry in taste as distinct from the official 'dry'.

Term used	Sugar (g/l)	Taste profile
brut nature	0–3	bone-dry
extra brut	0–6	bone-dry to dry
brut	0–12	bone-dry, to dry, to off-dry
extra dry	12–17	off-dry to medium-dry
dry	17–32	medium-dry
demi-sec	32–50	medium-sweet
sweet	> 50	sweet

EU wine dry–sweet regulations

Cap Classique. See *méthode champenoise*.

Chalk. Formed during the Upper Cretaceous period, around 70 million years ago, from marine plankton, chalk has a high active lime content, helping with natural acidity.

Chaptalization. Adding sugar to the must to raise the wine's potential alcohol.

Charmat method. The tank method, also known as Martinotti method and cuve close. The second fermentation of the base wine takes place in a large, closed pressurized tank.

Classic method. See *méthode champenoise*.

Col fondo. Also *sui lievite*. Refermented in the bottle and not disgorged, so left cloudy, with yeast lees part of the attraction.

Crayères. Cellars excavated from chalk quarries.

Criadera. See solera.

Cru. Broadly, a village or commune, more narrowly, a specific vineyard site.

Cuvée. 1. The blend. 2. The first fraction of the pressing.

DIAM. A technical microagglomerate cork that reduces or eliminates cork taint and bottle variation.

Disgorgement. Removal of the yeast sediment, or plug, collected in the neck of the bottle after the second fermentation in bottle, either *à la glace*, by freezing, or, *à la volée*, by hand.

Dosage. The sweet *liqueur d'expédition* added after disgorgement.

Fermentation. The process by which grape sugars are converted to alcohol and carbon dioxide by indigenous or selected yeasts.

Fining. Clarification of the juice by, e.g., casein, bentonite and gelatin-tannins.

Flocculation. The process by which tiny particles aggregate into a small number of larger particles, enabling yeast survival in harsh conditions.

Flotation. A solid–liquid separation process used for clarification.

Foudre. Large wooden vat.

Grande Marque. One of the group of top Champagne houses, officially disbanded in 1997, but still loosely referred to as such.

Growing season temperature (GST). The metric for wine-grape ripening based on calculating the overall average temperature of the growing season.

Haute Valeur Environnementale (HVE). French certification, recognizing sustainable and environmentally-friendly practices.

IWC. International Wine Challenge.

Jeroboam. 3-litre bottle, equal to four standard 75 centilitre bottles.

Judgment of Paris. The 1976 head-to-head blind tasting contest organized by Steven Spurrier in Paris in which California beat France.

Kimmeridgian. Late Jurassic period chalky marl and limestone geology (160–150 million years ago), which lends its name to the Kimmeridgian soils of Chablis, the Aube's Côte de Bar and parts of south-western England.

Late-disgorged. Also, recently disgorged. Bottle-fermented fizz that's spent a long time on its lees, gaining in complexity.

Layering. Provignage or marcottage in French, a traditional form of planting: the long cane of an ungrafted vine is buried to allow propagation from the same vine.

Lees. Yeast-based sediment in bottle or barrel.

Limestone. A range of sedimentary rock types consisting of carbonates, including chalk.

Liqueur d'expédition. Also liqueur de dosage, a blend of sugar and base or reserve wine added to sparkling wine after disgorgement.

Liqueur de tirage. A blend of wine, sugar, yeast and yeast nutrients added to the base wine at tirage to induce the bubbles.

Magnum. A 150-centilitre bottle. With a ratio of oxygen to wine that is half that of a standard bottle, the fizz ages more slowly and the wine stays fresher for longer.

Maillard reaction. Named after the French chemist Louis-Camille Maillard, who first described it in 1912, this is the gradual interaction of amino acids and sugars during autolysis for brioche, biscuit and toasty notes. It most likely continues post-disgorgement too.

Malolactic fermentation. Also malo, bacterial conversion of tart malic acid to softer lactic acid, during or after the first alcoholic fermentation.

Mannoproteins. Released during autolysis from the decomposition of the yeast cell walls, mannoproteins contribute towards texture and stability.

Marque d'Acheteur (MA). An 'own brand' wine label produced exclusively for a client such as a supermarket, celebrity or similar.

Melchizedek. See Midas.

Méthode champenoise. Also called the Champagne method, traditional method or classic method, this is the process of fizz creation by a second fermentation in the same bottle in which the wine is sold.

Methuselah. A 6-litre bottle (named 'impériale' in Bordeaux), the equivalent of eight standard bottles. Named for the grandfather of Noah, credited with having planted the very first vines and having lived to the ripe old age of 969 (Genesis 5.27).

Midas. A 30-litre bottle, equal to 40 standard 75-centilitre bottles. The biggest fizz bottle size known to humankind, the Midas is exclusive to Jay-Z's Armand de Brignac.

Minerality. A vague descriptor for a perceived salinity associated with the interpretation of terroir.

Muselet. Muzzle or wire cage holding the cork in place.

Natural wine. Broadly defined as a wine made with minimal intervention in the vineyard and cellar.

Nebuchadnezzar. A 15-litre bottle, equivalent to 20 standard 75 centilitre bottles.

Négociant. A company that mainly buys-in grapes, also a house or *maison* in Champagne.

Négociant-manipulant (NM). See négociant.

Nucleation. The nucleation or effervescence point is the birthplace of the bubble in the glass.

Oak barrel. The traditional Champagne barrel is 205 litres, Bordeaux barrique 225 litres, Burgundy barrel, or pièce, 228 litres, demi-muid 600 litres.

Organic wine. Made from grapes grown, broadly speaking, without the use of chemical inputs. Producers are subject to the rules of the relevant certifying organic body. Use of sulphur dioxide and copper sulphate is allowed.

Peptides. Peptides are organic compounds released during autolysis that consist of a number of amino acids.

Perpetual reserve. Wine of earlier vintages used for blending, replenished with the most recent wine of the vintage.

pH. Potential hydrogen-ion concentration, measuring the active acidity or alkalinity of a liquid on a scale of 0–14, 0 being the most acid, 14 the most alkaline.

Polysaccharides. Sugar-related compounds released during autolysis.

Primat. A 27-litre bottle, equal to 36 standard 75 centilitre bottles.

Prise de mousse. See tirage.

Protected Designation of Origin (PDO). The name used by the EU and the UK aimed at preserving the designations of origin of food- and wine-related products.

Rebêche. Discarded final fraction of the pressing (from which we get the word rubbish), usually going to distillation.

Récoltant coopérateur (RC). A cooperative grower who markets co-op produced Champagne under their own label.

Récoltant manipulant (RM). A grower who makes and markets Champagne under their own label from grapes sourced exclusively from their own vineyards and processed on their own premises. Co-op members can also sell wines made for them by their co-op as RM if the cooperative treats the wine from this grower separately from the RC wines.

Rectified Concentrated Grape Must (RCGM, or MCR, or RGM). A dense, relatively neutral, reduced grape-based sugar solution made up normally of fructose and glucose.

Rehoboam. A 4.5-litre bottle, equal to six standard 75-centilitre bottles.

Renaisssance des Appellations. Also known as Return to Terroir, the group was founded in 1971 by Nicolas Joly with the aim of guaranteeing the authenticity of terroir: https://renaissance-des-appellations.com/en/presentation-return-to-terroir/

Réserve individuelle, or qualitative. A back-up over and above the permitted base yield, allowing Champagne houses to use stock held back as an insurance policy in the event of reduced yields or increased sales. See Appendix 1.

Reserve wine. Still wine matured for blending with the new vintage before the second fermentation in bottle. Not permitted in vintage Champagne, but up to 15 per cent is allowed in the EU and up to 5 per cent in the USA.

Riddling (*remuage*). The manual or automated process of easing the sediment into the neck of the bottle ready for removal at disgorgement.

Rootstock. Since the phylloxera devastation of the nineteenth century, vineyards are routinely planted on resistant American rootstocks such as 41B, SO4 and 3309C.

Sabrage. Ostentatious opening of a bottle of sparkling wine with a knife or sword. Not necessary or recommended.

Salmanazar. A 9-litre bottle, equal to 12 standard 75-centilitre bottles.

Solera. Topping up separate tiers of barrels (criaderas) from the youngest to the oldest, as in Jerez, to maintain consistency of style. The word is bandied about in Champagne, but more often than not it refers to a perpetual reserve.

Solomon. An 18-litre bottle, the equivalent of 24 standard 75-centilitre bottles.

Sovereign. A 26.25-litre bottle, the equivalent of 35 standard 75-centilitre bottles. At the time, the biggest ever bottle of Champagne when made by Taittinger for the launch of the *Sovereign of the Seas* on 1 January 1988.

Sugars. The main sugars in wine are glucose and fructose. Fructose is the sweetest and most reactive of sugars and will degrade first in an acid solution. Sucrose has a higher purity. Other sugars relevant to the Maillard Reaction include arabinose, xylose, mannose, ribose and rhamnose.

Sui lievite. See *col fondo*.

Sulphur dioxide (SO$_2$). An antioxidant, typically added to the pressed juice before fermentation and after disgorgement to protect against oxidation.

Taille. 1. The pruning of the vines. 2. The second fraction of the pressing.

Tartrates. Tartrate crystals are deposits of tartaric acid.

TCA. 2,4,6-Trichloranisole, TCA for short, is cork taint.

Terroir. All the attributes of a vineyard location that contribute to the style and quality of a wine.

Tirage. The addition of yeast at bottling for the second fermentation, to which a mixture of sugar, nutrients and adjuvants is added to the clarified base wine (see also *liqueur de tirage*). Also known as *prise de mousse*.

Titratable acidity. The measurable amount of total acidity in a wine including fixed and volatile acidity, although in practice it is slightly lower than total acidity.

Traditional method. See *méthode champenoise*.

Transfer method. Also transvasage. After the second fermentation in bottle, the wine is decanted, filtered and rebottled under pressure in the required size.

Umami. Meaning mouthwatering or savoury, the fifth basic taste after sweet, salt, sour and bitter, derived from glutamic acid, discovered by Professor Ikunae Ikeda in Japan in 1908. The synergy between umami and IMP (inosinic acid: animal sources), GMP (guanylic acid: plant-based foods and mushrooms), and AMP (adenylic acid: fish and shellfish) is thought to account for the flavour 'booster effect' in matching umami-rich foods with lees-aged sparkling wines.

VDP. Vereinigung Deutscher Prädikatsweinguter. Union of some 200 top German wine estates (see www.vdp.de).

Veraison (Fr. *véraison*). The beginning of the ripening moment and changing of the colour of the grape as malic acid is gradually reduced in favour of sugars and tartaric acid.

Vin clair. The base wine that follows the first fermentation. If older than the most recent harvest, the *vin clair* is a reserve wine.

Vi.Te. An organization which brings together artisanal producers from around the world who aspire to express their terroir through their wines: https://vignaiolieterritori.it/en/#associazione.

Viticulture Durable en Champagne (VDC). Certification recognizing sustainable viticultural practices.

BUBBLIOGRAPHY

Alexandre, Hervé and Guilloux-Benatier, Michèle, 'Yeast autolysis in sparkling wine'. *Australian Journal of Grape and Wine Research*, March, 2008.

Amerine, Maynard, et al., *The Technology of Winemaking*. Fourth Edition, AVI Publishing Company Inc.,1980.

Avellan, Essie, Hugh Johnson, Simon Larkin and Anthony Rose, 'Myth or Magic? Prestige Cuvée Champagne. *The World of Fine Wine*, Issue 15, 2007, pp. 202–211. http://www.anthonyrosewine.com/sites/default/files/202_211_PerSeChampagne.pdf

Avellan, Essie, Simon Larkin and Anthony Rose, 'Rosé Champagne: Worth the Difference?' *The World of Fine Wine*, Issue 18, 2007, pp. 196–202. http://www.anthonyrosewine.com/sites/default/files/PerSeRosTChampagne.pdf

Barr, Andrew, *Drink*. Bantam Press, 1994.

Belfrage, Nicolas, *Life Beyond Lambrusco*. Sidgwick & Jackson, 1985.

Brook, Stephen (ed), *A Century of Wine*. Mitchell Beazley, 2000.

Campbell, Christy, *Phylloxera*. Harper Collins, 2004.

Clarke, Oz, *The History of Wine in 100 Bottles*. Pavilion, 2015.

Cserski, Helen, *Bubbles, A Ladybird Expert Book*. Michael Joseph, Penguin Random House UK, 2018.

Curtis, Charles, MW, *Vintage Champagne: 1899–2019*. WineAlpha, 2020.

Faith, Nicholas, *The Story of Champagne*. Hamish Hamilton, 1988.

Fallowfield, Giles, 'Are Warmer Harvests Causing Problems in Champagne?' *Canopy*, 5 November 2019.

Fallowfield, Giles, 'If You Can't Stand the Heat…'. *The Drinks Business Champagne Report*, 2020.

Gabay, Elizabeth, MW, *Rosé*. Infinite Ideas, 2018.

Goode, Jamie, 'Visiting Champagne Jacques Selosse, with Anselme Selosse'. Wine Anorak, 24 March 2015. https://Wineanorak. Com/2015/03/24/Teens-Use-Apps-To-Keep-Secrets.

Harcourt-Kelly, Maxine, *When Wine became English*. University of Chichester, 2020.

Kemp, Belinda, Bruna Condé, Sandrine Jégou, Kate Howell, Yann Vasserot and Richard Marchal, 'Chemical compounds and mechanisms involved in the formation and stabilization of foam in sparkling wines'. *Critical Reviews in Food Science and Nutrition* 59(13): 2072–94.

Kemp, Belinda, Hervé Alexandre, Bertrand Robillard, Richard Marchal, 'Effect of Production Phase on Bottle-Fermented Sparkling Wine'. *Journal of Agricultural and Food Chemistry*, 63(1):19–38. https:// pubmed.ncbi.nlm.nih.gov/25494838/

Krebiehl, Anne, MW, 'Champagne Soleras and Perpetual Reserves'. *The World of Fine Wine*, Issue 58, 2017.

Krebiehl, Anne, MW, *The Wines of Germany*. Infinite Ideas, 2019.

Liem, Peter, *Champagne*. Mitchell Beazley, 2017.

Liger-Belair, Gérard, *Uncorked*. Princeton University Press, 1970, revised 2004.

Lukacs, Paul, *Great Wines of America*. Wiley, 2005.

Matthews, Mark A., *Terroir and Other Myths of Winegrowing*. University of California Press, 2015.

Phillips, Rod, *A Short History of Wine*. Penguin, 2000.

Pinney, Thomas, *A History of Wine in America*. University of California Press, 2005.

Ray, Cyril, *Bollinger*. Heinemann Kingswood, 1971.

Rose, Anthony, *Sake and The Wines of Japan*. Infinite Ideas, 2018.

Saintsbury, George (1845–1933), *Notes on a Cellar Book*, First published 1920, University of California Press edition, 2008.

Schmitt, Patrick, MW, 'Changing dosages in brut nv Champagne: trends, causes and implications'. Research paper, IMW, 2014.

Shaw, T.G., *Wine, The Vine and the Cellar*. Longman, Green, Longman, Roberts, & Green, 2nd edition, 1864.

Simon, André, *Vintagewise*. Michael Joseph, 1945.

Skelton, Stephen, MW, *The Wines of Great Britain*. Infinite Ideas, 2019.

Sutcliffe, Serena, MW, *A Celebration of Champagne*. Mitchell Beazley, 1988.

Theise, Terry, 'The Sugar-Is-Bad-For-You Campaign Is Ruining Champagne'. *Robb Report*, 11 May 2019. https://robbreport.com/food-drink/wine/anti-sugar-campaign-is-ruining-Champagne-2850193/

Tiptree, Tim, MW, 'Reserve Wine Use in Brut NV Champagne'. Research paper, IMW, 2018.

Walker, Tony, *Vintage Tasmania*, Providore Island Tasmania, 2014.

Walters, Robert, *Bursting Bubbles*. Quiller, 2017.

Online articles and papers

'Nicholas Longworth: The "Father of the American Wine Industry"', Wine, Wit, and Wisdom (blog): http://winewitandwisdomswe.com/2021/01/03/guest-post-nicholas-longworth-the-father-of-the-american-wine-industry/

'Jean-Baptiste François', Grands Marques et Maisons de Champagne: https://maisons-Champagne.com/fr/encyclopedies/personnalites-du-Champagne/biographies/article/jean-baptiste-francois

Comité Champagne: https://www.Champagne.fr/en/homepage

Robinson, Jancis, 'Mystery wines: NV champagnes', 13 July 2019: https://www.jancisrobinson.com/articles/mystery-wines-nv-Champagnes

Robinson, Jancis, 'Pink champagne – a serious wine now', 28 September 2019: https://www.jancisrobinson.com/articles/pink-Champagne-serious-wine-now

THANKS

This book could not have been written without the cooperation of the many winemakers, viticulturalists and winery owners profiled, to whom I am immensely grateful for answering my questions, no matter how seemingly and actually trivial, for coming up with samples when requested, for enduring Zoom meetings and for that most precious resource of all, the generosity of time. I am indebted to Kazumi Suzuki for her unwavering support and assistance and to Richard Burton and Rebecca Clare at Infinite Ideas for their encouragement and necessarily skilful editing. I am particularly grateful to the following for their invaluable help with various sections of the book, notably Angela Lloyd (South Africa), Caroline Gilby MW (Central and Eastern Europe), Tony Aspler and Belinda Kemp (Canada), Jane Skilton MW (New Zealand), Ines Salpico (Portugal), Janet Wang (China) and Thomas Vaterlaus (Switzerland). I would also like to thank the following for their keen insights, contributions, corrections or suggestions: Brigitte Batonnet, Ian Bailey, Andrew Caillard MW, Hannah Charnock, Darrell Corti, David Crossley, Helen Czerski, Marjorie Dor, Michael Edwards, Julia Trustram Eve, Giles Fallowfield, Michael Garner, Justin Gibbs, Brad Greatrix, Tim Hall, Charlotte Hey, Huon Hooke, Chris Kissack, Fred Langdale, Peter Liem, Wink Lorch, Matthieu Longuère, Tony Milanowski, Françoise Perettti, Stuart Pigott, Xavier Rousset, Patrick Schmitt MW, Stephen Skelton MW, Matt Strugnell, Tim Triptree MW, Olly Whitfield.

INDEX

Note: Producers are filed under surnames.
Where family members appear only in the
producer description they are not indexed
separately. Champagne and France are
treated separately in subheadings.

Grange, The 68, 120–1
grape varieties 59–62
Graser family 176
Gratien, Alfred 165
Gratien, Champagne Alfred 14, 165–6
Gratiot Delugny, Champagne 61
Gray Monk 329
Great British Classic hallmark 108
Great Depression 22, 315
Great Western Champagne 78
Greatrix, Brad 32, 33, 52–3, 74, 133
Grenache *see* Garnacha/Garnatxa
Greno Champagne 24
Grier, Jeff 290
Grier family 281
Griesel 218
Griffin 274
Grimshaw, Tommy 130, 131
Grolleau 209
Gross, Vino 276–7
Grossard, Dom 12
growing season temperature (GST) 55–6
Grüner Veltliner 61, 265–7
Guiardel, Pehu 148
Guillaume, Pierre-Marie 114
Gunns 96
Gusbourne Estate 36, 68, 69, 105, 107–8, 121–3
Gut Hermannsberg 223–4
guyot 50
gyropalettes 43

Hall, Peter 58, 112–13
Halliday, James 65, 88
Halliday, Suzanne 88
Hambledon Wineries Ltd 62, 68, 69, 105, 123–4, 128
hand-harvesting 32, 51
Haraszthy, Agoston 25, 314
Haraszthy, Arpad 25, 314–15
Haraszthy & Co., Arpad 315
Harcourt, Laurent d' 185–6
Hardy, Geoff 82
Hardys 78, 81, 90
Harrow & Hope Marlow Winery 68, 107, 124–6
harvest
  climate change 56, 57, 58
  dates 51, 345
Hatch Mansfield 105
Hattingley Valley 105, 111, 121, 126–7, 131, 135
Hautvillers, Abbey of 9, 12–13, 157, 163

Hazek, Franz 315
Hearn, Lafcadio 113
Heemskerk 78, 81, 85, 91, 96
Heerema, Eric 132–3
Heidsieck, Champagne Charles 13, 36, 37–8, 57, 159, 166–7, 168, 187
Heidsieck, Charles-Camille and Jean-Marc 166–7
Henkell-Söhnlein 165, 218, 220, 224, 270, 271, 299
Henners Vineyard 68, 127–8
Henri III 10
Henrion, Arnaud and Marielle 207
Henriot, Champagne 14, 167–9
Henriot, Gilles de Larouzière and Joseph 167, 168, 169
Henriquez, Maggie 172
Henry of Pelham Family Estate 333–4
Henry VIII 103, 104, 132, 146
Herbreteau, Vincent 209
Hill, Andy 132
Hill Smith Family 91, 99
Himeur, Sofian 321
Hinterland Wine Company 328, 334–5
Hishiyama 339
history 1–2, 9–26
  Australia 24–5, 77–8
  Bulgaria 269
  Canada 327
  England 9–12, 14, 15, 17, 19, 103
  France 9–24
  Germany 217–18
  Hungary 26, 270
  Italy 25, 239–40, 247
  Japan 339
  Moldova 26, 272
  Slovenia 26, 273
  South Africa 281
  Spain 26, 293–4
  United States 25, 313–18
  see also individual producers
Hitchcock, Nicole 322
Hitler, Adolf 275
Hohnen, David 98
Holland, Charlie 106, 107–8, 122
Holloway, Shane 89
Hood, Andrew 86
Hubert 26, 270
Hubert, Johann Evangelist 26, 270
Huff Estate 328
Huget-Can Feixes 295
Humphries, Jason 117
Hungarovin 270